Lecture Notes in Computer Science 14544

Founding Editors

Gerhard Goos
Juris Hartmanis

Editorial Board Members

The series Lecture Notes in Computer Science (LNCS), including its subseries Lecture Notes in Artificial Intelligence (LNAI) and Lecture Notes in Bioinformatics (LNBI), has established itself as a medium for the publication of new developments in computer science and information technology research, teaching, and education.

LNCS enjoys close cooperation with the computer science R & D community, the series counts many renowned academics among its volume editors and paper authors, and collaborates with prestigious societies. Its mission is to serve this international community by providing an invaluable service, mainly focused on the publication of conference and workshop proceedings and postproceedings. LNCS commenced publication in 1973.

Jun Ma · Bo Wang

Editors

Fast, Low-resource, and Accurate Organ and Pan-cancer Segmentation in Abdomen CT

MICCAI Challenge, FLARE 2023
Held in Conjunction with MICCAI 2023
Vancouver, BC, Canada, October 8, 2023
Proceedings

 Springer

Editors
Jun Ma
Peter Munk Cardiac Centre
Toronto, ON, Canada

Bo Wang
Peter Munk Cardiac Centre
Toronto, ON, Canada

ISSN 0302-9743 ISSN 1611-3349 (electronic)
Lecture Notes in Computer Science
ISBN 978-3-031-58775-7 ISBN 978-3-031-58776-4 (eBook)
https://doi.org/10.1007/978-3-031-58776-4

This Springer imprint is published by the registered company Springer Nature Switzerland AG
The registered company address is: Gewerbestrasse 11, 6330 Cham, Switzerland

If disposing of this product, please recycle the paper.

Preface

This volume contains the proceedings of the international challenge on Fast, Low-Resource, and Accurate Organ and Pan-Cancer Segmentation in Abdomen CT (FLARE 2023), held in conjunction with the International Conference on Medical Image Computing and Computer Assisted Interventions (MICCAI) in 2023. By "proceedings", we mean to say that this volume contains the papers written by participants in the FLARE challenge to describe their solutions for automatic abdominal organ and pan-cancer segmentation using the official training dataset released for this purpose.

Abdomen organs are quite common cancer sites, examples include colorectal cancer and pancreatic cancer, which are the second and third most common causes of cancer death. Computed Tomography (CT) scanning yields important prognostic information for cancer patients and is a widely used technology for treatment monitoring. In both clinical trials and daily clinical practice, radiologists and clinicians measure the tumor and organ on CT scans based on manual two-dimensional measurements. However, this manual assessment is inherently subjective with considerable inter- and intra-expert variability. Moreover, existing challenges mainly focus on one type of tumor (e.g., liver cancer, kidney cancer). There are still no general and publicly available models for universal abdominal organ and cancer segmentation.

This challenge focuses on both organ and pan-cancer segmentation, which covers various abdominal cancer types. Specifically, the segmentation algorithm should segment 13 organs (liver, spleen, pancreas, right kidney, left kidney, stomach, gallbladder, esophagus, aorta, inferior vena cava, right adrenal gland, left adrenal gland, and duodenum) and one tumor class with all kinds of cancer types (such as liver cancer, kidney cancer, stomach cancer, pancreas cancer, colon cancer) in abdominal CT scans. The evaluation metrics contain both segmentation accuracy and efficiency, including Dice Similarity Coefficient (DSC) and Normalized Surface Dice (NSD), the inference speed and resource (GPU) consumption. Compared to the previous FLARE challenges, the dataset was larger and the segmentations targets were more challenging.

We received 37 successful Docker container submissions during the testing phase. Participants also submitted their methodology papers on the OpenReview platform. Each paper received three to six review comments. Based on the initial reviews and the authors' revisions and responses, we accepted 27 papers. The papers in this proceedings explain state-of-the-art methods for abdominal organ and pan-cancer segmentation in CT scans. We thank all the participants, reviewers, and the program committee whose incredible work made this possible.

February 2024

Jun Ma
Bo Wang

Organization

Organizing Committee

Jun Ma   University of Toronto and University Health
                            Network and Vector Institute, Canada
Bo Wang   University of Toronto and University Health
                            Network and Vector Institute, Canada

Program Committee

Yao Zhang   AI Lab, Lenovo Research, China
Song Gu   Nanjing Anke Medical Technology, China
Cheng Ge   Ocean University of China, China

Contents

Fast Abdomen Organ and Tumor Segmentation with nn-UNet

Yajun Wu[✉][iD], Ershuai Wang, and Zhenzhou Shao

Department of Research and Development, ShenZhen Yorktal DMIT Co. LTD.,
Shenzhen, China
`wuyj@yorktal.com`

Abstract. The medical imaging community generates a wealth of datasets, many of which are openly accessible and annotated for specific diseases and tasks such as multi-organ or lesion segmentation. However, most datasets are only partially annotated for particular purpose, which hinders the training of multi-talent models. We uses a combination of pseudo labels and partial annotations to generate reliable fully annotated data, avoiding data conflict issues. Then, we designed a fast segmentation method for abdominal organs and tumors based on localization and segmentation. To accelerate inference, we adopt a slice-like downsample for location. To obtain the satisfactory segmentation, we first trained two models for organs and tumors with different target spacing, then combine the results. We also designed a weighted compound loss function and training patches selection strategy to finetuning the model. On the public validation set, the average scores of organ DSC, organ DSC, tumor DSC and tumor NSD are 0.9164, 0.9597, 0.4856 and 0.4221, respectively. Under our development environments, the average inference time is 8.54 s, the average maximum GPU memory is 4221.49 M, the average area under the GPU memory-time curve is 15074.59. Our code is available at https://github.com/Shenzhen-Yorktal/flare23.

Keywords: Segmentation · nnU-Net · Pseudo label

1 Introduction

Abdomen organs are quite common cancer sites, such as colorectal cancer and pancreatic cancer, which are the 2nd and 3rd most common cause of cancer death. Computed Tomography (CT) scanning yields important prognostic information for cancer patients and is a widely used technology for treatment monitoring. In both clinical trials and daily clinical practice, radiologists and clinicians measure the tumor and organ on CT scans based on manual two-dimensional measurements (e.g., Response Evaluation Criteria In Solid Tumors (RECIST) criteria). However, this manual assessment is inherently subjective with considerable inter- and intra-expert variability. Besides, labeling medical images requires professional medical knowledge and rich experience, which makes manual labeling expensive and time consuming. Moreover, existing challenges mainly focus

© The Author(s), under exclusive license to Springer Nature Switzerland AG 2024
J. Ma and B. Wang (Eds.): FLARE 2023, LNCS 14544, pp. 1–14, 2024.
https://doi.org/10.1007/978-3-031-58776-4_1

on one type of tumor (e.g., liver cancer, kidney cancer). There are still no general and publicly available models for universal abdominal organ and cancer segmentation at present.

Different from existing tumor segmentation challenges, the FLARE2023 focuses on pan-cancer segmentation, which covers various abdominal cancer types. Specifically, the segmentation algorithm should segment 13 organs (liver, spleen, pancreas, right kidney, left kidney, stomach, gallbladder, esophagus, aorta, inferior ven cv, right adrenal gland, left adrenal gland, and duodenum) and one tumor class with all kinds of cancer types (such as liver cancer, kidney cancer, stomach cancer, pancreas cancer, colon cancer) in abdominal CT scans. Also, this challenge provides the largest abdomen training dataset, which includes 2200 3D CT partial labeled scans and 1800 unlabeled scans from 30+ medical centers. However, due to particular clinical purpose at different institutes, these partial labeled scans consists of 219 all organs labeled scans, 484 partial organs labeled scans, 888 only tumor labeled scans and 609 partial organs with tumor scans. What's more, 609 mixed scans only have 5 organs (liver, right kidney, spleen, pancreas, left kidney) and tumors, specifically only 592 of these have the all 5 organs, and the rest 17 scans missing some organ. Besides, the length of scans in axis-z is in range of 74 mm to 1983 mm which means the region is very different. In a word, the variety of organs, the difference of tumors, the partial annotations and the difference of regions make the segmentation a difficult challenge.

An intuitive strategy is extract each kind of label to make the original partially dataset into 14 binary labeled datasets, then train individual models on each dataset [8]. Afterwards, final segmentation results of all requested organs can be obtained by ensemble the outputs from individual networks. An alternative strategy is to train a single unified model with original partially labeled dataset, where the organs of interest can be segmented simultaneously. In comparison, the latter strategy yields three clear advantages. First, based on the demonstrated benefits of larger training dataset for deep learning models, a unified model trained on union of all partially labeled scans, is anticipated to outperform individual models trained on each binary labeled dataset. Second, during deployment, using a single unified model can lead to faster inference speeds and reduced storage requirements. Lastly, it does not require extra post-processing steps to address conflicting voxel predictions (a voxel being predicted as different classes), a challenge that may arise when using multiple models. Therefore, we adopt the single unified model. To expand training dataset, we also used public pseudo label generated by the best-accuracy-algorithm [17].

Because of significant differences in the scanning area, we adopt common localization followed by segmentation method. Specifically, we first use a light U-Net model to extract abdomen region under large spacing, then segment under fine spacing. To improve tiny organs and tumor segmentation performance, we also proposed a weighted compound loss based on focal loss and dice loss. Besides, we adopt fine-tuning and model ensemble to improve performance further.

2   Method

The outline of our method is shown in Fig. 1. Firstly, in order to train unified segmentation model, we generate fully annotated organs-tumor labels, as presented in top Fig. 1. Specifically, we replace pseudo annotation with official label at the same position. Secondly, we train a light model which named ROI extractor to locate the abdomen for reducing computation, resource usage and difference of regions. Besides, we cropped the scans to include abdomen exactly according to the combined labels and trained two segmentation models. Specifically, one named organs model is trained with high resolution, while the other named tumor model is trained with relative low resolution. Both can segment organs and tumors, but their performance are different. As shown in bottom Fig. 1, we ensemble the predictions at the end.

Afterward, we fine-tuning segmentation models to improve tumor and some small organs segmentation performance with particular training patches selection strategy. Specifically, we fine-tuning tumor model only with patches which have tumor at the center. The final prediction is the ensemble of these two models. Last but not the least, all of our models are trained based on nn-UNet [6], which is well known and one of the best baselines for medical image segmentation.

2.1   Preprocessing

Image preprocessing is very important for segmentation. Generally, it contains interpolation and normalization. The nn-UNet interpolates isotropic and anisotropic data differently [6]. Median spacing of all training cases is set as default target spacing. For isotropic data, nn-UNet [6] zooms data and segmentation maps with third order spline and nearest-neighbor interpolation respectively. For anisotropic data, nn-UNet [6] zooms data with third order spline in plane first, then interpolates across the out plane axis is done with the nearest interpolation. After that, nn-UNet [6] normalizes CT dataset in a global zero-score manner. Specifically, where a global normalization scheme is determined based on the intensities found in foreground voxels across all training cases.

For ROI extractor, we use a slightly different methods. Specifically, we sample the original data and segmentation maps with a step of 4 in the plane and an integer on the outer axis of plane that makes original spacing close to 5mm. Also, we clipped the data to $[-1024, 1024]$ then normalize it by global mean intensities and standard variance. For segmentation models, we adopt default methods in nn-UNet but change target spacing, $[4.0, 1.2, 1.2]$ for tumor and $[2.5, 0.82, 0.82]$ for organs, respectively.

2.2   Proposed Method

Network: As mentioned before, we adopt a two-stage segmentation method. The first stage is a ROI extractor, which treat all organs as foreground and the others as background. We followed the conventional nn-Unet configuration and got a 5-stages U-Net shown in Fig. 2.

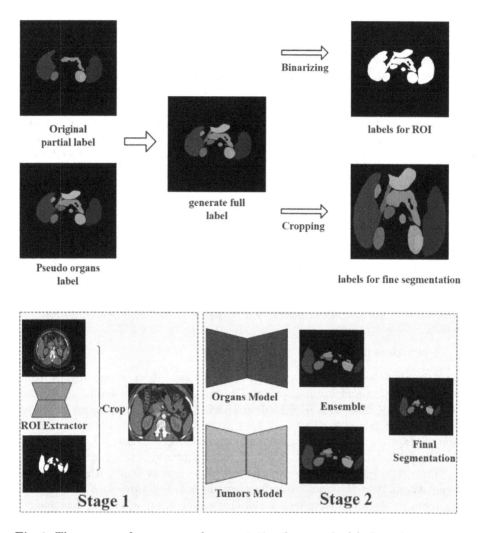

Fig. 1. The process of our proposed segmentation framework. (a) shows how we generate the training datasets. (b) shows the final inference pipeline.

Specifically, the encoder consists of an initial convolution layer and 5 encoder blocks with depths of 2, 2, 4, 6, and 4, respectively. Depth denotes number of the sequence of Conv-BatchNorm-ReLU-layers. Strides of the first convolution layer in each encoder block are 1, 2, 2, 2 and 2, respectively. The decoder consists of 4 decoder blocks, each of them consists of a transpose convolution layer which is used to upsample image, and 2 Conv-BatchNorm-ReLU sequential layers which is used to refine features. There are 4 short paths between the encoder and decoder for reusing low level features, enhancing model capacity, and avoiding gradient vanishing. It is worth noting that batch-Norm layer can be absorbed into convolution for acceleration during inference process [3].

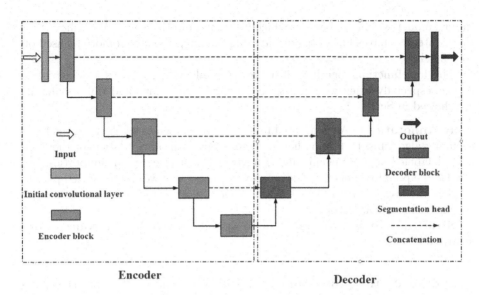

Fig. 2. U-Net

Our segmentation models are also based on U-Net, which have different configuration with extractor. Specifically, both models have 6 encoder blocks with depths of 2, 4, 6, 8, 8 and 8, respectively. The basic structure of encoder block is a residual block and the instance normalization is adopted in this model. Decoders are similar to the one in extractor, but with an extra decoder block with stride 2. The only difference is that tumor model has large target spacing while organs model has smaller spacing.

Loss Function and Training Data Selection. Recently, compound losses have been suggested as the most robust losses for medical image segmentation tasks [9]. For model prediction P and label G, we apply the sum of weighted Dice loss [15] and weighted focal loss [7] as the supervised segmentation loss:

$$L = l_d + \lambda l_f \tag{1}$$

$$l_d = -\frac{2\sum_{c=1}^{C} w_c \sum_{b=1}^{B} p_b^c g_b^c}{\sum_{c=1}^{C} \sum_{b=1}^{B} p_b^c + g_b^c} \tag{2}$$

$$l_f = -\sum_{c=1}^{C} \alpha w_c \sum_{b=1}^{B} (1 - p_{t,b}^c)^\gamma \log(p_{t,b}^c) \tag{3}$$

$$p_{t,b}^c = \begin{cases} p_b^c, & g_b^c = 1 \\ 1 - p_b^c & g_b^c = 0 \end{cases} \tag{4}$$

We also proposed a particular data selection strategy. Specifically, we dynamically selected patches during training by the location of organs and tumors. For organs model, we only choose those patches which have organ in the center. For tumors model, we choose patches which have tumor in the center. We believe that this strategy behaves like data oversampling, making the model more focused on specific class.

The loss function together with the data selection improves model performance, especially when we increase weights of small organs and tumors, details are showed in Sect. 4.1.

Fully Annotations: We generated fully annotated pseudo labels using the best-accuracy-algorithm [17], and then merged them with official labels of the 2200 partial labeled scans. Specifically, if a voxel has a foreground annotation, we replace the pseudo label with this annotation, otherwise we use generated pseudo label as the ground-truth. The 1800 unlabeled images were not used because of missing information of tumors.

Strategies to improve inference speed and reduce resource consumption

We improve inference from four aspects.

- **Interpolate the probability by GPU:** We found that restore the shape of predicted probability to the original shape was the most time-consuming. The reason behind this is that the computation is too huge for third order spline interpolation, especially interpolate by CPU. Therefore, we utilize the powerful parallel computing capabilities of GPU to reduce running time. Considering that computational load and memory usage increase with the number of target channels and volumes size, we adopted a block calculation method for large CT scans to avoid GPU memory overflow. Specifically, we restore probability every 150 slices each time.
- **Generate labels by GPU:** Default label generation method of nn-UNet is implemented on CPU. We use GPU again to make it faster.
- **Replace preprocessing by torch:** Default preprocessing is implemented by the toolkit for sciPy, which is slightly slower than torch. To reduce running time further, we decide to adopt interpolation of torch instead.
- **MultiThreading:** Another phenomenon is that even if the ROI model is smaller and there is less ROI data, ROI extraction expands much longer time than fine segmentation. We believe this is due to initialization of libraries of pytorch. To solve this problem, we use multithreading method to load models and complete initialization process when reading and preprocessing images.

Using these tricks, we were ultimately able to segment almost all of the validation cases within 15 s. Due to precise ROI and interpolate the large images by block, 4 GB GPU Memory is enough. Therefore, we did not make other changes for the GPU memory resource consumption.

2.3   Post-processing

Inspired by anatomy and the uniqueness of organs, the largest connected component-based post-processing is commonly used in medical image segmentation. In this work, we found that keep the largest connectivity component can improve the DSC scores of liver, spleen, pancreas, LAG, RAG and stomach. Due to the variety of tumors, retaining the largest connectivity component severely decrease the tumor DSC score. Therefore, we only keep the largest connected component for liver, spleen, pancreas, LAG, RAG and stomach, while keep the others unchanged.

3   Experiments

3.1   Dataset and Evaluation Measures

The FLARE 2023 challenge is an extension of the FLARE 2021–2022 [11,12], aiming to aim to promote the development of foundation models in abdominal disease analysis. The segmentation targets cover 13 organs and various abdominal lesions. The training dataset is curated from more than 30 medical centers under the license permission, including TCIA [2], LiTS [1], MSD [16], KiTS [4,5], and AbdomenCT-1K [13]. The training set includes 4000 abdomen CT scans where 2200 CT scans with partial labels and 1800 CT scans without labels. The validation and testing sets include 100 and 400 CT scans, respectively, which cover various abdominal cancer types, such as liver cancer, kidney cancer, pancreas cancer, colon cancer, gastric cancer, and so on. The organ annotation process used ITK-SNAP [18], nnU-Net [6], and MedSAM [10].

It is noticeable that we selected our training dataset for fine segmentation. Specifically, our training dataset only includes scans which have tumors and the tumor's bounding box must located in the bounding box of the organs.

The evaluation metrics encompass two accuracy measures-Dice Similarity Coefficient (DSC) and Normalized Surface Dice (NSD)-alongside two efficiency measures-running time and area under the GPU memory-time curve. These metrics collectively contribute to the ranking computation. Furthermore, the running time and GPU memory consumption are considered within tolerances of 15 s and 4 GB, respectively.

3.2   Implementation Details

Environment Settings. The development environments and requirements are presented in Table 1.

Table 1. Development environments and requirements.

Windows/Ubuntu version	Windows 10 pro
CPU	Intel(R) Core(TM) i7-10700kF CPU@3.80 GHz
RAM	16×4 GB; 2.67MT/s
GPU (number and type)	One NVIDIA RTX 3090 24G
CUDA version	11.1
Programming language	Python 3.8
Deep learning framework	Pytorch (Torch 1.10, torchvision 0.9.1)
Link to code	

Table 2. Training protocols for the ROI model.

Network initialization	"he" normal initialization
Batch size	2
Patch size	$80 \times 128 \times 128$
Total epochs	2000
Optimizer	SGD with nesterov momentum ($\mu = 0.95$)
Initial learning rate (lr)	0.01
Lr decay schedule	poly learning rate policy $lr = 0.01 * (1 - \frac{e}{m})^2$
Training time	76.5 h
Number of model parameters	10.66M
Number of flops	103.36G

Table 3. Training protocols for the refine model.

Network initialization	"he" normal initialization
Batch size	2 or 4 (fine-tuning)
Patch size	$32 \times 128 \times 192$
Total epochs	2000
Optimizer	SGD with nesterov momentum ($\mu = 0.95$)
Initial learning rate (lr)	0.01 or 0.0001 (fine-tuning)
Lr decay schedule	poly learning rate policy $lr = 0.01 * (1 - \frac{e}{m})^2$
Training time	104.5 h
Number of model parameters	68.34M
Number of flops	158.13G

Training Protocols. The training protocols of ROI extractor and fine segmentation model are listed in Table 2 and Table 3. We adopt data augmentation of additive brightness, gamma, rotation, mirroring, scaling and elastic deformation on the fly during training.

During training process, the batch size is 2 and 250 batches are randomly selected from the training set per epoch, the patch size is fixed as 32 * 128 * 192. For optimization, we train it for 2000 epochs using SGD with a learning rate of 0.01 and a momentum of 0.95. Besides, the learning rate is decayed following the poly learning rate policy. As for fine-tuning, we reduce the initial learning rate to 0.0001 and increase the batch size to 4.

4   Results and Discussion

4.1   Quantitative Results on Validation Set

At the very beginning, we trained a organ-only segmentation model using the 219 scans with fully organs annotation. The model was tested on public validation set which got 0.8715 average DSC score and 0.9342 NSD score. Due to limited training data and the presence of tumors, it is lower than the winner of FLARE2022.

Next, we constructed a larger training set with 2200 scans as described in Sect. 2 and trained a basic segmentation model. Benefit from more training data, the organ DSC, NSD, tumor DSC, and NSD scores of this model are 0.9078, 0.9461, 0.3841 and 0.2994, respectively. Then, we fine-tuned the model. Specifically, we increase the batch size to 4, set the initial learning rate to 0.0001, selected the patches with organs in the center and retrained the model for 1000 epochs. This increase the organs DSC and NSD scores to 0.9153 and 0.9558, which are 0.0075 and 0.0097 higher. Besides, the tumors DSC and NSD scores are 0.3886 and 0.3237, which are also slightly better.

Obviously, there are significant differences in segmentation performance between organs and tumors. We argue that it is caused by the variety of tumors, imprecise annotation of tumor especially of tumor boundaries and the data imbalance between organs and tumors. In order to improve performance of tumors, we increase the loss weights of tumors, increase the target spacing to [4.0, 1.2, 1.2] and retrain the model from scratch. As expected, the tumor DSC score and NSD score improved to 0.4426 and 0.3732, respectively, which were 0.0585 and 0.0738 higher than the organ model. Then, we also fine-tuned it with patches that have tumors in the center. This further improves the model, resulting in tumor DSC and tumor NSD scores of 0.4803 and 0.4201, respectively. Besides, this model got the organs DSC and NSD scores of 0.9055 and 0.9537, respectively.

To achieve better segmentation performance, we ensemble these two models. Specifically, if the prediction of the tumor model is a tumor, then the final label is a tumor, otherwise the final label is the prediction of the organ model, as showed in Eq. 5. Our final validation scores of organ DSC, organ NSD, tumor DSC and tumor NSD are 0.9165, 0.9597, 0.4803 and 0.4201 respectively, details are presented in Table 4.

$$L(x_i) = \begin{cases} \text{Tumor}, & M_{tumor}(x_i) = \text{Tumor} \\ M_{organ}(x_i), & else \end{cases} \tag{5}$$

4.2   Qualitative Results on Validation Set

Figure 3 presents some well-segmented cases in the public validation set. Similar to the DSC scores, there is little visual difference in the segmentation of liver, spleen, and aorta compared to the ground truth. We believe this is due to the intensity homogeneity, clear boundaries and good contrast. On the contrary, Fig. 4 presents some challenging cases, there are apparent difference in the segmentation of pancreas, gallbladder, duodenum, esophagus and tumors. We believe this is due to the smaller size, unclear boundaries and the heterogeneity, especially for tumors.

4.3   Results on Final Testing Set

The FLARE23 organizer collected 400 CT scans from several center sites as the final testing set. Our final performance on this hidden testing set are presented

Table 4. Quantitative evaluation results

Target	Public Validation		Online Validation		Testing	
	DSC (%)	NSD (%)	DSC (%)	NSD (%)	DSC (%)	NSD (%)
Liver	98.40 ± 0.44	99.26 ± 0.73	98.16	99.10	97.22	98.05
Right Kidney	95.07 ±7.45	96.25 ± 7.88	94.97	95.69	95.76	95.92
Spleen	98.24 ± 0.91	99.25 ± 1.30	98.19	99.30	97.90	99.05
Pancreas	87.93 ± 7.96	97.31 ± 4.09	87.28	96.72	90.47	96.91
Aorta	97.35 ± 1.84	99.22 ± 2.15	97.23	99.26	97.74	99.74
Inferior vena cava	93.30 ± 4.30	94.02 ± 4.60	92.11	92.43	92.81	93.73
Right adrenal gland	89.98 ± 4.25	98.22 ± 2.04	89.06	97.87	87.25	96.12
Left adrenal gland	89.03 ± 5.13	97.61 ± 2.84	87.90	96.45	89.26	96.56
Gallbladder	85.80 ± 23.77	86.58 ± 24.63	88.29	89.58	83.47	85.79
Esophagus	84.74 ± 15.70	93.88 ± 13.45	84.78	94.02	89.52	97.32
Stomach	94.36 ± 3.51	96.89 ± 4.16	94.73	97.37	94.88	97.25
Duodenum	83.76 ± 9.05	94.38 ± 6.46	83.56	94.48	87.63	95.88
Left kidney	95.61 ± 5.77	94.98 ± 8.69	95.01	95.38	96.05	96.70
Tumor	53.63 ± 37.10	47.82 ± 34.28	48.56	42.21	64.85	54.66
Average Organs	91.81 ± 5.21	95.99 ± 3.44	91.64	95.97	92.31	96.08

in Table 4. We can see the average organs DSC score, organs NSD score, tumors DSC score and NSD score are 0.9211, 0.9589, 0.6467 and 0.5432, respectively, which are very close to the scores on validation set. This means our models have good robustness.

4.4   Efficiency Analysis

As described in Sect. 2.2, we speed up the inference on four aspects, the inference running time details are present in Table 5. We can see that interpolating the probability to the original image size with GPU reduce the average running time by 23.88 s, generating the labels with GPU reduce the average running time by 2.88 s, preprocessing the image with torch reduce the average running time by 1.23 s and adopt multithreading reduce another 0.85 s.

Despite of using models ensemble, our method consumes less than 4GB GPU memory and can segment most of the scans within 15 s on official testing environment, except the extremely large cases.

4.5   Limitation and Future Work

As showed in Sect. 4.1, the DSC scores of gallbladder, esophagus, duodenum and pancreas are lower than 0.9, the DSC and NSD scores of tumor are much lower than organs. Besides, our final results are fused by two similar refine models, which is slightly time-consuming and complex. In the future, we will focus on improving the segmentation of small organs and tumors. Also, knowledge distillation maybe adopted to combine the two models into one (Table 6).

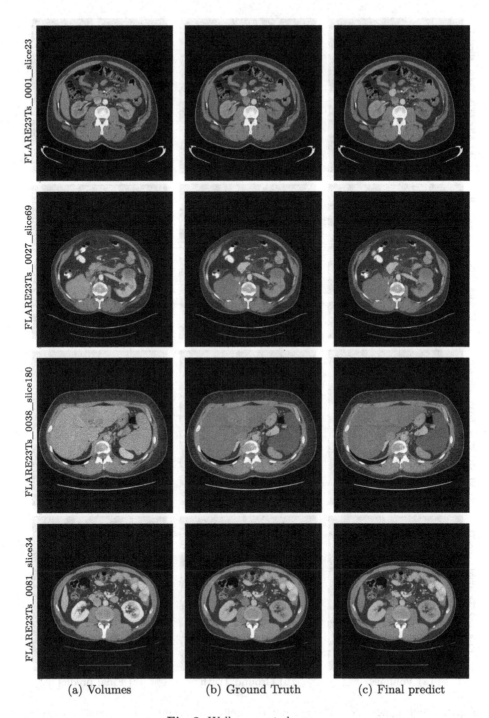

Fig. 3. Well-segmented cases.

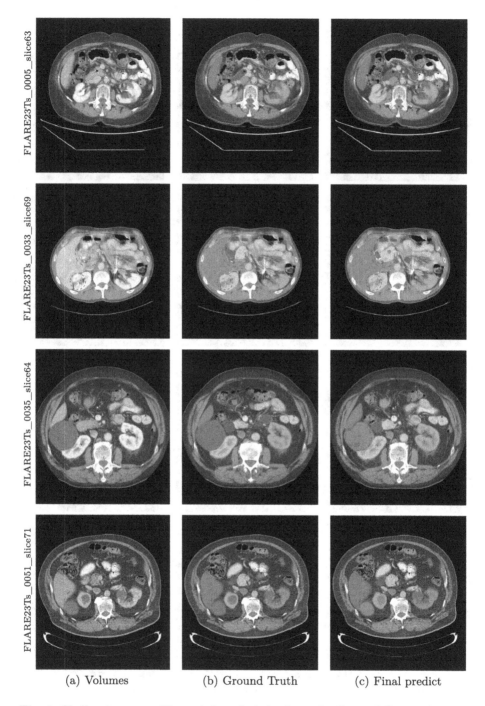

(a) Volumes   (b) Ground Truth   (c) Final predict

Fig. 4. Challenging cases. The red dotted circles have significant difference between ground-truth and prediction. (Color figure online)

Table 5. Comparison of accelerate strategies on local machine. Basic denotes inference with default nn-UNet. S1 denotes interpolating probability to original size with GPU. S2 denotes generating labels with GPU. S3 denotes preprocessing image with torch instead. S4 denotes multithreading, which means load models while reading and preprocessing images.

Strategies	Average Running Time (s)	Max Running Time (s)	Average GPU (MB)	Max GPU (MB)
Basic	37.14	95.35	4195	4624
+S1	13.26	25.41	4205	4625
+S2	10.68	18.41	4197	4624
+S3	9.45	14.14	4203	4624
+S4	8.60	11.74	4226	4721

Table 6. Quantitative evaluation of segmentation efficiency in terms of the running time and GPU memory consumption. Total GPU denotes the area under GPU Memory-Time curve. Evaluation GPU platform: NVIDIA QUADRO RTX5000 (16G).

Case ID	Image Size	Running Time (s)	Max GPU (MB)	Total GPU (MB)
0001	(512, 512, 55)	14.18	3674	17980
0051	(512, 512, 100)	9.75	3872	18538
0017	(512, 512, 150)	10.45	3816	16828
0019	(512, 512, 215)	9.08	3750	14843
0099	(512, 512, 334)	9.19	3426	15285
0063	(512, 512, 448)	10.81	3548	18534
0048	(512, 512, 499)	11.45	3638	20567
0029	(512, 512, 554)	14.05	3928	28659

5 Conclusion

In this work, we adopt pseudo labels to address the conflict of background and missing annotations. Then we proposed a weighted compound loss and a particular training-patches selection strategy to alleviate the class imbalance problem. Finally, we improve the performance by fine-tuning and model ensemble. These techniques may be helpful for other medical image segmentation tasks.

Acknowledgements. The authors of this paper declare that the segmentation method they implemented for participation in the FLARE 2023 challenge has not used any pre-trained models nor additional datasets other than those provided by the organizers. The proposed solution is fully automatic without any manual intervention. We thank all the data owners for making the CT scans publicly available and CodaLab [14] for hosting the challenge platform.

References

1. Bilic, P., et al.: The liver tumor segmentation benchmark (LiTS). Med. Image Anal. **84**, 102680 (2023)
2. Clark, K., et al.: The cancer imaging archive (TCIA): maintaining and operating a public information repository. J. Digit. Imaging **26**(6), 1045–1057 (2013)
3. Ding, X., Zhang, X., Ma, N., Han, J., Ding, G., Sun, J.: RepVGG: making VGG-style convnets great again. In: Proceedings of the IEEE/CVF Conference on Computer Vision and Pattern Recognition, pp. 13733–13742 (2021)
4. Heller, N., et al.: The state of the art in kidney and kidney tumor segmentation in contrast-enhanced CT imaging: results of the KiTS19 challenge. Med. Image Anal. **67**, 101821 (2021)
5. Heller, N., et al.: An international challenge to use artificial intelligence to define the state-of-the-art in kidney and kidney tumor segmentation in CT imaging. Proc. Am. Soc. Clin. Oncol. **38**(6), 626 (2020)
6. Isensee, F., Jaeger, P.F., Kohl, S.A., Petersen, J., Maier-Hein, K.H.: nnU-net: a self-configuring method for deep learning-based biomedical image segmentation. Nat. Methods **18**(2), 203–211 (2021)
7. Lin, T.Y., Goyal, P., Girshick, R., He, K., Dollár, P.: Focal loss for dense object detection. IEEE Trans. Pattern Anal. Mach. Intell. 2999–3007 (2017)
8. Liu, H., et al.: COSST: multi-organ segmentation with partially labeled datasets using comprehensive supervisions and self-training. IEEE Trans. Med. Imaging (2024)
9. Ma, J., et al.: Loss odyssey in medical image segmentation. Med. Image Anal. **71**, 102035 (2021)
10. Ma, J., He, Y., Li, F., Han, L., You, C., Wang, B.: Segment anything in medical images. Nat. Commun. **15**, 654 (2024)
11. Ma, J., et al.: Fast and low-GPU-memory abdomen CT organ segmentation: the flare challenge. Med. Image Anal. **82**, 102616 (2022)
12. Ma, J., et al.: Unleashing the strengths of unlabeled data in pan-cancer abdominal organ quantification: the flare22 challenge. arXiv preprint arXiv:2308.05862 (2023)
13. Ma, J., et al.: AbdomenCT-1k: is abdominal organ segmentation a solved problem? IEEE Trans. Pattern Anal. Mach. Intell. **44**(10), 6695–6714 (2022)
14. Pavao, A., et al.: CodaLab competitions: an open source platform to organize scientific challenges. J. Mach. Learn. Res. **24**(198), 1–6 (2023)
15. Ronneberger, O., Fischer, P., Brox, T.: U-net: convolutional networks for biomedical image segmentation. In: Navab, N., Hornegger, J., Wells, W.M., Frangi, A.F. (eds.) MICCAI 2015. LNCS, vol. 9351, pp. 234–241. Springer, Cham (2015). https://doi.org/10.1007/978-3-319-24574-4_28
16. Simpson, A.L., et al.: A large annotated medical image dataset for the development and evaluation of segmentation algorithms. arXiv preprint arXiv:1902.09063 (2019)
17. Wang, E., Zhao, Y., Wu, Y.: Cascade dual-decoders network for abdominal organs segmentation. In: Ma, J., Wang, B. (eds.) FLARE 2022. LNCS, vol. 13816, pp. 202–213. Springer, Cham (2022). https://doi.org/10.1007/978-3-031-23911-3_18
18. Yushkevich, P.A., Gao, Y., Gerig, G.: ITK-SNAP: an interactive tool for semi-automatic segmentation of multi-modality biomedical images. In: Annual International Conference of the IEEE Engineering in Medicine and Biology Society, pp. 3342–3345 (2016)

Exploiting Pseudo-labeling and nnU-Netv2 Inference Acceleration for Abdominal Multi-organ and Pan-Cancer Segmentation

Ziyan Huang[1,2], Jin Ye[2], Haoyu Wang[1,2], Zhongying Deng[2,3], Tianbin Li[2], and Junjun He[2(✉)]

[1] Shanghai Jiao Tong University, Shanghai, China
ziyanhuang@sjtu.edu.cn
[2] Shanghai AI Laboratory, Shanghai, China
hejunjun@pjlab.org.cn
[3] University of Cambridge, Cambridge, UK

Abstract. Deep-learning based models offer powerful tools for the automatic segmentation of abdominal organs and tumors in CT scans, yet they face challenges such as limited datasets and high computational costs. The FLARE23 challenge addresses these by providing a large-scale dataset featuring both partially and fully annotated data, and by prioritizing both segmentation accuracy and computational efficiency. In this study, we adapt the winning FLARE22 strategy to FLARE23 by utilizing a two-step pseudo-labeling approach. Initially, a large model trained on datasets with complete organ annotations generates pseudo-labels for datasets that originally contain only tumor annotations. These labels are then integrated to create a comprehensive training dataset. A smaller, more efficient model is subsequently trained on this enriched dataset for deployment, targeting both tumors and organs. Our approach, utilizing the FLARE23 dataset, has achieved notable results. On the online validation leaderboard, it reached an average DSC of 89.63% for organs and 46.07% for lesions, with an average processing time of 16.1 s for 20 selected validation cases. In the final testing set, our model demonstrated improved performance, achieving an organ DSC of 89.98% and lesion DSC of 62.61%, while reducing the average processing time to 12.02 s. The code and model are publicly available at https://github.com/Ziyan-Huang/FLARE23.

Keywords: Medical Image Segmentation · Computational Efficiency · Abdominal Tumors

1 Introduction

The abdomen is a prevalent site for tumor growth. Accurate annotation of tumors and relevant abdominal organs in CT scans is essential for the diagnosis and treatment of abdominal tumors. While deep-learning-based methods ease the

J. Ma and B. Wang (Eds.): FLARE 2023, LNCS 14544, pp. 15–27, 2024.
https://doi.org/10.1007/978-3-031-58776-4_2

task of manual annotation for radiologists, several challenges hinder their effectiveness. Firstly, there's a lack of comprehensive datasets that include annotations for both tumors and various abdominal organs. Many existing datasets focus either on organ-specific or tumor-specific annotations [8]. Therefore, learning accurate segmentations from these partially labeled and unlabeled datasets remains a challenge. Second, while state-of-the-art solutions [2,11,14,22] offer robust performance, they are often computationally intensive, thereby limiting their clinical utility. Recognizing these challenges, the FLARE23 challenge has been established. It offers a large-scale dataset that includes both partially annotated and unlabeled data, and it focuses on both segmentation accuracy and efficiency as evaluation metrics.

Given the challenge of insufficiently fully annotated datasets, semi-supervised and partial-label methods have increasingly garnered attention in the field of medical image segmentation. DoDNet [25] employs a dynamic on-demand network with a shared encoder-decoder architecture and a unique segmentation head, efficiently segmenting multiple organs and tumors from partially labeled datasets. In a similar vein, the Universal Model [12] employs Contrastive Language-Image Pretraining (CLIP) [19] to extract semantic relationships between abdominal structures, achieving high performance across multiple datasets. MultiTalent [21] adopts a multi-dataset learning approach, incorporating a class and dataset adaptive loss function to handle varying dataset characteristics and overlapping classes. As for using unlabeled data, the FLARE22 championship solution [10] demonstrates significant performance gains through pseudo-labeling and label-filtering techniques on unlabeled data. It also introduces a highly efficient, optimized version of nnU-Net [11]. However, the advent of nnU-Net v2, which excels in code usability, calls for new acceleration techniques tailored to this updated framework.

In this study, we extend the winning strategy of FLARE22 for application in the FLARE23 challenge by leveraging pseudo-labeling techniques. We employ partially-annotated and unannotated data to create datasets with comprehensive pseudo-labels. For efficiency, two different model sizes are utilized: a larger model for generating pseudo-labels and a smaller, deployable model for the final application. Specifically, we categorize the partially-labeled data into two main groups: one with comprehensive annotations for 13 types of abdominal organs, and another focused on tumor annotations. The pseudo-labeling process is executed in two stages. Initially, a larger model is trained on data with complete organ annotations to specialize in segmenting the 13 abdominal organs. This model then pseudo-labels organ annotations for datasets initially containing only tumor annotations. Subsequently, a full-annotation dataset is created by combining the new organ annotations with existing tumor annotations. A smaller, more efficient model is then trained on this comprehensive dataset for the final deployment. In this manner, we successfully generate organ and tumor labels for all 4000 complete datasets, while optimizing the inference speed of the latest nnU-Netv2 framework.

2 Method

2.1 Preprocessing

We employ the nnU-Net framework's default preprocessing. For anisotropic data resampling, trilinear interpolation is used in the axial plane and linear interpolation in the sagittal direction. Intensity normalization is performed by clipping values to the 0.5% (−970.0) and 99.5% (279.0) Hounsfield Unit levels, followed by z-normalization using a mean of 80.3 and a standard deviation of 141.4.

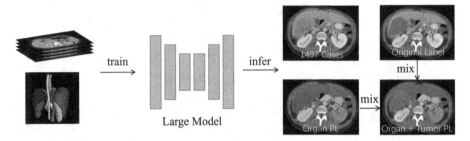

(1) Phase 1: Pseudo-Labeling Organs in 1497 Tumor-Annotated Images

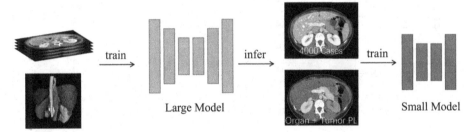

(2) Phase 2: Pseudo-Labeling Organs and Tumor in All 4000 Images

Fig. 1. Pipeline of our two-stage pseudo-labeling method. In the first stage, a large model trained for segmenting 13 organs assigns pseudo-labels to 1,497 tumor-annotated images. These images then receive combined organ and tumor labels. In the second stage, another large model trained on these 1,497 images assigns pseudo-labels for the remaining dataset. Finally, a small model is trained using the complete 4,000-image dataset.

2.2 Proposed Method

Inspired by the winning solution of FLARE 2022 from Huang et al. [10], we implement a two-stage approach for generating pseudo-labels and eventual model deployment. We employ varying sizes of STU-Net architectures [9] for these stages. For a comprehensive overview of our method, please refer to Fig. 1.

STU-Net with Different Scales. Figure 2 illustrates the architecture of our STU-Net, which serves as an extendable and transferable version of the nnU-Net. We achieve this by fixing certain configurations within the nnU-Net framework, adding residual connections to the basic blocks, and modifying the up-sampling and down-sampling techniques. In our experiments, we employed STU-Net-L for the generation of pseudo-labels and utilized STU-Net-B for the final inference deployment. These specific configurations are elaborated in the Table 1.

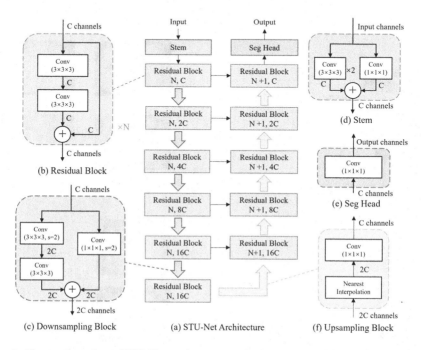

Fig. 2. Illustration of our STU-Net architecture which is built upon the nnU-Net architecture with several modifications to enhance its scalability and transferability. (a) An overview of the STU-Net architecture. The blue arrows denote downsampling while the yellow ones represent upsampling. (b) Residual blocks to achieve a large-scale model. (c) Downsampling in the first residual block of each encoder stage. (d–e) Stem and segmentation head for channel conversion of input and output. (f) Weight-free interpolation for upsampling, which effectively addresses the issue of weight mismatch across different tasks. (Color figure online)

Loss function: we use the summation between Dice loss and cross-entropy loss because compound loss functions have been proven to be robust in various medical image segmentation tasks [13].

Handling Partially-Labeled and Unlabeled Data. We divide the 2,200 partially-labeled FLARE23 images into three main categories, as summarized in

Table 1. Configurations of STU-Net-L and STU-Net-B models. Depth indicates the number of residual blocks at each resolution stage, and width denotes the channel count at each stage.

Model	depth	width	Params (M)	FLOPs (T)
STU-Net-B	(1, 1, 1, 1, 1, 1)	(32, 64, 128, 256, 512, 512)	58.26	0.51
STU-Net-L	(2, 2, 2, 2, 2, 2)	(64, 128, 256, 512, 1024, 1024)	440.30	3.81

Table 2. Categorization of Partially-labeled Data in FLARE23 Dataset: 2,200 images grouped into three categories

Category	Number of Cases
13-organs, no tumor	250
Tumor, some 5-organs	1,497
Only 5-organs	453

Table 2. We particularly focus on the subsets containing 250 and 1,497 images. Initially, a large STU-Net model (STU-Net-L) is trained on the 250 images annotated for 13 abdominal organs. This model is then applied to the set of 1,497 images, augmenting the organ annotations while preserving existing tumor labels.

For consistency, all pseudo-labels are generated by a large STU-Net model (STU-Net-L). Using the augmented 1,497-image set from the first stage, we train another STU-Net-L model to generate pseudo-labels for the remaining dataset. In the event of annotation conflicts, the original labels are preserved. Ultimately, we employ the fully augmented 4,000-image dataset to train a smaller STU-Net model (STU-Net-B) for efficient deployment and inference.

Inference Acceleration Based on NnU-Netv2. We build our efficient inference code upon the popular nnU-Net framework, particularly its latest version, v2. Several optimizations are made to accelerate the inference process. These include using larger target spacing, eliminating the cropping stage, and replacing the resampling function in skimage with torch.nn.interpolate to reduce computational load. Given that the FLARE2023 competition performs inference on a per-image basis, we transition from multi-threading to single-threaded inference to better align with the competition's structure. Additionally, we adopt last year's championship-winning efficient inference strategy, which involves skipping certain patches during patch-based inference.

2.3 Post-processing

During the pseudo-labeling generation phase, we employed Testing Time Augmentation (TTA) along the anatomical axes: sagittal, coronal, and axial, to enhance the quality of the generated labels.

However, in the final submission, we skipped post-processing for computational efficiency. The model's raw outputs serve as the final segmentation results without further modification.

3   Experiments

3.1   Dataset and Evaluation Measures

The FLARE 2023 challenge is an extension of the FLARE 2021–2022 [15,16], aiming to promote the development of foundation models in abdominal disease analysis. The segmentation targets cover 13 organs and various abdominal lesions. The training dataset is curated from more than 30 medical centers under the license permission, including TCIA [3], LiTS [1], MSD [20], KiTS [6,7], autoPET [4,5], TotalSegmentator [23], and AbdomenCT-1K [17]. The training set includes 4000 abdomen CT scans where 2200 CT scans with partial labels and 1800 CT scans without labels. The validation and testing sets include 100 and 400 CT scans, respectively, which cover various abdominal cancer types, such as liver cancer, kidney cancer, pancreas cancer, colon cancer, gastric cancer, and so on. The organ annotation process used ITK-SNAP [24], nnU-Net [11], and MedSAM [14].

The evaluation metrics encompass two accuracy measures-Dice Similarity Coefficient (DSC) and Normalized Surface Dice (NSD)-alongside two efficiency measures-running time and area under the GPU memory-time curve. These metrics collectively contribute to the ranking computation. Furthermore, the running time and GPU memory consumption are considered within tolerances of 15 s and 4 GB, respectively.

3.2   Implementation Details

Environment Settings. The development environments and requirements are presented in Table 3.

Training Protocols. To handle partially labeled and unlabeled data, we utilize the preprocessing and pseudo-labeling scheme discussed earlier. Alongside, we adopt extensive data augmentation techniques, including rotations, elastic deformations, and random cropping, to enhance our models' generalization capabilities. For training, a patch-based approach is employed. We use a balanced sampling mechanism in our patch sampling strategy to ensure equal representation of each class in each batch, effectively countering class imbalance issues. We do not conduct model selection (Tables 4 and 5).

Table 3. Development environments and requirements.

System	CentOS 7
CPU	Intel(R) Xeon(R) Platinum 8369B CPU @ 2.90 GHz
RAM	32×4 GB; 2.67MT/s
GPU (number and type)	one NVIDIA A100 80G
CUDA version	11.7
Programming language	Python 3.9
Deep learning framework	torch 2.0
Specific dependencies	nnU-Net 2.1
Code	https://github.com/Ziyan-Huang/FLARE23

Table 4. Training protocols for the STU-Net-L model.

Network initialization	He
Batch size	2
Patch size	$48 \times 192 \times 192$
Total epochs	2000
Optimizer	SGD with nesterov momentum ($\mu = 0.99$)
Initial learning rate (lr)	0.01
Lr decay schedule	poly decay
Training time	48 h
Loss function	Dice Loss + Cross Entropy
Number of model parameters	440M[a]
Number of flops	3.81T[b]
CO_2eq	114.02 Kg[c]

[a] https://github.com/sksq96/pytorch-summary
[b] https://github.com/facebookresearch/fvcore
[c] https://github.com/lfwa/carbontracker/

Table 5. Training protocols for the STU-Net-B model.

Network initialization	He
Batch size	2
Patch size	$48 \times 128 \times 160$
Total epochs	2000
Optimizer	SGD with nesterov momentum ($\mu = 0.99$)
Initial learning rate (lr)	0.01
Lr decay schedule	poly decay
Training time	24 h
Loss function	Dice Loss + Cross Entropy
Number of model parameters	58M[a]
Number of flops	510G[b]
CO_2eq	17.08 Kg[c]

[a] https://github.com/sksq96/pytorch-summary
[b] https://github.com/facebookresearch/fvcore
[c] https://github.com/lfwa/carbontracker/

Table 6. Quantitative evaluation results.

Target	Public Validation		Online Validation		Testing	
	DSC (%)	NSD (%)	DSC (%)	NSD (%)	DSC (%)	NSD (%)
Liver	97.70 ± 0.51	99.37 ± 0.48	97.61	99.29	96.43	98.09
Right Kidney	94.96 ± 5.19	96.84 ± 6.50	93.78	95.96	94.58	96.01
Spleen	96.64 ± 0.85	99.20 ± 1.32	96.67	99.41	96.08	98.46
Pancreas	87.07 ± 4.85	97.71 ± 2.95	85.82	96.97	90.20	98.08
Aorta	94.17 ± 2.18	98.64 ± 2.67	94.33	98.74	94.57	99.46
Inferior vena cava	92.84 ± 2.34	97.47 ± 2.32	92.81	97.34	93.24	98.35
Right adrenal gland	79.18 ± 12.52	94.93 ± 13.80	79.99	95.80	78.95	95.21
Left adrenal gland	80.41 ± 6.70	95.70 ± 4.18	79.94	94.97	79.89	95.07
Gallbladder	85.91 ± 19.62	88.06 ± 20.92	88.27	89.93	83.55	87.16
Esophagus	82.04 ± 15.17	93.95 ± 14.49	82.81	94.93	88.10	98.94
Stomach	93.92 ± 2.91	98.24 ± 3.25	94.19	98.34	93.47	97.96
Duodenum	84.65 ± 6.22	96.21 ± 4.65	85.47	96.75	88.22	97.89
Left kidney	94.00 ± 6.88	95.41 ± 9.33	93.46	95.59	94.69	96.52
Tumor	53.35 ± 34.22	45.24 ± 30.74	46.07	39.17	62.72	52.36
Average	86.92 ± 8.58	92.64 ± 8.40	86.52	92.37	88.19	93.54

Table 7. Performance Comparison: Partially Labeled vs. Total Data

Training Data	Organ DSC	Organ NSD	Tumor DSC	Tumor NSD
2200 Partial Label	89.45	96.20	45.91	40.04
4000 Total	89.63	96.46	46.07	39.17

4   Results and Discussion

4.1   Quantitative Results on Validation Set

Our final model's performance metrics are summarized in Table 6. Due to limitations in the online submission system, we present the average results obtained solely on a publicly labeled validation set of 50 cases.

Additionally, we conducted an ablation study to assess the impact of utilizing unlabeled data. Specifically, we compared the performance of STU-Net-L models trained on two different datasets: one with 2,200 partially labeled images and another with a total of 4,000 images. The results from the online leaderboard for both training scenarios are detailed in Table 7. As indicated by the data in Table 7, the inclusion of an extra 1,800 unlabeled images led to only minimal changes in performance metrics.

4.2   Qualitative Results on Validation Set

Qualitative results of two examples with good segmentation results and two examples with bad segmentation results in the validation set are shown in Fig. 3. As can be seen from the figure, our model performs well in segmenting larger

Table 8. Quantitative evaluation of segmentation efficiency in terms of the running them and GPU memory consumption. Total GPU denotes the area under GPU Memory-Time curve. Evaluation GPU platform: NVIDIA QUADRO RTX5000 (16G).

Case ID	Image Size	Running Time (s)	Max GPU (MB)	Total GPU (MB)
0001	(512, 512, 55)	22.03	2836	14975
0051	(512, 512, 100)	13.02	3144	16366
0017	(512, 512, 150)	28.82	3212	23825
0019	(512, 512, 215)	20.33	2974	16467
0099	(512, 512, 334)	14.13	3140	16904
0063	(512, 512, 448)	16.51	3210	19762
0048	(512, 512, 499)	16.17	3180	17090
0029	(512, 512, 554)	19.85	3394	23710

tumors that are situated on organs. However, for smaller tumors that are not located on organs, the model tends to miss the segmentation. Further investigation reveals that the model's limitations on smaller, isolated tumors could be attributed to the initial training set, which mainly consists of larger, organ-associated tumors.

4.3 Segmentation Efficiency Results on Validation Set

Efficiency results for multiple validation cases are presented in Table 8. As observed, our algorithm completes the segmentation in less than 30 s for all cases, with the majority finishing within 20 s. Additionally, the GPU memory consumption stays below 4 GB. These results demonstrate that our model not only performs well in terms of accuracy but also excels in computational efficiency.

4.4 Segmentation Efficiency Ablation

We conduct our experiments on a consistent setup featuring an Intel Core i9-13900K CPU and an NVIDIA RTX 4090 GPU. We analyze the time efficiency for Case FLARE23Ts_0063, a typically time-consuming case, with dimensions 448 × 512 × 512 and spacing 1.5 × 0.875 × 0.875.

Figure 4 illustrates the time consumption for various segmentation phases both before and after optimization. Before optimization, the process was most time-consuming in "Resample Logits", taking up to 54 s. After applying our optimization techniques, the time spent on this phase dramatically dropped to just 0.06 s. Similarly, "Sliding Window Inference" was reduced from 13.4 to 2 s.

Overall, the total time was reduced from approximately 92 s to about 11 s, demonstrating an 8-fold efficiency improvement in the segmentation process.

4.5   Results on Final Testing Set

We represent our final testing set in Table 9.

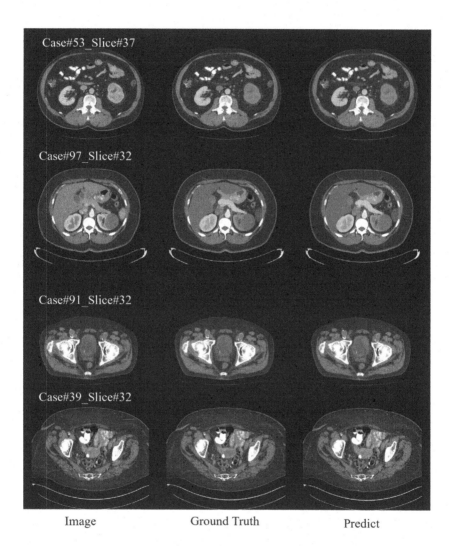

Image   Ground Truth   Predict

Fig. 3. Qualitative results of two examples with good segmentation results and two examples with bad segmentation results in the validation set.

Table 9. Results on final testing set

Organ DSC	Organ NSD	Lesion DSC	Lesion NSD	Time	GPU Memory
90.15	96.71	62.72	52.15	12.02	12033

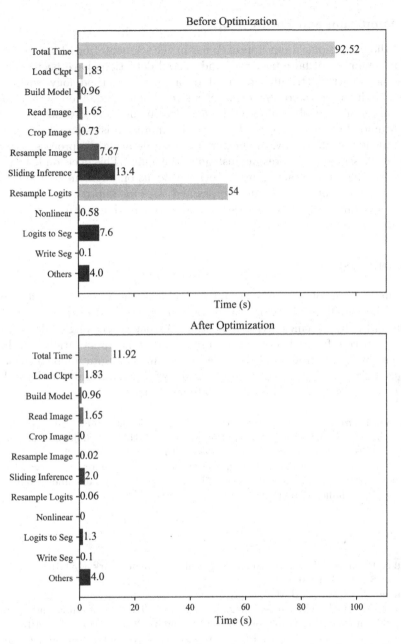

Fig. 4. Comparison of time consumption for various segmentation phases before and after optimization. The case analyzed is FLARE23Ts_0063, a typically time-consuming case.

4.6   Limitation and Future Work

One of the limitations of our approach lies in the segmentation of tumors, where a notable number of false negatives and missed detections have been observed. This issue is partly attributed to our data processing methodology, where cases marked with tumors were not comprehensively annotated. We operated under the assumption that all tumors were identified in such cases, which was a misstep. A more meticulous approach to tumor annotation is essential to overcome this challenge. Additionally, in our pursuit of accelerating the process, we opted to resize the segmentation results instead of the logits. This decision led to a significant decline in accuracy. Future work will focus on augmenting the training data to include more varied tumor types and sizes for improved generalization, alongside refining our data processing and segmentation methods to enhance precision and reliability.

5   Conclusion

The primary focus of our study has been to address the issue of partially labeled data in abdominal multi-organ and tumor segmentation. We explored a pseudo-labeling strategy to efficiently handle this challenge, breaking it down into a two-step process focused on separate organ and tumor annotations. Additionally, to reconcile the trade-off between accuracy and computational efficiency, we optimized the nnU-Netv2 segmentation framework. As a result, we have developed a methodology that is both accurate and efficient.

Acknowledgements. The authors of this paper declare that the segmentation method they implemented for participation in the FLARE 2023 challenge has not used any pre-trained models nor additional datasets other than those provided by the organizers. The proposed solution is fully automatic without any manual intervention. We thank all the data owners for making the CT scans publicly available and CodaLab [18] for hosting the challenge platform.

References

1. Bilic, P., et al.: The liver tumor segmentation benchmark (LiTS). Med. Image Anal. **84**, 102680 (2023)
2. Cheng, J., et al.: SAM-Med2D (2023)
3. Clark, K., et al.: The cancer imaging archive (TCIA): maintaining and operating a public information repository. J. Digit. Imaging **26**(6), 1045–1057 (2013)
4. Gatidis, S., et al.: The autoPET challenge: towards fully automated lesion segmentation in oncologic PET/CT imaging. Preprint at Research Square (Nature Portfolio) (2023). https://doi.org/10.21203/rs.3.rs-2572595/v1
5. Gatidis, S., et al.: A whole-body FDG-PET/CT dataset with manually annotated tumor lesions. Sci. Data **9**(1), 601 (2022)
6. Heller, N., et al.: The state of the art in kidney and kidney tumor segmentation in contrast-enhanced CT imaging: results of the KiTS19 challenge. Med. Image Anal. **67**, 101821 (2021)

7. Heller, N., et al.: An international challenge to use artificial intelligence to define the state-of-the-art in kidney and kidney tumor segmentation in ct imaging. Proc. Am. Soc. Clin. Oncol. **38**(6), 626 (2020)

8. Huang, Z., et al.: A-eval: a benchmark for cross-dataset evaluation of abdominal multi-organ segmentation (2023)

9. Huang, Z., et al.: STU-Net: scalable and transferable medical image segmentation models empowered by large-scale supervised pre-training. arXiv preprint arXiv:2304.06716 (2023)

10. Huang, Z., et al.: Revisiting nnU-net for iterative pseudo labeling and efficient sliding window inference. In: Ma, J., Wang, B. (eds.) FLARE 2022. LNCS, vol. 13816, pp. 178–189. Springer, Cham (2022). https://doi.org/10.1007/978-3-031-23911-3_16

11. Isensee, F., Jaeger, P.F., Kohl, S.A., Petersen, J., Maier-Hein, K.H.: nnU-net: a self-configuring method for deep learning-based biomedical image segmentation. Nat. Methods **18**(2), 203–211 (2021)

12. Liu, J., et al.: Clip-driven universal model for organ segmentation and tumor detection. In: 2023 IEEE/CVF International Conference on Computer Vision (ICCV), pp. 21095–21107. IEEE, Paris (2023)

13. Ma, J., et al.: Loss odyssey in medical image segmentation. Med. Image Anal. **71**, 102035 (2021)

14. Ma, J., He, Y., Li, F., Han, L., You, C., Wang, B.: Segment anything in medical images. Nat. Commun. **15**(1), 654 (2024)

15. Ma, J., et al.: Fast and low-GPU-memory abdomen CT organ segmentation: the flare challenge. Med. Image Anal. **82**, 102616 (2022)

16. Ma, J., et al.: Unleashing the strengths of unlabeled data in pan-cancer abdominal organ quantification: the flare22 challenge. arXiv preprint arXiv:2308.05862 (2023)

17. Ma, J., et al.: AbdomenCT-1k: is abdominal organ segmentation a solved problem? IEEE Trans. Pattern Anal. Mach. Intell. **44**(10), 6695–6714 (2022)

18. Pavao, A., et al.: CodaLab competitions: an open source platform to organize scientific challenges. J. Mach. Learn. Res. **24**(198), 1–6 (2023)

19. Radford, A., et al.: Learning transferable visual models from natural language supervision. In: International Conference on Machine Learning, pp. 8748–8763. PMLR (2021)

20. Simpson, A.L., et al.: A large annotated medical image dataset for the development and evaluation of segmentation algorithms. arXiv preprint arXiv:1902.09063 (2019)

21. Ulrich, C., Isensee, F., Wald, T., Zenk, M., Baumgartner, M., Maier-Hein, K.H.: MultiTalent: a multi-dataset approach to medical image segmentation. In: Greenspan, H., et al. (eds.) MICCAI 2023. LNCS, vol. 14222, pp. 648–658. Springer, Cham (2023). https://doi.org/10.1007/978-3-031-43898-1_62

22. Wang, H., et al.: SAM-Med3D (2023)

23. Wasserthal, J., et al.: TotalSegmentator: Robust segmentation of 104 anatomic structures in CT images. Radiol.: Artif. Intell. **5**(5), e230024 (2023)

24. Yushkevich, P.A., Gao, Y., Gerig, G.: ITK-SNAP: an interactive tool for semi-automatic segmentation of multi-modality biomedical images. In: Annual International Conference of the IEEE Engineering in Medicine and Biology Society, pp. 3342–3345 (2016)

25. Zhang, J., Xie, Y., Xia, Y., Shen, C.: DoDNet: learning to segment multi-organ and tumors from multiple partially labeled datasets. In: Proceedings of the IEEE/CVF Conference on Computer Vision and Pattern Recognition, pp. 1195–1204 (2021)

Context-Aware Cutmix is All You Need for Universal Organ and Cancer Segmentation

Qin Zhou[1,2], Peng Liu[1], and Guoyan Zheng[1(✉)]

[1] Institute of Medical Robotics, School of Biomedical Engineering, Shanghai Jiao Tong University, No. 800, Dongchuan Road, Shanghai 200240, China
guoyan.zheng@sjtu.edu.cn
[2] Department of Computer Science and Engineering, East China University of Science and Technology, Shanghai 200237, China

Abstract. Due to its important potential for various clinical applications, universal organ and cancer segmentation has attracted increasing attention recently. However, its performance is largely hindered due to issues such as (1) partial and noisy labels from different sources and (2) tremendously heterogeneous tumor cases. In this paper, we propose a novel partially supervised segmentation framework by introducing the $merge - max$ operation for hard mining among the unlabeled classes. Besides, to take full advantage of the expertly annotated tumor data, we design a novel context-aware CutMix scheme to dynamically perform tumor augmentation during training. We also introduce a useful data-cleaning strategy for self-training and adjust the nnU-Net framework for better efficiency. The average scores of organ DSC, organ NSD, tumor DSC and tumor NSD on the public validation set are 92.18%, 96.33%, 46.26% and 38.65%, respectively. And we achieve scores of 93.17% (organ DSC), 96.76% (organ NSD), 61.49% (tumor DSC) and 49.9% (tumor NSD) on the official test set. The average inference time is 13.95 s, the average maximum GPU memory is 2823 MB, and the average area under the GPU memory-time curve is 14112. Collectively, we ranked second among all submitted teams. Our code is available at https://github.com/luckieucas/FLARE23.

Keywords: Universal organ and cancer segmentation · Merge-max operation · Context-aware CutMix

1 Introduction

Automatic multi-organ and cancer segmentation plays a vital role in computer-aided diagnosis and treatment planning. Recently, deep learning based methods

This study was partially supported by the Natural Science Foundation of China via project U20A20199 and 62201341.
Q. Zhou and P. Liu—Contribute equally to this work.

J. Ma and B. Wang (Eds.): FLARE 2023, LNCS 14544, pp. 28–40, 2024.
https://doi.org/10.1007/978-3-031-58776-4_3

have made remarkable progress in solving organ and tumor segmentation tasks. However, most of them focus only on one type of tumor (e.g., liver cancer, kidney cancer). Pursuing a general and publicly available model for universal abdominal organ and cancer segmentation is rarely studied. Generally, multi-organ and cancer segmentation are faced with challenges from the following aspects: 1) Label inconsistency and partial annotations. Since the datasets are usually collected from different sources with varying purposes, not all the labels are annotated, and the same organ may be labeled as different indexes in different subsets; 2) Significant variations in the pan-cancer class. Due to different types of cancers, the non-rigidity of tumors and different disease progression across patients, the visual appearances of the pan-cancer class may vary dramatically among different individuals; 3) Label noise. Due to the requirement of expertise, noisy labels may occur in the forms of isolated points etc., especially in the annotations of pan-cancer class. This kind of noisy data can notoriously degrade the performance of NSD.

Many efforts have been devoted to solve the problems of label inconsistency and partial annotations. In PaNN [22], the average organ size distributions on the partially labeled datasets were constrained to resemble the prior statistics obtained from the fully labeled dataset. Another method was introduced in [17], where the non-overlapping characteristics between different organs was exploited to design the exclusion loss. Besides the prior-knowledege-based methods, co-training between two models with consistency constraints on soft pseudo labels [8], and multi-scale features learned in a pyramid-input and pyramid-output network [3] were both explored for partially supervised multi-organ segmentation. To allow effective training of the inconsistently labeled data, we introduce a $merge - max$ operation to perform hard mining on the unlabeled classes. Concretely, the labeled classes are constrained to be discriminative against each other and the hardest unlabeled class, where the hardest unlabeled class is identified as the index of the largest logits from the unlabeled classes.

To address the problem of tremendous intra-class variability (size, shape, positions and visual appearances etc.) of tumors, we propose a novel context-aware CutMix strategy to dynamically perform online tumor augmentation during training. Specifically, we locate all the tumor objects by finding each connected tumor regions, and cropping the tumor objects with neighboring regions to form a Context-aware Tumor Object (CTO) pool. These CTOs are then filtered and combined online with image cases not containing tumors for tumor augmentation during training.

To mitigate the effect of label noise, we introduce a novel data cleaning strategy to improve training data quality, which is proven to improve NSD segmentation performance without bells and whistles. (with only a small part of the unlabeled data, we can achieve equivalent performance compared to other methods that using all the unlabeled data. Besides, no post-processing is needed).

Our overall contributions can be summarized as follows:

- We propose a novel partially supervised segmentation framework by introducing the $merge - max$ operation for hard mining among the unlabeled classes.
- We design a novel context-aware CutMix scheme to dynamically perform tumor augmentation during training.
- We introduce a useful data-cleaning strategy for self-training and adjust the nnU-Net framework for better efficiency.

2   Method

In this section, we will elaborate on the training protocol of our method. Firstly, the partially labeled data is processed in a fine-resolution setting, and subsequently utilized to train a fine model for selecting the unlabeled data. Then a small part of the unlabeled data with confident pseudo labels are selected and combined with the partially labeled data to train a coarse model for final inference. During training, the $merge - max$ operation is introduced to perform hard mining on the unlabeled classes. Moreover, a novel context-aware CutMix is proposed for online tumor augmentation. Please note, data-cleaning is performed before coarse model training. We use the summation between Dice loss and cross-entropy loss, because compound loss functions have been proven to be robust in various medical image segmentation [11]. We also adapt the nnU-Net framework for better inference efficiency. Figure 1 illustrates our training protocol.

2.1   Preprocessing

We follow the standard preprocessing steps of nnU-Net to process the data before feeding into the network. For the fine-resolution and coarse-resolution preprocessing, the target spacing is (2.5, 0.82, 0.82) and (2.5, 1.5, 1.5) respectively.

2.2   Proposed Method

Hard Mining for Partially Supervised Segmentation. As many organs or tumors are not labeled in the challenge data, traditional segmentation losses (e.g., cross-entropy loss and Dice loss) can not be directly utilized for training. To enable effective training, we first group the data into different types considering their annotated label configurations. In our method, CT images with the same annotated classes are identified as the same type. During training, a certain labeling type is first selected with a probability proportional to its amount ratio, then a mini-batch of images from the selected type are randomly selected for partially supervised training. In this way, the annotated parts of images in a mini-batch are guaranteed to be the same.

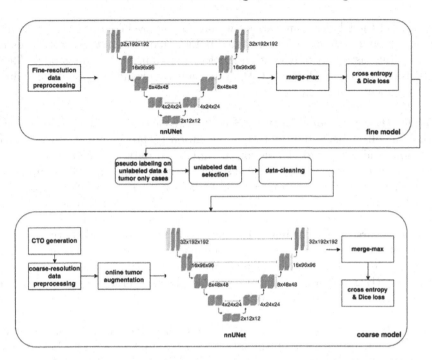

Fig. 1. A schematic illustration of our training protocol.

Merge-Max Operation. Mathematically, denote each input image as $\mathbf{I} \in \mathbb{R}^{Z \times H \times W}$, where Z, H, W refers to the number of slices along each dimension. Then the generated logits can be denoted as $\mathbf{P} \in \mathbb{R}^{C \times Z \times H \times W}$, where C is the total number of classes. Then $\mathbf{P}$ is split into labeled and unlabeled predictions $\mathbf{P}_l \in \mathbb{R}^{C_l \times Z \times H \times W}$ and $\mathbf{P}_u \in \mathbb{R}^{C_u \times Z \times H \times W}$, where $C_l + C_u = C$. $\mathbf{P}_l$ and $\mathbf{P}_u$ are further organized into a new prediction as,

$$\mathbf{P}' = [\mathbf{P}_l; max_{:C}(\mathbf{P}_u)], \tag{1}$$

where $[;]$ refers to concatenation along the first dimension, and $max_{:C}(\cdot)$ returns the max value along the C dimension. The final reorganized predictions and ground truth labels are of size $(C_l + 1) \times Z \times H \times W$. Then traditional cross-entropy loss and Dice loss are calculated as the training loss. Instead of using the summation over all the unlabeled predictions, our proposed $merge - max$ operation can help to select the hardest unlabeled class for distinguishing between labeled classes in current mini-batch.

Context-Aware CutMix for Online Tumor Augmentation. Another challenge in building a universal organ and tumor segmentation model is the lack of context-aware tumor cases, where a large fraction of the labeled tumor cases only contain tumors, while organs are labeled as background. To effectively take advantage of the labeled tumor cases, we propose a novel context-aware CutMix scheme for online tumor augmentation. Before that, we first generate pseudo labels for the cases that only contain labeled tumors using the fine model. Then Context-aware Tumor Objects (CTOs) are generated and processed for online tumor augmentation.

Unlabeled Data Selection. Following Sect. 2.2, we can get the fine model trained on the partially labeled data with fine-resolution preprocessing. Then we make predictions and get pseudo labels for the unlabeled data. As the tumor prediction confidence is low ($<50\%$), we first select the most confident 1000 samples by sorting their organ prediction uncertainty. Then 100 out of the 1000 cases with the least tumor uncertainty are selected as the pseudo labeled samples for subsequent training. On the remaining 900 cases, the tumor class is relabeled as background for coarse model training. For details of uncertainty calculation, please refer to [9]. Please note, we separately calculate the uncertainty for organs and tumors. During the uncertainty calculation of organs, the pseudo labels generated by the FLARE22 winning algorithm [9] and the best-accuracy-algorithm [19] are utilized together with our fine model.

Context-Aware Tumor Objects (CTOs) Generation. Since the shapes, positions, sizes and visual appearances of tumors may vary dramatically given the different disease types and progression in patients. Besides, for some cases, the tumors may be widely distributed in different parts of the body. It is not reasonable to use the tumor cases as a whole for online augmentation. To address this problem, we propose to generate context-aware tumor objects (CTOs), where each CTO contains only one connected tumor region. To further preserve the context of each tumor region, the neighboring regions with a predefined size are cropped together with the tumor object to form a context-aware tumor object. Figure 2 demonstrates some CTO slices on the transverse plane. In our paper, based on the statistics of tumor sizes, the neighboring extension sizes are randomly chosen between [8, 16] and [24, 32] along the Z and H, W dimension respectively. The cropped CTOs are processed following the same pre-processing steps as the coarse-resolution configurations, and saved offline for coarse model training.

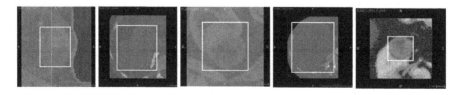

Fig. 2. Some sample slices of the generated CTO on the transverse plane. The middle-centered regions within each yellow bounding box are tumor objects. The neighboring areas are also cropped to capture context information. (Color figure online)

Online Tumor Augmentation. During the training of coarse model, for image cases with labeled tumors, they are directly optimized according to Sect. 2.2. As for images without labeled tumors, the offline generated CTOs are randomly selected and pasted into the abdominal regions of the current image for loss calculation. This is referred as the context-aware CutMix. Mathematically, denote the (image, label) pair of current image and the selected CTO as $\mathbf{I} \in \mathbb{R}^{Z \times H \times W}, \mathbf{Y} \in \mathbb{R}^{Z \times H \times W}$ and $\mathbf{I}_{CTO} \in \mathbb{R}^{Z1 \times H1 \times W1}, \mathbf{Y}_{CTO} \in \mathbb{R}^{Z1 \times H1 \times W1}$ respectively, where $Z1, H1, W1$ are varying according to the size of the selected CTO. To perform context-aware CutMix, we first generate a zero-centered mask $\mathcal{M} \in \{0,1\}^{Z \times H \times W}$, indicating whether the voxel comes from the CTO (0) or the current image (1). The size of the zero-value region is $Z1, H1, W1$. Please note the zero-center is constrained to be inside the abdominal region in our experiments. Formally, the image and label obtained using context-aware CutMix is formulated as,

$$\mathbf{I}_{CM} = \mathbf{I} \odot \mathcal{M} + \mathbf{I}_{CTO} \odot (1 - \mathcal{M}); \mathbf{Y}_{CM} = \mathbf{Y} \odot \mathcal{M} + \mathbf{Y}_{CTO} \odot (1 - \mathcal{M}), \quad (2)$$

where $\odot$ means element-wise multiplication. $\mathbf{I}_{CM}, \mathbf{Y}_{CM}$ are further utilized to train the coarse model according to Sect. 2.2.

Data-Cleaning for Robust Training. To further improve the training data quality, we introduce the data-cleaning strategy as follows. Firstly, we remove the very small isolated regions (100 voxels in our case), since they could be noise. Then we filter out the tumors that are not in the abdominal region. We further filter out tumor objects far away from all the organs to preserve context during training.

Efficient Adaptations to nnU-Net. To improve the inference efficiency, we make the following adaptations to the nnU-Net framework. We modify the cropping and resampling functions in the image preprocessing stage, where Pytorch interpolation is adopted for faster resampling. In [9], the authors assume that organs locate in the middle of the transverse plane in CT images. Inspired by this, we design a novel filtering strategy to filter out the sliding windows by only predicting a small fraction of the windows in the current transverse plane. In specific, when 2×2 (3×3) windows exist in current transverse plane, we select the windows indexed as 0,3 (4) as the indicator. If the selected windows only contain the background, then the other windows within the same transverse plane is directly set as background. This strategy can effectively improve the inference efficiency, especially for large image cases.

3   Experiments and Results

3.1   Datasets and Evaluation Measures

The FLARE 2023 challenge is an extension of the FLARE 2021–2022 [13,14], aiming to promote the development of foundation models in abdominal disease analysis. The segmentation targets cover 13 organs and various abdominal lesions. The training dataset is curated from more than 30 medical centers under the license permission, including TCIA [2], LiTS [1], MSD [18], KiTS [6,7], autoPET [4,5], TotalSegmentator [20], and AbdomenCT-1K [15]. The training set includes 4000 abdomen CT scans where 2200 CT scans with partial labels and 1800 CT scans without labels. The validation and testing sets include 100 and 400 CT scans, respectively, which cover various abdominal cancer types, such as liver cancer, kidney cancer, pancreas cancer, colon cancer, gastric cancer, and so on. The organ annotation process used ITK-SNAP [21], nnU-Net [10], and MedSAM [12].

The evaluation metrics encompass two accuracy measures—Dice Similarity Coefficient (DSC) and Normalized Surface Dice (NSD)—alongside two efficiency measures—running time and area under the GPU memory-time curve. These metrics collectively contribute to the ranking computation. Furthermore, the running time and GPU memory consumption are considered within tolerances of 15 s and 4 GB, respectively.

3.2   Implementation Details

Environment Settings. The development environments and requirements are presented in Table 1.

Table 1. Development environments and requirements.

System	Ubuntu 20.04 LTS
CPU	Dual Intel Xeon Platinum 8168, 2.7 GHz, 24 cores
RAM	1.5 TB
GPU (number and type)	16x NVIDIA Tesla V100
CUDA version	11.7
Programming language	Python 3.10
Deep learning framework	torch 2.0, torchvision 0.15.1
Specific dependencies	nnU-Net 2.0
Code	https://github.com/luckieucas/FLARE23

Training Protocols. During training, we first train a fine model on fine-resolution data (where the target spacing is set as (2.5, 0.82, 0.82)). Then, we generate pseudo labels for the unlabeled data using the trained fine model, and 1000 out of the 1800 unlabeled data are selected according to their organ prediction uncertainty. 100 out of the selected 1000 samples with least tumor uncertainty are further chosen as the pseudo labeled samples for training the coarse model (where the target spacing is set as (2.5, 1.5, 1.5)). While on the remaining 900 cases, online tumor augmentation is performed to enhance the tumor diversity during coarse model training. We adopt extensive data augmentations

Table 2. Training protocols.

Network initialization	"He" normal initialization
Batch size	4
Patch size	$32 \times 192 \times 192$
Total epochs	1200
Optimizer	SGD with nesterov momentum ($\mu = 0.99$)
Initial learning rate (lr)	0.01
Lr decay schedule	Poly learning rate policy: $(1 - epoch/1000)^{0.9}$
Training time	24 h
Loss function	Dice loss and cross-entropy loss
Number of model parameters	88.62M[a]
Number of flops	2036G[b]
CO_2eq	1 Kg[c]

[a] https://github.com/sksq96/pytorch-summary
[b] https://github.com/facebookresearch/fvcore
[c] https://github.com/lfwa/carbontracker/

(including rotations, elastic deformations, and random cropping) to enhance our models' generalization capabilities. In our patch-based training, we over-sample the foreground classes with the oversampling percent set as 0.7. Our training batch size is set as 4. And the optimal models are selected based on their segmentation performance on the public validation set. More details of the training protocol are presented in Table 2.

4 Results and Discussion

4.1 Quantitative Results on Validation Set

Table 3 shows the quantitative results on validation set. Our method achieves a mean Dice Similarity Coefficient (DSC) of 88.90% and a Normalized Surface Dice (NSD) of 92.21% on the FLARE 2023 online validation dataset. Table 4 shows the effectiveness of using unlabeled data. One can see that by using unlabeled data for training, the segmentation performance improved.

4.2 Qualitative Results on Validation Set

We analyze the samples with relatively good predictions and those with poor predictions. Figure 3 shows the results. Cases #0017 and #0053 are good cases, it can be observed that the well-segmented cases have clear organ and tumor boundaries. Case #0067 and #0035 are bad cases, they often have poor predictions of results on tumors, this may due to the large differences in tumor size of different organs. Furthermore, when training with both labeled and unlabeled data, the segmentation results are more consistent with the ground truth

Table 3. Quantitative evaluation results.

Target	Public Validation		Online Validation		Testing	
	DSC (%)	NSD (%)	DSC (%)	NSD (%)	DSC (%)	NSD (%)
Liver	98.40 ± 0.57	99.13 ± 0.99	98.39	99.15	97.26	98.17
Right Kidney	95.71 ± 8.65	95.86 ± 8.49	95.55	95.73	95.49	95.16
Spleen	98.37 ± 0.69	99.31 ± 1.20	98.47	99.51	97.71	98.81
Pancreas	88.13 ± 6.82	97.27 ± 4.79	87.50	96.91	92.03	97.99
Aorta	97.37 ± 1.64	99.13 ± 1.88	97.39	99.08	98.06	99.68
Inferior vena cava	96.01 ± 1.81	97.96 ± 2.36	95.97	97.86	96.63	98.70
Right adrenal gland	88.76 ± 2.99	97.78 ± 1.83	87.45	96.08	88.46	96.60
Left adrenal gland	88.09 ± 5.11	97.31 ± 3.58	88.01	96.58	89.59	97.15
Gallbladder	91.66 ± 7.88	92.26 ± 9.59	87.41	87.98	85.59	87.75
Esophagus	84.26 ± 14.91	92.90 ± 15.57	85.28	94.35	91.73	98.78
Stomach	93.89 ± 5.95	96.71 ± 6.57	94.74	97.52	95.00	97.81
Duodenum	86.20 ± 6.59	95.62 ± 4.53	86.87	96.13	90.99	97.82
Left Kidney	95.67 ± 5.67	95.07 ± 9.10	95.30	95.39	94.35	94.55
Tumor	52.76 ± 34.21	43.92 ± 31.68	46.26	38.65	61.49	49.90
Average Organ	92.50 ± 5.33	96.64 ± 5.42	92.18	96.33	93.17	96.76
Average	89.66 ± 7.39	92.87± 7.30	88.90	92.21	90.91	93.41

Table 4. The effect of using unlabeled data.

Target	Train without unlabeled data		Train with both labeled and unlabeled data	
	DSC (%)	NSD (%)	DSC (%)	NSD (%)
Liver	98.34	99.00	98.39	99.15
Right Kidney	95.20	95.84	95.55	95.73
Spleen	98.38	99.43	98.47	99.51
Pancreas	86.66	96.51	87.50	96.91
Aorta	96.99	98.61	97.39	99.08
Inferior vena cava	94.84	96.29	95.97	97.86
Right adrenal gland	87.97	97.35	87.45	96.08
Left adrenal gland	86.40	95.83	88.01	96.58
Gallbladder	84.43	84.86	87.41	87.98
Esophagus	83.72	93.08	85.28	94.35
Stomach	93.89	96.65	94.74	97.52
Duodenum	84.45	94.80	86.87	96.13
Left kidney	94.52	95.16	95.30	95.39
Tumor	42.65	34.90	46.26	38.65
Average Organ	91.20	95.65	92.18	96.33
Average	87.74	91.31	88.90	92.21

compared to the segmentation results achieved by training with only labeled data.

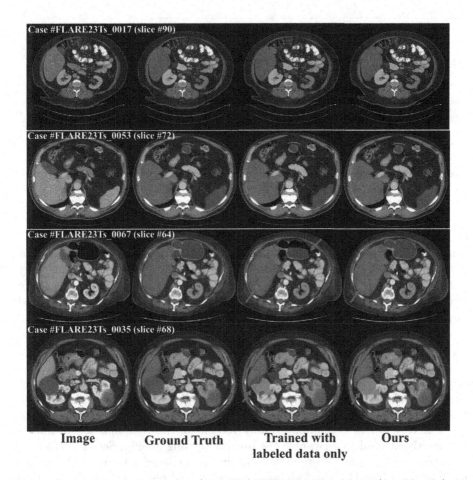

Fig. 3. Qualitative results on easy (case FLARETs #0017 and#0053) and hard (case FLARETs #0035 and #0067) examples. Please note that the results in the third column are generated by the model trained using only the partially labeled data.

4.3   Segmentation Efficiency Results on Validation Set

The average running time in validation set is 16.10 s per case in inference phase, and average used GPU memory is 2823 MB. The area under GPU memory-time curve is 18720. Table 5 lists segmentation efficiency of some typical cases.

Table 5. Quantitative evaluation of segmentation efficiency in terms of the running time and GPU memory consumption. Total GPU denotes the area under GPU Memory-Time curve. Evaluation GPU platform: NVIDIA QUADRO RTX5000 (16G).

Case ID	Image Size	Running Time (s)	Max GPU (MB)	Total GPU (MB)
0001	(512, 512, 55)	15.02	2688	11549
0051	(512, 512, 100)	13.47	2962	14673
0017	(512, 512, 150)	24.04	3022	23779
0019	(512, 512, 215)	17.27	2810	19026
0099	(512, 512, 334)	19.24	2958	23661
0063	(512, 512, 448)	23.27	3020	30148
0048	(512, 512, 499)	24.74	2994	33037
0029	(512, 512, 554)	31.57	3184	43774

4.4   Results on Final Testing Set

We obtained scores of 93.37% (organ DSC), 96.95% (organ NSD), 61.58% (tumor DSC), and 50.26% (tumor NSD) on the official test set. The average time latency and memory usage on the test set were 13.95 s and 2823 MB, with an average area under the GPU memory-time curve of 14112. Collectively, we ranked second among all submitted teams.

4.5   Discussion on Unlabeled Data

In our framework, the unlabeled data contributes from the following two aspects. Firstly, we select 100 pseudo labeled data with highest confidence to improve the data diversity, especially for tumors. Considering that the DSC performance of tumor is very low (less than 50%), only 100 out of the 1800 unlabeled samples are directly utilized to guarantee the pseudo labeling quality. Secondly, to take advantage of the confident organ parts from the unlabeled set, we select another 900 cases with best DSC performance on organs, and reset the tumor prediction as background. During training, the 900 cases will perform online CutMix with our generated CTOs to achieve dynamic tumor augmentation. In this way, we can effectively utilize the unlabeled data without introducing too much labeling noise.

4.6   Limitation and Future Work

We summarize the limitations of our method as follows: 1) Given that only 100 samples with tumors are utilized, the tumor cases in the unlabeled data is not fully exploited. 2) Due to different types of cancers, the non-rigidity of tumors and different disease progression across patients, the visual appearances of the pan-cancer class may vary dramatically among different individuals. Therefore, directly classifying the tumors as one unified class may be not the best choice.

To address the first issue, we will resort to the noisy learning tricks to directly learn the knowledge from noisy pseudo labels. As for the second issue, we will try to incorporate more prior knowledge (e.g., typical positional correlation between each organ and the corresponding tumor) into our framework to enhance the tumor learning process.

5 Conclusion

In this paper, we propose a novel framework to achieve universal organ and tumor segmentation. Specifically, we introduce the merge-max operation to perform hard-mining on unlabeled classes. Furthermore, to properly utilize the labeled tumor cases, we propose a novel context-aware CutMix scheme. This online tumor augmentation strategy is demonstrated to boost the segmentation performance. We further validate that the data cleaning step is crucial to improve the NSD performance, especially for organs.

Acknowledgements. The authors of this paper declare that the segmentation method they implemented for participation in the FLARE 2023 challenge has not used any pre-trained models nor additional datasets other than those provided by the organizers. The proposed solution is fully automatic without any manual intervention. We thank all the data owners for making the CT scans publicly available and CodaLab [16] for hosting the challenge platform.

References

1. Bilic, P., et al.: The liver tumor segmentation benchmark (LiTS). Med. Image Anal. **84**, 102680 (2023)
2. Clark, K., et al.: The cancer imaging archive (TCIA): maintaining and operating a public information repository. J. Digit. Imaging **26**(6), 1045–1057 (2013)
3. Fang, X., Yan, P.: Multi-organ segmentation over partially labeled datasets with multi-scale feature abstraction. IEEE Trans. Med. Imaging **39**(11), 3619–3629 (2020). https://doi.org/10.1109/TMI.2020.3001036
4. Gatidis, S., et al.: The autoPET challenge: towards fully automated lesion segmentation in oncologic PET/CT imaging. Preprint at Research Square (Nature Portfolio) (2023). https://doi.org/10.21203/rs.3.rs-2572595/v1
5. Gatidis, S., et al.: A whole-body FDG-PET/CT dataset with manually annotated tumor lesions. Sci. Data **9**(1), 601 (2022)
6. Heller, N., et al.: The state of the art in kidney and kidney tumor segmentation in contrast-enhanced CT imaging: results of the KiTS19 challenge. Med. Image Anal. **67**, 101821 (2021)
7. Heller, N., et al.: An international challenge to use artificial intelligence to define the state-of-the-art in kidney and kidney tumor segmentation in CT imaging. Proc. Am. Soc. Clin. Oncol. **38**(6), 626 (2020)
8. Huang, R., Zheng, Y., Hu, Z., Zhang, S., Li, H.: Multi-organ segmentation via co-training weight-averaged models from few-organ datasets. In: Martel, A.L., et al. (eds.) MICCAI 2020. LNCS, vol. 12264, pp. 146–155. Springer, Cham (2020). https://doi.org/10.1007/978-3-030-59719-1_15

9. Huang, Z., et al.: Revisiting nnU-net for iterative pseudo labeling and efficient sliding window inference. In: Ma, J., Wang, B. (eds.) FLARE 2022. LNCS, vol. 13816, pp. 178–189. Springer, Cham (2022). https://doi.org/10.1007/978-3-031-23911-3_16

10. Isensee, F., Jaeger, P.F., Kohl, S.A., Petersen, J., Maier-Hein, K.H.: nnU-net: a self-configuring method for deep learning-based biomedical image segmentation. Nat. Methods **18**(2), 203–211 (2021)

11. Ma, J., et al.: Loss odyssey in medical image segmentation. Med. Image Anal. **71**, 102035 (2021)

12. Ma, J., He, Y., Li, F., Han, L., You, C., Wang, B.: Segment anything in medical images. Nat. Commun. **15**, 654 (2024)

13. Ma, J., et al.: Fast and low-GPU-memory abdomen CT organ segmentation: the flare challenge. Med. Image Anal. **82**, 102616 (2022)

14. Ma, J., et al.: Unleashing the strengths of unlabeled data in pan-cancer abdominal organ quantification: the FLARE22 challenge. arXiv preprint arXiv:2308.05862 (2023)

15. Ma, J., et al.: AbdomenCT-1k: is abdominal organ segmentation a solved problem? IEEE Trans. Pattern Anal. Mach. Intell. **44**(10), 6695–6714 (2022)

16. Pavao, A., et al.: CodaLab competitions: an open source platform to organize scientific challenges. J. Mach. Learn. Res. **24**(198), 1–6 (2023)

17. Shi, G., Xiao, L., Chen, Y., Zhou, S.K.: Marginal loss and exclusion loss for partially supervised multi-organ segmentation. Med. Image Anal. **70**, 101979 (2021). https://doi.org/10.1016/j.media.2021.101979

18. Simpson, A.L., et al.: A large annotated medical image dataset for the development and evaluation of segmentation algorithms. arXiv preprint arXiv:1902.09063 (2019)

19. Wang, E., Zhao, Y., Wu, Y.: Cascade dual-decoders network for abdominal organs segmentation. In: Ma, J., Wang, B. (eds.) FLARE 2022. LNCS, vol. 13816, pp. 202–213. Springer, Cham (2022). https://doi.org/10.1007/978-3-031-23911-3_18

20. Wasserthal, J., et al.: TotalSegmentator: robust segmentation of 104 anatomic structures in CT images. Radiol.: Artif. Intell. **5**(5), e230024 (2023)

21. Yushkevich, P.A., Gao, Y., Gerig, G.: ITK-SNAP: an interactive tool for semi-automatic segmentation of multi-modality biomedical images. In: Annual International Conference of the IEEE Engineering in Medicine and Biology Society, pp. 3342–3345 (2016)

22. Zhou, Y., et al.: Prior-aware neural network for partially-supervised multi-organ segmentation. In: 2019 IEEE/CVF International Conference on Computer Vision, ICCV 2019, Seoul, Korea (South), 27 October–2 November 2019, pp. 10671–10680. IEEE (2019). https://doi.org/10.1109/ICCV.2019.01077

Abdomen Multi-organ Segmentation Using Pseudo Labels and Two-Stage

Xinye Yang, Xuru Zhang, Xiaochao Yan, Wangbin Ding, Hao Chen, and Liqin Huang(✉)

College of Physics and Information Engineering, Fuzhou University, Fuzhou, China
hlq@fzu.edu.cn

Abstract. Recently, the nnU-Net network had achieved excellent performance in many medical image segmentation tasks. However, it also had some obvious problems, such as being able to only perform fully supervised tasks, excessive resource consumption in the predict. Therefore, in the abdominal multi-organ challenge of FLARE23, only incomplete labeled data was provided, and the size of them was too large, which made the original nnU-Net difficult to run. Based on this, we had designed a framework that utilized generated pseudo labels and two-stage segmentation for fast and effective prediction. Specifically, we designed three nnU-Net, one for generating high-quality pseudo labels for unlabeled data, the other for generating coarse segmentation to guide cropping, and the third for achieving effective segmentation. Our method achieved an average DSC score of 88.87% and 38.00% for the organs and lesions on the validation set and the average running time and area under GPU memory-time cure are 45 s and 3000 MB, respectively.

Keywords: Pseudo Label · Two-stage · Low Consumption

1 Introduction

The segmentation of abdomen organs plays an important role in the field of medical imaging. Abdomen organs are common cancer sites, including colorectal and pancreatic cancer, which are the second and third major causes of cancer deaths worldwide. Therefore, accurate segmentation of abdominal CT images is crucial for early diagnosis, treatment planning, and efficacy evaluation of cancer. Since the advent of CT (computer tomography), it has been frequently used for the treatment and monitoring of cancer. Through CT scanning, doctors can obtain detailed three-dimensional images of the patient's internal organs in a non-invasive manner, thereby helping doctors locate and develop treatment plans. These tasks all rely on the accurate segmentation of abdominal organs. For example, in the process of cancer treatment, doctors need to quantitatively evaluate the volume changes of lesions to monitor efficacy, which requires precise lesions segmentation. In addition, organ segmentation before surgery can help doctors plan surgical paths and predict surgical risks, thereby improving the success rate of surgery.

© The Author(s), under exclusive license to Springer Nature Switzerland AG 2024
J. Ma and B. Wang (Eds.): FLARE 2023, LNCS 14544, pp. 41–53, 2024.
https://doi.org/10.1007/978-3-031-58776-4_4

Traditional manual segmentation methods have many limitations. This manual evaluation is subjective, resulting in significant differences between experts, and low consistency of results. Secondly, the manual segmentation process consumes a lot of time and labor, especially for large-scale datasets, which reduces work efficiency. In addition, manual segmentation may face many difficulties for complex anatomical structures and lesions, resulting in unsatisfactory segmentation results. Therefore, researchers have proposed some traditional abdominal segmentation methods, such as region growth algorithm, graph cut, morphological, and level set method, which have achieved good results. However, due to its reliance on manually designed features and rules, it has poor segmentation performance for complex organ structures and lesions and slow speed for processing large-scale data.

The introduction of deep learning technology has brought new hope for abdominal organ segmentation. Deep learning models can automatically learn the features in images, and accurately segment abdominal organs and lesions at the pixel level, greatly improving the efficiency and accuracy of segmentation. Therefore, deep learning technology is widely used in the segmentation of abdominal CT images and has achieved remarkable results in many studies. For example, the U-Net model adopts an encoding decoding structure, which effectively captures features at different scales, significantly improving the segmentation effect of organs and lesions [16]. The Seg-Net model adopts a lightweight encoding decoding structure, which is suitable for low computational resource scenarios while maintaining good segmentation accuracy [1]. Cao et al. proposed a network based on self-attention mechanism for abdominal organ segmentation [3], which can capture long-distance dependencies of images and improve generalization ability through self-supervised pre-training. This method has also achieved good results in multi-organ and tumor segmentation tasks. However, it requires a large amount of computing resources and time to train the model, which may not be feasible in practical applications. Chen et al. proposed a deep network based on incremental learning [21], which can recall old knowledge without saving old data and dynamically extends to new categories. It also utilizes visual semantic information embedded in text to enhance training effectiveness. It demonstrates superior performance in multi-organ and tumor segmentation tasks. However, as to this method, it is necessary to design a reasonable pseudo label generation strategy and parameter-sharing mechanism to alleviate catastrophic forgetting problems, select appropriate text descriptions and embedding methods to extract effective visual semantic information, balance the learning rate and weight between new and old categories to avoid overfitting or underfitting problems.

One of the most important and well-performing baselines among these methods is nnU-Net [10], namely no-new-Net. It can automatically configure parameters and conduct network training based on data. The nnU-Net places more emphasis on image preprocessing, automatically determining image modality and performing corresponding normalization operations, and resampling different voxel intervals based on cubic spline interpolation. And it can automatically set hyperparameters, such as training batch size, image block size, downsampling frequency, etc. In recent years, many top-level solutions have been established based on it to address the challenges of medical image segmentation. Although nnU-Net can achieve state-of-the-art performance in a fully supervised manner, it is also limited to fully supervised training. Faced with complex datasets, it is difficult for nnU-Net to achieve the expected results. Generally speaking, it can be observed that nnU-Net has the following problems:

– The default nnU-Net has a high computational complexity, which takes a long time to perform preprocessing or prediction. At the same time, the device is prone to memory overflow;
– The default nnU-Net does not support training other than fully supervised.

However, in real clinical scenarios, the time budget inferred by the model and the amount of labeled data is limited. Therefore, we urgently need a framework that can utilize all types of data and perform effective inference simultaneously.

Inspired by [20,23], in this article, we designed a two-stage framework consisting of three 3D nnU-Net. Firstly, by using incomplete labeled data to generate pseudo labels and overlaying existing labels to generate more reliable pseudo labels which serve as the basis for fully supervised data in subsequent stages; Secondly, in the first stage, coarse segmentation is performed to generate the abdominal ROI region, guiding the data crop in the second stage, thereby reducing the initial size of the data. Thirdly, perform final fully supervised fine segmentation.

Our main contributions are summarized as follows:

– We have designed a simple pseudo-labels generation framework based on nnU-Net;
– We propose an effective cropping strategy that utilizes coarse segmentation results to locate and crop ROI regions. This strategy can greatly reduce the initial data size and is beneficial for improving inference speed and reducing resource consumption.

2   Method

2.1   Preprocessing

We analyzed the original labeled data and found that some data contained partial organ labels, some data only contained tumor labeling, and some data contained both organ and tumor labeling. Due to the fact that no label in the original data contained both the tumor and all abdominal organs, we extracted the data of labels containing all organs (a total of 13 categories) as the first category data. As to the remaining data which had incomplete organ labels, we continued to divide it into two parts, one of which contained both organs and tumors as the second category. In subsequent strategies, we would use these two types of data in sequence.

We didn't use unlabeled images and the pseudo labels generated by the FLARE22 winning algorithm [9] and the best-accuracy-algorithm [18].

2.2   Proposed Method

As shown in the Fig. 1, this is the overall framework of our method. First, use the first category data which has 13 organ-labels for training nnU-Net-14 to generate pseudo labels for the organs(According to the number of categories required in the corresponding segmentation task, we add number-suffixes to the "nnU-Net" used to distinguish different nnU-Net we used. For example, if the task has 13 labels, the number of categories is 14 and it is named nnU-Net-14. The latter two nnU-Net are also the same). Second, the pseudo labels are added to the second category data to obtain a more reliable pseudo labels. Third, unify all the pseudo labels obtained in the second step into similar labels, which used for nnU-Net-2 training for coarse segmentation of background and abdominal regions. Finally, under the guidance of nnU-Net-2 coarse segmentation, the pseudo labels got in second step with its' corresponding data are cropped and used for nnU-Net-15 training to obtain a network that can segment tumors and all organs.

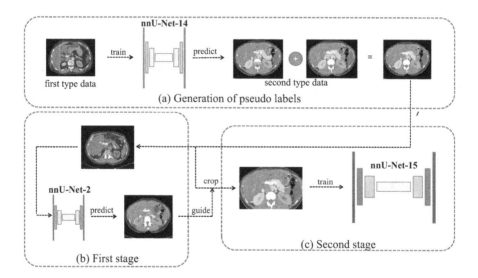

Fig. 1. This is the overall framework of our method. Part (a) is pseudo label generation, (b) is the first stage coarse segmentation, and (c) is the second stage fine segmentation.

Generation of Pseudo Labels. Previously, we had already divided the dataset into several parts. For the first type of data, we used threshold algorithms to roughly remove the areas outside the torso to reduce excess areas and training costs. Firstly, the first type of data containing 13 organ labels after processing was used for fully supervised training of the first nnU-Net-14 network. Secondly, the network was used to predict the second type of data and generate corresponding organ pseudo labels. Thirdly, used the generated pseudo labels to guide the filling of real labels, forming 14-type labels including all organs and tumors, like Fig. 2. This process could also use data that only contain tumor label to be filled by predicted pseudo organ labels, getting 14-type labels. But we didn't choose it. This was because the quality of real labels was better than that of pseudo labels, the more real organ labels there were during the process, the better the quality of the final pseudo labels.

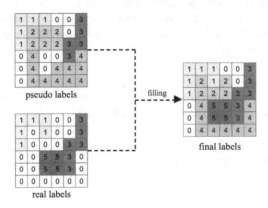

Fig. 2. We introduce our label-filling strategy. As shown in the figure, first identify which types of real labels are missing compared to the generated pseudo labels. In our schematic, it is obvious that the real labels do not contain two types of labels: 2 and 4. Then, we will only fill in these types of labels based on the real labels. When filling in, first determine whether the location already has a label. If not, fill it in. Otherwise not to avoid overwriting the original real labels.

First Stage Segmentation. We converted the final labels of these 14 categories into labels with only one category, and reduced them and the corresponding data's size to 1/4 of the original size to lower the consumption of training and predict processes. We used the reduced data and labels to train the nnU-Net-2 network and used it to predict any reduced data to obtain simple abdominal region segmentation results. Finally, by expanding the segmentation result to the initial size, we obtained the final coarse segmentation result.

Second Stage Segmentation. We could use the first stage coarse segmentation network to predict the second type of data, and guided cropping for the second type of data based on the abdominal region labels in the coarse segmentation results. Due to the high amount of impurities in the coarse segmentation results, there were many misclassified areas, and the abdominal organs'label did not stick together, these factors would affect our strategy of finding the abdominal range. Therefore, we first dilated the labels of the coarse segmentation results to make the abdominal organs as connected as possible. Then counted all connected domains, among which the largest connected domain was basically the abdominal region. We took its range to guide subsequent data cropping and used these data for the training of nnU-Net-15.

2.3   Our Method Used in Inference

In inference, we first reduced the input data size to 1/4. Then used nnU-Net-2 for the first prediction on the reduced data to obtain the coarse segmentation result, then restored its size. Secondly, we got the spatial range of the largest connected domain in the coarse segmentation results, which was very likely abdomen, to guide the cropping of the original validation data. Finally, nnU-Net-15 was used to predict the validation data after the cropping, obtaining a fine segmentation. The size of the fine segmentation result was filled to the same size as the original data to obtain the final segmentation result. Although our method used two predictions, it did not take more time than end-to-end nnU-Net. Moreover, we used different methods before each stage to greatly reduce the size of input data, resulting in improved inference speed and lower resource consumption in each stage.

3   Experiments

3.1   Dataset and Evaluation Measures

The FLARE 2023 challenge is an extension of the FLARE 2021–2022 [12,13], aiming to aim to promote the development of foundation models in abdominal disease analysis. The segmentation targets cover 13 organs and various abdominal lesions. The training dataset is curated from more than 30 medical centers under the license permission, including TCIA [4], LiTS [2], MSD [17], KiTS [7,8], autoPET [5,6], TotalSegmentator [19], and AbdomenCT-1K [14]. The training set includes 4000 abdomen CT scans where 2200 CT scans with partial labels and 1800 CT scans without labels. The validation and testing sets include 100 and 400 CT scans, respectively, which cover various abdominal cancer types, such as liver cancer, kidney cancer, pancreas cancer, colon cancer, gastric cancer, and so on. The organ annotation process used ITK-SNAP [22], nnU-Net [10], and MedSAM [11].

The evaluation metrics encompass two accuracy measures-Dice Similarity Coefficient (DSC) and Normalized Surface Dice (NSD)-alongside two efficiency measures-running time and area under the GPU memory-time curve. These metrics collectively contribute to the ranking computation. Furthermore, the running time and GPU memory consumption are considered within tolerances of 15 s and 4 GB, respectively.

3.2   Implementation Details

Environment Settings. The development environments and requirements are presented in Table 1.

Table 1. Development environments and requirements.

System	Ubuntu 20.04.2
CPU	Intel(R) Core(TM) i9-12900X CPU@3.13 GHz
RAM	$16 \times 4\,\mathrm{GB/s}$
GPU (number and type)	NVIDIA GeForce RTX 4090 24G
CUDA version	11.7
Programming language	Python 3.9
Deep learning framework	Pytorch (Torch 2.0.1)

Training Protocols. The training protocols for three nnU-Net are shown in Table 2.

Table 2. Training protocols.

	Labels generation	Stage 1	Stage 2
Batch size	2		
Initial learning rate (lr)	0.01		
Lr decay schedule	polylrscheduler for nnU-Net		
Patch size	$64 \times 128 \times 224$	$96 \times 160 \times 160$	$112 \times 128 \times 160$
Total epochs	1000	50	500
Training time	36 h	2 h	14 h
Optimizer	SGD with nesterov momentum ($\mu = 0.99$)		
Loss	RobustCrossEntroyLoss + MeomoryEfficientSoftDiceLoss		

4 Results and Discussion

4.1 Quantitative Results on Validation Set

The performance of trained nnU-Net-14 and nnU-Net-15 on the validation is shown in the Table 3. It can be seen that nnU-Net-15, trained after label filling, performs better on most organ segmentation in the validation than nnU-Net-14 which only segments organs.

4.2 Qualitative Results on Validation Set

In the two cases with the best segmentation performance, like Fig. 3, it can be seen that the organ and tumor are well segmented. In the two cases with the worst segmentation performance, we found that our model's prediction results clearly had regular boundaries, causing the segmentation results to appear as if some parts have been removed, as shown in the red box in the Fig. 4.

Table 3. Quantitative evaluation results.

Target	nnU-Net-14		nnU-Net-15	
	DSC (%)	NSD (%)	DSC (%)	NSD (%)
Liver	0.9363	0.9539	0.9663	0.9599
Right Kidney	0.9032	0.9168	0.9229	0.9204
Spleen	0.9121	0.9169	0.9673	0.9658
Pancreas	0.8062	0.9365	0.8445	0.9462
Aorta	0.9439	0.9676	0.9558	0.9744
Inferior vena cava	0.9171	0.9303	0.9323	0.9435
Right adrenal gland	0.7938	0.9275	0.8284	0.9457
Left adrenal gland	0.7676	0.9008	0.7853	0.9117
Gallbladder	0.7471	0.7159	0.7849	0.7721
Esophagus	0.8063	0.9175	0.8146	0.9218
Stomach	0.8895	0.9305	0.9003	0.9346
Duodenum	0.8895	0.9199	0.8269	0.9411
Left kidney	0.8956	0.8943	0.9240	0.9196
Tumor	/	/	0.3914	0.3286
Average	0.8547	0.9100	0.8810	0.9274

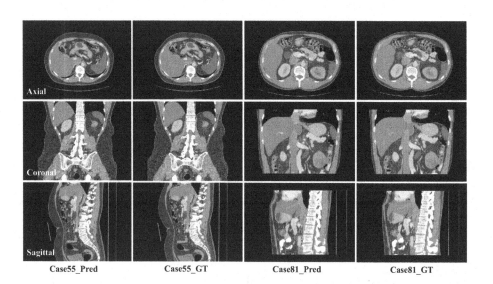

Case55_Pred   Case55_GT   Case81_Pred   Case81_GT

Fig. 3. Two best examples from our segmentation results.

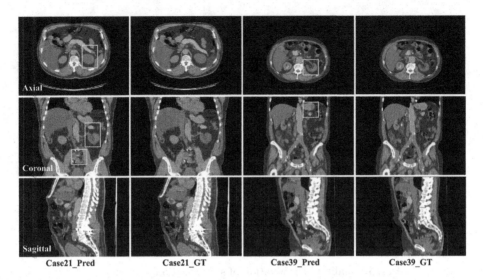

Fig. 4. Two worst examples from our segmentation results.

4.3   Segmentation Efficiency Results on Validation Set

After observation, most of the data show similar utilization rates in CPU, GPU, and RAM, so we randomly select two of them for analysis, like Fig. 5. Because this is a two-stage segmentation network, there are two prediction stages, which will occupy a lot of RAM and GPU. Therefore, there will be two peaks in the variation of GPU and RAM occupancy over time. The first smaller peak is due to the coarse segmentation, while the second larger peak is due to the fine segmentation in the second stage.

Table 4. Quantitative evaluation of segmentation efficiency in terms of the running them and GPU memory consumption.

Case ID	Image Size	Running Time (s)	Max GPU (MB)	Total GPU (MB)
0001	(512, 512, 55)	93.76	3882	16384
0051	(512, 512, 100)	107.06	4174	16384
0017	(512, 512, 150)	127.36	4394	16384
0019	(512, 512, 215)	111.72	3946	16384
0099	(512, 512, 334)	129.2	3848	16384
0063	(512, 512, 448)	162.63	3922	16384
0048	(512, 512, 499)	173.74	3794	16384
0029	(512, 512, 554)	225.18	4554	16384

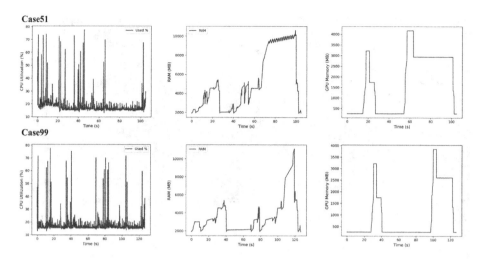

Fig. 5. Qualitative evaluation of segmentation efficiency.

4.4   Results on Final Testing Set

The Table 5 is our testing results during MICCAI (2023.10.8).

4.5   Limitation and Future Work

For limitation, from examples of poor segmentation, we can easily conclude that the segmentation performance of our method not only depends on the quality of the pseudo labels, but also on the accuracy of the first stage coarse segmentation. Poor quality of coarse segmentation can lead to incomplete coverage to the abdominal area after cropping, resulting in segmentation fragmentary. For future work, on the one hand, we plan to adopt the idea of iterative learning and continuously utilize better models to generate more accurate pseudo labels; On the other hand, we plan to improve the performance of the coarse segmentation network and improve the post-processing strategy of it (Table 4).

5   Conclusion

This article designs a two-stage segmentation framework based on nnU-Net, which utilizes partially labeled data for fully supervised data construction, training, and effective predict. This method can solve the problem of excessive consumption of nnU-Net.

Acknowledgements. The authors of this paper declare that the segmentation method they implemented for participation in the FLARE 2023 challenge has not used any pre-trained models nor additional datasets other than those provided by the organizers. The proposed solution is fully automatic without any manual intervention. We

Table 5. Results on final testing set

Accuracy measures	DSC	NSD
Liver	0.9646	0.9656
RK	0.9447	0.9423
Spleen	0.9252	0.9311
Pancreas	0.8925	0.9659
Aorta	0.9672	0.9842
IVC	0.9540	0.9704
RAG	0.8305	0.9445
LAG	0.8014	0.9270
Gallbladder	0.7894	0.8033
Esophagus	0.8743	0.9690
Stomach	0.9074	0.9505
Duodenum	0.8610	0.9561
LK	0.9127	0.9168
Organ	0.8940	0.9407
Lesion	0.3379	0.2474

thank all the data owners for making the CT scans publicly available and CodaLab [15] for hosting the challenge platform.

This work was supported by National Natural Science Foundation of China (62271149), Fujian Provincial Natural Science Foundation project (2021J02019, 2021J01578).

References

1. Badrinarayanan, V., Kendall, A., Cipolla, R.: SegNet: a deep convolutional encoder-decoder architecture for image segmentation. IEEE Trans. Pattern Anal. Mach. Intell. **39**(12), 2481–2495 (2017)
2. Bilic, P., et al.: The liver tumor segmentation benchmark (LiTS). Med. Image Anal. **84**, 102680 (2023)
3. Cao, H., et al.: Swin-Unet: Unet-like pure transformer for medical image segmentation. In: Karlinsky, L., Michaeli, T., Nishino, K. (eds.) ECCV 2022. LNCS, vol. 13803, pp. 205–218. Springer, Cham (2022). https://doi.org/10.1007/978-3-031-25066-8_9
4. Clark, K., et al.: The cancer imaging archive (TCIA): maintaining and operating a public information repository. J. Digit. Imaging **26**(6), 1045–1057 (2013)
5. Gatidis, S., et al.: The AutoPET challenge: towards fully automated lesion segmentation in oncologic PET/CT imaging. Preprint at Research Square (Nature Portfolio) (2023). https://doi.org/10.21203/rs.3.rs-2572595/v1

6. Gatidis, S., et al.: A whole-body FDG-PET/CT dataset with manually annotated tumor lesions. Sci. Data **9**(1), 601 (2022)
7. Heller, N., et al.: The state of the art in kidney and kidney tumor segmentation in contrast-enhanced CT imaging: results of the KiTS19 challenge. Med. Image Anal. **67**, 101821 (2021)
8. Heller, N., et al.: An international challenge to use artificial intelligence to define the state-of-the-art in kidney and kidney tumor segmentation in CT imaging. Proc. Am. Soc. Clin. Oncol. **38**(6), 626 (2020)
9. Huang, Z., et al.: Revisiting nnU-net for iterative pseudo labeling and efficient sliding window inference. In: Ma, J., Wang, B. (eds.) FLARE 2022. LNCS, vol. 13816, pp. 178–189. Springer, Cham (2022). https://doi.org/10.1007/978-3-031-23911-3_16
10. Isensee, F., Jaeger, P.F., Kohl, S.A., Petersen, J., Maier-Hein, K.H.: nnU-net: a self-configuring method for deep learning-based biomedical image segmentation. Nat. Methods **18**(2), 203–211 (2021)
11. Ma, J., He, Y., Li, F., Han, L., You, C., Wang, B.: Segment anything in medical images. Nat. Commun. **15**, 654 (2024)
12. Ma, J., et al.: Fast and low-GPU-memory abdomen CT organ segmentation: the flare challenge. Med. Image Anal. **82**, 102616 (2022)
13. Ma, J., et al.: Unleashing the strengths of unlabeled data in pan-cancer abdominal organ quantification: the FLARE22 challenge. arXiv preprint arXiv:2308.05862 (2023)
14. Ma, J., et al.: AbdomenCT-1k: is abdominal organ segmentation a solved problem? IEEE Trans. Pattern Anal. Mach. Intell. **44**(10), 6695–6714 (2022)
15. Pavao, A., et al.: CodaLab competitions: an open source platform to organize scientific challenges. J. Mach. Learn. Res. **24**(198), 1–6 (2023)
16. Ronneberger, O., Fischer, P., Brox, T.: U-net: convolutional networks for biomedical image segmentation. In: Navab, N., Hornegger, J., Wells, W.M., Frangi, A.F. (eds.) MICCAI 2015. LNCS, vol. 9351, pp. 234–241. Springer, Cham (2015). https://doi.org/10.1007/978-3-319-24574-4_28
17. Simpson, A.L., et al.: A large annotated medical image dataset for the development and evaluation of segmentation algorithms. arXiv preprint arXiv:1902.09063 (2019)
18. Wang, E., Zhao, Y., Wu, Y.: Cascade dual-decoders network for abdominal organs segmentation. In: Ma, J., Wang, B. (eds.) FLARE 2022. LNCS, vol. 13816, pp. 202–213. Springer, Cham (2022). https://doi.org/10.1007/978-3-031-23911-3_18
19. Wasserthal, J., et al.: TotalSegmentator: robust segmentation of 104 anatomic structures in CT images. Radiol.: Artif. Intell. **5**(5), e230024 (2023)
20. Wu, M., Ding, W., Yang, M., Huang, L.: Multi-depth boundary-aware left atrial scar segmentation network. In: Zhuang, X., Li, L., Wang, S., Wu, F. (eds.) LAScarQS 2022. LNCS, vol. 13586, pp. 16–23. Springer, Cham (2022). https://doi.org/10.1007/978-3-031-31778-1_2
21. You, C., Xiang, J., Su, K., Zhang, X., Dong, S., Onofrey, J., Staib, L., Duncan, J.S.: Incremental learning meets transfer learning: application to multi-site prostate MRI segmentation. In: Albarqouni, S., et al. (eds.) DeCaF FAIR 2022. LNCS, vol. 13573, pp. 3–16. Springer, Cham (2022). https://doi.org/10.1007/978-3-031-18523-6_1

22. Yushkevich, P.A., Gao, Y., Gerig, G.: ITK-SNAP: an interactive tool for semi-automatic segmentation of multi-modality biomedical images. In: Annual International Conference of the IEEE Engineering in Medicine and Biology Society, pp. 3342–3345 (2016)

23. Zhang, X., Yang, X., Huang, L., Huang, L.: Two stage of histogram matching augmentation for domain generalization: application to left atrial segmentation. In: Zhuang, X., Li, L., Wang, S., Wu, F. (eds.) LAScarQS 2022. LNCS, vol. 13586, pp. 60–68. Springer, Cham (2022). https://doi.org/10.1007/978-3-031-31778-1_6

A Two-Step Deep Learning Approach for Abdominal Organ Segmentation

Jianwei Gao(✉)(iD), Juan Xu, Honggao Fei, and Dazhu Liang

Digital Health China Technologies Co., LTD., Beijing, China
`{gaojw,xujuan,feihg,liangdz}@dhctech.com`

Abstract. Accurate delineation and analysis of anatomical structures within medical images are essential in various clinical applications, with medical image segmentation playing a key role. In the context of abdominal imaging, the precise segmentation of organs like the liver, spleen, and kidneys holds significant importance for tasks such as diagnosis, treatment planning, and surgical interventions. However, achieving precise and efficient segmentation of abdominal organs poses significant challenges due to the variability in organ shape, size, and appearance across different patients and imaging modalities. The MICCAI FLARE23 segmentation paper presents a solution to the challenging problem of segmenting 13 organs and tumor from CT scans, provided 2200 CT scans with partial labels and 1800 CT scans without labels, while balancing model performance and resource consumption. To address these challenges, the paper proposes a two-step segmentation approach that combines organ segmentation and tumor segmentation, which are both accomplished with nnU-Net model. We also crop some top and bottom slices for faster process. Experimental results on the FLARE 2023 test dataset achieved a mean Dice Similarity Coefficient of 0.0361, Normalized Sum of Differences of 0.0331 for organ, a mean Dice Similarity Coefficient of 0.005, Normalized Sum of Differences of 0 for lesion. Besides, our method cost 80.28 s and 158993 MB GPU.

Keywords: Abdominal organ segmentation · Supervised Learning · nnU-Net

1 Introduction

Medical image segmentation plays a pivotal role in various clinical applications, enabling the accurate delineation and analysis of anatomical structures within medical images. However, achieving precise and efficient segmentation of abdominal organs poses significant challenges, because it typically requires a large amount of labeled data to train an accurate model, while manually annotating organs from CT scans is a time-consuming and labor-intensive process, furthermore, abdominal organs may have complex morphological structures and heterogeneous lesions, which segmentation a more difficult task.

In recent years, deep learning became the mainstream method for medical image analysis, demonstrating remarkable capabilities in automated organ segmentation tasks. [8] Specifically, the nnU-Net model [7] has emerged as a powerful framework for achieving state-of-the-art results in medical image segmentation. nnU-Net combines the strengths of the U-Net architecture with advancements in neural network design and training strategies, allowing for improved accuracy and robustness. Semi-supervised segmentation [14] is a type of segmentation where the training set consists of both labeled and unlabeled data. The goal is to assign pseudo-labels to the pixels of unlabeled images. This approach is useful when obtaining labeled data is expensive or time-consuming, which is perfect for this challenge.

Because there are no full 14 classes labeled data but 13 classes organ segmentation labeled data, in this paper, we break it down into two tasks: organ segmentation and tumour segmentation. Therefor, we propose an approach which involved training two nnUnet model with labeled data, which are used to segment organs and tumours respectively. A post-process is used to merge two Deep Learning results when inferencing.

2   Method

2.1   Preprocessing

We use several pre-processing strategies as follows.

- Data choose and preprocessing
  We choose train data with full 13 organ label and data with tumor label, thus get 222 data for organ segment and 735 for tumor segment. Then we split them by 8:2 ratio for train and validation.
- Cropping strategy
  We use the CT scans as the data source to generate the bounding box of foreground, and then crop only the foreground object of the images.
- Resampling method for anisotropic data
  We resample the original data to unify the voxel spacing into $[1.0, 1.0, 1.0]$.
- Intensity normalization method
  We collect intensity values from the foreground classes (all but the background and ignore) from all training cases, compute the mean, standard deviation as well as the 0.5 and 99.5 percentile of the values. Then clip to the percentiles, followed by subtraction of the mean and division with the standard deviation. The normalization that is applied is the same for each training case (for this input channel).

2.2   Deep Network

Figure 1 illustrates the applied 3D nnU-Net [7], where a 3D U-Net architecture is adopted. We use the leaky ReLU function with a negative slope of 0.01 as the activation function. Our first 3D nnU-Net has 14 out channels, corresponding to the background and 13 organs, while our second 3D nnU-Net has 2 out channels, corresponding to the background and the tumor. In this case, only data with 13 organ label and data with tumor label are used, the others is abandon. Unlabeled images were not used.

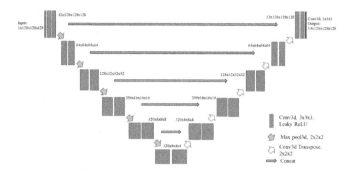

Fig. 1. Our 3D U-Net architecture

We use the sum of Dice loss (after applying a softmax function) and Cross Entropy Loss as the loss function, because it's a popular choice for loss fuction and have been proven to be robust in various medical image segmentation tasks.

When predicting a single image with the trained segmentation model, we first resample it to a voxel spacing of [1.0, 1.0, 1.0], as we did during training, and try to predict. In order to improving inference speed and reducing resource consumption, we crop top and bottom slices of the data in predicting, only keep only the middle 50 slices.

2.3 Post-processing

During model prediction, we select the label (from 0 to 13) corresponding to the largest of the 13 outputs for each voxel, after that, we combine predictions of two model to get the final result. When one pixel is both predicted as tumor and organ, it will be considered as tumor. Finally, we add full 0 array as top and bottom slices.

3 Experiments

3.1 Dataset and Evaluation Measures

The FLARE 2023 challenge is an extension of the FLARE 2021–2022 [10,11], aiming to aim to promote the development of foundation models in abdominal disease analysis. The segmentation targets cover 13 organs and various abdominal lesions. The training dataset is curated from more than 30 medical centers under the license permission, including TCIA [2], LiTS [1], MSD [13], KiTS [5,6], autoPET [3,4], TotalSegmentator [15], and AbdomenCT-1K [12]. The training set includes 4000 abdomen CT scans where 2200 CT scans with partial labels and 1800 CT scans without labels. The validation and testing sets include 100 and 400 CT scans, respectively, which cover various abdominal cancer types, such as liver cancer, kidney cancer, pancreas cancer, colon cancer, gastric cancer, and so on. The organ annotation process used ITK-SNAP [16], nnU-Net [7], and MedSAM [9].

The evaluation metrics encompass two accuracy measures-Dice Similarity Coefficient (DSC) and Normalized Surface Dice (NSD)-alongside two efficiency measures-running time and area under the GPU memory-time curve. These metrics collectively contribute to the ranking computation. Furthermore, the running time and GPU memory consumption are considered within tolerances of 15 s and 4 GB, respectively.

3.2 Implementation Details

Environment Settings. The development environments and requirements are presented in Table 1.

Table 1. Development environments and requirements.

Windows/Ubuntu version	Ubuntu 20.04.4 LTS
CPU	Intel(R) Xeon(R) Gold 5218R CPU @ 2.10 GHz
RAM	128G
GPU (number and type)	1* NVIDIA Tesla T4 (16G)
CUDA version	11.6
Programming language	Python 3.9
Deep learning framework	Pytorch (Torch 1.13.1, torchvision 0.14.1)
Specific dependencies	numpy 1.25.2, SimpleITK 2.2.1, nnunetv2 2.1 nibabel 5.1.0

Training Protocols. As described below.

Random flipping strategy (only for initial training stage): each image has a 20% probability of flipping along the x-axis and a 20% probability of flipping along the y-axis.

Random Gaussian smooth (only for initial training stage): each image has a 10% probability of being Gaussian smoothed with sigma in (0.5, 1.15) for every spatial dimension.

Random Gaussian noise (only for initial training stage): each image has a 20% probability of being added with Gaussian noise with mean in (0, 0.5) and standard deviation in (0, 1).

Random intensity change (only for initial training stage): each image has a 10% probability of changing intensity with gamma in (0.5, 2.5).

Random intensity shift (only for initial training stage): each image has a 10% probability of shifting intensity with offsets in (0, 0.3).

Patch sampling strategy: 2 patches of size [128, 128, 128] are randomly cropped from each image. The center of each patch has 50% probability in the foreground and 50% probability in the background.

As described above, only data with 13 organ label and data with tumor label are used, the others is abandon. Unlabeled images were not used.

Some details of the initial training stage and the fine-tuning stage are shown in Table 2 and Table 3 respectively.

Table 2. Training protocols (initial training stage).

Network initialization	"he" normal initialization
Batch size	2
Patch size	$128 \times 128 \times 128$
Total epochs	1000
Optimizer	Adam
Initial learning rate (lr)	0.0001
Lr decay schedule	initial learning rate $\times (1 - epoch/500)^{0.9}$
Training time	20 h
Loss function	the sum of dice loss and cross entropy loss
Number of model parameters	31.42M

Table 3. Training protocols (fine-tuning stage).

Network initialization	model after initial training
Batch size	2
Patch size	$128 \times 128 \times 128$
Total epochs	40
Optimizer	Adam
Initial learning rate (lr)	0.00005
Lr decay schedule	initial learning rate $\times (1 - epoch/500)^{0.9}$
Training time	39 h
Loss function	the sum of dice loss and cross entropy loss
Number of model parameters	31.42M

Table 4. Results on validation set.

Target	Public Validation		Online Validation		Testing	
	DSC (%)	NSD (%)	DSC (%)	NSD (%)	DSC (%)	NSD (%)
Liver	0.600 ± 0.600	0.000 ± 0.000	5.500	4.400	0.310	0.160
RK	1.500 ± 1.500	1.110 ± 1.110	5.500	8.900	2.710	2.130
Spleen	0.000 ± 0.000	0.000 ± 0.000	10.000	10.000	0.850	0.800
Pancreas	0.440 ± 0.440	0.540 ± 0.540	5.100	7.500	0.340	0.410
Aorta	8.860 ± 8.860	9.570 ± 9.570	6.870	7.460	12.340	12.240
IVC	0.980 ± 0.980	0.820 ± 0.820	14.500	14.000	3.450	2.860
RAG	4.000 ± 4.000	4.000 ± 4.000	2.000	2.000	0.250	0.250
LAG	2.000 ± 2.000	2.000 ± 2.000	1.000	1.000	1.000	1.000
Gallbladder	8.000 ± 8.000	8.000 ± 8.000	10.000	9.000	8.800	9.000
Esophagus	0.000 ± 0.000	0.000 ± 0.000	0.0000	0.0000	0.560	0.580
Stomach	0.000 ± 0.000	0.000 ± 0.000	0.0000	0.0000	0.450	0.340
Duodenum	5.500 ± 5.500	9.400 ± 9.400	0.280	0.470	0.140	0.150
LK	11.930 ± 11.930	11.480 ± 11.480	12.210	11.090	14.270	11.930
Tumor	0.000 ± 0.000	0.000 ± 0.000	0.000	0.000	0.005	0.000
Average	3.129 ± 3.129	3.351 ± 3.351	5.211	5.401	3.510	3.220

Table 5. Quantitative evaluation of segmentation efficiency in terms of the running them and GPU memory consumption. Total GPU denotes the area under GPU Memory-Time curve.

Case ID	Image Size	Running Time (s)	Max GPU (MB)	Total GPU (MB)
0001	(512, 512, 55)	133.13	3746	30428
0051	(512, 512, 100)	143.65	3806	14327
0017	(512, 512, 150)	121.93	3590	24825
0019	(512, 512, 215)	85.79	3323	14863
0099	(512, 512, 334)	73.7	3374	11619
0063	(512, 512, 448)	72.57	3370	10082
0048	(512, 512, 499)	70.87	3316	10466
0029	(512, 512, 554)	74.38	3382	11035

4   Results and Discussion

4.1   Quantitative Results on Validation Set

DSC and NSD results on validation set are shown in Table 4. It can be seen from the table that Aorta and LK have best proformance, while others has worst proformance. A possible reason of it is that Aorta and LK is larger organ and more likely in the center, therefore not be croped by preprocessing.

4.2   Qualitative Results on Validation Set

Two examples of good segmentation are shown in Fig. 2 and two examples of bad segmentation are shown in Fig. 3. Visualization is achieved with ITK-SNAP [17] version 3.6.0.

From the perspective of images, some potential reasons for the bad-segmentation cases are listed below.

(1) The size of the case is very large, so we have to reduce the size of the case by cutting top and bottom slice to process it in 60 s.
(2) The case is not clear, distorted, or skewed.
(3) There are rare structures in the case that are not in the training set.

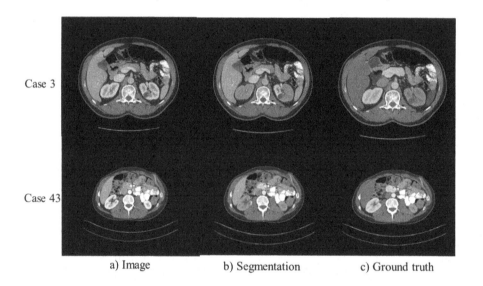

a) Image   b) Segmentation   c) Ground truth

Fig. 2. Good segmentation examples

4.3   Segmentation Efficiency Results on Validation Set

Table 5 show the efficiency results on 8 validation sets. Due to the crop of top and bottom slices, the data which has larger thrid-dimension also have fast running times.

4.4 Results on Final Testing Set

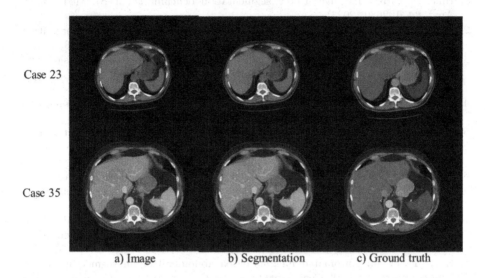

Case 23

Case 35

a) Image   b) Segmentation   c) Ground truth

Fig. 3. Bad segmentation examples

4.5 Limitation and Future Work

In terms of model accuracy, first, we does not use pseudo-labels for unlabeled image at present. In the future, we are going to use pseudo-labels for unlabeled image. Second, we consider using some post-processing methods, such as largest connected component extraction, hole filling, open operation and closed operation, which are not used at present.

To reduce the time consumption, we simply cut top and bottom slices, which caused a large loss of accuracy. To deal with it, we consider using some optimization methods to improve the running speed of the model in the future.

5 Conclusion

In this paper, we have explored the application of the nnU-Net model for Flare23 abdominal organ segmentation. Due to the limitation of time, we could not Leverage the power of deep learning and the architectural advancements of nnU-Net, but we will explore better deep learning methods in the future.

Acknowledgements. The authors of this paper declare that the segmentation method they implemented for participation in the FLARE 2023 challenge has not used any pre-trained models nor additional datasets other than those provided by the organizers. The proposed solution is fully automatic without any manual intervention.

References

1. Bilic, P., et al.: The liver tumor segmentation benchmark (LiTS). Med. Image Anal. **84**, 102680 (2023)
2. Clark, K., et al.: The cancer imaging archive (TCIA): maintaining and operating a public information repository. J. Digit. Imaging **26**(6), 1045–1057 (2013)
3. Gatidis, S., et al.: The AutoPET challenge: towards fully automated lesion segmentation in oncologic PET/CT imaging. Preprint at Research Square (Nature Portfolio) (2023). https://doi.org/10.21203/rs.3.rs-2572595/v1
4. Gatidis, S., et al.: A whole-body FDG-PET/CT dataset with manually annotated tumor lesions. Sci. Data **9**(1), 601 (2022)
5. Heller, N., et al.: The state of the art in kidney and kidney tumor segmentation in contrast-enhanced CT imaging: results of the KiTS19 challenge. Med. Image Anal. **67**, 101821 (2021)
6. Heller, N., et al.: An international challenge to use artificial intelligence to define the state-of-the-art in kidney and kidney tumor segmentation in CT imaging. Proc. Am. Soc. Clin. Oncol. **38**(6), 626 (2020)
7. Isensee, F., Jaeger, P.F., Kohl, S.A., Petersen, J., Maier-Hein, K.H.: nnU-net: a self-configuring method for deep learning-based biomedical image segmentation. Nat. Methods **18**(2), 203–211 (2021)
8. Kart, T., et al.: Automated imaging-based abdominal organ segmentation and quality control in 20,000 participants of the UK biobank and German national cohort studies. Sci. Rep. (2022)
9. Ma, J., He, Y., Li, F., Han, L., You, C., Wang, B.: Segment anything in medical images. Nat. Commun. **15**(1), 654 (2024)
10. Ma, J., et al.: Fast and low-GPU-memory abdomen CT organ segmentation: the flare challenge. Med. Image Anal. **82**, 102616 (2022)
11. Ma, J., et al.: Unleashing the strengths of unlabeled data in pan-cancer abdominal organ quantification: the FLARE22 challenge. arXiv preprint arXiv:2308.05862 (2023)
12. Ma, J., et al.: AbdomenCT-1k: is abdominal organ segmentation a solved problem? IEEE Trans. Pattern Anal. Mach. Intell. **44**(10), 6695–6714 (2022)
13. Simpson, A.L., et al.: A large annotated medical image dataset for the development and evaluation of segmentation algorithms. arXiv preprint arXiv:1902.09063 (2019)
14. Wang, Y., et al.: Semi-supervised semantic segmentation using unreliable pseudo-labels (2022)
15. Wasserthal, J., et al.: TotalSegmentator: robust segmentation of 104 anatomic structures in CT images. Radiol.: Artif. Intell. **5**(5), e230024 (2023)
16. Yushkevich, P.A., Gao, Y., Gerig, G.: ITK-SNAP: an interactive tool for semi-automatic segmentation of multi-modality biomedical images. In: Annual International Conference of the IEEE Engineering in Medicine and Biology Society, pp. 3342–3345 (2016)
17. Yushkevich, P.A., et al.: User-guided 3D active contour segmentation of anatomical structures: significantly improved efficiency and reliability. Neuroimage **31**(3), 1116–1128 (2006)

Semi-supervised Two-Stage Abdominal Organ and Tumor Segmentation Model with Pseudo-labeling

Li Mao[✉][ID]

AI Lab, Deepwise Healthcare, Beijing 100081, China
molly_maoli2024@foxmail.com

Abstract. In real-world scenarios, such as abdominal organ and tumor segmentation, obtaining complete labels for all classes often presents significant challenges. Additionally, optimizing GPU efficiency emerges as another critical factor in the abdominal organ and tumor segmentation process.

To address the challenge of partial labeling, a semi-supervised approach was employed. Initially, a larger model was trained using complete labels, which was then utilized to generate pseudo-labels. Subsequently, a smaller model was trained on these pseudo-labels. To mitigate GPU memory consumption, a two-stage strategy was implemented. Firstly, an abdomen location model was trained to accurately identify the abdominal area. Subsequently, the segmentation process was restricted to this localized area, thereby reducing the GPU memory requirements.

Experiments on the FLARE23 challenge exhibited promising performance, with an average actual running time of 25.971 s, an average AUC-GPU (Area Under the Curve of GPU memory consumption) of 28463.7 MB, and an average maximum GPU memory usage of 2.6 GB on the validation set, and the average running time on the testing set was 18.95 s, with AUC-GPU of 20790 MB. Moreover, the model achieved a Dice coefficient (DSC) of 79.99% for organ segmentation and 27.99% for tumor segmentation on the public validation dataset, and 80.84% and 24.26% for the DSC of organ and tumor segmentation on the testing result.

Keywords: Segmentation · Partial-label Segmentation · Computational efficiency

1 Introduction

In recent years, there has been an increasing adoption of deep learning-based segmentation models in the field of medicine [1–5]. However, the exorbitant cost entailed in the annotation of medical images has given rise to an increasingly acute dearth of labeled data. Furthermore, owing to the frequent collection of medical data from disparate centers, the predicament of incomplete data labeling has become a pervasive and recurrent concern.

© The Author(s), under exclusive license to Springer Nature Switzerland AG 2024
J. Ma and B. Wang (Eds.): FLARE 2023, LNCS 14544, pp. 63–75, 2024.
https://doi.org/10.1007/978-3-031-58776-4_6

Currently, there have been several studies addressing the training of models on partial-labeled data. Zhang et al. [6] designed a propagated self-training method that further guarantees the quality of the pseudo-labels and improves the richness of the labeled data. Petit et al. [7]introduce an iterative confidence self-training approach inspired by curriculum learning to relabel missing pixel labels. Li et al. [8] proposed the Conditional Dynamic Attention Network (CDANet) that fusing the conditional and multiscale information to better distinguish among different tasks and promoting more attention to task-related features.

On the other hand, reducing GPU utilization is crucial for the practical implementation of the model. More efficient implementations are necessary, as most segmentation methods are computationally expensive, and the amount of medical imaging data is growing [9]. The approach involves the design of efficient models, wherein the architecture is meticulously crafted and developed. ENet [10] serves as an exemplar of this approach. Conversely, another approach revolves around network compression, wherein lightweight models such as ICNet [11] are devised, employing pruning methods [12] that are extensively employed in image classification models.

The Fast, Low-resource, and Accurate oRgan and Pan-cancer sEgmentation in Abdomen CT (MICCAI FLARE 2023) is a competition that aims at efficiently segmenting of 13 organs (liver, spleen, pancreas, right kidney, left kidney, stomach, gallbladder, esophagus, aorta, inferior vena cava, right adrenal gland, left adrenal gland, and duodenum) and pan-cancer, i.e., all kinds of cancer types (such as liver cancer, kidney cancer, stomach cancer, pancreas cancer, colon cancer). The FLARE competition provided a training set includes 4000 3D CT scans from 30+ medical centers. 2200 cases have partial labels and 1800 cases are unlabeled. Despite providing a substantial amount of multi-center data, the dataset suffers from incomplete labeling, necessitating consideration of this issue during model training.

In this paper, we proposed a weakly supervised approach based on pseudo-labeling. Firstly, a large parameterized organ segmentation model was trained, enabling the generation of pseudo labels. Subsequently, leveraging these pseudo labels, a small parameterized segmentation model was trained. To mitigate the GPU memory consumption, an abdomen region location model was trained aimed at minimizing the size of segmentation model input tensor.

2   Method

As illustrated in Fig. 1, this study begins by training a large parameterized model for organ segmentation (organ segmentation model), then this model is utilized to annotate the remaining data with missing labels. An abdominal region classification model was trained to identify the abdominal slices. Eventually, by leveraging the pseudo-labeled data, we train an efficient lightweight model for both organ and tumor segmentation.

2.1 Preprocessing

Before being fed into the 3D U-Net model, a preprocessing step was performed on the CT images to enhance their suitability for analysis. This involved applying z-score normalization, which effectively standardized the pixel intensity values across the dataset. By normalizing the images, any variations in brightness and contrast were minimized, ensuring consistent and reliable input for subsequent processing.

Following the normalization step, an additional resampling procedure was conducted to achieve uniformity in voxel spacing. The images were resampled to a unified spacing of $2 \times 2 \times 3$ for the x, y, and z axes. This adjustment not only facilitated easier comparison and analysis of the data but also eliminated any potential distortions caused by variations in voxel dimensions.

To further optimize the input for the 3D U-Net model, the patch size of the image slices was carefully chosen. Specifically, a patch size of $96 \times 128 \times 160$ was selected for the x, y, and z axes, respectively. This choice ensured that the model received an appropriate and informative region of interest, enabling it to effectively capture relevant features and patterns during the segmentation process.

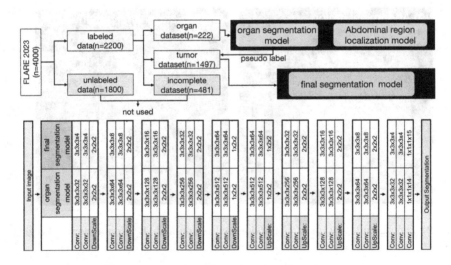

Fig. 1. The workflow of our study and the network architecture.

2.2 Proposed Method

As was shown in Fig. 1, we divided the dataset of 2200 cases from MICCAI into three categories: 222 cases with complete organ labels but no tumor labels (**organ dataset**), 1497 cases with tumor labels but incomplete organ labels (**tumor dataset**), and 481 cases with incomplete organ labels and no tumor labels (**incomplete dataset**). Our pipeline including three models.

The two-stage pipeline in our study was composed of abdominal region localization and abdominal segmentation. Firstly, the abdominal region localization model as employed to identify the abdominal slices. Then, the segmentation model only performed on abdominal region.

Abdominal Region Localization Model

In abdominal segmentation tasks, certain images incur significant GPU memory consumption. These images encompass non-abdominal regions. This insight motivates us to construct an abdominal region localization model that selectively retains and segments only the abdominal region. The model was trained on organ dataset, as was shown in Fig. 1.

In this study, we adopt a mask-based segmentation approach to extract labels that signify the presence of the abdominal region in a given CT image. Specifically, if a CT slice contains a mask, it is classified as representing the abdominal region; conversely, if no mask is present, it is classified as representing a non-abdominal region. Figure 2 illustrate a typical example of the abdominal region and the non-abdominal region.

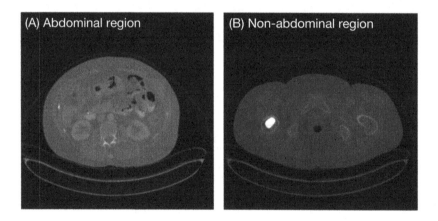

Fig. 2. The example of typical (A) abdominal region and (B) Non-abdominal region.

For the organ dataset used in this study, a split of 4/5 and 1/5 was employed for training and testing the Abdominal region localization model, respectively. Initially, the input data undergoes preprocessing steps. The CT images are normalized using a window width of 400 and a window level of 40, enhancing the visibility of soft tissue regions. Subsequently, the images are resampled to a size of 256×256 and expanded to 3 channels, resulting in a tensor size of $3 \times 256 \times 256$, which serves as the input to the model. The model architecture employed in this study is based on ResNet18 [13].

During the model training process, data augmentation techniques are employed to prevent overfitting and improve generalization. These techniques help in generating additional training samples by applying transformations such as rotations, translations, and scaling to the input data.

Considering that the abdominal localization model itself consumes computational resources, during the inference stage, CT images larger than 50MB in file size are processed layer by layer to obtain predictions for each slice. The maximum and minimum predicted values among all the slices identified as the abdominal region are used to define a continuous region of interest for subsequent segmentation of abdominal organs and cancer region.

Organ Segmentation Model

An organ segmentation model was trained on an organ dataset using the nnU-Net framework [14]. The model architecture is based on the 3D U-Net architecture, which consists of 5 downsampling modules and 5 upsampling modules. To improve the accuracy of pseudo label generation, the model has a large number of parameters. Within the nnU-Net framework, the model was trained for a total of 500 epochs with an initial learning rate of 0.01. To achieve robust performance in various medical image segmentation tasks, a compound loss function combining Dice loss and cross-entropy loss was employed, as it has been proven effective [15]. Data augmentation techniques such as mirroring, scaling, rotation, and translation were applied to prevent overfitting.

During training, 4/5 of the organ dataset was used for training the model, while the remaining 1/5 was used for validation. The model with the highest Dice coefficient on the validation set was selected as the optimal organ segmentation model. After training, this model was utilized to annotate a tumor dataset, providing segmentation labels for regions where the tumor dataset was lacking annotations, based on the model's predictions.

Final Segmentation Model

To obtain an efficient lightweight model for organ and tumor segmentation, we first reduced the number of parameters of the 3D UNet model. Subsequently, we pretrained the model on the organ dataset using the same training approach as described earlier for the organ segmentation model. After the pretraining procedure, we modified the model's parameters by adding a tensor of the same size to the final output convolutional layer, resulting in 15 output channels representing the background, 13 organs, and tumors. This additional tensor was initialized to zero.

Subsequently, model optimization was performed on the tumor dataset after completing the segmentation label augmentation. A total of 500 epochs were trained with an initial learning rate of 0.01. The loss function, optimizer, and other settings remained consistent with the organ segmentation model. After training, the model with the highest Dice coefficient on the validation set was selected as the final model.

The Remaining Dataset

The incomplete dataset and the unlabeled images were not used, as well as any pseudo labels generated by the FLARE21 winning algorithm [16,17].

2.3   Post-processing

To reduce computational load, this study employed GPU-based resampling to ensure that the size of the output segmented images matched that of the original images and corresponded to the abdominal region. No post-processing techniques were employed beyond this to maintain computational efficiency.

3   Experiments

3.1   Dataset and Evaluation Measures

The FLARE 2023 challenge is an extension of the FLARE 2021–2022 [18,19], aiming to promote the development of foundation models in abdominal disease analysis. The segmentation targets cover 13 organs and various abdominal lesions. The training dataset is curated from more than 30 medical centers under the license permission, including TCIA [20], LiTS [21], MSD [22], KiTS [23,24], autoPET [25,26], TotalSegmentator [1], and AbdomenCT-1K [27]. The training set includes 4000 abdomen CT scans where 2200 CT scans with partial labels and 1800 CT scans without labels. The validation and testing sets include 100 and 400 CT scans, respectively, which cover various abdominal cancer types, such as liver cancer, kidney cancer, pancreas cancer, colon cancer, gastric cancer, and so on. The organ annotation process used ITK-SNAP [28], nnU-Net [14], and MedSAM [29].

The evaluation metrics encompass two accuracy measures-Dice Similarity Coefficient (DSC) and Normalized Surface Dice (NSD)-alongside two efficiency measures-running time and area under the GPU memory-time curve. These metrics collectively contribute to the ranking computation. Furthermore, the running time and GPU memory consumption are considered within tolerances of 15 s and 4 GB, respectively.

3.2   Implementation Details

Environment Settings. The development environments and requirements are presented in Table 1.

Training Protocols. The training protocals of the final segmentation models can be found in Table 2. As for the abdominal region location model, the optimization process utilizes the Adam optimizer with an initial learning rate of 0.0001. The Cross Entropy Loss function is employed as the objective function for training the model.

4   Results and Discussion

4.1   Performance of Abdominal Region Localization Model

The organ dataset composed of 56989 images (17716 labeled non-abdominal image, and 39273 labeled abdominal image), and was splitted into training set

Table 1. Development environments and requirements.

System	Ubuntu 16.04.3 LTS
CPU	Intel(R) Xeon(R) CPU E5-2685 v3 @ 2.60 GHz
RAM	16 × 16 GB; (the memory speed is not available)
GPU (number and type)	One TITAN Xp 12G
CUDA version	10.1
Programming language	Python 3.6.8
Deep learning framework	torch 1.6.0, torchvision 0.7.0
Specific dependencies	NA
Code	https://github.com/MollyMaoli/MiccaiFLARE23

Table 2. Training protocols.

Network initialization	InitWeights_He
Batch size	2
Patch size	96×128×160
Total epochs	500
Optimizer	Adam
Initial learning rate (lr)	0.01
Lr decay schedule	Polynomial Learning Rateschedule
Training time	11.25 h
Loss function	$0.5 \times L_{BCE} + 0.5 \times L_{Dice}$
Number of model parameters	1.385M[a]
Number of flops	34.185G[b]
CO_2eq	2.6 Kg[c]

[a] https://github.com/sksq96/pytorch-summary
[b] https://github.com/facebookresearch/fvcore
[c] https://github.com/lfwa/carbontracker/

(13585 labeled non-abdominal image, and 31078 labeled abdominal image) and testing set (4131 labeled non-abdominal image, and 8195 labeled abdominal image). On the testing set, the abdominal region localization model reached a area under the receiver operating characteristic curve (AUC) of 0.994, accuracy of 0.959, sensitivity of 0.954, and specificity of 0.969.

4.2 Segmentation Efficiency Results on Validation Set

The efficiency performance on validation set can be found in Table 3. In our approach, we leveraged abdominal localization models to enhance segmentation efficiency in case 0019, 0099, 0063, 0048, and 0029. We observed that the running time was shorter in case 0001 and 0019 compared to the other cases. Additionally, the maximum GPU usage and total GPU usage were also lower in these two cases. In case 0019, for example, out of the total 215 slices, the abdominal region predicted by the abdominal region localization model only spanned from slice 106 to slice 214. This means that only 108 slices were available for segmentation, which resulted in a reduced workload and potentially improved the efficiency of GPU utilization.

Table 3. Quantitative evaluation of segmentation efficiency in terms of the running them and GPU memory consumption. Total GPU denotes the area under GPU Memory-Time curve. Evaluation GPU platform: NVIDIA QUADRO RTX5000 (16G).

Case ID	Image Size	Running Time (s)	Max GPU (MB)	Total GPU (MB)
0001	(512, 512, 55)	18.85	1796	16313
0051	(512, 512, 100)	28.21	2454	34003
0017	(512, 512, 150)	36.33	2946	47435
0019	(512, 512, 215)	16.54	2470	17208
0099	(512, 512, 334)	42.7	2992	27054
0063	(512, 512, 448)	20.15	3444	24857
0048	(512, 512, 499)	23.07	4090	31461
0029	(512, 512, 554)	23.83	4222	33770

4.3   Quantitative Results on Validation Set

Figure 3 presents four samples of the segmentation results. The first two rows depict well-segmented slices, whereas the last two rows exhibit unsatisfactory segmentation outcomes. In case 0073, the liver was not fully recognized, and in case 0025, the presence of vessels within the liver misled the model.

The quantitative performance can be found in Table 4. The model proposed in this paper demonstrated favorable performance on organs such as the liver, kidney, spleen, and stomach, achieving Dice Similarity Coefficient (DSC) and Normalized Surface Dice (NSD) scores of over 85% on the validation set. However, the segmentation results for tumors were less satisfactory, with a DSC of only 27.99%. This lower performance could be attributed to the significant intraclass heterogeneity and smaller volumes of tumors. The same trend can be found in online validation result.

4.4   Ablation Study

The performance of the organ segmentation model is elaborated in Table 5. The DSC and NSD of the organ segmentation model was inferior than the final segmentation model. The average DSC and NSD performance of the organic region was 82.20 % and 86.52 %, lower than that of final segmentation model (88.38% and 94.52.

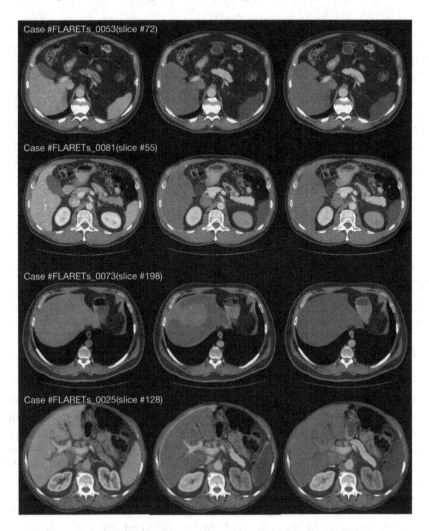

Fig. 3. The sample of four cases in validation set.

4.5 Results on Final Testing Set

The average actual running time on final testing set is 18.95 s, with an average AUC-GPU (Area Under the Curve of GPU memory consumption) of 20790 MB. Our model reached a DSC of 80.67% and a NSD of 85.61% for the segmentation of organs. However, the tumor segmentation was relative hard, resulting in a DSC of 24.26% and a NSD of 12.33%.

4.6 Limitation and Future Work

The objective of this study is to minimize GPU memory usage while ensuring accurate prediction outcomes. The average execution time and AUC-GPU achieved notable efficiency, measuring 18.95 s and 20790 MB, respectively, on the testing set. However, compared with the organ region, the segmentation performance of tumor region was relatively low.

Table 4. Quantitative evaluation results.

Target	Public Validation		Online Validation		Testing	
	DSC(%)	NSD(%)	DSC(%)	NSD(%)	DSC(%)	NSD (%)
Liver	95.43 ± 3.08	95.59 ± 5.17	97.32	98.75	93.23	93.09
Right Kidney	87.74 ± 18.95	86.46 ± 19.52	93.34	94.54	90.68	88.79
Spleen	93.53 ± 4.16	92.92 ± 7.03	97.00	99.06	91.78	91.79
Pancreas	75.05 ± 10.22	88.7 ± 9.2	83.70	95.47	73.97	86.21
Aorta	87.36 ± 9.29	85.63 ± 15.1	94.91	98.40	90.25	91.69
Inferior vena cava	80.42 ± 15.29	77.72 ± 18.02	92.03	95.26	81.87	79.13
Right adrenal gland	68.44 ± 16.59	81.89 ± 17.24	80.58	94.40	67.21	80.15
Left adrenal gland	64.27 ± 21.62	76.07 ± 24.16	80.21	93.82	65.09	76.37
Gallbladder	74.2 ± 25.74	70.63 ± 28.05	79.80	79.64	71.71	69.47
Esophagus	72.06 ± 16.93	83.29 ± 16.86	82.18	93.86	79.03	91.02
Stomach	85.65 ± 11.25	87.6 ± 13.3	92.61	96.60	86.05	88.91
Duodenum	68.11 ± 15.2	86.36 ± 11.48	81.92	94.46	69.74	86.33
Left kidney	87.59 ± 18.6	86.33 ± 19.85	93.30	94.56	89.72	89.01
Tumor	27.99 ± 36.29	18.17 ± 25.31	39.78	31.11	24.26	12.33
Average	76.27 ± 24.35	79.81 ± 25.40	88.38	94.52	80.84	85.61

The ablation study compared the organ segmentation model and the final segmentation model. In the online validation set, the organ segmentation model exhibited inferior performance compared to the final segmentation model, even in the organic region. The difference indicated that the final segmentation model, trained on the pseudo-labeled dataset, benefited from the organ segmentation model.

This study still have some limitations. Firstly, only two subsets from the FLARE 2023 dataset was used for modeling. During the restriction of deadline, the remaining data was not used. In our future study, the utilization of these data can be performed to enhance the model performance. Secondly, the semi-supervised algorithm in our study is primitively. The state-of-the-art semi-supervised algorithm can be used in our future study. Finally, the pseudo label from the FLARE 2022 models was not used in our study.

Table 5. Organ segmentation model performance.

Target	Online Validation	
	DSC(%)	NSD(%)
Liver	93.32	92.34
Right Kidney	86.83	86.72
Spleen	93.42	93.12
Pancreas	77.65	89.86
Aorta	94.83	96.63
Inferior vena cava	91.83	92.94
Right adrenal gland	70.34	87.48
Left adrenal gland	72.79	86.80
Gallbladder	72.09	67.73
Esophagus	76.92	89.64
Stomach	81.17	78.37
Duodenum	70.45	79.11
Left kidney	86.90	83.97
Average	82.20	86.52

5 Conclusion

This paper adopts a straightforward and simple approach for partially labeled data segmentation. The organ segmentation model is trained using fully labeled data with complete organ labels. Subsequently, this model is utilized to augment the missing organ labels in the data with tumor labels. This process enables the training of a comprehensive organ-tumor segmentation model. The utilization of the abdominal localization model further enhances the prediction efficiency of the model.

Acknowledgements. The authors of this paper declare that the segmentation method they implemented for participation in the FLARE 2023 challenge has not used any pre-trained models nor additional datasets other than those provided by the organizers. The proposed solution is fully automatic without any manual intervention. We thank all the data owners for making the CT scans publicly available and CodaLab [30] for hosting the challenge platform.

References

1. Wasserthal, J., et al.: TotalSegmentator: robust segmentation of 104 anatomic structures in CT images. Radiol. Artif. Intell. **5**(5), e230024 (2023)
2. Xiao, H., Ran, Z., Mabu, S., Li, Y., Li, L.: SAUNet++: an automatic segmentation model of Covid-19 lesion from CT slices. Vis. Comput. **39**(6), 2291–2304 (2023)
3. Pan, S., et al.: Abdomen CT multi-organ segmentation using token-based MLP-mixer. Med. Phys. **50**(5), 3027–3038 (2023)

4. Li, J., et al.: Eres-UNet++: liver CT image segmentation based on high-efficiency channel attention and Res-UNet++. Comput. Biol. Med. **158**, 106501 (2023)

5. Bougourzi, F., Distante, C., Dornaika, F., Taleb-Ahmed, A.: PDAtt-UNet: pyramid dual-decoder attention UNet for Covid-19 infection segmentation from CT-scans. Med. Image Anal. **86**, 102797 (2023)

6. Zhang, L., Lu, W., Zhang, J., Wang, H.: A semisupervised convolution neural network for partial unlabeled remote-sensing image segmentation. IEEE Geosci. Remote Sens. Lett. **19**, 1–5 (2022)

7. Petit, O., Thome, N., Soler, L.: Iterative confidence relabeling with deep convnets for organ segmentation with partial labels. Comput. Med. Imaging Graph. **91**, 101938 (2021)

8. Li, L., Lian, S., Lin, D., Luo, Z., Wang, B., Li, S.: Learning multi-organ and tumor segmentation from partially labeled datasets by a conditional dynamic attention network. Concurr. Comput. Pract. Experience e7869 (2023)

9. Smistad, E., Falch, T.L., Bozorgi, M., Elster, A.C., Lindseth, F.: Medical image segmentation on GPUs-a comprehensive review. Med. Image Anal. **20**(1), 1–18 (2015)

10. Paszke, A., Chaurasia, A., Kim, S., Culurciello, E.: ENet: a deep neural network architecture for real-time semantic segmentation. arXiv preprint arXiv:1606.02147 (2016)

11. Li, G., Liu, Z., Ling, H.: ICNet: information conversion network for RGB-D based salient object detection. IEEE Trans. Image Process. **29**, 4873–4884 (2020)

12. Molchanov, P., Mallya, A., Tyree, S., Frosio, I., Kautz, J.: Importance estimation for neural network pruning. In: Proceedings of the IEEE/CVF Conference on Computer Vision and Pattern Recognition, pp. 11264–11272 (2019)

13. He, K., Zhang, X., Ren, S., Sun, J.: Deep residual learning for image recognition. In: Proceedings of the IEEE Conference on Computer Vision and Pattern Recognition, pp. 770–778 (2016)

14. Isensee, F., Jaeger, P.F., Kohl, S.A., Petersen, J., Maier-Hein, K.H.: nnU-Net: a self-configuring method for deep learning-based biomedical image segmentation. Nat. Methods **18**(2), 203–211 (2021)

15. Ma, J., et al.: Loss odyssey in medical image segmentation. Med. Image Anal. **71**, 102035 (2021)

16. Huang, Z., et al.: Revisiting nnU-net for iterative pseudo labeling and efficient sliding window inference. In: Ma, J., Wang, B. (eds.) FLARE 2022. LNCS, vol. 13816, pp. 178–189. Springer, Cham (2022). https://doi.org/10.1007/978-3-031-23911-3_16

17. Wang, E., Zhao, Y., Wu, Y.: Cascade dual-decoders network for abdominal organs segmentation. In: Ma, J., Wang, B. (eds.) FLARE 2022. LNCS, vol. 13816, pp. 202–213. Springer, Cham (2022). https://doi.org/10.1007/978-3-031-23911-3_18

18. Ma, J., et al.: Fast and low-GPU-memory abdomen CT organ segmentation: the flare challenge. Med. Image Anal. **82**, 102616 (2022)

19. Ma, J., et al.: Unleashing the strengths of unlabeled data in pan-cancer abdominal organ quantification: the flare22 challenge. arXiv preprint arXiv:2308.05862 (2023)

20. Clark, K., et al.: The cancer imaging archive (TCIA): maintaining and operating a public information repository. J. Digit. Imaging **26**(6), 1045–1057 (2013)

21. Bilic, P., et al.: The liver tumor segmentation benchmark (LiTS). Med. Image Anal. **84**, 102680 (2023)

22. Simpson, A.L., et al.: A large annotated medical image dataset for the development and evaluation of segmentation algorithms. arXiv preprint arXiv:1902.09063 (2019)

23. Heller, N., et al.: The state of the art in kidney and kidney tumor segmentation in contrast-enhanced CT imaging: results of the kits19 challenge. Med. Image Anal. **67**, 101821 (2021)

24. Heller, N., et al.: An international challenge to use artificial intelligence to define the state-of-the-art in kidney and kidney tumor segmentation in CT imaging. Proc. Am. Soc. Clin. Oncol. **38**(6), 626 (2020)

25. Gatidis, S., et al.: A whole-body FDG-PET/CT dataset with manually annotated tumor lesions. Sci. Data **9**(1), 601 (2022)

26. Gatidis, S., et al.: The autopet challenge: towards fully automated lesion segmentation in oncologic PET/CT imaging. preprint at Research Square (Nature Portfolio) (2023). https://doi.org/10.21203/rs.3.rs-2572595/v1

27. Ma, J., et al.: AbdomenCT-1K: is abdominal organ segmentation a solved problem? IEEE Trans. Pattern Anal. Mach. Intell. **44**(10), 6695–6714 (2022)

28. Yushkevich, P.A., Gao, Y., Gerig, G.: ITK-SNAP: an interactive tool for semi-automatic segmentation of multi-modality biomedical images. In: Annual International Conference of the IEEE Engineering in Medicine and Biology Society, pp. 3342–3345 (2016)

29. Ma, J., He, Y., Li, F., Han, L., You, C., Wang, B.: Segment anything in medical images. Nat. Commun. **15**, 654 (2024)

30. Pavao, A., et al.: Codalab competitions: an open source platform to organize scientific challenges. J. Mach. Learn. Res. **24**(198), 1–6 (2023)

2.5D U-Net for Abdominal Multi-organ Segmentation

Ruixiang Lei⬛ and Mingjing Yang$^{(\boxtimes)}$

Intelligent Image processing and Analysis Laboratory, Fuzhou University,
Fuzhou 350108, Fujian, China
yangmj5@fzu.edu.cn

Abstract. Accurate and efficient segmentation of multiple abdominal organs from medical images is crucial for clinical applications such as disease diagnosis and treatment planning. In this paper, we propose a novel approach for abdominal organ segmentation using the U-Net architecture. Our method addresses the challenges posed by anatomical variations and the proximity of organs in the abdominal region. To improve the segmentation accuracy, we introduce an attention mechanism into the U-Net architecture. This mechanism allows the network to focus on salient regions and suppress irrelevant background regions, enhancing the overall segmentation performance. Additionally, we incorporate 3D information by connecting three consecutive slices as 3-dimensional inputs. This enables us to exploit the spatial context across the slices while minimizing the increase in GPU memory usage. We evaluate our proposed method on the MICCAI FLARE 2023 validation dataset, the mean DSC is 0.3683 and the mean NSD is 0.3668.

Keywords: organ segmentation · U-Net · attention mechanism

1 Introduction

Medical image segmentation is important for clinical applications, including disease diagnosis, treatment planning, and image-guided interventions. Accurate and efficient segmentation of abdominal organs from medical images is important for assessing organ function, detecting abnormalities, and guiding surgical procedures. However, multi- organ segmentation is a challenging task due to the complex anatomical structures, variabilities in organ shapes and sizes, and the presence of noise and artifacts. Further more, it is difficult to obtain labeled data, unlabeled data is easier to access. In recent years, deep learning based method are widely used for abdominal multi-organ segmentation with good results, among which nnU-Net [7] is one of the most used methods. But nnU-Net's high resource consumption and low inference speed, it does not meet the Challenge's requirements for fast and low-resource. In this work, the main contributions are summarized as follows:

- We use a 2.5D segmentation framework, which can utilize 3D information from CT and does not increasing the computing complexity.
- Introduce an attention mechanism into the U-Net architecture to better capture salient regions and suppress irrelevant background regions.

2   Method

2.1   Preprocessing

Our method includes the following preprocessing steps:

- **Threshold truncation:** In our opinion, it will encounters difficulties when it comes to segmenting small organs, particularly, more focus is needed on accurately segmenting extremely small organs with unclear boundaries, such as the inferior vena cava (IVC) and duodenum. One possible approach to address this challenge is through threshold value to distinguish the target organ from the surrounding tissues. This technique can help improve the segmentation accuracy for small and indistinct boundary organs.
- **Cropping strategy:** We crop the images and labels based on the slices containing labels and discard the slices without labels. Along the z-axis, we reduce the number of slices to the power of 2 to speed up the subsequent data reading.
- **Resamping method for anisotropic data:** We use this method to resize the slice to reduce GPU memory usage.
- **Intensity normalization method.**

2.2   Proposed Method

As shown in Fig. 1, our method follows the standard U-Net [14] design to achieve the organ segmentation. Specifically, We introduce the attention mechanism into the UNet segmentation network to enhance its ability to focus on region of interest while suppressing irrelevant background region. The attention module can be well embedded in skip connection, which can improve the performance of the model without adding too much computation. In terms of details, we connect three consecutive slices to form a 3D input, which allowing us to fully utilize the 3D information without significantly increasing the GPU memory usage. This approach optimizes memory usage while preserving the spatial context across slices.

Network Architecture Details. Our proposed UNet-CBAM network consists of a combination of UNet network and CBAM module, which consists of spatial attention module and channel attention module. The network input first goes through 5 convolution modules and 4 max pooling layers to complete the downsampling process, and then goes through 5 convolution modules and four upsampling to get the output. The output of each layer of the downsampling path is connected by the features of the skip connection and the upsampling

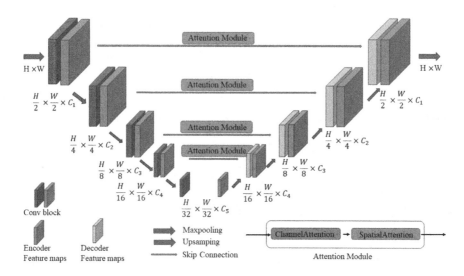

Fig. 1. Network architecture

path, respectively. The skip connection performs channel-wise and spatial-wise feature correction on the features through the CBAM module.

Loss Function: we use the summation between Dice loss and cross-entropy loss because compound loss functions have been proven to be robust in various medical image segmentation tasks [8].

Strategies to Deal with the Partial Labels. The dataset provided by the FLARE 2023 challenge included 2200 CT scans with partial labels, and we did not know which organ was labeled in each case, but due to the amount of the data was sufficient, our method did not make special treatment for the data with partial labels.

Strategies to Use the Unlabeled Data. Unlabeled images were not used.

Strategies to Improve Inference Speed and Reduce Resource Consumption. We have introduced attention modules in skip connection of U-Net, which can speed up inference and reduce parameters compared to other attention modules. In order to avoid the problem that the loss of 3D information and the low segmentation accuracy of the pure 2D method, we use multiple slices. We also resize the image to reduce resolution to improve inference speed and reduce resource consumption.

2.3   Post-processing

We use connected component-based post-process to remove noise and isolated pixels and improve segmentation results.

3   Experiments

3.1   Dataset and Evaluation Measures

The FLARE 2023 challenge is an extension of the FLARE 2021–2022 [10,11], aiming to aim to promote the development of foundation models in abdominal disease analysis. The segmentation targets cover 13 organs and various abdominal lesions. The training dataset is curated from more than 30 medical centers under the license permission, including TCIA [2], LiTS [1], MSD [15], KiTS [5,6], autoPET [3,4], TotalSegmentator [16], and AbdomenCT-1K [12]. The training set includes 4000 abdomen CT scans where 2200 CT scans with partial labels and 1800 CT scans without labels. The validation and testing sets include 100 and 400 CT scans, respectively, which cover various abdominal cancer types, such as liver cancer, kidney cancer, pancreas cancer, colon cancer, gastric cancer, and so on. The organ annotation process used ITK-SNAP [17], nnU-Net [7], and MedSAM [9].

The evaluation metrics encompass two accuracy measures-Dice Similarity Coefficient (DSC) and Normalized Surface Dice (NSD)-alongside two efficiency measures-running time and area under the GPU memory-time curve. These metrics collectively contribute to the ranking computation. Furthermore, the running time and GPU memory consumption are considered within tolerances of 15 s and 4 GB, respectively.

3.2   Implementation Details

Environment Settings. The development environments and requirements are presented in Table 1.

Table 1. Development environments and requirements.

System	Windows10/Ubuntu 20.04.4 LTS
CPU	Intel(R) Core(TM) i9-12900K CPU@3.20 GHz
RAM	4×4 GB; 2400MT/s
GPU (number and type)	One RTX 2080Ti 8G
CUDA version	11.4
Programming language	Python 3.8
Deep learning framework	Pytorch(torch 1.7.0, torchvision 0.8.2)
Specific dependencies	medicaltorch, pandas, scipy, collections
Code	

Training Protocols. The Training protocols and details (e.g., batch size, epoch, optimizer) are presented in Table 2. In the training process, the batch size is 16 and the patch size is fixed as 3*192*192 for optimization, we train it for 150 epochs using Adam with a learning rate of 0.001 and the learning rate reduction strategy using CosineAnnealingLR.

Table 2. Training protocols.

Network initialization	
Batch size	16
Patch size	$3 \times 192 \times 192$
Total epochs	150
Optimizer	Adam
Initial learning rate (lr)	0.001
Lr decay schedule	CosineAnnealingLR
Training time	82 h
Loss function	
Number of model parameters	74.1M[a]
Number of flops	8.22G[b]
CO_2eq	1 Kg[c]

[a] https://github.com/sksq96/pytorch-summary
[b] https://github.com/facebookresearch/fvcore
[c] https://github.com/lfwa/carbontracker/

Table 3. Quantitative evaluation results. While the proposed method shows promising results in segmenting large organs like the liver, spleen, and kidneys, it still faces significant challenges when it comes to segmenting small organs. Specifically, more attention needs to be paid to extremely small and indistinct boundary organs such as the right adrenal gland (RAG) and esophagus.

Target	Public Validation		Online Validation		Testing	
	DSC(%)	NSD(%)	DSC(%)	NSD(%)	DSC(%)	NSD (%)
Liver	97.66 ± 0.40	97.51 ± 1.08	83.45	83.45	94.84	93.21
Right Kidney	97.35 ± 1.92	97.19 ± 3.01	95.24	93.30	90.68	86.81
Spleen	98.20 ± 0.11	96.69 ± 4.16	87.86	82.30	94.78	93.23
Pancreas	77.38 ± 12.25	83.59 ± 13.02	72.98	81.95	75.67	83.63
Aorta	0	0	14.95	15.30	13.02	12.20
Inferior vena cava	0	0	0.00	0.00	0.00	0.00
Right adrenal gland	0	0	0.20	0.20	0.23	0.23
Left adrenal gland	0	0	1.00	1.00	0.93	0.93
Gallbladder	45.65 ± 53.28	49.46 ± 51.22	10.00	10.00	9.49	9.49
Esophagus	0	0	0.00	0.00	0.46	0.46
Stomach	53.56 ± 37.14	56.85 ± 37.43	14.83	16.25	9.21	8.39
Duodenum	0	0	0.00	0.00	0.00	0.00
Left kidney	95.06 ± 2.13	94.42 ± 0.33	85.58	82.44	90.18	87.96
Tumor	0	0	19.41	11.29	18.55	9.37
Average	43.45	44.29	36.83	36.68	37.03	36.81

4   Results and Discussion

4.1   Qualitative Results on Validation Set

Figure 2 shows the segmentation results of our method. It clearly illustrates that our method can obtain better segmentation results on large organs than on small organs. However, our segmentation results are clearly missing some organ labels.

Table 4. Quantitative evaluation of segmentation efficiency in terms of the running them and GPU memory consumption. Total GPU denotes the area under GPU Memory-Time curve. Evaluation GPU platform: NVIDIA QUADRO RTX5000 (16G).

Case ID	Image Size	Running Time (s)	Max GPU (MB)	Total GPU (MB)
0001	(512, 512, 55)	14.7	1570	14158
0051	(512, 512, 100)	20.69	1570	22391
0017	(512, 512, 150)	28.79	1570	33231
0019	(512, 512, 215)	38.65	1570	46742
0099	(512, 512, 334)	57.79	1570	72527
0063	(512, 512, 448)	74.66	1570	95581
0048	(512, 512, 499)	88.88	1570	114971
0029	(512, 512, 554)	101.26	1570	131953

4.2   Segmentation Efficiency Results on Validation Set

We evaluated the segmentation efficiency on validation set, some of the results are shows in Table 4.

4.3   Results on Final Testing Set

As shown in Table 3, our method achieves a mean DSC of 0.3703 and a mean NSD of 0.3681 on the FLARE 2023 final testing set.

4.4   Limitation and Future Work

Our proposed method for abdominal organ segmentation does not achieve good segmentation results, the limitation of our method is that we are not taking full advantage of unlabeled data, and trained on the data with partial labels may introduce noise and inconsistencies in the training process, leading to reduce model performance. Therefore, we will focus on some techniques such as active learning or semi-supervised learning to iteratively select and annotate the most informative instances, improving the model's performance with partial labeled data.

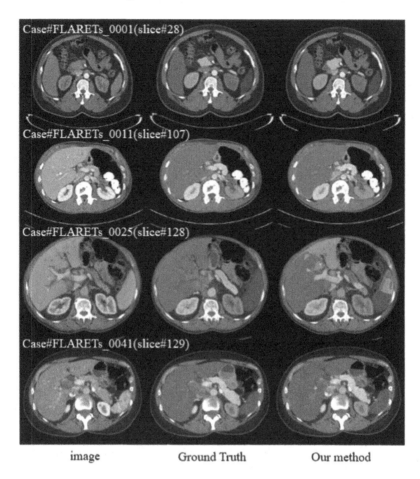

Fig. 2. Example cases from the MICCAI FLARE 2023 validation set. Our method does not achieve good segmentation results on the validation set, and here are just two examples that seem to have slightly better segmentation results (No. 0001 and No. 0011) and two examples that have poor segmentation results (No. 0025 and No. 0041).

5   Conclusion

In this work, we propose a 2.5D-based U-Net for abdominal multi-organ segmentation. By utilizing partial label data during the training process, we have overcome the challenges of incomplete data annotating. Future research can further extend this method and validate it in a broader range of medical image segmentation tasks.

Acknowledgements. The authors of this paper declare that the segmentation method they implemented for participation in the FLARE 2023 challenge has not used any pre-trained models nor additional datasets other than those provided by the organizers. The proposed solution is fully automatic without any manual intervention. We thank all the data owners for making the CT scans publicly available and CodaLab [13] for hosting the challenge platform. This study is supported by National Natural Science Foundation of China (62271149), Fujian Provincial Natural Science Foundation project (2021J02019, 2021J01578).

References

1. Bilic, P., et al.: The liver tumor segmentation benchmark (LiTS). Med. Image Anal. **84**, 102680 (2023)
2. Clark, K., et al.: The cancer imaging archive (TCIA): maintaining and operating a public information repository. J. Digit. Imaging **26**(6), 1045–1057 (2013)
3. Gatidis, S., et al.: The autopet challenge: towards fully automated lesion segmentation in oncologic PET/CT imaging. Preprint at Research Square (Nature Portfolio) (2023). https://doi.org/10.21203/rs.3.rs-2572595/v1
4. Gatidis, S., et al.: A whole-body FDG-PET/CT dataset with manually annotated tumor lesions. Sci. Data **9**(1), 601 (2022)
5. Heller, N., et al.: The state of the art in kidney and kidney tumor segmentation in contrast-enhanced CT imaging: results of the kits19 challenge. Med. Image Anal. **67**, 101821 (2021)
6. Heller, N., et al.: An international challenge to use artificial intelligence to define the state-of-the-art in kidney and kidney tumor segmentation in CT imaging. Proc. Am. Soc. Clin. Oncol. **38**(6), 626 (2020)
7. Isensee, F., Jaeger, P.F., Kohl, S.A., Petersen, J., Maier-Hein, K.H.: nnU-Net: a self-configuring method for deep learning-based biomedical image segmentation. Nat. Methods **18**(2), 203–211 (2021)
8. Ma, J., et al.: Loss odyssey in medical image segmentation. Med. Image Anal. **71**, 102035 (2021)
9. Ma, J., He, Y., Li, F., Han, L., You, C., Wang, B.: Segment anything in medical images. Nat. Commun. **15**, 654 (2024)
10. Ma, J., et al.: Fast and low-GPU-memory abdomen CT organ segmentation: the flare challenge. Med. Image Anal. **82**, 102616 (2022)
11. Ma, J., et al.: Unleashing the strengths of unlabeled data in pan-cancer abdominal organ quantification: the flare22 challenge. arXiv preprint arXiv:2308.05862 (2023)
12. Ma, J., et al.: AbdomenCT-1K: is abdominal organ segmentation a solved problem? IEEE Trans. Pattern Anal. Mach. Intell. **44**(10), 6695–6714 (2022)
13. Pavao, A., et al.: CodaLab competitions: an open source platform to organize scientific challenges. J. Mach. Learn. Res. **24**(198), 1–6 (2023)
14. Ronneberger, O., Fischer, P., Brox, T.: U-net: convolutional networks for biomedical image segmentation. In: International Conference on Medical Image Computing and Computer-Assisted Intervention, pp. 234–241 (2015)
15. Simpson, A.L., et al.: A large annotated medical image dataset for the development and evaluation of segmentation algorithms. arXiv preprint arXiv:1902.09063 (2019)
16. Wasserthal, J., et al.: TotalSegmentator: robust segmentation of 104 anatomic structures in CT images. Radiol. Artif. Intell. **5**(5), e230024 (2023)
17. Yushkevich, P.A., Gao, Y., Gerig, G.: ITK-snap: an interactive tool for semi-automatic segmentation of multi-modality biomedical images. In: Annual International Conference of the IEEE Engineering in Medicine and Biology Society, pp. 3342–3345 (2016)

Advancing Multi-organ and Pan-Cancer Segmentation in Abdominal CT Scans Through Scale-Aware and Self-attentive Modulation

Pengju Lyu[1,2], Junchen Xiong[2], Wei Fang[2], Weifeng Zhang[2],
Cheng Wang[2(✉)], and Jianjun Zhu[2,3(✉)]

[1] City University of Macau, Macau, China
[2] Hanglok-Tech Co., Ltd., Hengqin 519000, China
{pj.lv,cheng.wang,jj.zhu}@hanglok-tech.cn
[3] Zhongda Hospital, Medical School, Southeast University, Nanjing 210009, China

Abstract. Accurately segmenting abdominal organs and tumors within computed tomography (CT) scans holds paramount significance for facilitating computer-aided diagnosis and devising treatment plans. However, inherent challenges such as lesion heterogeneity and the scarcity of adequately annotated data hamper model development. In this study, we present a two-phase cascaded framework to address the complexities of multi-organ and pan-cancer segmentation. A lightweight CNN first generates candidate regions of interest (ROIs) followed by a hybrid CNN-Transformer model culminating in refined segmentation by synergizing scale-aware modulation for local features and self-attention for global context. Our proposed method secured the 5th position in the MICCAI FLARE23 final test set, showcasing its competitive edge in achieving precise target segmentation with mean Dice Similarity Coefficients of 90.69% for multi-organ and 53.16% for pan-cancer respectively. Additionally, efficient inference is exhibited with an average runtime of 18 s per 512 × 512 × 215 3D volume with less than 2G GPU memory consumption. Our code is available at: https://github.com/lyupengju/Flare23.

Keywords: Multi-organ and pan-cancer segmentation · Hybrid CNN-Transformer model · Scale-aware and self-attention modulation

1 Introduction

Medical image segmentation plays a crucial role in clinical diagnosis. Accurate organ and cancer segmentation in abdomen computed tomography (CT) as one of the most commonly used modalities for the abdominal diagnosis can assist clinicians in identifying distinct anatomical regions as well as assessing the structure of lesions which assumes critical significance in computer-aided diagnosis,

---

P. Lyu and J. Xiong—Equal contribution.

J. Ma and B. Wang (Eds.): FLARE 2023, LNCS 14544, pp. 84–101, 2024.
https://doi.org/10.1007/978-3-031-58776-4_8

treatment planning, and image-guided interventions. For instance, the efficacy of radiotherapy treatment planning (RTP), to a great extent, hinges upon the precise demarcation of both the organ at risk (OAR) and the target tumor [45]. Moreover, segmentation on pan-cancer enables the identification of common features and patterns across different cancer types, facilitating the development of targeted therapies and personalized medicine approaches, e.g., identification of unique gene expression signatures associated with different cancers are valuable as diagnostic biomarkers and therapeutic targets [17].

In the deep learning era, the application of convolutional neural network (CNN) or Transformer-based U-Net represents a seminal milestone in the field of medical image segmentation. By virtue of its expansive encoder-decoder structure, U-Net [29] effectively captures both local and global contextual information, enabling the precise delineation of anatomical structures. Its hierarchical approach, coupled with skip connections, facilitates the fusion of multi-scale features, empowering U-Net to discern fine-grained details and accurately segment complex structures in medical images. CNN-based U-Net variants [11,25] leverage the power of convolutional layers to extract spatial features, enabling the network to discern intricate patterns and variations in tumor morphology, with remarkable precision. On the other hand, Transformer-based U-Net models [7,31,44] exploit self-attention mechanisms to capture long-range dependencies and contextual relationships, facilitating a comprehensive understanding of anatomical structures. The hybridization of CNN and Transformer [4,39]stands to the pursuit of synthesizing the best of both paradigms, aiming to forge a sophisticated framework that pushes the boundaries of segmentation accuracy and efficiency.

Abdominal multi-organ and pan-cancer segmentation, however, continues to pose several challenges due to the inherent complexity and variability of cancer lesions, e.g., inter- and intra-tumor heterogeneity coupled with the presence of surrounding anatomical structures that can confound accurate segmentation [24]. On top of that, the scarcity of cancer annotated datasets, especially for rare cancer types, poses a significant hurdle in training accurate and generalizable models. MICCAI FLARE23[1] (Fast, Low-resource, and Accurate oRgan and Pan-cancer sEgmentation in Abdomen CT) makes a significant contribution with the availability of an extensive partial labeled dataset, enabling comprehensive research and analysis in the field. To mitigate the requirement for fully labeled data, which aligns with FLARE23 challenge's objectives, self-training with pseudo labeling and semi-supervised learning emerge as a valuable strategy [20]. Self-training entails the generation of surrogate labels through models trained on partially labelled datasets, thereby offering a bridge towards the realm of fully supervised methodologies. Lian et al. [18] introduces a novel approach that employs partially labelled single-organ datasets to generate pseudo labels for multi-organ segmentation, utilizing partial and mutual priors to enhance organ segmentation performance. Though iterative pseudo labeling with one resource-intensive nnU-Net and selecting reliable ones, Huang et al. [12], under this knowledge distillation framework, ultimately attain a lightweight model

---

[1] https://codalab.lisn.upsaclay.fr/competitions/12239.

achieving accuracy and efficiency tradeoff in FLARE22 [23]. Semi-supervised learning leverages unlabeled samples to improve generalization [16] where consistency regularization is a popular approach enforcing invariant predictions under input perturbations [15,32]. Other than that, Pan et al. [26] adopt adversarial training [43] that focuses on training a generator against a discriminator that tries to differentiate segmented outputs derived from labeled versus unlabeled data to promote outputs distribution convergence. On the other hand, the majority of extant deep learning architectures for medical image segmentation, such as APAU-Net [36], TransBTS [35], albeit achieving impressive precision optimized on high-compute laboratory settings with GPUs, typically manifest immense computational demands and parametric complexity. While in bed-side setting with on-device processing of limited computational resources and memory capacities., e.g., point-of-care imaging [33] or interventional surgeries demanding immediate decision-making [45], developing light-weighted, yet competent and scalable models for robust and reliable segmentation becomes paramount.

In this work, we aim to develop a fast, low-resource, and accurate organ and pan-cancer segmentation framework. Our approach is based on the classic two-phase (location-segmentation) cascaded processing stream wherein a lightweight CNN in phase one employing partial convolution and a novel hybrid CNN-Transformer model with synergistic amalgamation of scale-aware modulator and self-attention in phase two are proposed. We trained both models with forementioned simple self-training with pseudo labeling technique. The obtained results on validation set not only demonstrate superior performance on Dice Similarity Coefficient (DSC) and Normalized Surface Dice (NSD) but also showcase favorable inference speeds, underscoring the efficacy and practicality of our proposed method.

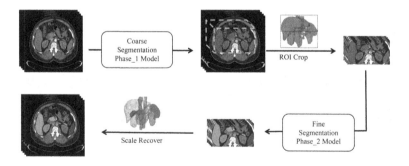

Fig. 1. An overview of the two-phase cascade network.

2   Method

We adopted localization and segmentation strategy to instantiate multi-phase cascade methodologies which has been proven useful in the past FLARE challenges [34,36], the overall framework is as shown in the Fig. 1. The first phase of the network bestows invaluable location information, furnishing a candidate frame that subsequently facilitates the precise cropping of the image's region of interest (ROI). This localized region (i.e., hard attention [14,42]), thus extracted, serves as the input for the second-stage network, wherein the process of fine segmentation ensues. This sequential strategy imparts the profound advantage of confining the segmentation focus solely to the target organ, effectively excluding any perturbations arising from unrelated organs or background noise.

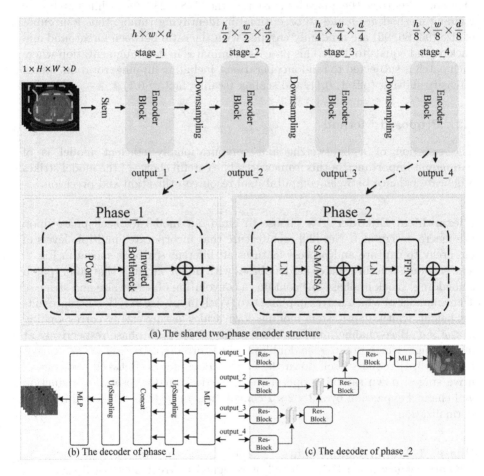

Fig. 2. The schematic illustration of proposed models. (a) The shared two-phase backbone structure with Phase_1 model residual inverted bottleneck block where partial convolution (PConv) efficiently conduct spatial token mixing while Phase_2 model utilizing scale-aware modulator (SAM) or Multi-head Self-Attention (MSA) in Metaformer structure; (b) Phase_1 decoder adapted from [38]; (c) Phase_2 decoder adapted from [7].

2.1   Preprocessing

This preprocessing workflow commences with a percentile-based rescaling (percentile values: 5th and 95th) constraining intensity range to crop region containing salient features while suppressing outliers. It is followed by respacing to (1.5 mm, 1.5 mm, 2 mm) rectifies inter-slice spacing disparities, imparting uniformity to the image domain. Image intensities are further Z-normalized to ameliorate convergence dynamics and numerical stability during model training. For phase one, we resize the image dimension to the (128, 128, 128), while patch-wise training method are found to be optimal in identifying tumor, thus four cubes of size (96, 96, 96) are randomly cropped with the ratio between foreground and background equals to 3 : 1. This process culminates in data augmentation where each patch is subjected to random operations, including flipping, rotation, affine, intensity shifting (offset: 0.1), and scaling (scaling factor: 0.1).

2.2   Proposed Method

The selection of a lightweight and computationally efficient model is of paramount importance in this framework. The careful choice of the model strikes a delicate balance between computational resource utilization and precision.

Hierarchical Encoder. We choose to build our model for each phase upon the macro design of U-Net [29] architecture that incorporates multiple levels of hierarchy to capture and process features at different scales as shown in Fig. 2. The encoder structure shares across phases with minor variance that stem (patch embedding) block in phase one contains a convolution of kernel size and stride of 4, the number of which halves in phase two. With input size $H \times W \times D$ representing height, width, depth, stem module down scales feature size to corresponding $h \times w \times d$. Base channel number is set as 32/60 for each phase respectively at initial stage, which progressive doubles and feature map size $\frac{h}{2^{i-1}} \times \frac{w}{2^{i-1}} \times \frac{d}{2^{i-1}}$, $i \in \{1, 2, 3, 4\}$ reduces itself down the four encoder stages. Between two consecutive stages, down sampling operations is carried out for resolution reduction and channel expansion by a $2 \times 2 \times 2$ convolution with stride 2 followed by layer normalization.

Phase_1 Model Components. The localization network is represented by a binary segmentation U-Net, which is designed to treat all labeled organs as the foreground label. To obtain a coarse ROI, we resort to partial convolution (PConv) [2] as choice of spatial token mixing. PConv improves the efficiency by applying filters on only a subset of input channels (first quarter in our case) while preserving the remaining ones. This reduces computational redundancy and the number of memory accesses, resulting in lower FLOPs than regular convolution and higher FLOPS than depthwise convolution. With the completion of shortcut connection and two successive pointwise convolutions, the Phase_1 encoder presents itself as a stacking of residual inverted bottleneck blocks in which channel expansion ratio is 2 and the number of such block is set 2 per stage.

For the decoding of this phase_1, we employ the streamlined MLP decoder from Segformer [38] for efficient information aggregation. Specifically, the multi-level features derived from encoder blocks undergo channel wise compression to base channel number via MLP layers before being upsampled to the size of $h \times w \times d$ and a second MLP layer condenses the concatenated features channels to the number equivalent to that of output classes, trilinear interpolation is ultimately applied to recover to full image size.

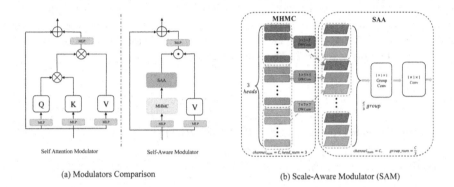

(a) Modulators Comparison

(b) Scale-Aware Modulator (SAM)

Fig. 3. (a) Spatial modulation comparison between self-attentive and scale-aware operator. self-attention first generates the key K, query Q, and value V using MLP layers and the weights to modulate the V representations are determined by attention weights computed by measuring the similarity between Q and K. SAM instead directly obtain the weights with Multi-Head Mixed Convolution (MHMC) and a Scale-Aware Aggregation (SAA) blocks. (b) Evolving from [19], the schematic illustration of SAM integrating multi-scale contexts via a MHMC and adapts token representations through a SAA.

Phase_2 Model Components. For fine segmentation, by taking advantage of the strengths of both CNNs and Transformers in Meta-former style [40], which contains a spatial token mixing layer and a feed-forward layer (FFN) [28]. We adopt Scale-Aware Modulator (SAM) [19] to reweight the value representations for lower-level local feature extraction in early stages while Multi-head Self-Attention (MSA) [7] dedicated to global information in later stages, see Fig. 3 for details. SAM consists of a Multi-Head Mixed Convolution (MHMC) and a Scale-Aware Aggregation (SAA) module to enable the integration of multi-scale contexts and adaptive modulation of tokens. Together, SAM and MSA provide complementary modeling of multi-scale local features and long-range global contexts. Their combination enables extracting both localized fine details and overall spatial relationships.

The MHMC introduces multiple depth-wise convolutions with different kernel sizes, enabling it to capture various spatial features across multiple scales.

Figure 3 illustrates the structure of MHMC, wherein the input channels are divided into multiple groups (heads), each subjected to depth-wise separable convolutions with diverse kernel sizes respectively, which are able to discern a diverse spectrum of granularity features in an adaptive fashion.

The SAA module engages in a practice of cross-group information aggregation across all features to harmonize diverse insights from distinct groups. Specifically, three mixed groups are curated with each selecting one channel from previously partitioned group, and the inverse bottleneck structure (expansion ratio = 2) with point-wise convolutions are subsequently leveraged fostering a holistic synergy of knowledge propagation and enriched representation, which, by means of the Hadamard product operation, eventually serves as weight modulator of the value V in contrast to yielding attention matrices via a matrix multiplication between the query and key in self-attention. The whole process of SAM can be summarized in the following steps:

$$
\begin{aligned}
&\textbf{\textit{Input}}: \ \boldsymbol{z} \in \mathbb{R}^{C \times H' \times W' \times D'} \\
&\textbf{\textit{MHMC}}: \ H_j^i = DWConv_{k_j \times k_j \times k_j}\left(\boldsymbol{z}_j^i\right), j \in \{1, 2, \cdots, M\}, i \in \{1, 2, \cdots, C/M\} \\
&\textbf{\textit{SAA}}: \ G_i = Relu\left(IN\left(Conv_{1 \times 1 \times 1}\left(\left[H_1^i, H_2^i, \cdots, H_M^i\right]\right)\right)\right) \\
&\qquad\quad W = Conv_{1 \times 1 \times 1}\left(\left[G_1, G_2, \cdots, G_{C/M}\right]\right) \\
&\textbf{\textit{Output}}: \ \hat{\boldsymbol{z}} = W \odot \left(Conv_{1 \times 1 \times 1}\left(z\right)\right)
\end{aligned}
\tag{1}
$$

Let $\boldsymbol{z} \in \mathbb{R}^{C \times H' \times W' \times D'}$ denote the input tensor to the SAM module with C channels and spatial dimensions $H' \times W' \times D'$ for the current layer. We divide the channels into $M = 3$ heads, indexed by $j \in \{1, 2, 3\}$, with C/M channels in each head. The output is denoted as $\hat{\boldsymbol{z}}$ with the same dimensions as $\boldsymbol{z}$. Within each head j, we have single-channel feature maps $\boldsymbol{z}_j^i \in \mathbb{R}^{1 \times H' \times W' \times D'}$ for $i \in \{1, 2, \cdots, C/M\}$. These are convolved with learned depth-wise kernels $DWConv$ of size k_j, where we set $k_j \in \{3, 5, 7\}$ for the 3 heads respectively. $\odot$ denotes dot product operation.

SAM blocks reside only in the initial two stages. During the penultimate stage, triple of SAM blocks and Multi-Head Self-Attention (MSA) blocks are alternatively stacked, effectively capturing the transition from local to global dependencies. In the ultimate stage, exclusively MSA blocks are employed, thereby ensuring proficient capture of long-range dependencies. The number of such blocks in each stage amounts to 2, 4, 6, 2 correspondingly.

We adopted phase_2 decoder similar to that from UNETR [7]. A residual block, composed of two consecutive sequences of Conv + InstanceNorm + LeakyRelu, is applied to skip connections as well as subsequent concatenated features. Upsampling is realized with transpose convolution.

2.3   Post-processing

After phase one, we remove objects of size smaller than $(20 \times 20 \times 20)$, which might be outliers affecting a precise ROI cropping for phase two whose result are refined by preserving solely the largest components of organs. Based on the observation that predicted tumor mask could appear separate with abdominal organs though within the ROI defined by bounding box. This contradicts a well-established fact that tumors originate on organs. We have tumor mask through basic morphological operations of dilation and subtraction to identify any organs in proximity, thereby filtering out those isolated components as shown in Fig. 4. The resultant mask are finally mapped back to the same size of input image.

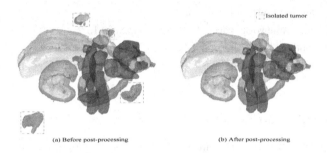

(a) Before post-processing   (b) After post-processing

Fig. 4. Feasibility analysis of post-processing operations. It is evident that the proposed post-processing applied to the predictive mask effectively eliminates isolated tumors.

3 Experiments

3.1 Dataset

The FLARE23 challenge constitutes an extension of its precursor, the FLARE 2021–2022 initiative [22,23]. Its primary objective is to foster the advancement of foundational models in the realm of abdominal disease analysis. The delineation objectives encompass a spectrum of 13 distinct organs including liver, spleen, pancreas, right kidney, left kidney, stomach, gallbladder, esophagus, aorta, inferior vena cava, right adrenal gland, left adrenal gland, and duodenum in addition to diverse abdominal lesions, namely pan-cancer. The training dataset is curated from more than 30 medical centers under the license permission, including TCIA [3], LiTS [1], MSD [30], KiTS [8,9], autoPET [5,6], TotalSegmentator [37], and AbdomenCT-1K [24]. The training dataset consists of a total of 4000 abdominal CT scans in which 2200 scans with partial annotations and 1800 scans devoid of annotations. Two sets of 4000 pseudo labels of multi organs, generated by two top-performance teams during FLARE22 [12,34], were appended afterwards. The validation and testing sets include 100 and 400 CT scans, respectively, which cover various abdominal cancer types, such as liver cancer, kidney cancer, pancreas cancer, colon cancer, gastric cancer, and so on. The organ annotation process used ITK-SNAP [41], nnU-Net [13], and MedSAM [21].

Table 1. Development environments and requirements.

System	Ubuntu 20.04.5 LTS
CPU	Intel(R) Xeon(R) Platinum 8358 CPU @ 2.60 GHz
RAM	1.0 Ti; 3200 MT/S
GPU (number and type)	Two NVIDIA A800 80G
CUDA version	11.8
Programming language	Python 3.8.16
Deep learning framework	torch 2.0.1, torchvision 0.15.2
Specific dependencies	monai 1.2.0
Code	https://github.com/lyupengju/Flare23

3.2 Implementation Details

Throughout the entire experimental process, we implemented our code based on PyTorch library[2] and MONAI framework[3]. All models were trained on two Nvidia A800 GPUs. To accelerate model training, the CacheDataset method in the MONAI was utilized for data pre-loading. During the training phase, the Adam optimizer was adopted with weight decay of $1e^{-5}$ to minimize the most widely used joint loss function, i.e., dice and cross entropy [7]. Initial learning rate was set as $3e^{-4}$ scheduled by cosine annealing strategy. The number of training epochs was up to 300 with batch size of 4. See Table 1, 2 for more training and environment settings.

Table 2. Training protocols.

Network initialization	Random
Batch size	4
Patch size (Phase_2 model)	$96 \times 96 \times 96$
Resized size (Phase_1 model)	$128 \times 128 \times 128$
Total epochs	300
Optimizer	AdamW
Initial learning(lr)	$3e^{-4}$
Lr decay schedule	Cosine annealing
Training time for each model	36 h
Loss function	Dice loss and Cross entropy loss
Number of model parameters (Phase_1/Phase_2)	1.38 M/35.84 M
Number of flops (Phase_1/Phase_2)	1.56 G/374.77 G

---

[2] http://pytorch.org/.
[3] https://monai.io/.

3.3   Training Protocols

Leveraging the entire dataset comprising 4000 cases and one set of their corresponding organ pseudo labels from FLARE22 winning algorithm [12], we are able to obtain our Phase_1 model by means of a label filtering technique, along with a pre-trained Phase_2 model, the specific process is as depicted in Fig. 5. Similar to [12], we adopted self-training with pseudo labeling strategy to obtain final Phase_2 model. Specially, we reassigned pseudo annotations in conjunction with 2200 partial ground truth for the whole dataset to update the segmentation model. This process facilitated the creation of a comprehensive dataset, complete with fully annotated organs and tumors. The process of pseudo labeling was executed iteratively 3 times, thereby enabling the iterative enhancement of the quality of pseudo annotations, which is pivotal in advancing the model's performance. In practice, we first split the renewed dateset into two folds, the updating pseudo labels was then formed by ensembling two branch networks through soft voting, which are later utilized to train our final Phase_2 model. We empirically selected the model that tend to produce oversegmented results on pan-cancer, which generally yield better Dice score on online validation leaderboard.

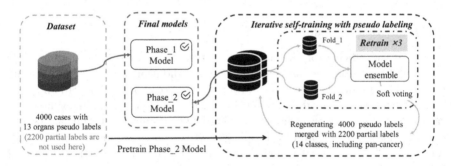

Fig. 5. Training pipeline.

4   Results and Discussion

We conducted comprehensive quantitative evaluation of our proposed model using standard segmentation and efficiency metrics. Regarding accuracy, we report the Dice similarity coefficient (DSC) and normalized surface Dice (NSD) between predicted and ground truth organ and lesion masks with DSC elucidating overall overlap and NSD focusing on boundary alignment precision [31]. Efficiency-wise, running time and the GPU memory consumption, are integral for assessing the algorithm's practicality and real-world applicability. The running time and GPU memory consumption are considered within tolerances of 15 s and 4 GB, respectively.

Table 3. Quantitative evaluation results in terms of DSC and NSD for organs and tumor respectively.

Target	Public Validation		Online Validation		Testing	
	DSC (%)	NSD (%)	DSC (%)	NSD (%)	DSC (%)	NSD (%)
Liver	97.68 ± 0.54	99.28 ± 0.77	97.64	99.24	97.05	97.81
Right Kidney	95.90 ± 2.94	96.95 ± 4.27	94.86	95.95	95.15	96.17
Spleen	96.89 ± 1.57	98.46 ± 4.13	96.19	98.06	96.48	98.42
Pancreas	85.96 ± 7.20	96.67 ± 6.09	84.63	95.79	88.89	97.15
Aorta	94.17 ± 4.39	97.34 ± 5.82	94.72	98.08	95.32	99.30
Inferior vena cava	90.16 ± 5.63	92.93 ± 5.77	89.46	91.88	90.64	93.72
Right adrenal gland	83.66 ± 1.25	95.93 ± 1.39	83.97	96.58	83.43	96.11
Left adrenal gland	84.67 ± 5.47	96.73 ± 4.13	83.98	95.90	84.36	96.02
Gallbladder	88.28 ± 19.06	90.81 ± 20.10	88.92	91.09	84.06	87.43
Esophagus	80.78 ± 17.86	91.23 ± 17.34	82.04	92.84	87.85	97.36
Stomach	94.46 ± 3.09	97.75 ± 3.42	94.50	97.70	94.59	97.34
Duodenum	83.07 ± 8.72	94.74 ± 6.59	83.41	94.70	86.08	95.22
Left kidney	93.06 ± 14.38	94.05 ± 15.32	93.60	94.80	95.11	96.76
Organ Average	89.90	95.61	89.84	95.56	90.69	96.06
Tumor	54.25 ± 36.10	49.65 ± 33.51	50.26	45.31	53.16	44.68

4.1 Quantitative Results

To validate the efficacy of the model, we present in Table 3 the details of 50 cases from the validation dataset, the online validation and the final testing outcomes. Our model demonstrates strong performance on both organ and pan-cancer segmentation from abdominal CTs. For the 13 organs on online validation, we achieve competitive accuracy score with DSC ranging from 82.04% (Esophagus) to 97.64% (liver), and NSD all over 90%, which highlight our model's ability to capture fine anatomical details. Specifically, our model in Phase_2 with only 35.84M parameters achieves considerable gains on average Dice over prior arts spanning CNN-based V-Net (67.70M) [25], nnUNet (30.74M) [13], and Transformer-based Swin UNETR (69.94M) [31], nnFormer (158.9M) [44] as well as their hybrid CoTr (41.93M) [39], as presented in Fig. 6. This again validates the benefits of synergistically combining SAM and MSA from both paradigms.

With regards to pan-cancer segmentation, although our approach attains a relatively high average DSC of 50.26% across all lesion types, since the fact that best model was selected based on its performance on the public 50 cases, the divergence on tumor metrics between it and full validation set coupling with a high standard variance (36.10%) indicates that model's weak capacity of learning generalizable representations of pan-cancer. Our methodology distinguished itself by securing a commendable 5th position in the final test set, quantified by elevated mean Dice on both multi-organ (90.69%) and tumor (53.16%).

To analyze the impact of training set size, an ablation study was conducted comparing validation performance between models trained on the full 4000 case dataset versus the 2200 partially labeled cases alone. Despite nearly doubling the training data through pseudo-labeling, the models seem not to learn novel

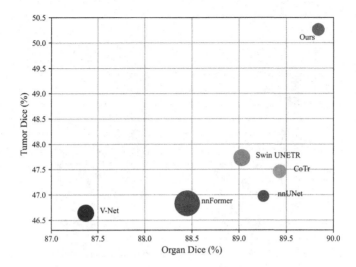

Fig. 6. Phase_2 models comparison with prior arts on online validation. The diameter of the circular data points is proportional to the total number of parameters in each respective model.

anatomical representations but rather fine-tuning of existing feature spaces, exemplified by both DSC and NSD metrics on either scenario revealing negligible differences regarding organs (0.1%) and tumor (0.5%), as shown in Fig. 7, which indicates that model's learned features might not be universally applicable, resulting in limited generalization to different cases, which in turn impacts the overall effectiveness of pseudo labeling.

4.2   Qualitative Results on Validation Set

We supplement our quantitative results with qualitative analysis to gain further insights, as shown in Fig. 8. Notably, the segmentation performance exhibits variability across organs. In contrast to near perfect demonstration (Case #27), our model generates fragmentary or inaccurate contours with smaller structures like esophagus and duodenum (Case #69), echoed by their relatively lower Dice scores on validation set. For pan-cancer, while some tumor instances (Case #35) are effectively segmented, showcasing a robust alignment with ground truth annotations, others exhibit violent segmentation inconsistencies (Case #99). This variance in tumor segmentation proficiency is indicative of the complexity inherent in cancer lesions, often characterized by diverse morphological traits and inter-tumor heterogeneity. Column (c) represents the segmentation result by model trained only with partial-label 2200 cases demonstrating similar performance with that of column (d) using all 4000 cases.

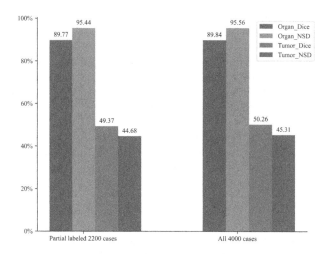

Fig. 7. Performance comparison on online validation using 2200 partially labeled examples and 4000 fully labeled examples for training.

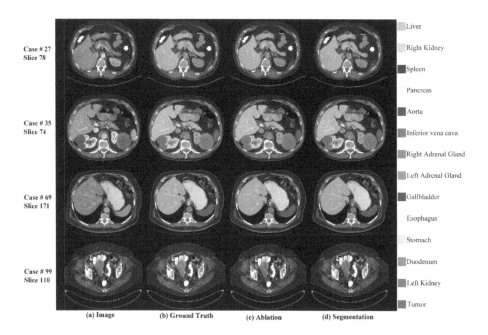

Fig. 8. Qualitative evaluation on four cases from validation set.

4.3   Segmentation Efficiency Results on Online Validation

Our two-phase cascaded network provides major speed and memory benefits. Table 4 provides the efficiency for certain examples from the validation dataset. For the majority of test cases, our proposed method can complete the inference process requiring extra seconds (8 in average) than the prescribed time budget of 15 s, while maintaining GPU memory consumption well under the allotted 4 GB limit. Moreover, running time appears to exhibit a positive correlation with input image size owing to the serial scanning nature of the sliding window, traversing spatially across the input, consequently inflicting a computational burden that scales directly with image area, as evidenced by the near 31 s run time for the largest case 0029 scan, resulting in greater cumulative GPU utilization.

Table 4. Quantitative evaluation of segmentation efficiency in terms of the run-ning time and GPU memory consumption. Total GPU denotes the area under GPUMemory-Time curve. Evaluation GPU platform: NVIDIA QUADRO RTX5000 (16 GB).

Case ID	Image Size	Running Time (s)	Max GPU (MB)	Total GPU (MB)
0001	(512, 512, 55)	15.17	2020	17200
0051	(512, 512, 100)	16.73	2020	22141
0017	(512, 512, 150)	17.84	2020	23832
0019	(512, 512, 215)	18.01	2020	23875
0099	(512, 512, 334)	20.61	2020	27427
0063	(512, 512, 448)	24.40	2020	32647
0048	(512, 512, 499)	25.36	2020	33937
0029	(512, 512, 554)	30.87	2020	43991

4.4   Limitation and Future Work

While our method shows promise for multi-organ and tumor segmentation, enabling clinical utilization through efficient computation and memory usage. These validation results highlight areas for continued future refinement, especially enhancing delineation of tiny organs and handling greater tumor heterogeneity. For that, tumor synthesis technique [10] could be employed to artificially generate additional lesion examples. This data augmentation approach may facilitate greater robustness in the segmentation model, allowing it to generalize more effectively to the heterogeneity inherent in pathological anatomy. Since our pseudo labeling approach is mostly off-line making impossible real time updating, we should further explore online semi-supervised method as well as mechanisms to enhance the fidelity and reliability of generated pseudo labels such as applying confidence thresholding, and detecting out-of-distribution pseudo labels [20].

5   Conclusion

In the pursuit of advancing the state of the art in multi-organ and pan-cancer image segmentation, we have made significant strides in this realm by our participation in the MICCAI FLARE23 challenge through the development and application of a two-phase cascade framework. Phase_1 model built upon partial convolution enjoys computational efficiency while yielding credible segmented ROI. The harmonious fusion of scale-aware and self-attentive modulation forms the foundation of our Phase_2 model backbone, enabling enhanced segmentation accuracy. Through meticulous model selection, tuning, and optimization, our algorithm has shown promising overall results with reference to precision and efficiency metrics on the online validation and test datasets, substantiating its efficacy in target segmentation. We believe our approach holds the promise of enhancing clinical practices and contributing to the broader scientific understanding of complex medical image analysis in abdominal oncology.

Acknowledgements. The authors of this paper declare that the segmentation method they implemented for participation in the FLARE 2023 challenge has not used any pre-trained models nor additional datasets other than those provided by the organizers. The proposed solution is fully automatic without any manual intervention. We thank all the data owners for making the CT scans publicly available and CodaLab [27] for hosting the challenge platform.

The study was supported by National Natural Science Foundation of China (81827805, 82130060, 61821002, 92148205), National Key Research and Development Program (2018YFA0704100, 2018YFA0704104). The project was funded by China Postdoctoral Science Foundation (2021M700772), Zhuhai Industry-University-Research Collaboration Program (ZH22017002210011PWC), Jiangsu Provincial Medical Innovation Center (CXZX202219), Collaborative Innovation Center of Radiation Medicine of Jiangsu Higher Education Institutions, and Nanjing Life Health Science and Technology Project (202205045). The funding sources had no role in the writing of the report, or decision to submit the paper for publication.

References

1. Bilic, P., et al.: The liver tumor segmentation benchmark (LiTS). Med. Image Anal. **84**, 102680 (2023)
2. Chen, J., et al.: Run, don't walk: chasing higher flops for faster neural networks. In: Proceedings of the IEEE/CVF Conference on Computer Vision and Pattern Recognition, pp. 12021–12031 (2023)
3. Clark, K., et al.: The cancer imaging archive (TCIA): maintaining and operating a public information repository. J. Digit. Imaging **26**(6), 1045–1057 (2013)
4. Gao, Y., Zhou, M., Metaxas, D.N.: UTNet: a hybrid transformer architecture for medical image segmentation. In: de Bruijne, M., et al. (eds.) MICCAI 2021. LNCS, vol. 12903, pp. 61–71. Springer, Cham (2021). https://doi.org/10.1007/978-3-030-87199-4_6
5. Gatidis, S., et al.: The autopet challenge: towards fully automated lesion segmentation in oncologic PET/CT imaging. Preprint at Research Square (Nature Portfolio) (2023). https://doi.org/10.21203/rs.3.rs-2572595/v1

6. Gatidis, S., et al.: A whole-body FDG-PET/CT dataset with manually annotated tumor lesions. Sci. Data **9**(1), 601 (2022)
7. Hatamizadeh, A., et al.: UNETR: transformers for 3D medical image segmentation. In: Proceedings of the IEEE/CVF Winter Conference on Applications of Computer Vision, pp. 574–584 (2022)
8. Heller, N., et al.: The state of the art in kidney and kidney tumor segmentation in contrast-enhanced CT imaging: results of the KiTS19 challenge. Med. Image Anal. **67**, 101821 (2021)
9. Heller, N., et al.: An international challenge to use artificial intelligence to define the state-of-the-art in kidney and kidney tumor segmentation in CT imaging. Proc. Am. Soc. Clin. Oncol. **38**(6), 626 (2020)
10. Hu, Q., et al.: Label-free liver tumor segmentation. In: Proceedings of the IEEE/CVF Conference on Computer Vision and Pattern Recognition, pp. 7422–7432 (2023)
11. Huang, H., et al.: UNet 3+: a full-scale connected UNet for medical image segmentation. In: 2020 IEEE International Conference on Acoustics, Speech and Signal Processing (ICASSP), ICASSP 2020, pp. 1055–1059. IEEE (2020)
12. Huang, Z., et al.: Revisiting nnU-Net for iterative pseudo labeling and efficient sliding window inference. In: Ma, J., Wang, B. (eds.) FLARE 2022. LNCS, vol. 13816, pp. 178–189. Springer, Cham (2022). https://doi.org/10.1007/978-3-031-23911-3_16
13. Isensee, F., Jaeger, P.F., Kohl, S.A., Petersen, J., Maier-Hein, K.H.: nnU-Net: a self-configuring method for deep learning-based biomedical image segmentation. Nat. Methods **18**(2), 203–211 (2021)
14. Jiang, Y., Zhang, Z., Qin, S., Guo, Y., Li, Z., Cui, S.: APAUNet: axis projection attention UNet for small target in 3D medical segmentation. In: Proceedings of the Asian Conference on Computer Vision, pp. 283–298 (2022)
15. Lai, H., Wang, T., Zhou, S.: DLUNet: semi-supervised learning based dual-light UNet for multi-organ segmentation. In: Ma, J., Wang, B. (eds.) FLARE 2022. LNCS, vol. 13816, pp. 64–73. Springer, Cham (2022). https://doi.org/10.1007/978-3-031-23911-3_7
16. Li, S., Wang, H., Meng, Y., Zhang, C., Song, Z.: Multi-organ segmentation: a progressive exploration of learning paradigms under scarce annotation. arXiv preprint arXiv:2302.03296 (2023)
17. Li, Y., et al.: A comprehensive genomic pan-cancer classification using the cancer genome atlas gene expression data. BMC Genom. **18**, 1–13 (2017)
18. Lian, S., Li, L., Luo, Z., Zhong, Z., Wang, B., Li, S.: Learning multi-organ segmentation via partial-and mutual-prior from single-organ datasets. Biomed. Signal Process. Control **80**, 104339 (2023)
19. Lin, W., Wu, Z., Chen, J., Huang, J., Jin, L.: Scale-aware modulation meet transformer. In: Proceedings of the IEEE/CVF International Conference on Computer Vision, pp. 6015–6026 (2023)
20. Liu, X., Qu, L., Xie, Z., Zhao, J., Shi, Y., Song, Z.: Towards more precise automatic analysis: a comprehensive survey of deep learning-based multi-organ segmentation. arXiv preprint arXiv:2303.00232 (2023)
21. Ma, J., He, Y., Li, F., Han, L., You, C., Wang, B.: Segment anything in medical images. Nat. Commun. **15**(1), 654 (2024)
22. Ma, J., et al.: Fast and low-GPU-memory abdomen CT organ segmentation: the flare challenge. Med. Image Anal. **82**, 102616 (2022)
23. Ma, J., et al.: Unleashing the strengths of unlabeled data in pan-cancer abdominal organ quantification: the flare22 challenge. arXiv preprint arXiv:2308.05862 (2023)

24. Ma, J., et al.: AbdomenCT-1K: is abdominal organ segmentation a solved problem? IEEE Trans. Pattern Anal. Mach. Intell. **44**(10), 6695–6714 (2022)
25. Milletari, F., Navab, N., Ahmadi, S.A.: V-net: fully convolutional neural networks for volumetric medical image segmentation. In: 2016 Fourth International Conference on 3D Vision (3DV), pp. 565–571. IEEE (2016)
26. Pan, Y., Zhu, J., Huang, B.: Unlabeled abdominal multi-organ image segmentation based on semi-supervised adversarial training strategy. In: Ma, J., Wang, B. (eds.) FLARE 2022. LNCS, vol. 13816, pp. 11–22. Springer, Cham (2022). https://doi.org/10.1007/978-3-031-23911-3_2
27. Pavao, A., et al.: CodaLab competitions: an open source platform to organize scientific challenges. J. Mach. Learn. Res. **24**(198), 1–6 (2023)
28. Ren, S., Zhou, D., He, S., Feng, J., Wang, X.: Shunted self-attention via multi-scale token aggregation. In: Proceedings of the IEEE/CVF Conference on Computer Vision and Pattern Recognition, pp. 10853–10862 (2022)
29. Ronneberger, O., Fischer, P., Brox, T.: U-net: convolutional networks for biomedical image segmentation. In: Navab, N., Hornegger, J., Wells, W.M., Frangi, A.F. (eds.) MICCAI 2015. LNCS, vol. 9351, pp. 234–241. Springer, Cham (2015). https://doi.org/10.1007/978-3-319-24574-4_28
30. Simpson, A.L., et al.: A large annotated medical image dataset for the development and evaluation of segmentation algorithms. arXiv preprint arXiv:1902.09063 (2019)
31. Tang, Y., et al.: Self-supervised pre-training of swin transformers for 3D medical image analysis. In: Proceedings of the IEEE/CVF Conference on Computer Vision and Pattern Recognition, pp. 20730–20740 (2022)
32. Tarvainen, A., Valpola, H.: Mean teachers are better role models: weight-averaged consistency targets improve semi-supervised deep learning results. In: Advances in Neural Information Processing Systems, vol. 30 (2017)
33. Valanarasu, J.M.J., Patel, V.M.: UNeXt: MLP-based rapid medical image segmentation network. In: Wang, L., Dou, Q., Fletcher, P.T., Speidel, S., Li, S. (eds.) MICCAI 2022. LNCS, vol. 13435, pp. 23–33. Springer, Cham (2022). https://doi.org/10.1007/978-3-031-16443-9_3
34. Wang, E., Zhao, Y., Wu, Y.: Cascade dual-decoders network for abdominal organs segmentation. In: Ma, J., Wang, B. (eds.) FLARE 2022. LNCS, vol. 13816, pp. 202–213. Springer, Cham (2022). https://doi.org/10.1007/978-3-031-23911-3_18
35. Wang, W., Chen, C., Ding, M., Yu, H., Zha, S., Li, J.: TransBTS: multimodal brain tumor segmentation using transformer. In: de Bruijne, M., et al. (eds.) MICCAI 2021. LNCS, vol. 12901, pp. 109–119. Springer, Cham (2021). https://doi.org/10.1007/978-3-030-87193-2_11
36. Wang, Y., Zhao, L., Wang, M., Song, Z.: Organ at risk segmentation in head and neck CT images using a two-stage segmentation framework based on 3D U-Net. IEEE Access **7**, 144591–144602 (2019)
37. Wasserthal, J., et al.: TotalSegmentator: robust segmentation of 104 anatomic structures in CT images. Radiol. Artif. Intell. **5**(5), e230024 (2023)
38. Xie, E., Wang, W., Yu, Z., Anandkumar, A., Alvarez, J.M., Luo, P.: Segformer: Simple and efficient design for semantic segmentation with transformers. In: Advances in Neural Information Processing Systems, vol. 34, pp. 12077–12090 (2021)
39. Xie, Y., Zhang, J., Shen, C., Xia, Y.: CoTr: efficiently bridging CNN and transformer for 3D medical image segmentation. In: de Bruijne, M., et al. (eds.) MICCAI 2021. LNCS, vol. 12903, pp. 171–180. Springer, Cham (2021). https://doi.org/10.1007/978-3-030-87199-4_16

40. Yu, W., et al.: MetaFormer is actually what you need for vision. In: Proceedings of the IEEE/CVF Conference on Computer Vision and Pattern Recognition, pp. 10819–10829 (2022)
41. Yushkevich, P.A., Gao, Y., Gerig, G.: ITK-snap: an interactive tool for semi-automatic segmentation of multi-modality biomedical images. In: Annual International Conference of the IEEE Engineering in Medicine and Biology Society, pp. 3342–3345 (2016)
42. Zhang, D., Chen, B., Chong, J., Li, S.: Weakly-supervised teacher-student network for liver tumor segmentation from non-enhanced images. Med. Image Anal. **70**, 102005 (2021)
43. Zhang, Y., Yang, L., Chen, J., Fredericksen, M., Hughes, D.P., Chen, D.Z.: Deep adversarial networks for biomedical image segmentation utilizing unannotated images. In: Descoteaux, M., Maier-Hein, L., Franz, A., Jannin, P., Collins, D.L., Duchesne, S. (eds.) MICCAI 2017. LNCS, vol. 10435, pp. 408–416. Springer, Cham (2017). https://doi.org/10.1007/978-3-319-66179-7_47
44. Zhou, H.Y., Guo, J., Zhang, Y., Yu, L., Wang, L., Yu, Y.: nnFormer: interleaved transformer for volumetric segmentation. arXiv preprint arXiv:2109.03201 (2021)
45. Zhu, J., et al.: Embedding expertise knowledge into inverse treatment planning for low-dose-rate brachytherapy of hepatic malignancies. Med. Phys. (2023)

Combine Synergetic Approach with Multi-scale Feature Fusion for Boosting Abdominal Multi-organ and Pan-Cancer Segmentation

Shuo Wang and Yanjun Peng[✉]

College of Computer Science and Engineering, Shandong University of Science and Technology, Qingdao 266590, China
pengyanjuncn@163.com

Abstract. Due to the capability of abdominal images to accurately represent the spatial distribution and size relationships of lesion components in the body, precise segmentation of these images can significantly assist doctors in diagnosing illnesses. To address issues such as high computational resource consumption and inaccurate boundary delineation, we propose a two-stage segmentation framework with multi-scale feature fusion. This approach aims to enhance segmentation accuracy while reducing computational complexity. In the initial stage, a coarse segmentation network is employed to identify the location of segmentation targets with minimal computational overhead. Subsequently, in the second stage, we introduce a multi-scale feature fusion module that incorporates cross-layer connectivity. This method enhances the network's context-awareness capabilities and improves its ability to capture boundary information of intricate medical structures. Our proposed method has achieved notable results, with an average Dice Similarity Coefficient (DSC) score of 85.60% and 37.26% for organs and lesions, respectively, on the validation set. Additionally, the average running time and area under the GPU memory-time curve are reported as 11 s and 24,858.1 megabytes, demonstrating the efficiency and effectiveness of our approach in both accuracy and resource utilization.

Keywords: Deep learning · Abdominal organ segmentation · Feature fusion · Tumor segmentation

1 Introduction

Cancers affecting abdominal organs are a significant medical concern, particularly with colorectal and pancreatic malignancies ranking as the second and third leading causes of cancer-related mortality [5]. Computed Tomography (CT) scanning plays a crucial role in providing prognostic insights for oncological patients and remains a widely used technique for therapeutic monitoring. In both clinical research trials and routine medical practice, the assessment of tumor dimensions [2] and organ characteristics on CT scans often relies on manual two-dimensional measurements, following criteria such as the Response Evaluation Criteria In Solid Tumors (RECIST) guidelines [23]. However, this method of evaluation introduces inherent subjectivity and is susceptible to significant inter and intra-professional variations. Furthermore, existing challenges tend to focus predominantly on specific tumor categories, such as hepatic or renal malignancies.

Convolutional neural networks (CNNs) [1] possess the capability to autonomo-usly acquire image features by conducting convolution operations, thereby facilitating automated feature extraction. Yuan et al. [25] proposed a two-branch UNet architecture, adding a branch to the original network to learn global features. The 3D-based coarse-to-fine framework [30] enables the gradual processing of input data at various granularity levels, progressively enhancing segmentation results while conserving computational resources. Yuan et al. [26] designed a better combination of convolutional neural network and Transformer to capture dual attention features. Complementary features were generated in the Transformer and CNN domains. Feature fusion is crucial in medical image segmentation, as it integrates various pieces of information, addresses image complexity, and enhances model accuracy and generalization. UNet++ [29] improved skip connections by nesting them layer and layer, and experiments on several datasets achieved perfect performance. FFA-Net [18] combines features from different levels, directing the network's attention towards more effective information. It assigns greater weight to important features while preserving shallow features. In addition, it also proposed skip connections [21] that can combine the original features while recovering the resolution. Han et al. [8] utilize deep semi-supervised learning with a precision-focused pseudo-labeling approach, effectively expanding the training dataset for liver CT image segmentation. Achieving superior results with minimal labeled data from the LiTS dataset. SS-Net [24] addresses the challenges of semi-supervised medical image segmentation by enforcing pixel-level smoothness, promoting inter-class separation, and achieving state-of-the-art performance on LA and ACDC datasets. GEPS-Net [12] combines graph-enhanced segmentation with semi-super-vised learning, notably improving pancreas segmentation on CT scans, surpassing methods with limited data, and aiding early diagnoses and adaptive therapy.

We intensity normalize and resample the size of the original image and perform extensive data enhancement. Abdominal organs as well as tumors are segmented and post-processed using a two-stage segmentation framework. The two-stage segmentation method is used to segment 3D abdominal organs and tumor images to improve accuracy, especially when dealing with complex anatomical structures, the error rate can be effectively reduced by the first stage of localization and initial segmentation, while the second stage can segment tumors and organs more finely. For large datasets, this method can reduce the computational burden and improve efficiency.

2   Method

Our proposed method is a whole-volume-based two-stage framework. Details about the method are described as follows:

Firstly, for the localization of organs and tumors, we adopt a lightweight model to optimize the model with fewer parameters and computational requirements; Secondly, we use mixed precision training to represent the model parameters with low accuracy, which can reduce computational overhead without significant performance loss. Finally, for duplicate inputs, cache the output results of the model to reduce duplicate calculations and improve inference speed.

2.1   Preprocessing

The proposed method includes the following pre-processing steps:

- Resize the image to a right-anterior-inferior (RAI) view.
- Remove the background (label 0) by threshold segmentation.
- Considering the memory constraints of the current training process, we resampled the image to a fixed size [160, 160, 160] and applied it to coarse and fine segmentation inputs.
- Intensity normalization: all images are cropped to $[-500, 500]$, and z-score normalization is applied based on the mean and standard deviation of the intensity values.
- Our framework employs a mixed-precision approach throughout the workflow to improve the efficiency of the training and testing procedures.

2.2   Proposed Method

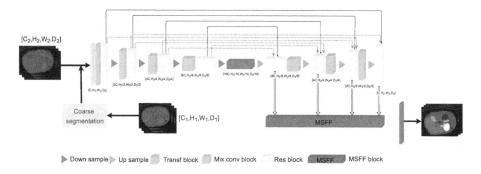

Fig. 1. The whole architecture of our proposed methods. The MSFF block is the multi-scale feature fusion block, the Mixed conv block is the hybrid convolution block consisting of Conv-IN-Drop-ReLU, and the Res block represents the residual block.

The proposed network is shown in Fig. 1. For abdominal medical images, the anatomical structures and lesion locations are complex and variable. The varying

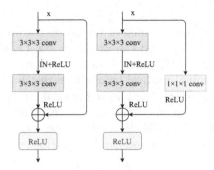

Fig. 2. Comparison of different residual connection methods.

sizes of tumors tend to lead to category imbalance problems, and have a certain degree of artifacts and noise. To solve this issue, we design a two-stage network [30] with multi-scale feature fusion network. We first use a lightweight U-shaped network [3] to obtain the approximate location and distribution of segmented targets. The network input is $x \in R^{B \times C \times H_1 \times W_1 \times D_1}$, where B denotes the size of the batch, C denotes the number of input channels and $H_1 \times W_1 \times D_1$ denotes the size after re-sampling. After localization, Specific optimization of the segmented target edges is performed. The network input is $x \in R^{B \times C \times H_2 \times W_2 \times D_2}$. Importantly, we design a multi-scale feature fusion module. It is used to enhance the important features in the encoding stage and improve the context-awareness of the network. It can effectively reduce the loss of information and blurred edges caused during the decoding process, thus enhancing the overall segmentation of medical images.

2.3 Backbone Network

The two-stage framework is illustrated in Fig. 1. We use a coarse segmentation network for initial localization of the segmentation target. As shown in Fig. 2, a $1 \times 1 \times 1$ convolution is added to the connected path of the residuals. Compared to the original residual connection, this solves the semantic loss problem. In the deeper layers of the network, it can enhance the transfer and expression of information. It is also effective in preventing the gradient from disappearing. After pre-processing, the edges of the segmentation target are then finely segmented. Different organs or structures vary greatly in shape and size. The network channels are increased from $[8, 16, 32, 64, 128]$ to $[16, 32, 64, 128, 256]$ to extract richer features. This improves the ability to accurately locate details of segmented target edges.

Abdominal medical data [7] have differences in images due to differences in acquisition equipment. We combine the two residual approaches in Fig. 2 to form a mixed convolution block. This block incorporates two at each layer in the encoding stage and one at each layer in the decoding stage. We use instancenorm to reinforce detailed features and enhance the consistency of intensity distribution within the region of interest. It reduces the impact of variability on feature extraction and enables better learning of the image feature representation. The final input to the network is passed through a $1 \times 1 \times 1$ convolution to obtain a segmented probability map utilizing a sigmoid function.

Loss function: Abdominal medical images face the challenges of overlapping tissue structures and organ deformation, complicating network training. Therefore, our loss function uses a combination of binary cross entropy (BCE) loss and dice coefficient (Dice) loss [13]. It effectively solves the category imbalance problem. Our loss function expression can be described as follows:

$$L_{total} = L_{BCE} + L_{Dice} \tag{1}$$

$$L_{BCE} = -\frac{1}{N} \sum_i \sum_{c=1}^{M} y_{ic} \log P_{ic} \tag{2}$$

$$L_{Dice} = 1 - \frac{2|X \cap Y| + \varepsilon}{|X| + |Y| + \varepsilon} \tag{3}$$

Unlabeled data play a role in our experiments, involving the utilization of 1800 instances for inference. We divided the model training into two distinct phases, employing partially labeled data. Subsequent to model saving, predictions were applied to the entire pool of unlabeled data to generate pseudo-images and credible scores. We selected the top fifty percent most dependable instances during the prediction process. Furthermore, a new pseudo dataset is crafted by amalgamating this selection with a partially labeled dataset.

However, the outcomes didn't meet our expectations as they fell notably short. We reverted to the fully supervised approach, which yielded a 3–5% enhancement compared to previous results.

Due to time and equipment constraints, we did not use untagged images. Pseudo-labels generated by the FLARE22 winning algorithm [11] and the best-accuracy-algorithm [20] are used during the research and exploration of the methodology, and the segmentation of organs and tumors is performed using the pseudo-labeled data and the data from FLARE2023.

2.4   Post-processing

Utilizing the Python connected-components-3d and fastremap3 packages [28], we extract the largest connected component of the segmentation mask per each class for both coarse and fine outputs, ensuring noise impact avoidance by employing the connected component analysis and selecting the maximum connected component as the final segmentation outcome.

3   Experiments

3.1   Dataset and Evaluation Measures

FLARE2023 is an extension of the FLARE2021 [15] and FLARE2022 [16] challenges. This challenge aims to promote the development of universal organ and tumor segmentation [9] in abdominal CT scans. In FLARE2023, add the lesion segmentation task. Different from existing tumor segmentation challenges [2], FLARE2023 focuses on pan-cancer segmentation, which covers various abdominal cancer types. The segmentation targets cover 13 organs and various abdominal lesions. The training dataset is curated from more than 30 medical centers under the license permission, including TCIA [4], LiTS [2], MSD [19], KiTS [9,10], autoPET [6], TotalSegmentator [22], and AbdomenCT-1K [17]. 2200 cases have partial labels and 1800 cases are unlabeled. The validation set consists of 100 CT scans of various cancer types. The test set consists of 400 CT scans of various cancer types. Specifically, the segmentation algorithm should segment 13 organs (liver, spleen, pancreas, right kidney, left kidney, stomach, gallbladder, esophagus, aorta, inferior vena cava, right adrenal gland, left adrenal gland, and duodenum) and one tumor class with all kinds of cancer types (such as liver cancer, kidney cancer, stomach cancer, pancreas cancer, colon cancer) in abdominal CT scans. All the CT scans only have image information and the center information is not available. The organ annotation process used ITK-SNAP [27], and MedSAM [14].

The evaluation metrics consist of segmentation accuracy metrics and segmentation efficiency metrics. The segmentation accuracy metricsconsist of two measures: Dice Similarity Coefficient (DSC) and Normalized Surface Dice (NSD). The segmentation efficiency metrics consist of two measures: running time (s) and area under GPU memory-time curve (MB). All measures will be used to compute the ranking. Moreover, the GPU memory consumption has a 4 GB tolerance.

3.2   Implementation Details

Environment Settings. The development environments and requirements are presented in Table 1.

Table 1. Development environments and requirements.

System	Ubuntu 18.04.5 LTS
CPU	Intel(R) Xeon(R) Silver 4210 CPU @ 2.20 GHz($\times$8)
RAM	16 $\times$ 4 GB; 2.67MT/s
GPU (number and type)	NVIDIA GeForce RTX 2080Ti 11G($\times$4)
CUDA version	11.6
Programming language	Python 3.9
Deep learning framework	Pytorch (Torch 1.13.0)

Training Protocols. The training protocols of the baseline method is shown in Table 2 and Table 3.

Table 2. Training protocols.

Network initialization	"he" normal initialization
Batch size	1
Patch size	$160 \times 160 \times 160$
Total epochs	200
Optimizer	Adam with betas(0.9, 0.99), L2 penalty: 0.00001
Initial learning rate (lr)	0.0001
Lr decay schedule	halved by 20 epochs
Training time	48 h
Loss function	Dice loss + BCE loss
Number of model parameters	28.82M
Number of flops	41.54G

Table 3. Training protocols for the refine model.

Network initialization	"he" normal initialization
Batch size	1
Patch size	$160 \times 160 \times 160$
Total epochs	200
Optimizer	Adam with betas(0.9, 0.99), L2 penalty: 0.00001
Initial learning rate (lr)	0.0001
Lr decay schedule	halved by 20 epochs
Training time	48 h
Number of model parameters	36.32M
Number of flops	48.14G

4   Results and Discussion

Table 4. The performance on the validation set is represented by the average values in the table.

Target	Public Validation		Online Validation	
	DSC(%)	NSD(%)	DSC(%)	NSD(%)
Liver	97.69 ± 0.51	98.50 ± 1.57	97.78	87.87
Right Kindney	91.74 ± 6.79	91.19 ± 8.31	90.32	84.61
Spleen	95.13 ± 1.02	96.61 ± 2.06	97.32	94.02
Pancreas	83.09 ± 6.44	93.87 ± 5.14	84.09	70.21
Aorta	94.60 ± 1.25	96.84 ± 1.98	91.99	87.59
Inferior vena cava	91.90 ± 2.89	92.89 ± 3.46	90.28	83.95
Right adrenal gland	77.96 ± 6.91	90.09 ± 2.45	76.46	80.36
Left adrenal gland	72.24 ± 8.56	85.89 ± 5.76	73.46	77.89
Gallbladder	74.02 ± 20.45	73.09 ± 24.56	73.73	62.93
Esophagus	74.41 ± 15.67	85.70 ± 19.48	71.31	62.21
Stomach	89.70 ± 2.14	92.28 ± 3.14	88.75	67.27
Duodenum	77.19 ± 8.19	90.61 ± 5.13	75.46	62.41
Left kidney	93.09 ± 4.23	93.17 ± 2.54	91.94	85.83
Tumor	37.26 ± 23.14	29.09 ± 30.41	39.94	26.47
Average	82.14 ± 7.11	86.41 ± 7.53	81.63	73.83

Table 5. Quantitative evaluation of segmentation efficiency in terms of the running them and GPU memory consumption

Case ID	Image Size	Running time(s)	Max GPU(MB)	Total GPU(MB)
0001	(512, 512, 55)	5.79	1005	11145
0051	(512, 512, 100)	7.12	1293	10536
0017	(512, 512, 150)	8.41	1940	10549
0019	(512, 512, 215)	10.55	2138	11474
0099	(512, 512, 334)	13.33	2620	12965
0063	(512, 512, 448)	16.81	2838	12863
0048	(512, 512, 499)	19.22	2985	13425
0029	(512, 512, 554)	23.71	3241	14562

4.1   Quantitative Results on Validation Set

Table 4 illustrates the results of this work on the validation cases whose ground truth are publicly provided by FLARE2023. Our method performs well in the task of segmenting multiple abdominal organs. The Dice similarity coefficients (DSC) of key organs such as the liver, kidney, spleen, and aorta are all above 0.9, and the Normalized Surface Distance (NSDs) also remain above 0.9. This highlights the superior ability of our method in capturing organ contours and morphology, proving our significant advantage in organ segmentation.

Tumor segmentation presented challenges due to uncertainties in tumor number and size, leading to recognition errors and omissions during segmentation. Consequently, the method achieved a DSC coefficient of 37.26% and an NSD coefficient of 29.09%, highlighting room for improvement in tumor recognition and delineation. Our method fully utilizes the strategy of multi-scale feature fusion, which is one of the keys to our success. By integrating image information at different scales, our model can capture the details and structures of organs more accurately. This strategy results in very satisfactory DSC and NSD values for most organs, which is a clear indication of the advantages of our method in segmentation tasks. Although we have achieved remarkable results, we recognize that there is room for further improvement in the results of tumor segmentation. Table 5 presents a quantitative evaluation of runtime and GPU memory consumption.

In our final submission, we exclusively utilized labeled data for the segmentation of abdominal organs and tumors. Our segmentation approach involved a two-stage network, which encompasses the entire segmentation process. Furthermore, we conducted ablation study to substantiate the benefits of employing this two-stage network. The results of our approach are presented in Table 6.

Table 6. Ablation study in our methodology (s represents training using a single stage network, and d represents training using a two-stage network.)

Number	Organ DSC	Organ NSD	Tumor DSC	Tumor NSD
1(s)	81.40	79.51	10.25	9.88
2(d)	86.50	90.88	37.26	29.09

4.2   Qualitative Results on Validation Set

In Fig. 3, the upper two layers (ID53 and ID81) exhibit favorable segmentation, while the lower two layers (ID35 and ID51) display suboptimal segmentation results. The horizontal axis represents the original image, Ground Truth, ablation study outcomes, and segmentation results achieved through our proposed method. In instances characterized by effective segmentation, the contours of organs are distinctly delineated, highlighting the robust performance of our multi-scale method during the feature recovery phase. Conversely, for cases demonstrating inadequate segmentation, the accurate identification of organ sizes poses a challenge. Specifically, organs such as the gallbladder, duodenum, adrenal gland, and esophagus have not been precisely delineated.

Our proposed method has demonstrated effectiveness in the segmentation of multiple abdominal organs and their associated tumors. Particularly, when confronted with large abdominal tumors characterized by a relatively flat contour

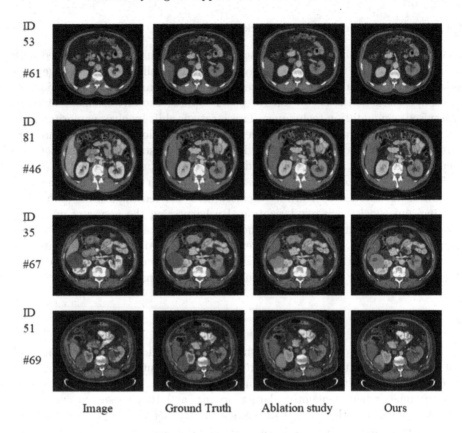

Image   Ground Truth   Ablation study   Ours

Fig. 3. Visualization results for some cases.

and a normal tumor count, our method exhibits high-performance segmentation, achieving notable results for both organs and tumors. Acknowledging the significance of addressing instances of segmentation failure, we delve into potential causes, including our method's limitation in accurately determining the number of tumors within the abdomen. This limitation can lead to misidentification and the overlooking of tumors. Furthermore, during the model training process, a disparity arises between tumors and organs: organs typically have fixed positions and shapes, allowing for more comprehensive feature learning, while tumors exhibit diverse positions and shapes, resulting in insufficiently learned features. To address this, we plan to enhance the model's training frequency, aiming to attain higher levels of segmentation accuracy.

4.3 Segmentation Efficiency Results on Validation Set

The average running time is 11.0 s per case in inference phase, and average used GPU memory is 2654 MB. The area under GPU memory-time curve is 24858.1 and the area under CPU utilization-time curve is 1240.5.

4.4 Limitation and Future Work

In our future research endeavors, we acknowledge the challenges associated with the time-consuming and labor-intensive nature of labeling medical image data for abdominal organ and tumor segmentation. Recognizing the limitations of fully supervised methods, we aim to pivot towards the advancement of semi-supervised segmentation techniques. This strategic shift involves exploring innovative approaches that effectively leverage a combination of limited annotated data and a larger pool of unlabeled data, aiming to strike a balance between accuracy and practicality in real-world medical image processing.

To address the complexities of labeling, our research will delve into the integration of advanced deep learning architectures and techniques, including self-training and consistency regularization. By harnessing the power of unlabeled data, we seek to enhance the robustness and generalization capabilities of our segmentation model. Through these efforts, our objective is to contribute significantly to the field of medical image processing, offering more accurate and efficient solutions for the segmentation of abdominal organs and tumors.

5 Conclusion

In this paper, our proposed network shows excellent efficacy in abdominal medical image segmentation. Through extensive experiments, we have verified the effectiveness of two-stage segmentation. Particularly, ours have achieved impressive outcomes when segmenting larger organs, and they've shown even more promising results in the context of segmenting smaller tissues. However, in the case of organ tumors, there is still a relatively long way to go.

Acknowledgements. The authors of this paper declare that the segmentation method they implemented for participation in the FLARE 2023 challenge has not used any pre-trained models nor additional datasets other than those provided by the organizers. The proposed solution is fully automatic without any manual intervention.

References

1. Albawi, S., Mohammed, T.A., Al-Zawi, S.: Understanding of a convolutional neural network. In: 2017 International Conference on Engineering and Technology (ICET), pp. 1–6. IEEE (2017)
2. Bilic, P., et al.: The liver tumor segmentation benchmark (LiTS). Med. Image Anal. **84**, 102680 (2023)
3. Çiçek, Ö., Abdulkadir, A., Lienkamp, S.S., Brox, T., Ronneberger, O.: 3D U-net: learning dense volumetric segmentation from sparse annotation. In: Ourselin, S., Joskowicz, L., Sabuncu, M.R., Unal, G., Wells, W. (eds.) MICCAI 2016. LNCS, vol. 9901, pp. 424–432. Springer, Cham (2016). https://doi.org/10.1007/978-3-319-46723-8_49
4. Clark, K., et al.: The cancer imaging archive (TCIA): maintaining and operating a public information repository. J. Digit. Imaging **26**(6), 1045–1057 (2013)

5. Ferlay, J., et al.: Cancer statistics for the year 2020: an overview. Int. J. Cancer **149**(4), 778–789 (2021)
6. Gatidis, S., et al.: A whole-body FDG-PET/CT dataset with manually annotated tumor lesions. Sci. Data **9**(1), 601 (2022)
7. Gibson, E., et al.: Automatic multi-organ segmentation on abdominal CT with dense v-networks. IEEE Trans. Med. Imaging **37**(8), 1822–1834 (2018)
8. Han, K., et al.: An effective semi-supervised approach for liver CT image segmentation. IEEE J. Biomed. Health Inform. **26**(8), 3999–4007 (2022). https://doi.org/10.1109/JBHI.2022.3167384
9. Heller, N., et al.: The state of the art in kidney and kidney tumor segmentation in contrast-enhanced CT imaging: results of the KiTS19 challenge. Med. Image Anal. **67**, 101821 (2021)
10. Heller, N., et al.: An international challenge to use artificial intelligence to define the state-of-the-art in kidney and kidney tumor segmentation in CT imaging. Proc. Am. Soc. Clin. Oncol. **38**(6), 626 (2020)
11. Huang, Z., et al.: Revisiting nnU-net for iterative pseudo labeling and efficient sliding window inference. In: Ma, J., Wang, B. (eds.) FLARE 2022. LNCS, vol. 13816, pp. 178–189. Springer, Cham (2022). https://doi.org/10.1007/978-3-031-23911-3_16
12. Liu, S., Liang, S., Huang, X., Yuan, X., Zhong, T., Zhang, Y.: Graph-enhanced U-net for semi-supervised segmentation of pancreas from abdomen CT scan. Phys. Med. Biol. **67**(15), 155017 (2022)
13. Ma, J., et al.: Loss odyssey in medical image segmentation. Med. Image Anal. **71**, 102035 (2021)
14. Ma, J., He, Y., Li, F., Han, L., You, C., Wang, B.: Segment anything in medical images. Nat. Commun. **15**(1), 654 (2024)
15. Ma, J., et al.: Fast and low-GPU-memory abdomen CT organ segmentation: the flare challenge. Med. Image Anal. **82**, 102616 (2022)
16. Ma, J., et al.: Unleashing the strengths of unlabeled data in pan-cancer abdominal organ quantification: the flare22 challenge. arXiv preprint arXiv:2308.05862 (2023)
17. Ma, J., et al.: AbdomenCT-1K: is abdominal organ segmentation a solved problem? IEEE Trans. Pattern Anal. Mach. Intell. **44**(10), 6695–6714 (2022)
18. Qin, X., Wang, Z., Bai, Y., Xie, X., Jia, H.: FFA-net: feature fusion attention network for single image dehazing. In: Proceedings of the AAAI Conference on Artificial Intelligence, vol. 34, pp. 11908–11915 (2020)
19. Simpson, A.L., et al.: A large annotated medical image dataset for the development and evaluation of segmentation algorithms. arXiv preprint arXiv:1902.09063 (2019)
20. Wang, E., Zhao, Y., Wu, Y.: Cascade dual-decoders network for abdominal organs segmentation. In: Ma, J., Wang, B. (eds.) FLARE 2022. LNCS, vol. 13816, pp. 202–213. Springer, Cham (2022). https://doi.org/10.1007/978-3-031-23911-3_18
21. Wang, H., Cao, P., Wang, J., Zaiane, O.R.: UCTransNet: rethinking the skip connections in u-net from a channel-wise perspective with transformer. In: Proceedings of the AAAI Conference on Artificial Intelligence, vol. 36, pp. 2441–2449 (2022)
22. Wasserthal, J., et al.: TotalSegmentator: robust segmentation of 104 anatomic structures in CT images. Radiol. Artif. Intell. **5**(5), e230024 (2023)
23. Watanabe, H., et al.: New response evaluation criteria in solid tumours-revised RECIST guideline (version 1.1). Gan to Kagaku Ryoho. Cancer Chemother. **36**(13), 2495–2501 (2009)
24. Wu, Y., Wu, Z., Wu, Q., Ge, Z., Cai, J.: Exploring smoothness and class-separation for semi-supervised medical image segmentation. In: Wang, L., Dou, Q., Fletcher,

P.T., Speidel, S., Li, S. (eds.) MICCAI 2022. LNCS, vol. 13435, pp. 34–43. Springer, Cham (2022). https://doi.org/10.1007/978-3-031-16443-9_4

25. Yuan, F., Zhang, L., Xia, X., Wan, B., Huang, Q., Li, X.: Deep smoke segmentation. Neurocomputing **357**, 248–260 (2019)

26. Yuan, F., Zhang, Z., Fang, Z.: An effective CNN and transformer complementary network for medical image segmentation. Pattern Recogn. **136**, 109228 (2023)

27. Yushkevich, P.A., Gao, Y., Gerig, G.: ITK-snap: an interactive tool for semi-automatic segmentation of multi-modality biomedical images. In: Annual International Conference of the IEEE Engineering in Medicine and Biology Society, pp. 3342–3345 (2016)

28. Zhang, F., Wang, Y., Yang, H.: Efficient context-aware network for abdominal multi-organ segmentation. arXiv preprint arXiv:2109.10601 (2021)

29. Zhou, Z., Rahman Siddiquee, M.M., Tajbakhsh, N., Liang, J.: UNet++: a nested U-net architecture for medical image segmentation. In: Stoyanov, D., et al. (eds.) DLMIA/ML-CDS -2018. LNCS, vol. 11045, pp. 3–11. Springer, Cham (2018). https://doi.org/10.1007/978-3-030-00889-5_1

30. Zhu, Z., Xia, Y., Shen, W., Fishman, E., Yuille, A.: A 3D coarse-to-fine framework for volumetric medical image segmentation. In: 2018 International Conference on 3D Vision (3DV), pp. 682–690. IEEE (2018)

Coarse to Fine Segmentation Method Enables Accurate and Efficient Segmentation of Organs and Tumor in Abdominal CT

Hui Meng[1]([✉])(ID), Haochen Zhao[2](ID), Deqian Yang[1](ID), Songping Wang[2](ID), and Zhenpeng Li[2](ID)

[1] School of Intelligent Science and Technology, Hangzhou Institute for Advanced Study, University of Chinese Academy of Sciences, Hangzhou 310024, China
huimeng@ucas.ac.cn
[2] Hangzhou Innovation Institute of Beihang University, Hangzhou 310051, China

Abstract. Automatic segmentation of organs and tumor in abdominal CT scans is essential for cancer diagnosis and treatment monitoring. However, there does not exist an accurate and efficient method for universal organ and tumor segmentation in abdominal CT scans. Therefore, we propose a coarse to fine segmentation (CFS) method based on pseudo labels. Specifically, the CFS consists of a coarse segmentation model (CSM), a tumor segmentation model (TSM), and an organ segmentation model (OSM). The CSM is trained to segment abdominal regions in CT scans. The TSM and the OSM are trained to generate segmentation masks of organs and tumor. The outputs of the TSM and the OSM are merged to generate the final segmentation results. To improve efficiency of the CFS, we optimize the inference process by streamlining intricate steps. On validation set of FLARE23 challenge, our method achieves mean DSC of 91.59% and mean NSD of 95.74% on organ segmentation, and mean DSC of 47.12% and mean NSD of 39.94% on tumor segmentation. The mean inference time is 24.12 s, and the mean area under the GPU memory-time curve is 39543.46 MB.

Keywords: segmentation · abdominal CT · coarse to fine

1 Introduction

Abdominal organs are quite common cancer sites, such as colorectal cancer and pancreatic cancer, which are the 2nd and 3rd most common cause of cancer death [23]. Computed Tomography (CT) scanning is widely used for diagnosis and treatment monitoring of abdominal cancers. Nowadays, radiologists and clinicians measure the tumor and organs on CT scans based on manual two-dimensional measurements, which is inherently subjective with considerable

J. Ma and B. Wang (Eds.): FLARE 2023, LNCS 14544, pp. 115–129, 2024.
https://doi.org/10.1007/978-3-031-58776-4_10

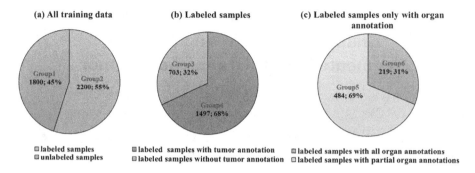

Fig. 1. Data distribution of training set in FLARE23 challenge. (a) Distribution of labeled samples and unlabeled samples. (b) Data partitioning of labeled samples. (c) Data partitioning of labeled samples only with organ annotation.

inter- and intra-expert variability. Therefore, it is necessary to develop an automatic segmentation method for simultaneous segmentation of organs and tumor in abdominal CT scans.

For segmentation of abdominal CT scans, the difficulty of data annotation leads to a lack of public large-scale labeled datasets. Thus, researchers try to improve segmentation accuracy using unlabeled data and partial-label data. To effectively utilize unlabeled data, Zhou et al. proposed a deep multi-plane co-training approach [26] to generate dependable pseudo labels. Similarly, Lee et al. devised an advanced pseudo-label quality discriminator to effectively guide and regulate network learning of unlabeled data [16]. Additionally, participants of FLARE22 challenge proposed many semi-supervised methods for organ segmentation in abdominal CT scans, including pseudo label-based methods [1,6,13], consistency learning-based methods [9,15,21], and cross pseudo supervision-based methods [4,12]. Compared with the consistency learning-based methods and the cross pseudo supervision-based methods, the pseudo label-based methods achieved more accurate segmentation results.

Although the above researches improved semi-supervised segmentation accuracy, the tasks of them mainly focus on segmentation of organs or one type of tumor whose distribution in CT scans is relatively fixed. In FLARE23 challenge, the segmentation task focuses on 13 organ segmentation and pan-cancer segmentation. Different from existing researches, the FLARE23 aims to segment various abdominal cancer types and 13 organs simultaneously. Compared with organ segmentation, the pan-cancer segmentation faces two major challenges. The first one is that the tumor location, tumor shape, and the tumor number are various among different CT scans, which make the tumor feature complex. The second one is lack of cases with both organ and tumor annotations. Therefore, it is necessary to make full use of cases with tumor annotation.

To achieve accurate organ and pan-cancer segmentation, we propose a coarse to fine segmentation (CFS) method based on pseudo labels. The CFS consists of a coarse segmentation model (CSM), a tumor segmentation model (TSM), and an organ segmentation model (OSM), whose architectures are all nnU-Net [14].

The CSM is first trained using cases with full organ annotations. Then, cases with only tumor labels are inferenced to generate pseudo labels of organs based on the trained CSM. Next, we use the cases with tumor labels and pseudo labels of organs to train the TSM. The OSM is trained using all 4000 cases with ground truth and pseudo labels generated by the [13]. During inference, we first segment input CT scans using the CSM to obtain abdominal regions. Then, the abdominal regions are segmented by the TSM and the OSM separately. Last, the segmentation masks given by the TSM and the OSM are merged to generate the final segmentation results. To improve efficiency of the CFS, we optimize the inference process by streamlining intricate steps.

2   Method

2.1   Preprocessing

In our method, preprocessing operations include data grouping, image cropping, data resampling, intensity normalization, and data augmentation. The details of the preprocessing operations are listed as follows:

- Data grouping:
  The training set is analysed and grouped based on annotations. As shown in Fig. 1(a), the training set consists of 1800 unlabeled samples (*Group* 1) and 2200 labeled samples (*Group* 2). For the *Group* 2, we further divide labeled samples based on whether annotations contain tumor labels. As shown in Fig. 1(b), there are 703 labeled samples without tumor annotations (*Group* 3) and 1497 labeled samples with tumor annotations (*Group* 4). Furthermore, we divide the *Group* 3 into 484 samples with partial organ annotations (*Group* 5) and 219 samples with all organ annotations (*Group* 6) (Fig. 1(c)).
- Cropping strategy:
  Before model training, the training CT scans are cropped along the z-axis direction based on ground truth or pseudo labels. Specifically, the indices of start slice and the end slice of region containing targets are first calculated based on labels. To reserve context information of segmentation targets, we reduce the index of the start slice by 10 and add the index of the end slice by 10. During model training, the cropped CT scans are further cropped based on non-zero region introduced by nnU-Net [14].
- Resampling method for anisotropic data:
  We perform image redirection to the desired orientation, followed by resampling all CT scans to match the median voxel spacing of the training dataset. Specifically, third-order spline interpolation is used for image resampling, and the nearest neighbor interpolation is employed for label resampling.
- Intensity normalization approach:
  We gather pixel values in the cropped CT scans and subsequently truncate all data to fall within [0.5, 99.5] of foreground voxel values. Following that, z-score normalization is applied.

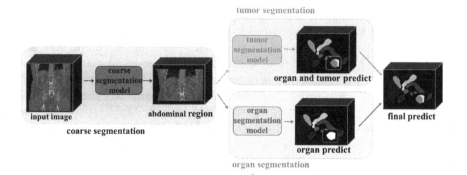

Fig. 2. The overall architecture of the CFS method. The CFS consists of three models: the CSM, the TSM, and the OSM. The three models are all based on nnU-Net architecture, but trained with different data.

– Data augmentation:
  In our method, random rotation, random scaling, elastic transformation, brightness transformation, contrast transformation, and gamma transformation are used for data augmentation.

2.2 Proposed Method

As shown in Fig. 2, the architecture of our proposed method contains three segmentation models, i.e. the CSM, the TSM, and the OSM. Noted that the three segmentation models are all based on the nnU-Net framework [14]. We combine Dice loss and cross-entropy loss to train all models. The details of model training and inference process are described in the following.

Training of the CSM. To reduce redundant information in CT scans and extract abdominal regions, we first train the CSM using 219 labeled samples with all organ annotations (*Group* 6). Based on the trained CSM, we predict pseudo labels of 13 organs on *Group* $1 - 5$ and merge them with the corresponding ground truth. Then, we obtain 4000 training data with all organ annotations (real labels or pseudo labels), which is termed as *Dataset* 1.

Training of the TSM. To train the TSM, we first extract the 1497 samples of the *Group* 4 from *Dataset* 1. The 1497 samples are randomly divided into training data and validation data by 4:1. The TSM is trained to segment 13 organs and tumor. The best weights are saved every 50 epochs based on the highest segmentation accuracy of tumor on validation data. Then, we evaluate the saved weights on online validation set (100 samples) and select the best weight (*tumor_weight*1) with the highest segmentation accuracy of tumor. To further improve accuracy of tumor segmentation, we train the TSM with random initialization again and save another weight (*tumor_weight*2) following the above method.

Training of the OSM. The OSM is trained using all training data with the pseudo labels generated by the FLARE22 winning algorithm [13]. The 4000 samples are randomly divided into training set and validation set by 4:1. The model is trained to segment 13 organs and the best weights are saved based on the performance of validation set every 50 epochs. Finally, we evaluate the saved weights on the online validation and choose the weight with the highest segmentation accuracy as the weight of the OSM.

Inference Process. During inference, the test CT scans are first segmented by the CSM, and the abdominal regions of the CT scans are cropped based on the segmentation masks of 13 organs. Then, the abdominal regions are segmented by the TSM with $tumor\_weight1$ and $tumor\_weight2$, respectively. The segmentation masks given by the two weights are merged to obtain the masks of tumor and 13 organs ($mask1$). Next, the abdominal regions are segmented by the OSM and the masks of 13 organs are generated ($mask2$). Finally, we modify the $mask1$ with $mask2$ for organ labels and obtain the final segmentation results.

To improve the efficiency of the CFS, we optimize the inference process of conventional nnU-Net by streamlining intricate steps while ensuring faster sampling without compromising accuracy. During the employment of sliding window inference, we omit Gaussian weighting and mirror inference. Compared with the conventional inference of the nnU-Net, our inference strategy achieves a significant reduction in inference time. To reduce resource consumption, we use abdominal regions rather than whole CT scans as input of the TSM and the OSM.

2.3 Post-processing

Based on the segmentation mask, we retain the largest connected region for each segmentation organ based on centroid distances. The small connected regions of segmented organs are removed to reduce false positive islands. Noted that the segmented tumor regions are not processed because there are might multiple tumors in one CT scan.

3 Experiments

3.1 Dataset and Evaluation Measures

The FLARE 2023 challenge is an extension of the FLARE 2021–2022 [19,20], aiming to promote the development of foundation models in abdominal disease analysis. The segmentation targets cover 13 organs and various abdominal lesions. The training dataset is curated from more than 30 medical centers under the license permission, including TCIA [5], LiTS [3], MSD [2], KiTS [10,11], autoPET [7,8], TotalSegmentator [24], and AbdomenCT-1K [18]. The training set includes 4000 abdomen CT scans where 2200 CT scans with partial labels and 1800 CT scans without labels. The validation and testing sets include 100 and

400 CT scans, respectively, which cover various abdominal cancer types, such as liver cancer, kidney cancer, pancreas cancer, colon cancer, gastric cancer, and so on. The organ annotation process used ITK-SNAP [25], nnU-Net [14], and MedSAM [17].

The evaluation metrics encompass two accuracy measures-Dice Similarity Coefficient (DSC) and Normalized Surface Dice (NSD)-alongside two efficiency measures-running time and area under the GPU memory-time curve. These metrics collectively contribute to the ranking computation. Furthermore, the running time and GPU memory consumption are considered within tolerances of 15 s and 4 GB, respectively.

3.2   Implementation Details

Environment Settings. The development environments and requirements are presented in Table 1.

Table 1. Development environments and requirements.

System	Ubuntu 20.04
CPU	13th Gen Intel(R) Core(TM) i7-13700KF 3.40 GHz
RAM	8×4 GB; 2.67MT/s
GPU (number and type)	NVIDIA 4070Ti 12G
CUDA version	12.1
Programming language	Python 3.10
Deep learning framework	Pytorch (Torch 1.12, torchvision 0.2.3)
Specific dependencies	nnU-Net 1.7.0
Code	https://github.com/zhuji423/MICCAI2023_Flare2023

Training Protocols The data processing of unlabeled data and samples with partial labels has been described in Sect. 2.2. We adopt nnU-Net's data augmentation to train the CSM, the TSM, and the OSM. The best weights of the three models are determined based on the online validation, and the details have been introduced in Sect. 2.2. The detailed training protocols of the three models are listed in Table 2.

Table 2. Training protocols for the three segmentation models.

	CSM	TSM	OSM
Network initialization	"he" normal initialization		
Batch size	2	2	2
Patch size	$64 \times 160 \times 224$	$96 \times 128 \times 192$	$96 \times 160 \times 192$
Total epochs	1500	2500	2000
Optimizer	SGD with nesterov momentum ($\mu = 0.99$)		
Initial learning rate (lr)	0.01	0.01	0.01
Lr decay schedule	halved by 200 epochs		
Training time	48 h	65 h	55.5 h
Number of model parameters	41.22M	41.22M	41.22M
Number of flops	59.32G	59.32G	59.32G
CO_2eq	1.23 Kg	2.34 Kg	1.56 Kg

4   Results and Discussion

In this section, we assess the CFS method using FLARE23 dataset. Ablation studies on utilization of unlabeled data and effectiveness of the three models are conducted. We present quantitative results, qualitative results, and efficiency results on validation set. Additionally, results on final testing set are presented. Last, we discuss limitations of the CFS method and our future work.

Table 3. Quantitative evaluation results of CFS method.

Target	Public Validation		Online Validation		Testing	
	DSC(%)	NSD(%)	DSC(%)	NSD(%)	DSC(%)	NSD (%)
Liver	98.62 ± 0.40	99.28 ± 0.89	98.56	99.23	97.83	98.17
Right Kidney	96.59 ± 5.46	96.54 ± 0.41	95.65	95.84	95.74	95.52
Spleen	97.98 ± 4.09	98.69 ± 4.04	97.07	97.96	97.76	98.51
Pancreas	87.88 ± 4.88	97.08 ± 3.65	86.71	96.19	91.32	97.22
Aorta	97.62 ± 1.15	99.42 ± 0.40	97.57	99.31	98.12	99.73
Inferior vena cava	92.33 ± 8.52	93.17 ± 8.81	92.13	92.74	92.70	94.12
Right adrenal gland	87.03 ± 12.47	95.91 ± 13.32	87.40	96.52	88.26	96.73
Left adrenal gland	88.82 ± 5.31	97.70 ± 3.09	88.06	96.7	89.32	96.77
Gallbladder	88.49 ± 19.27	89.68 ± 20.6	89.01	89.92	86.14	87.90
Esophagus	83.03 ± 16.47	91.38 ± 16.40	83.59	92.36	89.50	87.90
Stomach	94.37 ± 4.72	97.07 ± 4.83	94.83	97.34	97.46	95.64
Duodenum	84.57 ± 8.48	94.96 ± 6.45	84.80	94.99	96.83	89.36
Left kidney	95.03 ± 11.56	94.70 ± 13.59	95.26	95.54	95.16	94.75
Tumor	54.45 ± 34.80	47.31 ±31.78	47.12	39.94	63.43	51.02
Average	89.05 ± 9.82	92.34 ± 9.72	91.59	95.74	92.64	96.10

4.1   Quantitative Results on Validation Set

In our method, the CSM is trained using 219 labeled data with all organ annotations. The TSM is trained using 1497 labeled data with tumor annotation and
pseudo labels of 13 organs. To further improve the segmentation performance,
we train the OSM using all 4000 CT scans including unlabeled data. To verify
the effectiveness of the utilization of the unlabeled data, we evaluate the segmentation results given by the CSM and the TSM (two-stage method). The mean
and standard deviation (SD) of DSC and NSD on 50 validation data (public validation) are calculated based on the official evaluation code. The mean of DSC
and NSD on 100 validation data are calculated on CodaLab platform.

Table 4. Quantitative evaluation results of two-stage method.

Target	Public Validation		Online Validation	
	DSC(%)	NSD(%)	DSC(%)	NSD(%)
Liver	95.49 ± 5.94	99.09 ± 0.89	97.21	98.59
Right Kidney	96.59 ± 5.46	96.54 ± 0.41	93.74	93.57
Spleen	96.22 ± 10.12	97.37 ± 10.44	94.28	96.26
Pancreas	86.63 ± 6.96	96.38 ± 6.16	84.45	95.54
Aorta	96.78 ± 2.43	98.6 ± 3.54	95.98	97.88
Inferior vena cava	92.84 ± 6.77	94.41 ± 7.20	93.00	95.28
Right adrenal gland	84.10 ± 15.2	94.25 ± 16.42	81.73	93.67
Left adrenal gland	85.01 ± 10.54	95.72 ± 10.04	80.63	93.17
Gallbladder	85.44 ± 22.4	86.52 ± 23.53	79.96	80.19
Esophagus	82.13 ± 16.26	91.13 ± 16.23	81.98	92.54
Stomach	93.83 ± 4.68	97.16 ± 4.68	93.54	97.53
Duodenum	83.74 ± 7.81	94.84 ± 5.76	82.85	94.67
Left kidney	94.12 ± 10.23	93.67 ± 12.91	92.91	92.89
Tumor	54.45 ± 34.8	47.31 ± 31.78	47.12	39.94
Average	87.66 ± 11.4	91.64 ± 9.72	85.67	90.12

Table 3 and Table 4 list quantitative results of the CFS method and the two-
stage method, respectively. Because pseudo labels of unlabeled data lack tumor
label, the tumor segmentation accuracy of the CFS method is same as that of
the two-stage method. Compared with the two-stage method, the organ segmentation accuracy is improved by the CFS method. For right adrenal gland, left
adrenal gland, and gallbladder, the CFS method yields results of 87.4%, 88.06%,
and 89.01% in mean DSC on online validation, which outperforms the two-stage
method by 5.67%, 7.43%, and 9.05%, respectively. These results demonstrate
that the unlabeled data have great potential to improve segmentation accuracy
of organs, especially small organs.

Furthermore, we implement an ablation study to evaluate the effectiveness
of the three models in our method. The quantitative results are list in Table 5.
Compared with the CSM, the TSM significantly improves the mean organ DSC
and the mean organ NSD. Additionally, the OSM achieves higher organ DSC

and higher organ NSD than the two-stage method. Furthermore, we evaluate the effectiveness of the two weights used in the TSM. The quantitative results (Table 6) demonstrate that inference using two weights obtains the highest tumor segmentation accuracy. All these results illustrate the effectiveness of the TSM and the OSM.

Table 5. Quantitative results of ablation study on the three models.

CSM	TSM	OSM	organ_DSC	organ_NSD	tumor_DSC	tumor_NSD
√			66.97%	70.19%	\	\
√	√		90.35%	95.70%	47.12%	39.94%
√	√	√	91.59%	95.74%	47.12%	39.94%

Table 6. Quantitative results of ablation study on tumor segmentation weights.

tumor_weight1	tumor_weight2	organ_DSC	organ_NSD	tumor_DSC	tumor_NSD
√		91.58%	95.75%	43.09%	36.87%
	√	91.60%	95.75%	46.14%	38.82%
√	√	91.59%	95.74%	47.12%	39.94%

4.2   Qualitative Results on Validation Set

Figure 3 shows two examples with good segmentation results and two examples with bad segmentation results given by the CFS and the two-stage method, respectively. In Case #FLARETs_0019 (slice #155) and Case #FLARETs_0099 (slice #290), both the two-stage method and the CFS achieve accurate organ segmentation. However, the two-stage method and the CFS fail to segment small organs accurately in Case #FLARETs_0001 (slice #99) and Case #FLARETs_0029 (slice #290). Additionally, we present three examples with bad organ segmentation results in Fig. 4. In Case #FLARETs_0001 (slice #31), stomach (green label) and pancreas (yellow label) are not completely segmented. In Case #FLARETs_0029 (slice #290), duodenum in the upper right corner and gallbladder are not segmented. Additionally, the stomach and the pancreas are not fully segmented in the Case #FLARETs_0011 (slice #97). These results indicate that our method still has room for improvement in organ segmentation, especially in small organ segmentation.

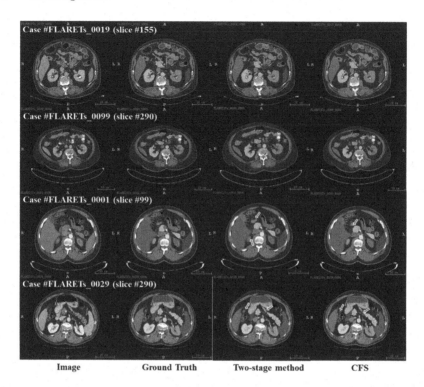

| Image | Ground Truth | Two-stage method | CFS |

Fig. 3. Qualitative results given by the two-stage method and the CFS, respectively. Case #FLARETs_0019 and Case #FLARETs_0099 are examples with good segmentation results. Case #FLARETs_0001 and Case #FLARETs_0029 are examples with bad segmentation results. Red arrows indicate regions with bad segmentation. (Color figure online)

Besides qualitative results of organ segmentation, we present three examples with tumor segmentation results in Fig. 5. In Case #FLARETs_0051 (slice #73), the tumor in the right kidney is segmented as liver by the CFS. In Case #FLARETs_0071 (slice #104), the tumor in the liver is not segmented. Additionally, the tumor in the Case #FLARETs_0048 (slice #297) is segmented as liver or stomach. These results demonstrate that tumors have similar features with organs and it is difficult for the CFS to segment tumors accurately.

4.3   Segmentation Efficiency Results on Validation Set

Table 7 lists quantitative efficiency results in terms of the running time and GPU memory consumption. Total GPU denotes the area under GPU Memory-Time curve. Evaluation GPU platform is NVIDIA QUADRO RTX5000 (16G). The average running time of the CFS is 24.12 s, while the two-stage method obtains shorter average running time (18.17 s). Additionally, the GPU memory consumption of the two-stage method and the CFS is both within 4 GB. Furthermore, quantitative efficiency results of eight examples given by the CFS and the two-stage method are listed in Table 8 and Table 9, respectively. All results demonstrate that our methods achieve efficient segmentation.

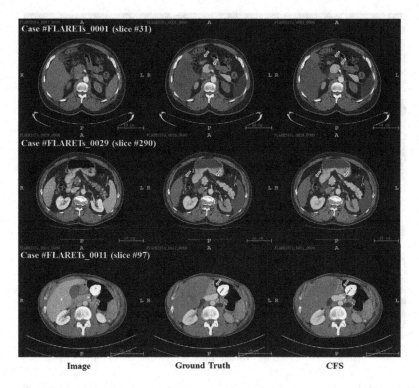

Fig. 4. Qualitative results of three examples with bad organ segmentation results given by the CFS. Red arrows indicate regions with bad segmentation. (Color figure online)

Table 7. Quantitative efficiency results on online validation (Mean ± SD).

Efficiency index	two-stage method	CFS
Running Time (s)	18.17 ± 4.78	24.12 ± 5.39
Max GPU (MB)	3137.16 ± 232.18	3480.48 ± 150.48
Total GPU (MB)	26314.9 ± 8457.26	39543.46 ± 9845.58

Table 8. Quantitative efficiency results given by the CFS.

Case ID	Image Size	Running Time (s)	Max GPU (MB)	Total GPU (MB)
0001	(512, 512, 55)	21	3452	36129
0051	(512, 512, 100)	26.31	3452	47694
0017	(512, 512, 150)	26.24	3452	46555
0019	(512, 512, 215)	24.03	3452	37880
0099	(512, 512, 334)	28.09	3452	42890
0063	(512, 512, 448)	34.86	3452	54187
0048	(512, 512, 499)	35.65	3452	52391
0029	(512, 512, 554)	44.23	4064	69970

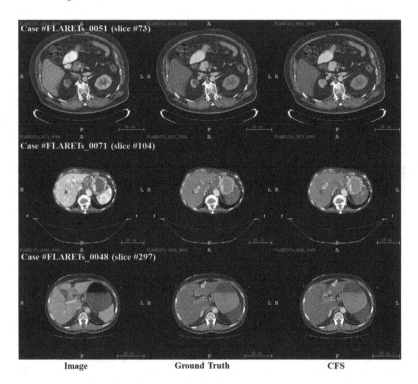

Image   Ground Truth   CFS

Fig. 5. Qualitative results of three examples with tumor segmentation results given by the CFS. Red arrows indicate tumor regions. (Color figure online)

Table 9. Quantitative efficiency results given by the two-stage method.

Case ID	Image Size	Running Time (s)	Max GPU (MB)	Total GPU (MB)
0001	(512, 512, 55)	18.26	3071	23535
0051	(512, 512, 100)	23.67	3071	39243
0017	(512, 512, 150)	22.97	3097	37210
0019	(512, 512, 215)	17.45	3071	23727
0099	(512, 512, 334)	22.51	3071	33945
0063	(512, 512, 448)	26.1	3229	37647
0048	(512, 512, 499)	23.59	3223	31547
0029	(512, 512, 554)	34.15	4025	49582

4.4   Results on Final Testing Set

The quantitative results of the CFS on final testing set are listed in Table 3. The mean DSC and the mean NSD are 92.64% and 96.10%, respectively. Compared with the results on online validation set, the CFS achieves higher tumor DSC (63.43%) and higher tumor NSD (51.02%) on the final testing set. Additionally, the CFS obtains mean organ DSC of 92.64% and mean organ NSD of 96.10% on the final testing set, respectively.

4.5   Limitation and Future Work

The major limitation of the CFS is that the tumor segmentation accuracy is much lower than the organ segmentation accuracy. It is valuable to propose novel methods to improve the tumor segmentation accuracy. Besides that, the training of the CFS is cumbersome because the three models are trained separately. Furthermore, the segmentation accuracy of the small organs is low, and the robustness of the segmentation results is poor.

In the future, we will continue working on segmentation of abdominal organs and tumor in CT scans. We will further investigate semi-supervised methods for segmentation of abdominal CT scans. Specifically, we will mainly focus on improvement of tumor segmentation and small organ segmentation.

5   Conclusion

In this study, we propose a novel CFS method for multi-organ and tumor segmentation in abdominal CT scans. The CFS consists of the CSM, the TSM, and the OSM, which are trained with different data. During inference, test samples are first segmented by the CSM to obtain abdominal regions. Then, the abdominal regions are segmented by the TSM and the OSM, respectively. Finally, the segmentation masks of the TSM and the OSM are merged to generate the final segmentation results. Besides that, we optimize the inference process by streamlining intricate steps to improve the efficiency of the CFS.

To validate segmentation performance of the CFS, we implement ablation studies on utilization of unlabeled data and effectiveness of the three models. The experimental results demonstrate that the unlabeled data can improve segmentation accuracy of organs, especially small organs. Additionally, the TSM achieves higher tumor segmentation accuracy using two weights than using one weight. The organ segmentation model further improves the organ segmentation accuracy given by the TSM. Furthermore, the quantitative results of segmentation efficiency demonstrate that the two-stage method and the CFS achieve fast multi-organ and tumor segmentation in CT scans.

Acknowledgements. The authors of this paper declare that the segmentation method they implemented for participation in the FLARE 2023 challenge has not used any pre-trained models nor additional datasets other than those provided by the organizers. The proposed solution is fully automatic without any manual intervention. We thank all the data owners for making the CT scans publicly available and CodaLab [22] for hosting the challenge platform. This work was supported in part by the National Natural Science Foundation of China under Grant Nos. 62303127 and 62273009.

References

1. Alves, N., de Wilde, B.: Uncertainty-guided self-learning framework for semi-supervised multi-organ segmentation. In: Ma, J., Wang, B. (eds.) FLARE 2022. LNCS, vol. 13816, pp. 116–127. Springer, Cham (2022). https://doi.org/10.1007/978-3-031-23911-3_11
2. Simpson, A.L., Antonelli, M., Bakas, S., et al.: A large annotated medical image dataset for the development and evaluation of segmentation algorithms. arXiv preprint arXiv:1902.09063 (2019)
3. Bilic, P., Christ, P., Li, H.B., et al.: The liver tumor segmentation benchmark (LiTS). Med. Image Anal. **84**, 102680 (2023)
4. Choi, J.W.: Knowledge distillation from cross teaching teachers for efficient semi-supervised abdominal organ segmentation in CT. In: Ma, J., Wang, B. (eds.) FLARE 2022. LNCS, vol. 13816, pp. 101–115. Springer, Cham (2022). https://doi.org/10.1007/978-3-031-23911-3_10
5. Clark, K., Vendt, B., Smith, K., et al.: The cancer imaging archive (TCIA): maintaining and operating a public information repository. J. Digit. Imaging **26**(6), 1045–1057 (2013)
6. Gao, J., Xu, J., Fei, H.: A pseudo-labeling approach to semi-supervised organ segmentation. In: Ma, J., Wang, B. (eds.) FLARE 2022. LNCS, vol. 13816, pp. 318–326. Springer, Cham (2022). https://doi.org/10.1007/978-3-031-23911-3_28
7. Gatidis, S., Früh, M., Fabritius, M., et al.: The autopet challenge: towards fully automated lesion segmentation in oncologic PET/CT imaging. Preprint at Research Square (Nature Portfolio) (2023). https://doi.org/10.21203/rs.3.rs-2572595/v1
8. Gatidis, S., Hepp, T., Früh, M., et al.: A whole-body FDG-PET/CT dataset with manually annotated tumor lesions. Sci. Data **9**(1), 601 (2022)
9. Han, M., Qu, Y., Luo, X.: Efficient semi-supervised multi-organ segmentation using uncertainty rectified pyramid consistency. In: Ma, J., Wang, B. (eds.) FLARE 2022. LNCS, vol. 13816, pp. 307–317. Springer, Cham (2022). https://doi.org/10.1007/978-3-031-23911-3_27
10. Heller, N., Isensee, F., Maier-Hein, K.H., et al.: The state of the art in kidney and kidney tumor segmentation in contrast-enhanced CT imaging: results of the kits19 challenge. Med. Image Anal. **67**, 101821 (2021)
11. Heller, N., McSweeney, S., Peterson, M.T., et al.: An international challenge to use artificial intelligence to define the state-of-the-art in kidney and kidney tumor segmentation in CT imaging. Proc. Am. Soc. Clin. Oncol. **38**(6), 626 (2020)
12. Huang, Y., Zhang, H., Yan, Y., Hassan, H.: 3D cross-pseudo supervision (3D-CPS): a semi-supervised nnU-net architecture for abdominal organ segmentation. In: Ma, J., Wang, B. (eds.) FLARE 2022. LNCS, vol. 13816, pp. 87–100. Springer, Cham (2022). https://doi.org/10.1007/978-3-031-23911-3_9
13. Huang, Z., et al.: Revisiting nnU-Net for iterative pseudo labeling and efficient sliding window inference. In: Ma, J., Wang, B. (eds.) FLARE 2022. LNCS, vol. 13816, pp. 178–189. Springer, Cham (2022). https://doi.org/10.1007/978-3-031-23911-3_16
14. Isensee, F., Jaeger, P.F., Kohl, S.A., et al.: nnU-Net: a self-configuring method for deep learning-based biomedical image segmentation. Nat. Methods **18**(2), 203–211 (2021)
15. Lai, H., Wang, T., Zhou, S.: DLUNet: semi-supervised learning based dual-light UNet for multi-organ segmentation. In: Ma, J., Wang, B. (eds.) FLARE 2022.

LNCS, vol. 13816, pp. 64–73. Springer, Cham (2022). https://doi.org/10.1007/978-3-031-23911-3_7

16. Lee, H.H., Tang, Y., Tang, O., et al.: Semi-supervised multi-organ segmentation through quality assurance supervision. In: Medical Imaging 2020: Image Processing, vol. 11313, pp. 363–369. SPIE (2020)

17. Ma, J., He, Y., Li, F., Han, L., You, C., Wang, B.: Segment anything in medical images. Nat. Commun. **15**, 654 (2024)

18. Ma, J., Zhang, Y., Gu, S., et al.: AbdomenCT-1K: is abdominal organ segmentation a solved problem? IEEE Trans. Pattern Anal. Mach. Intell. **44**(10), 6695–6714 (2022)

19. Ma, J., Zhang, Y., Gu, S., et al.: Fast and low-GPU-memory abdomen CT organ segmentation: the flare challenge. Med. Image Anal. **82**, 102616 (2022)

20. Ma, J., Zhang, Y., Gu, S., et al.: Unleashing the strengths of unlabeled data in pan-cancer abdominal organ quantification: the flare22 challenge. arXiv preprint arXiv:2308.05862 (2023)

21. Meng, H., Zhao, H., Yu, Z., Li, Q., Niu, J.: Uncertainty-aware mean teacher framework with inception and squeeze-and-excitation block for MICCAI FLARE22 challenge. In: Ma, J., Wang, B. (eds.) FLARE 2022. LNCS, vol. 13816, pp. 245–259. Springer, Cham (2022). https://doi.org/10.1007/978-3-031-23911-3_22

22. Pavao, A., Guyon, I., Letournel, A.C., et al.: CodaLab competitions: an open source platform to organize scientific challenges. J. Mach. Learn. Res. **24**(198), 1–6 (2023)

23. Siegel, R.L., Miller, K.D., Fuchs, H.E., et al.: Cancer statistics, 2022. CA Cancer J. Clin. **72**(1), 7–33 (2022)

24. Wasserthal, J., Breit, H.C., Meyer, M.T., et al.: TotalSegmentator: robust segmentation of 104 anatomic structures in CT images. Radiol. Artif. Intell. **5**(5), e230024 (2023)

25. Yushkevich, P.A., Gao, Y., Gerig, G.: ITK-snap: an interactive tool for semi-automatic segmentation of multi-modality biomedical images. In: Annual International Conference of the IEEE Engineering in Medicine and Biology Society, pp. 3342–3345 (2016)

26. Zhou, Y., Wang, Y., Tang, P., et al.: Semi-supervised 3D abdominal multi-organ segmentation via deep multi-planar co-training. In: 2019 IEEE Winter Conference on Applications of Computer Vision (WACV), pp. 121–140. IEEE (2019)

Abdominal Organs and Pan-Cancer Segmentation Based on Self-supervised Pre-training and Self-training

He Li[1], Meng Han[1], and Guotai Wang[1,2(✉)]

[1] School of Mechanical and Electrical Engineering, University of Electronic Science and Technology of China, Chengdu, China
guotai.wang@uestc.edu.cn
[2] Shanghai Artificial Intelligence Laboratory, Shanghai, China

Abstract. Despite the effective progress in automatic abdominal multi-organ segmentation methods based on deep learning, there are still few studies on general models for abdominal organ and pan-cancer segmentation. Additionally, the manual annotation of organs and tumors from CT scans is a time-consuming and labor-intensive process. To deal with these problems, an efficient two-stage framework combining self-supervised pre-training and self-training is proposed. Specifically, in the first stage, we adopt the Model Genesis method for image reconstruction to promote the model to learn effective anatomical representation information, thereby improving the model's perception of anatomical structures in downstream segmentation tasks and generating high-quality tumor pseudo-labels. Afterward, we fuse partial organ fine-standard of labeled data with pseudo-labels to improve the organ labeling quality. In the second stage, we overlay the generated tumor pseudo-labels onto the corresponding regions of the organ pseudo-labels, and the final pseudo-label images are used to train the nnU-Net model for efficient inference. The proposed method has been evaluated on the FLARE2023 validation cases, and get a relatively good segmentation performance. The average DSC and NSD for organs are 91.51% and 95.52%, respectively. For tumors, the average DSC is 43.47%, and the average NSD is 33.81%. In addition, the average running time and area under the GPU memory-time curve are 85.4 s and 246157.2 MB, respectively. On the test set, we achieved average organ and tumor DSC of 92.17% and 54.99%, respectively, and average inference time of 95.83 s. Our code is publicly available at https://github.com/lihe-CV/HiLab_FLARE23

Keywords: Semi-supervised learning · Self-supervised learning · Pseudo labels

1 Introduction

Abdominal organ and tumor segmentation is a critically important task in abdominal disease diagnosis, cancer treatment, and radiation therapy planning [11]. The abdomen is a common site for the occurrence of cancer, and

© The Author(s), under exclusive license to Springer Nature Switzerland AG 2024
J. Ma and B. Wang (Eds.): FLARE 2023, LNCS 14544, pp. 130–142, 2024.
https://doi.org/10.1007/978-3-031-58776-4_11

accurate segmentation results can provide valuable information for clinical diagnosis and surgical planning, like the size and location of organs and tumors, the spatial relationship of multiple organs, etc. In recent years, deep learning-based methods have been widely used for automatic segmentation of organs and tumors [16]. However, these methods heavily rely on a large amount of annotated data for training purposes. In past clinical practice, segmentation labels for organs and tumors was usually performed manually by radiologists. It is time-consuming and labor-intensive. Thus, it is often challenging to obtain a large number of labeled cases. In light of this situation, semi-supervised semantic segmentation aims to utilize limited labeled data and abundant unlabeled data for model training. It addresses the issue of label scarcity by exploring valuable information from the unlabeled data.

FLARE [13] is an international challenge focusing on abdominal scene segmentation. Compared with FLARE22, the challenge for FLARE23 adds the pan-cancer segmentation task and provides only partial organ segmentation labels for the labeled data in semi-supervised segmentation. The organizer of FLARE23 provided the largest abdomen CT dataset, including 4000 3D CT scans from 30+ medical centers. 2200 cases have partial labels and 1800 cases are unlabeled. For the task scenario combining semi-supervised and partial-label segmentation, the main solutions can be divided into two types: (1) consistency-regularization-based methods [3]. (2) pseudo-label-based methods [10,19]. Since the organizer invited the FLARE22 champion team to generate pseudo labels for FLARE23 data. We choose the pseudo-labeling-based approach and integrate it with the nnU-Net framework [9] to train organ segmentation model. However, due to the uncertainty in tumor shape, size, and location, as well as the scarcity of tumor labels, we attempt to incorporate self-supervised strategies to learn effective representation information from images, thereby enhancing the model's perception of tumor category.

In this work, we propose a two-stage training framework that combines self-supervised and semi-supervised learning to generate high-quality pseudo-labels and improve the segmentation performance of the model, respectively. Specifically, in the first stage, we employ the Model Genesis method [23] for image reconstruction to learn effective anatomical representation information. From 2200 labeled images, 735 tumor-containing images and corresponding labels were further selected, and the pre-trained model was transferred to the tumor segmentation task to generate high-quality pseudo-labels for 3265 tumor-free labeled data [2]. For the pseudo-label generation of organs, we simply fused the pseudo-labels provided by the organizer with partial organ segmentation annotations, and achieved good segmentation results. In the second stage, we overlay the generated tumor pseudo-labels onto the corresponding regions of the organ pseudo-labels, and the final pseudo-labeled images are used to train nnU-Net model [9] for inference.

In summary, we make the following three contributions:

- We design a two-stage training framework based on nnU-Net to generate high-quality pseudo-labels and improve the segmentation performance of the model.
- We adopt self-supervised learning strategy to learn anatomical representation information, enabling the model to generate high-quality pseudo-labels.
- We optimize the organ segmentation task by fusing pseudo-labels and partial organ segmentation annotations. Models trained with our fused labels perform better.

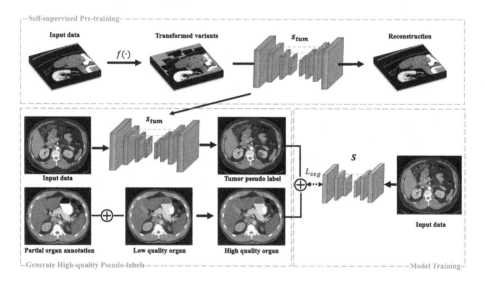

Fig. 1. Overview of our proposed framework.

2   Method

To deal with a training dataset with partial labels on a small part of images, we propose a two-stage training framework that combines self-supervised and semi-supervised learning, as shown in Fig. 1. We adopt self-supervised learning and image fusion strategies to generate high-quality pseudo-labels. The self-training [10] is adopted for semi-supervised semantic segmentation. The detailed description of this framework is as follows.

2.1   Preprocessing

The preprocessing strategies for labeled data and pseudo-labeled data in the two-stage segmentation framework are as follows:

Table 1. Comparison of different segmentation models. The order of axes of input patch size and spacing is (z,y,x).

Settings	Default	Tumor	Organ&Pan-cancer
convolution kernel sizes	(1, 3, 3)	(3, 3, 3)	(1, 3, 3)
step size for sliding window	0.5	0.5	1
input patch size	(64×160×192)	(112×160×160)	(56×160×192)
input spacing	(2.0, 0.8, 0.8)	(1.8, 1.8, 1.8)	(2.5, 0.8, 0.8)

- Image cropping: Crop the bounding box of the image to the non-zero area, thereby reducing the image size and improving computational efficiency.
- We adopt image resampling to ensure that the actual physical space of each voxel is consistent across different image data.
- We applied z-score normalization based on the mean and standard deviation of foreground intensity values across the training set.
- The detailed configurations and the comparison with default nnU-Net are listed in Table 1.

2.2   Generate High-Quality Pseudo-labels

We employ pseudo-label generation as a simple and effective method to utilize unlabeled data for model training. Specifically, we make full use of the pseudo-labels of abdominal organs provided by the organizer. To improve the labeling quality, we fuse partial organ fine-standard of labeled data with pseudo-labels. However, tumor category is difficult to segment due to the uncertainty of tumor shape, size and location, as well as the scarcity of tumor labels. We utilize self-supervised learning strategy to facilitate tumor segmentation model S_{tum} to understand local and global features, thereby boosting the model's awareness of tumor category and generating high-quality tumor pseudo-labels.

Self-supervised Pre-training. Model Genesis [23] learns from scratch on unlabeled images with the goal of learning a universal visual representation that can be generalized and transferred across diseases, organs, and modalities. In order to improve the model's transfer and perception capabilities for tumor category, we use similar self-supervised training strategies as the Model Genesis [23] to pre-train S_{tum} with the provided FLARE23 dataset. Throughout the pre-training process, S_{tum} reconstructs the original patches according to the augmented variants, thereby learning anatomical representation information of 3D abdominal CT images. The generation process of augmented variants is shown in Fig. 2.

Specifically, four transformations are randomly combined and applied to the original patch to generate augmented variants. The transformations include: 1) Non-linear transformation. By integrating Bézier Curve [17] to assign a uniquely determined value to each pixel, to encourage self-supervision focusing on the

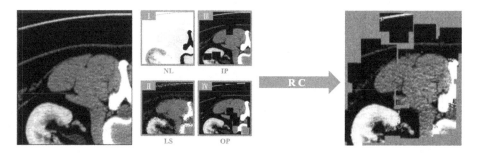

Fig. 2. The transformations made to the original patch during the pre-training. I: Nonlinear transformation, II: local pixels shuffling, III: in-painting, IV: out-painting. (RC: random combine.)

information of image appearance, shape and intensity distribution. 2) Local pixel shuffling. By sampling a window smaller than the model's receptive field in the patch and rearranging the internal pixels, to encourage model learning the local texture and boundary of the image. 3) Out-painting and In-painting. By blending windows of different sizes to create a complex shape. Out-painting sets the outer pixels of the shape to random values, while the inner pixels retain their original intensities. In-painting is the opposite.

Then, the pre-training model S_{tum} will learn the anatomical representation information by reconstructing the original patch. The mean squared error (MSE) loss is used for training S_{tum} by minimizing a reconstruction error $\mathcal{L}_{rec}$:

$$\mathcal{L}_{rec} = \frac{1}{N} \sum_{i=1}^{N} |X_i - \hat{X}_i| \tag{1}$$

where i is the voxel index, N is the number of the voxels, X_i is original patch and $\hat{X}_i$ is the prediction of the model. Finally, we screened out 735 tumor-containing images and corresponding labels from 2200 labeled data, and transferred the pre-trained model S_{tum} to the tumor segmentation task. We adopt an average of cross-entropy loss and Dice loss to supervise the tumor segmentation model:

$$\mathcal{L}_{seg} = \frac{1}{2N^t} \sum_{i=1}^{N^t} \left(\mathcal{L}_{Dice}(p_i, y_i) + \mathcal{L}_{ce}(p_i, y_i) \right) \tag{2}$$

where y_i is the tumor label, N^t is the number of training images and p_i is the prediction of the model S_{tum}.

Label Fusion. Due to the organizer invited FLARE22 champion team to use its docker to generate pseudo labels for FLARE23 data. Therefore, we adopt a simple but effective label fusion strategy. Specifically, we achieve high-quality fusion by replacing the corresponding organ regions in the pseudo-labels with accurately annotated organ parts from the labeled data.

$$\hat{y} = y_p \oplus y_q \tag{3}$$

where y_p is ground truth and y_q is pseudo label. At the same time, the unlabeled data retains the corresponding pseudo-labels as supervision signals.

2.3 Model Training and Inference

We adopt similar label fusion strategy to the high-quality organ and tumor pseudo-labels obtained in the first stage, generating a dataset $\mathcal{D} = \{x_i, y_i\}_{i=1}^{N}$ for training organ and pan-cancer segmentation model S. In addition, in order to improve the inference efficiency of the model S, we try using small patch size as in Table 1 to increase the training and inference speed of each patch and reduce GPU memory. Finally, the segmentation model S learns from organ and pan-cancer data by minimizing a supervised loss function:

$$\mathcal{L}_{seg} = \frac{1}{2N^d} \sum_{j=1}^{N^d} \left(\mathcal{L}_{Dice}(p_j, y_j) + \mathcal{L}_{ce}(p_j, y_j) \right) \qquad (4)$$

where y_j is the organ and pan-cancer label, N^d is the number of training images and p_j is the prediction of the model S.

Due to the high resolution of 3D medical images, nnU-Net [9] adopts the slidingwindow strategy for inference. However, this strategy significantly consumes the time and space complexity. Therefore, we set the step-size to 1 during inference to effectively improve inference speed and reduce resource consumption while ensuring accuracy.

2.4 Post-processing

A connected component analysis of segmentation mask is applied on the outputs to remove small connected areas. And then the results are resampled back to original spacing for the convenience of the following evaluation.

3 Experiments

3.1 Dataset and Evaluation Measures

The FLARE 2023 challenge is an extension of the FLARE 2021–2022 [13,14], aiming to promote the development of foundation models in abdominal disease analysis. The segmentation targets cover 13 organs and various abdominal lesions. The training dataset is curated from more than 30 medical centers under the license permission, including TCIA [4], LiTS [1], MSD [20], KiTS [7,8], autoPET [5,6], TotalSegmentator [21], and AbdomenCT-1K [15]. The training set includes 4000 abdomen CT scans where 2200 CT scans with partial labels and 1800 CT scans without labels. The validation and testing sets include 100 and 400 CT scans, respectively, which cover various abdominal cancer types, such as liver cancer, kidney cancer, pancreas cancer, colon cancer, gastric cancer, and so on. The organ annotation process used ITK-SNAP [22], nnU-Net [9], and MedSAM [12].

The evaluation metrics encompass two accuracy measures—Dice Similarity Coefficient (DSC) and Normalized Surface Dice (NSD)—alongside two efficiency measures—running time and area under the GPU memory-time curve. These metrics collectively contribute to the ranking computation. Furthermore, the running time and GPU memory consumption are considered within tolerances of 15 s and 4 GB, respectively.

3.2   Implementation Details

Environment Settings. The development environments and requirements are presented in Table 2.

Table 2. Development environments and requirements.

System vision	Ubuntu 18.04.5 LTS
CPU	Intel(R) Xeon(R) Gold 6248 CPU@2.50 GHz
RAM	16×4 GB; 2.67MT/s
GPU (number and type)	One NVIDIA V100 32G
CUDA version	11.0
Programming language	Python 3.10.8
Deep learning framework	torch 2.0.0, torchvision 0.15.1
Specific dependencies	nnU-Net 2.1.1
Code	https://github.com/lihe-CV/HiLab_FLARE23

Training Protocols. The training protocols of S_{tum} and S are shown in Table 3 and 4 respectively. During the training process, we dynamically adopt elastic deformation, rotation, random cropping, Gaussian noise transformation, Gamma transformation, contrast transformation, morphological transformation and other data enhancement strategies. In addition, we applied mirror test time data augmentation during inference.

4   Results and Discussion

4.1   Quantitative Results on Validation Set

Quantitative result is illustrated in Table 5, it can be observed that the two-stage framework can achieve very promising segmentation results for large regional organs, such as liver, spleen, kidney, stomach, etc. However, the segmentation of small and structurally complex organs such as the duodenum, esophagus, and adrenal glands remains challenging in comparison. Moreover, the strong uncertainty in tumor shapes, sizes, and locations in the pan-cancer segmentation

Table 3. Training protocols for tumor segmentation model S_{tum}.

Network initialization	"He" normal initialization
Batch size	2
Patch size	112×160×160
Total epochs	2000
Step size	1
Optimizer	SGD with nesterov momentum ($\mu = 0.99$)
Initial learning rate (lr)	0.01
Lr decay schedule	Poly learning rate policy: $(1 - epoch/2000)^{0.9}$
Training time	132.5 h
Loss function	Dice loss and cross entropy loss
Number of model parameters	88.21 M
Number of flops	913.4 G
CO_2eq	41.05 Kg

Table 4. Training protocols for organ and pan-cancer segmentation model S.

Network initialization	"He" normal initialization
Batch size	2
Patch size	56×160×192
Total epochs	1000
Optimizer	SGD with nesterov momentum ($\mu = 0.99$)
Initial learning rate (lr)	0.01
Lr decay schedule	Poly learning rate policy: $(1 - epoch/1000)^{0.9}$
Training time	41.5 h
Loss function	Dice loss and cross entropy loss
Number of model parameters	71.02M
Number of flops	727.76G
CO_2eq	35.02 Kg

task added to the FLARE23 challenge makes the segmentation task extremely challenging. Indeed, there is a problem of missing in the segmentation results, particularly for small tumors, where the segmentation model fails to predict their presence.

Table 5. Quantitative results of validation set in terms of DSC and NSD. (Public Validation: the performance on the 50 validation cases with ground truth. Online Validation: the leaderboard results. Testing: the performance on the testing cases.)

Target	Public Validation		Online Validation		Testing	
	DSC (%)	NSD (%)	DSC (%)	NSD (%)	DSC (%)	NSD (%)
Liver	98.43 ± 0.0102	98.91 ± 0.0231	98.30	98.77	96.61	96.82
Right Kidney	93.25 ± 12.12	94.13 ± 11.83	93.47	93.47	94.47	94.18
Spleen	96.52 ± 11.39	96.74 ± 13.23	95.82	96.53	96.56	96.81
Pancreas	85.43 ± 10.89	95.35 ± 10.06	86.84	96.54	91.35	97.37
Aorta	97.45 ± 1.82	99.41 ± 2.55	97.68	99.29	97.75	99.10
Inferior vena cava	93.02 ± 7.29	92.66 ± 6.91	93.21	93.87	93.62	95.07
Right adrenal gland	88.94 ± 9.21	97.88 ± 10.23	89.09	97.89	87.90	96.07
Left adrenal gland	87.89 ± 9.63	96.17 ± 8.31	87.58	95.61	89.60	96.76
Gallbladder	88.95 ± 20.48	90.79 ± 21.38	89.79	90.54	84.85	86.68
Esophagus	84.22 ± 10.06	93.76 ± 10.18	84.19	93.30	89.42	96.57
Stomach	95.01 ± 3.71	97.90 ± 6.65	94.66	97.18	94.91	96.72
Duodenum	83.74 ± 10.01	94.98 ± 8.24	84.53	95.21	88.71	96.36
Left kidney	94.81 ± 12.69	93.31 ± 12.80	94.44	93.60	94.85	94.52
Tumor	43.86 ± 25.98	33.27 ± 23.56	43.47	33.81	55.17	42.51
Average (Organ)	91.62 ± 9.73	95.38 ± 14.70	91.51	95.52	92.35	95.62

Then, Table 6 and Table 7 showed the Dice and NSD metrics calculated on the validation set. Evidently, compared with models trained using labeled data with only partial organ segmentation annotations, training the model using the Label Fusion strategy can significantly improve segmentation performance. Moreover, the introduction of self-supervised pretraining strategy has significantly improved the performance of the two-stage framework on tumor classes, as evidenced by the achieved Dice Similarity Coefficient (DSC) of 43.47%.

Table 6. Ablation study of Dice(%) metrics on validation set. (BaseLine: Training nnU-Net with labeled images only. LF: Label Fusion. SP: Self-supervised Pre-training.)

Methods	Liver	RK	Spleen	Pancreas	Aorta	IVC	RAG	LAG
Baseline	97.58	92.71	94.96	85.94	97.01	91.29	82.32	83.69
Baseline+LF	**98.46**	**95.98**	**97.10**	86.72	97.51	**93.34**	88.46	**88.77**
Baseline+LF+SP	98.30	93.47	95.82	**86.84**	**97.68**	93.21	**89.09**	87.58
Methods	GBD	EPG	Stomach	Duodenum	LK	Average	Tumor	
Baseline	85.11	**85.69**	91.24	80.65	93.29	89.38	33.06	
Baseline+LF	88.34	84.35	94.35	**84.64**	**95.22**	**91.68**	37.52	
Baseline+LF+SP	**89.79**	84.19	**94.66**	84.53	94.44	91.51	**43.47**	

Table 7. Ablation study of NSD(%) metrics on validation set. (BaseLine: Training nnU-Net with labeled images only. LF: Label Fusion. SP: Self-supervised Pre-training.)

Methods	Liver	RK	Spleen	Pancreas	Aorta	IVC	RAG	LAG
Baseline	97.83	92.12	96.12	95.24	98.35	91.67	92.29	92.41
Baseline+LF	**99.05**	**96.16**	**98.25**	96.46	99.25	**94.01**	97.69	**96.85**
Baseline+LF+SP	98.77	93.47	96.53	**96.54**	**99.29**	93.87	**97.89**	95.61

Methods	GBD	EPG	Stomach	Duodenum	LK	Average	Tumor
Baseline	85.74	92.98	94.62	91.33	92.01	93.91	22.07
Baseline+LF	89.84	**93.55**	96.92	**95.33**	**95.08**	**96.07**	28.52
Baseline+LF+SP	**90.54**	93.30	**97.18**	95.21	93.60	95.52	**33.81**

Finally, we quantitatively evaluated the segmentation efficiency of the model, as shown in Table 8. It can be found that the three evaluation metrics show an increasing trend as the input instances grow larger. Although the inference time is mostly within 60 s, the proportion of inference times below 15 s is relatively low. Therefore, further optimization is needed in terms of model inference efficiency to strive for achieving clinical usability standards.

Table 8. Quantitative evaluation of segmentation efficiency in terms of the running them and GPU memory consumption.(Total GPU: the area under GPU Memory-Time curve. Evaluation GPU platform: NVIDIA QUADRO RTX5000 (16G).)

Case ID	Image Size	Running Time (s)	Max GPU (MB)	Total GPU (MB)
0001	(512, 512, 55)	8.47	4266	17433
0051	(512, 512, 100)	11.12	5290	34759
0017	(512, 512, 150)	20.29	5526	70528
0019	(512, 512, 215)	23.62	4722	64923
0099	(512, 512, 334)	30.20	5282	96292
0063	(512, 512, 448)	42.10	5506	144037
0048	(512, 512, 499)	49.15	5420	150701
0029	(512, 512, 554)	97.21	6142	247289

4.2 Qualitative Results on Validation Set

Figure 3 displays the qualitative results on the validation set. The first and second rows depict relatively easy segmentation cases, while the third and fourth rows showcase challenging segmentation cases. It can be observed that in the first and second rows, the organ boundaries are clear, there is good contrast, and there are no complex tumor lesions within the organs. Compared with well-segmented instances, challenging instances often have complex tumor lesions (row 3) and noise (row 4), which bring difficulties to accurate segmentation of organs and pan-cancer.

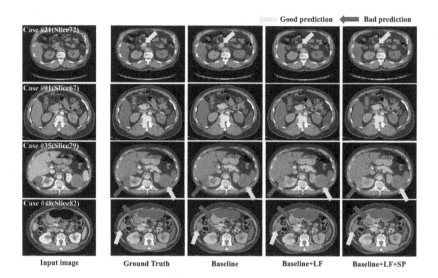

Fig. 3. Qualitative evaluation of model performance on validation set. Row 1 and 2: Well-segmented examples. Row 3 and 4: challenging examples.

4.3 Segmentation Efficiency Results on Validation Set

We combine efficient inference schemes to build nnU-Net [9] as the final submitted Docker image. The average running time per instance during the inference phase is 85.4 s, and average used GPU memory is 2352 MB. The area under the GPU memory-time curve is 246157.2 MB, and the area under CPU utilization-time curve is 2973.

4.4 Results on Final Testing Set

Table 5 show the detailed evaluation metrics of our method in the final testing set. It can be observed that the two-stage framework achieved average DSC scores of 92.17% for organs and 54.99% for lesions, along with NSD scores averaging 95.44% for organs and 42.45% for lesions. Additionally, the average running time was 95.83 s, and the area under the GPU memory-time curve was 227770 MB.

4.5 Limitation and Future Work

While ensuring accuracy, we can explore the use of the following advanced processing strategies to speed up inference and reduce resource consumption:

– Model Pruning. Identify and remove redundant or less important model parameters, reducing the model size and improving inference speed without significant loss in accuracy.

- Model Quantization. Convert the model from floating-point precision to lower-precision fixed-point representation, reducing memory usage and improving inference speed.
- Filter Data Augmentation. Select specific data enhancement strategies based on organ and tumor characteristics to prevent redundancy.

5 Conclusion

In this work, we propose a two-stage training framework that combines self-supervised and semi-supervised learning to efficiently perform training and inference on organ and pan-cancer segmentation tasks. Experiments show that our method achieves good segmentation performance. In the future, we hope to optimize the model framework to further improve the segmentation accuracy of difficult tumor samples, improve inference speed and reduce resource consumption.

Acknowledgements. The authors of this paper declare that the segmentation method they implemented for participation in the FLARE 2023 challenge has not used any pre-trained models nor additional datasets other than those provided by the organizers. The proposed solution is fully automatic without any manual intervention. We thank all the data owners for making the CT scans publicly available and CodaLab [18] for hosting the challenge platform.

References

1. Bilic, P., et al.: The liver tumor segmentation benchmark (lits). Med. Image Anal. **84**, 102680 (2023)
2. Chen, H., Lundberg, S.M., Erion, G., Kim, J.H., Lee, S.I.: Forecasting adverse surgical events using self-supervised transfer learning for physiological signals. NPJ Digit. Med. **4**(1), 167 (2021)
3. Chen, X., Yuan, Y., Zeng, G., Wang, J.: Semi-supervised semantic segmentation with cross pseudo supervision. In: Proceedings of the IEEE/CVF Conference on Computer Vision and Pattern Recognition, pp. 2613–2622 (2021)
4. Clark, K., et al.: The cancer imaging archive (TCIA): maintaining and operating a public information repository. J. Digit. Imaging **26**(6), 1045–1057 (2013)
5. Gatidis, S., et al.: The autopet challenge: towards fully automated lesion segmentation in oncologic PET/CT imaging. preprint at Research Square (Nature Portfolio) (2023). https://doi.org/10.21203/rs.3.rs-2572595/v1
6. Gatidis, S., et al.: A whole-body FDG-PET/CT dataset with manually annotated tumor lesions. Sci. Data **9**(1), 601 (2022)
7. Heller, N.: The state of the art in kidney and kidney tumor segmentation in contrast-enhanced CT imaging: results of the kits19 challenge. Med. Image Anal. **67**, 101821 (2021)
8. Heller, N., et al.: An international challenge to use artificial intelligence to define the state-of-the-art in kidney and kidney tumor segmentation in CT imaging. Proc. Am. Soc. Clin. Oncol. **38**(6), 626–626 (2020)
9. Isensee, F., Jaeger, P.F., Kohl, S.A., Petersen, J., Maier-Hein, K.H.: nnu-net: a self-configuring method for deep learning-based biomedical image segmentation. Nat. Methods **18**(2), 203–211 (2021)

10. Lee, D.H., et al.: Pseudo-label: the simple and efficient semi-supervised learning method for deep neural networks. In: Workshop on Challenges in Representation Learning, ICML, vol. 3, p. 896. Atlanta (2013)
11. Luo, X., et al.: Word: a large scale dataset, benchmark and clinical applicable study for abdominal organ segmentation from CT image. Med. Image Anal. **82**, 102642 (2022)
12. Ma, J., He, Y., Li, F., Han, L., You, C., Wang, B.: Segment anything in medical images. Nat. Commun. **15**(1), 654 (2024)
13. Ma, J., et al.: Fast and low-GPU-memory abdomen CT organ segmentation: the flare challenge. Med. Image Anal. **82**, 102616 (2022)
14. Ma, J., et al.: Unleashing the strengths of unlabeled data in pan-cancer abdominal organ quantification: the flare22 challenge. arXiv preprint arXiv:2308.05862 (2023)
15. Ma, J., et al.: Abdomenct-1k: is abdominal organ segmentation a solved problem? IEEE Trans. Pattern Anal. Mach. Intell. **44**(10), 6695–6714 (2022)
16. Ma, J., et al.: Abdomenct-1k: is abdominal organ segmentation a solved problem? IEEE Trans. Pattern Anal. Mach. Intell. **44**(10), 6695–6714 (2021)
17. Mortenson, M.E.: Mathematics for computer graphics applications. Industrial Press Inc. (1999)
18. Pavao, A.: Codalab competitions: an open source platform to organize scientific challenges. J. Mach. Learn. Res. **24**(198), 1–6 (2023)
19. Sime, D.M., Wang, G., Zeng, Z., Peng, B.: Uncertainty-aware and dynamically-mixed pseudo-labels for semi-supervised defect segmentation. Comput. Ind. **152**, 103995 (2023)
20. Simpson, A.L., et al.: A large annotated medical image dataset for the development and evaluation of segmentation algorithms. arXiv preprint arXiv:1902.09063 (2019)
21. Wasserthal, J., et al.: Totalsegmentator: robust segmentation of 104 anatomic structures in CT images. Radiol.: Artif. Intell. **5**(5), e230024 (2023)
22. Yushkevich, P.A., Gao, Y., Gerig, G.: ITK-SNAP: an interactive tool for semi-automatic segmentation of multi-modality biomedical images. In: Annual International Conference of the IEEE Engineering in Medicine and Biology Society, pp. 3342–3345 (2016)
23. Zhou, Z., Sodha, V., Pang, J., Gotway, M.B., Liang, J.: Models genesis. Med. Image Anal. **67**, 101840 (2021)

Two-Stage Hybrid Supervision Framework for Fast, Low-Resource, and Accurate Organ and Pan-Cancer Segmentation in Abdomen CT

Wentao Liu[1]([✉])[iD], Tong Tian[2][iD], Weijin Xu[1][iD], Lemeng Wang[1][iD],
Haoyuan Li[1][iD], and Huihua Yang[1,3][iD]

[1] School of Artificial Intelligence, Beijing University of Posts and
Telecommunications, Beijing 100876, China
liuwentao@bupt.edu.cn
[2] State Key Laboratory of Structural Analysis, Optimization and CAE Software for
Industrial Equipment, School of Aeronautics and Astronautics, Dalian University of
Technology, Dalian 116024, China
[3] School of Computer Science and Information Security, Guilin University of
Electronic Technology, Guilin, China

Abstract. Abdominal organ and tumour segmentation has many important clinical applications, such as organ quantification, surgical planning, and disease diagnosis. However, manual assessment is inherently subjective with considerable inter- and intra-expert variability. In the paper, we propose a hybrid supervised framework, StMt, that integrates self-training and mean teacher for the segmentation of abdominal organs and tumors using partially labeled and unlabeled data. We introduce a two-stage segmentation pipeline and whole-volume-based input strategy to maximize segmentation accuracy while meeting the requirements of inference time and GPU memory usage. Experiments on the testing set of FLARE2023 demonstrate that our method achieves excellent segmentation performance as well as fast and low-resource model inference. Our method achieved an average DSC score of 90.66% and 50.14% for the organs and lesions on the testing set and the average running time and area under GPU memory-time cure are 11.1 s and 8979 MB, respectively.

Keywords: Abdominal organ segmentation · Pan-cancer segmentation · Self-training · Mean teacher

1 Introduction

Abdomen organs are quite common cancer sites, such as colorectal cancer and pancreatic cancer, which are the 2nd and 3rd most common cause of cancer death [22]. Computed Tomography (CT) scanning provides important prognostic information for cancer patients and is a widely used technology for treatment

J. Ma and B. Wang (Eds.): FLARE 2023, LNCS 14544, pp. 143–154, 2024.
https://doi.org/10.1007/978-3-031-58776-4_12

monitoring. In both clinical trials and daily clinical practice, radiologists and clinicians measure the tumor and organ on CT scans based on manual two-dimensional measurements (e.g., Response Evaluation Criteria In Solid Tumors (RECIST) criteria) [5]. However, this manual assessment is inherently subjective with considerable inter- and intra-expert variability. Moreover, existing challenges mainly focus on one type of tumor (e.g., liver cancer, kidney cancer). There are still no general and publicly available models for universal abdominal organ and cancer segmentation at present.

The organizer of FLARE2022 curated a large-scale and diverse abdomen CT dataset, including 4000+ 3D CT scans from 30+ medical centers where 2200 cases have partial labels and 1800 cases are unlabeled. The challenge task is to segment 13 organs (liver, spleen, pancreas, right kidney, left kidney, stomach, gallbladder, esophagus, aorta, inferior vena cava, right adrenal gland, left adrenal gland, and duodenum) and one tumor class with all kinds of cancer types (such as liver cancer, kidney cancer, stomach cancer, pancreas cancer, colon cancer) in abdominal CT scans. Typically, semi-supervised segmentation (SSS) can be employed to resolve this issue. SSS aims to explore tremendous unlabeled data with supervision from limited labeled data. Recently, self-training methods [17,26] have dominated this field. Furthermore, methods employing consistency regularization strategies [3,19,26] improve the generalization ability by encouraging high similarity in predictions from two perturbed networks for the same input image.

In this challenge, due to the fact that the annotation data only includes annotations for partial organs or tumors, traditional SSS methods struggle to achieve excellent segmentation results. The key to developing segmentation algorithms lies in fully leveraging the semantic representation in partially labeled data and extending it to unlabeled cases to enhance the algorithm's generalization. Segmentation of multiple organs and tumors is a generally recognized difficulty in medical image analysis [28], particularly when there is no large-scale fully labeled datasets. To address this issue, [6,21] formulate the partially labeled issue as a multi-class segmentation task and treat unlabeled organs as the background, which may be misleading since the organ unlabeled in this dataset is indeed the foreground on another task. Moreover, most of these methods adopt the multi-head architecture, which is composed of a shared backbone network and multiple segmentation heads for different tasks. Each head is either a decoder [2] or the last segmentation layer [21]. In the paper, we propose a hybrid supervised framework, StMt, that integrates self-training and mean teacher for the segmentation of abdominal organs and tumors using partially labeled and unlabeled data. We introduce a two-stage segmentation pipeline and whole-volume-based input strategy to maximize segmentation accuracy while meeting the requirements of inference time and GPU memory usage.

2   Method

We conducted an analysis of the distribution of labels in the labeled data, as depicted in Fig. 1. We define datasets that include labels for all 13 organs as

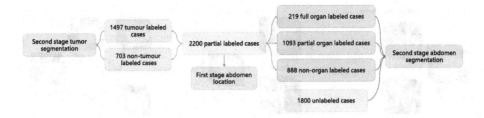

Fig. 1. The statistics and utilization of partial labeled data and unlabeled data.

'fully organ labeled cases'. Those without any organ annotations are termed 'non-organ labeled data', and data with annotations for some but not all of the 13 organs are referred to as 'partially labeled organ Data'. Similarly, the data is categorized based on the presence or absence of tumors into two distinct groups: 'Tumor-Annotated Data' and 'Non-Tumor-Annotated Data'. Specifically focusing on abdominal organs, we found that out of a total of 219 cases, all 13 organs were fully annotated. Moreover, there were 1093 cases with partial annotations, indicating that only specific organ categories were annotated. The remaining 888 cases had no annotations. For tumors, 1497 cases have annotations, and the remaining 703 cases do not. It is worth noting that within the annotated cases, there may still be unlabeled regions that potentially contain tumors. We introduce a two-stage segmentation pipeline [14] to maximize segmentation accuracy while meeting the requirements of inference time and GPU memory usage, in where the first-stage aims to obtain the rough location of the abdomen and the second-stage achieves precise segmentation of abdominal organs and tumour based on the first-stage location. Considering the uncertainty in the distribution of tumors, we divided second-stage segmentation task into two subtasks: semi-supervision organ segmentation and tumor segmentation. The method is described in detail in the following subsections.

2.1 Preprocessing

The preprocessing strategy for input data in the two-stage segmentation framework is as follows:

– Resampling images to uniform sizes. We use small-scale images as the input of the two-stage segmentation to improve the segmentation efficiency. First-stage input: [128, 128, 128]; Second-stage input: [192, 192, 192].
– We uses the 0.5 and 99.5 percentiles of the foreground voxels for clipping as well as the global foreground mean and s.d. for the normalization of all images [12].
– In training phase, considering that the purpose of first-stage segmentation is to roughly extract the locations of abdomen, we set the voxels whose intensity values are greater than 1 in the resampled ground truth to 1, which converts the multi-classification abdominal organ and tumour segmentation

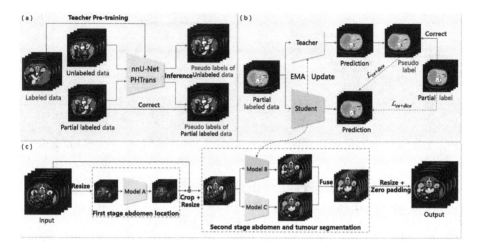

Fig. 2. (a) Self-training with partially annotated data and unlabeled data. (b) Tumor segmentation based on Mean Teacher with hybrid supervision. (c) Two-stage inference pipeline for abdominal organ and tumor segmentation.

into a simple two-classification integrated abdomen segmentation. Furthermore, we set the label of tumors in the input data for the second-stage organ segmentation as 0, while setting the label of organs in the input data for tumor segmentation as 0.

2.2   Proposed Method

We follow self-training to segment abdominal organs in both the first and second stages: 1) train a teacher using fully annotated abdominal organ data, 2) generate pseudo-labels for partial labeled and unlabeled data, 3) train a student using both labeled data and pseudo-labeled data. In order to obtain high-accuracy pseudo-labels, PHTrans [13], a hybrid network consisting of CNN and Swin Transformer, replaces U-Net as the network within the nnU-Net framework for training the teacher and generating generate precise pseudo labels for partial labeled data and unlabeled data. The student model employ a smaller Res-UNet to reduce memory consumption and utilizes a whole-volume-based input strategy to improve inference efficiency. As shown in the Fig. 2(a), in step 2), we use partial annotations to correct pseudo-labels. Specifically, we calculate the category set A of organ annotations in the partial labels. We set the voxels in the pseudo-labels with values belonging to set A to 0. Finally, we assign the same label to the pseudo-labels based on the position indices of the annotated voxels in the partial labels. As a result, we obtained three types of labeled data: fully labeled cases, corrected pseudo-labeled (CPL) cases, and pseudo-labeled (PL) cases. We fed them into the student model, where the input batch for model training consisted of these three types of data in equal proportions. We calculated the loss function for each of these three types of data separately. Finally, the training objective $\mathcal{L}_o$ of organ segmentation is formulated as

$$\mathcal{L}_o = \mathcal{L}_{ol} + \lambda_1 \mathcal{L}_{cpl} + \lambda_2 \mathcal{L}_{pl} \tag{1}$$

where, λ_1 and λ_2 are the weight of loss components $\mathcal{L}_{cpl}$ and $\mathcal{L}_{pl}$.

The tumor segmentation task cannot follow traditional SSS settings due to the possibility of tumors being unannotated in partial labels. Pan-cancer Segmentation of the abdomen includes various types such as liver cancer and kidney cancer. Each annotated case only contains some types of tumors, and there may be unannotated tumors. As shown in the Fig. 2(b), we follow the idea of model weight aggregation in the mean teacher approach. The teacher model utilizes Exponential Moving Average (EMA) on the student model to update itself, aggregating all the previously learned representation information. Thanks to the updating mechanism of the teacher model, the model can explore the semantic representation of potential unannotated tumors. Therefore, in each training iteration, we use the predictions generated by the teacher model as pseudo-labels to provide additional supervision information. Specifically, similar to the pseudo-labels for organ segmentation, we make real-time corrections to the pseudo-labels. The training objective $\mathcal{L}_t$ of tumour segmentation is formulated as

$$\mathcal{L}_t = \mathcal{L}_{tl} + \lambda \mathcal{L}_{cpl} \tag{2}$$

where, λ is the weight of loss components $\mathcal{L}_{cpl}$.

Similarly, both the teacher and the student for tumor segmentation employ a smaller Res-UNet and a whole-volume-based input strategy to improve inference efficiency. Due to the poor performance of the tumor segmentation model trained using labeled data, unlabeled images were not used. The objective of each model training is to minimize the composite loss function, which is a combination of dice loss and cross-entropy loss. Moreover, We not used the pseudo labels generated by the FLARE22 winning algorithm [11] and the best-accuracy-algorithm [24]. As shown in the Fig. 2(c), in inference phase, the segmentation model of first-stage obtain the rough location of the abdomen from the whole CT volume. The second-stage achieves precise segmentation of abdominal organs and tumour based on cropped ROIs from the first-stage segmentation result. Then, the results of abdominal organ segmentation and tumor segmentation are merged, i.e., overlaying the segmented tumor onto the organ segmentation results. Finally, the result is restored to the size of the original data by resampling and zero padding.

2.3   Post-processing

Connected component-based post-processing is commonly used in medical image segmentation. Especially in organ image segmentation, it often helps to eliminate the detection of spurious false positives by removing all but the largest connected component. We applied it to the output of the second-stage organ segmentation.

3   Experiments

3.1   Dataset and Evaluation Measures

The FLARE 2023 challenge is an extension of the FLARE 2021–2022 [16,17], aiming to aim to promote the development of foundation models in abdominal disease analysis. The segmentation targets cover 13 organs and various abdominal lesions. The training dataset is curated from more than 30 medical centers under the license permission, including TCIA [4], LiTS [1], MSD [23], KiTS [9,10], autoPET [7,8], TotalSegmentator [25], and AbdomenCT-1K [18]. The training set includes 4000 abdomen CT scans where 2200 CT scans with partial labels and 1800 CT scans without labels. The validation and testing sets include 100 and 400 CT scans, respectively, which cover various abdominal cancer types, such as liver cancer, kidney cancer, pancreas cancer, colon cancer, gastric cancer, and so on. The organ annotation process used ITK-SNAP [27], nnU-Net [12], and MedSAM [15].

The evaluation metrics encompass two accuracy measures—Dice Similarity Coefficient (DSC) and Normalized Surface Dice (NSD)—alongside two efficiency measures—running time and area under the GPU memory-time curve. These metrics collectively contribute to the ranking computation. Furthermore, the running time and GPU memory consumption are considered within tolerances of 15 s and 4 GB, respectively.

3.2   Implementation Details

The training and inference of the teacher model in self-training utilize the default configuration of nnU-Net. For organ segmentation, the loss weights λ_1 and λ_2 for the student model are set as 1 and 0.5, respectively. The loss weight λ for correcting pseudo labels in tumor segmentation is set to 1. To achieve model lightweight, the base number of channels of Res-UNet is set to 16 and the number of up-sampling and down-sampling is 5. The development environments and requirements are presented in Table 1. The training protocols for first-stage and second-stage segmentation are presented in Table 2. To alleviate the over-fitting of limited training data, we employed online data argumentation, including random rotation, scaling, adding white Gaussian noise, Gaussian blurring, adjusting rightness and contrast, simulation of low resolution, Gamma transformation, and elastic deformation.

4   Results and Discussion

4.1   Quantitative Results on Validation Set

We used the default nnU-Net with full supervision to train on 2200 labeled data as the baseline. We conducted the following experiments: 1) two-stage segmentation experiments using the **F**ully **S**upervised method on 219 full **O**rgans labeled data (FSO); 2) two-stage segmentation experiments using the self-training method on 219 full organs labeled data and 1093 partial labeled data;

Table 1. Development environments and requirements.

System	Ubuntu 20.04.3 LTS
CPU	AMD EPYC 7742 64-Core Processor
RAM	94 GB; 2933 MT/s
GPU (number and type)	One NVIDIA A100 80G
CUDA version	11.6
Programming language	Python 3.10.11
Deep learning framework	Pytorch (Torch 2.0.0, torchvision 0.15.0)
Specific dependencies	nnU-Net

Table 2. The training protocols of two-stage segmentation framework.

Model	first-stage model/organ seg model/ tumour seg model
Batch size	2/3/2
Patch size	$128 \times 128 \times 128/192 \times 192 \times 192/192 \times 192 \times 192$
Total epochs	500
Optimizer	SGD with nesterov momentum ($\mu = 0.99$)
Initial learning rate (lr)	0.01
Lr decay schedule	Poly LR
Training time (hours)	17.28/47.88/ 31
Number of model parameters	45.87 M[a]
Number of flops	372.55/1886.03/ 1257.35G[b]
CO_2eq	1.40/7.27/5.00 kg[c]

[a] https://github.com/sksq96/pytorch-summary
[b] https://github.com/facebookresearch/fvcore
[c] https://github.com/lfwa/carbontracker/

Table 3. Ablation studies. (FSO: two-stage segmentation experiments using the Fully Supervised method on 219 full Organs labeled data; FST: two-stage segmentation experiments using the Fully Supervised method on 1497 Tumor labeled data.)

Methods	Organ		Tumour	
	DSC (%)	NSD (%)	DSC (%)	NSD (%)
nnU-Net	38.76	40.32	46.8	35.47
FSO	87.86	94.27	–	–
Self-training with part label	89.1	95.58	–	–
Self-training with part label and unlabel	89.6	96.19	–	–
FST	–	–	46.69	39.02
Mean teacher	–	–	52.08	42.82
StMt	89.6	96.19	52.08	42.82

3) two-stage segmentation experiments introducing 888 + 1800 unlabeled data based on experiment 2); 4) two-stage segmentation experiments using the Fully Supervised method on 1497 Tumor labeled data (FST); 5) two-stage segmentation experiments using mean teacher and pseudo-label supervision based on experiment 4); 6) hybird supervision of Self-training and Mean teacher for organ-tumor segmentation (StMt), which is the combination of experiments 3) and 5).

Table 3 shows that the average organ DSC on the validation set of nnU-Net is only 38.76%. The reason for this result is that when training partial labeled data in a fully supervised manner, the unlabeled organs are considered as background, which can lead to ambiguity during training optimization and result in lower performance. With FSO training using only full organ labeled data, the DSC for organs is 87.86%. By introducing pseudo-label data from partial labeled data through self-training, the DSC improves to 89.1%. Furthermore, with the additional introduction of pseudo-labels from unlabeled data, the DSC further increases to 89.6%. The NSD exhibits a similar changing trend. These results fully demonstrate that both partial label and unlabeled data are beneficial for performance improvement. Using Mean teacher for tumor segmentation has shown improvements of 5.39% in DSC and 3.8% in NSD compared to FST. StMt integrates self-training and mean teacher to achieve the best segmentation results. Table 4 presents detailed results for StMt in terms of public Validation, online validation, and test submission.

Table 4. Quantitative evaluation results.

Target	Public Validation		Online Validation		Testing	
	DSC (%)	NSD (%)	DSC (%)	NSD (%)	DSC (%)	NSD (%)
Liver	97.41 ± 0.60	99.32 ± 0.51	97.40	99.21	96.33	97.94
Right Kidney	94.18 ± 6.14	95.74 ± 8.13	93.78	95.51	93.60	94.62
Spleen	95.29 ± 1.93	97.94 ± 2.99	95.78	98.45	95.37	98.04
Pancreas	85.95 ± 5.22	97.50 ± 3.71	85.42	97.01	89.05	98.15
Aorta	94.87 ± 0.97	99.09 ± 1.13	94.77	98.91	95.31	99.68
Inferior vena cava	92.81 ± 2.09	97.38 ± 2.14	92.86	97.35	93.21	98.05
Right adrenal gland	82.76 ± 5.03	96.98 ± 2.47	81.67	96.50	81.19	95.21
Left adrenal gland	81.54 ± 5.14	96.26 ± 3.37	80.91	95.31	81.36	94.38
Gallbladder	87.12 ± 18.85	89.15 ± 19.90	89.92	91.40	87.26	90.44
Esophagus	92.39 ± 14.93	93.29 ± 14.72	83.56	94.76	89.53	98.89
Stomach	93.40 ± 5.11	97.49 ± 5.68	93.98	98.03	94.53	98.10
Duodenum	83.60 ± 6.68	95.69 ± 4.75	84.72	96.27	88.40	97.87
Left kidney	93.49 ± 6.24	94.68 ± 8.91	92.55	94.40	92.26	93.97
Tumor	52.08 ± 34.09	42.82 ± 28.69	45.55	37.82	50.00	38.32
Average	86.92 ± 8.07	92.38 ± 7.65	86.63	92.21	87.59	92.35

4.2 Qualitative Results on Validation Set

We visualize the segmentation results of the validation set. The representative samples in Fig. 3 demonstrate the success of identifying organ details by StMt, which is the closest to the ground truth compared to other methods due to retaining most of the spatial information of abdominal organs and tumour. In particular, it outperforms FSO significantly by leveraging partial labeled and unlabeled data with self-training, which enhances the generalization of the segmentation model. Compared to FST, mean Teacher achieves more complete tumor segmentation. Furthermore, we show representative examples of poor segmentation. The third row demonstrates that none of the methods were able to segment the tumor (atrovirens region) in the lower abdomen. Due to the fact that the 13 organ classes in the Flare2023 dataset are primarily focused on the upper abdomen, it is difficult to accurately locate the approximate position of the abdominal area containing the tumor in the first stage by relying solely on the tumor. The fourth row shows another case where none of the methods accurately detected the spleen (blue region).

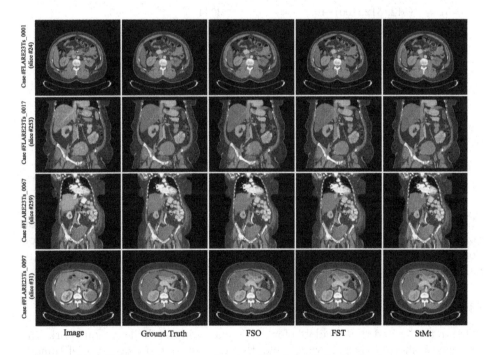

Fig. 3. Visualization of segmentation results of abdominal organs and tumour.

4.3   Segmentation Efficiency Results on Validation Set

In the official segmentation efficiency evaluation, the average inference time of 100 cases in the validation set is 11.25 s, the average maximum GPU memory is 3519.06 MB, and the area under the GPU memory-time curve is 9627.82MB. Thanks to the two-stage framework and the whole-volume-based input strategy, the inference time for each test case is within 15 s. Additionally, the small Res-UNet and input size ensure that the GPU memory usage remains below 4GB. The detailed quantitative results of the segmentation efficiency for some cases are shown in Table 5.

Table 5. Quantitative evaluation of segmentation efficiency in terms of the running them and GPU memory consumption. Total GPU denotes the area under GPU Memory-Time curve. Evaluation GPU platform: NVIDIA QUADRO RTX5000 (16G).

Case ID	Image Size	Running Time (s)	Max GPU (MB)	Total GPU (MB)
0001	(512, 512, 55)	11.76	3220	10849
0051	(512, 512, 100)	10.2	3044	8833
0017	(512, 512, 150)	10.62	3200	9204
0019	(512, 512, 215)	11.14	3800	9557
0099	(512, 512, 334)	11.92	3800	9941
0063	(512, 512, 448)	13.51	3582	10614
0048	(512, 512, 499)	13.85	3800	10724
0029	(512, 512, 554)	14.6	3800	11134

4.4   Results on Final Testing Set

In the testing set, the StMt model achieved average DSC scores of 90.66% for organs and 50.14% for lesions, along with NSD scores averaging 96.69% for organs and 38.77% for lesions. Additionally, the average running time was 11.1 s, and the area under the GPU memory-time curve was 8979 MB.

4.5   Limitation and Future Work

Due to the limited time available for participating in the challenge, our work still has many shortcomings. For example, the segmentation performance of tumors is poor, partly due to the fact that the tumor in the lower abdomen was not successfully segmented in the first stage. It is possible to try performing tumor segmentation independently in the first stage and then integrating the results with organ segmentation, similar to the second stage. Furthermore, selecting high-quality pseudo-labeled data may contribute to improving segmentation performance, and it is worth a try.

5   Conclusion

In the paper, we propose a hybrid supervised framework, StMt, that integrates self-training and mean teacher for the segmentation of abdominal organs and tumors using partially labeled and unlabeled data. We introduce a two-stage segmentation pipeline and whole-volume-based input strategy to maximize segmentation accuracy while meeting the requirements of inference time and GPU memory usage. Experiments on the validation set of FLARE2023 demonstrate that our method achieves excellent segmentation performance as well as fast and low-resource model inference. Our method achieved an average DSC score of 89.79% and 45.55% for the organs and lesions on the validation set and the average running time and area under GPU memory-time cure are 11.25 s and 9627.82MB, respectively.

Acknowledgements. The authors of this paper declare that the segmentation method they implemented for participation in the FLARE 2023 challenge has not used any pre-trained models nor additional datasets other than those provided by the organizers. The proposed solution is fully automatic without any manual intervention. We thank all the data owners for making the CT scans publicly available and CodaLab [20] for hosting the challenge platform.

References

1. Bilic, P., et al.: The liver tumor segmentation benchmark (lits). Med. Image Anal. **84**, 102680 (2023)
2. Chen, S., Ma, K., Zheng, Y.: Med3d: transfer learning for 3d medical image analysis. arXiv preprint arXiv:1904.00625 (2019)
3. Chen, X., Yuan, Y., Zeng, G., Wang, J.: Semi-supervised semantic segmentation with cross pseudo supervision. In: Proceedings of the IEEE/CVF Conference on Computer Vision and Pattern Recognition, pp. 2613–2622 (2021)
4. Clark, K., et al.: The cancer imaging archive (TCIA): maintaining and operating a public information repository. J. Digit. Imaging **26**(6), 1045–1057 (2013)
5. Eisenhauer, E.A., et al.: New response evaluation criteria in solid tumours: revised RECIST guideline (version 1.1). Eur. J. Cancer **45**(2), 228–247 (2009)
6. Fang, X., Yan, P.: Multi-organ segmentation over partially labeled datasets with multi-scale feature abstraction. IEEE Trans. Med. Imaging **39**(11), 3619–3629 (2020)
7. Gatidis, S., et al.: The autoPET challenge: towards fully automated lesion segmentation in oncologic PET/CT imaging. preprint at Research Square (Nature Portfolio) (2023). https://doi.org/10.21203/rs.3.rs-2572595/v1
8. Gatidis, S., et al.: A whole-body FDG-PET/CT dataset with manually annotated tumor lesions. Sci. Data **9**(1), 601 (2022)
9. Heller, N., et al.: The state of the art in kidney and kidney tumor segmentation in contrast-enhanced CT imaging: results of the kits19 challenge. Med. Image Anal. **67**, 101821 (2021)
10. Heller, N., et al.: An international challenge to use artificial intelligence to define the state-of-the-art in kidney and kidney tumor segmentation in ct imaging. Proc. Am. Soc. Clin. Oncol. **38**(6), 626–626 (2020)

11. Huang, Z., et al.: Revisiting nnU-Net for iterative pseudo labeling and efficient sliding window inference. In: Ma, J., Wang, B. (eds.) FLARE 2022. LNCS, vol. 13816, pp. 178–189. Springer, Cham (2022). https://doi.org/10.1007/978-3-031-23911-3_16

12. Isensee, F., Jaeger, P.F., Kohl, S.A., Petersen, J., Maier-Hein, K.H.: nnU-Net: a self-configuring method for deep learning-based biomedical image segmentation. Nat. Methods **18**(2), 203–211 (2021)

13. Liu, W., et al.: PHTrans: parallelly aggregating global and local representations for medical image segmentation. In: Wang, L., Dou, Q., Fletcher, P.T., Speidel, S., Li, S. (eds.) MICCAI 2022. LNCS, vol. 13435, pp. 235–244. Springer, Cham (2022). https://doi.org/10.1007/978-3-031-16443-9_23

14. Liu, W., Xu, W., Yan, S., Wang, L., Li, H., Yang, H.: Combining self-training and hybrid architecture for semi-supervised abdominal organ segmentation. In: Ma, J., Wang, B. (eds.) FLARE 2022. LNCS, vol. 13816, pp. 281–292. Springer, Cham (2022). https://doi.org/10.1007/978-3-031-23911-3_25

15. Ma, J., He, Y., Li, F., Han, L., You, C., Wang, B.: Segment anything in medical images. Nat. Commun. **15**, 654 (2024)

16. Ma, J., et al.: Fast and low-GPU-memory abdomen CT organ segmentation: the flare challenge. Med. Image Anal. **82**, 102616 (2022)

17. Ma, J., et al.: Unleashing the strengths of unlabeled data in pan-cancer abdominal organ quantification: the flare22 challenge. arXiv preprint arXiv:2308.05862 (2023)

18. Ma, J., et al.: Abdomenct-1k: Is abdominal organ segmentation a solved problem? IEEE Trans. Pattern Anal. Mach. Intell. **44**(10), 6695–6714 (2022)

19. Ouali, Y., Hudelot, C., Tami, M.: Semi-supervised semantic segmentation with cross-consistency training. In: Proceedings of the IEEE/CVF Conference on Computer Vision and Pattern Recognition, pp. 12674–12684 (2020)

20. Pavao, A., et al.: Codalab competitions: an open source platform to organize scientific challenges. J. Mach. Learn. Res. **24**(198), 1–6 (2023)

21. Shi, G., Xiao, L., Chen, Y., Zhou, S.K.: Marginal loss and exclusion loss for partially supervised multi-organ segmentation. Med. Image Anal. **70**, 101979 (2021)

22. Siegel, R.L., Miller, K.D., Fuchs, H.E., Jemal, A.: Cancer statistics, 2022. CA: Cancer J. Clin. **72**(1), 7–33 (2022). https://doi.org/10.3322/caac.21708, https://acsjournals.onlinelibrary.wiley.com/doi/abs/10.3322/caac.21708

23. Simpson, A.L.,et al.: A large annotated medical image dataset for the development and evaluation of segmentation algorithms. arXiv preprint arXiv:1902.09063 (2019)

24. Wang, E., Zhao, Y., Wu, Y.: Cascade dual-decoders network for abdominal organs segmentation. In: Ma, J., Wang, B. (eds.) FLARE 2022. LNCS, vol. 13816, pp. 202–213. Springer, Cham (2022). https://doi.org/10.1007/978-3-031-23911-3_18

25. Wasserthal, J., et al.: Totalsegmentator: robust segmentation of 104 anatomic structures in CT images. Radiol. Artif. Intell. **5**(5), e230024 (2023)

26. Yang, L., Zhuo, W., Qi, L., Shi, Y., Gao, Y.: St++: make self-training work better for semi-supervised semantic segmentation. In: Proceedings of the IEEE/CVF Conference on Computer Vision and Pattern Recognition, pp. 4268–4277 (2022)

27. Yushkevich, P.A., Gao, Y., Gerig, G.: ITK-SNAP: an interactive tool for semi-automatic segmentation of multi-modality biomedical images. In: Annual International Conference of the IEEE Engineering in Medicine and Biology Society, pp. 3342–3345 (2016)

28. Zhang, J., Xie, Y., Xia, Y., Shen, C.: Dodnet: learning to segment multi-organ and tumors from multiple partially labeled datasets. In: Proceedings of the IEEE/CVF Conference on Computer Vision and Pattern Recognition, pp. 1195–1204 (2021)

Semi-Supervised Learning Based Cascaded Pocket U-Net for Organ and Pan-Cancer Segmentation in Abdomen CT

Tao Wang[✉], Xiaoling Zhang, Wei Xiong, Shuoling Zhou, and Xinyue Zhang

School of Biomedical Engineering, Southern Medical University, Guangzhou 510515, China
wangtao_9802@sina.cn

Abstract. In clinical practice, CT scans are frequently employed as the primary imaging modality for detecting prevalent tumors arising from the abdominal organs. Hence, the accomplishment of simultaneous organ segmentation and pan-cancer segmentation in abdominal CT scans holds significant importance in decreasing the workload of clinical practitioners. To maximize the utilization of partially labeled and unlabeled data, a iterative training strategy through a semi-supervised approach based on pseudo labels is employed in this work. Furthermore, to reduce parameter size of model and increase efficiency of GPU utilization, the proposed method is built upon the pocket U-Net architecture. The methodology involves a cascaded network consisting of two parts: initially, a segmentation network trained on labeled data refines the low-resolution pocket U-Net to reduce image dimensions; subsequently, the high-resolution pocket U-Net conducts intricate segmentation to precisely delineate organ and tumor regions. As demonstrated by the evaluation outcomes on the FLARE 2023 validation dataset, the proposed method achieves an average dice similarity coefficient (DSC) of 88.94% for organs and 15.92% for tumors, along with normalized surface dice (NSD) values of 93.31% for organs and 0.0816% for tumors, with minimal parameter size. Furthermore, the average inference time is 82.61 s, with an average maximum GPU memory usage of 3560M. Codes are available at https://github.com/wt812549723/FLARE2023_solution.

Keywords: Organ and pan-cancer segmentation · Semi-supervised learning · Minimal parameter size

1 Introduction

Accurate and fast segmentation of abdominal organs and pan-cancer in abdominal CT scans is crucial to reduce the clinician's workload and improve the efficiency of diagnosis and treatment. However, abdominal organ and pan-cancer segmentation faces several challenges: (1) Obtaining labels is both time-consuming and labor-intensive. (2) A significant amount of unlabeled and partially labeled data is available to improve segmentation performance. (3) Balancing segmentation performance, rapid inference speed, and efficient GPU utilization. (4) The segmentation performance of certain organs and pan-cancers is limited by the variations in size and morphology among different organs and the morphological differences and heterogeneity of tumors within various organs.

As a result of the unlabeled and partially labeled data available, the proposed method adopts a semi-supervised learning framework. Semi-supervised methods can be categorized into three groups: pseudo-label-based [5,10], consistency-based [3,11], and hybrid methods [19]. Among these methods, pseudo-label based methods are often devoid of introducing supplementary parameters and burdens to the model. In consideration of the model size and inference speed, the proposed method incorporates a pseudo-label based semi-supervised learning framework. Moreover, many existing medical segmentation models have been extended upon the foundation of nnU-Net, which has proven to be an excellent solution capable of addressing a variety of medical segmentation tasks [9]. However, the default configuration of nnU-Net employs the traditional U-Net architecture, often leading to concerns about large model parameter sizes and slow inference speed. Furthermore, nnU-Net was originally designed for fully supervised segmentation tasks, necessitating extensions to incorporate aspects of semi-supervised learning.

Therefore, a semi-supervised learning based cascaded pocket U-Net is proposed to achieve abdominal multi-organ and pan-cancer segmentation. First, the proposed method builds on the nnU-Net framework and extends it to introduce a pseudo-label-based semi-supervised learning strategy through iterative training. This strategy effectively utilizes a substantial amount of unlabeled and partially labeled data. In addition, the use of the pocket U-Net reduces the network parameters, thereby decreasing the GPU utilization and increasing the compatibility with a wide range of devices. Subsequently, a cascaded network is employed to accelerate segmentation: the first-tier network performs a region-of-interest (ROI) segmentation to reduce image dimensions, followed by the second-tier network to perform a refined segmentation. Finally, the proposed method achieves efficient segmentation of abdominal organs and pan-cancer.

The main contributions of the proposed method are as follows:

- We integrated a semi-supervised training strategy based on pseudo labels into the nnU-Netv2 framework.
- We implemented a two-stage cascaded architecture to enhance the inference speed.
- We employed the Pocket U-Net architecture as the backbone network, resulting in a significant reduction in the model's parameter size. This optimization ensures efficient GPU utilization.

2   Method

2.1   Preprocessing

The preprocessing steps in our proposed method align with the approach for handling CT data as defined by nnU-Net [9]. These steps encompass the following procedures: (a) the exclusion of irrelevant background regions through cropping; (b) the application of CT value truncation to eliminate superfluous information; (c) the utilization of mean and standard deviation computed from all training samples for normalization; (d) the resampling of all images to ensure a consistent target (targets are set to $4.0\,\text{mm} \times 1.2\,\text{mm} \times 1.2\,\text{mm}$ and $2.5\,\text{mm} \times 0.8\,\text{mm} \times 0.8\,\text{mm}$ for ROI segmentation network and detail segmentation network in the proposed method, respectively).

2.2   Proposed Method

Pocket U-Net. As shown in Fig. 1, traditionally, in the U-Net architecture, it is customary to double the number of feature channels following each downsampling operation. However, this practice significantly contributes to the increase in the parameter size of model. Moreover, previous research in medical image segmentation has demonstrated that controlling the expansion of feature channels can maintain satisfactory performance while effectively managing parameter size [2]. Inspired by this study, a specialized variant of U-Net, named as Pocket U-Net, was introduced as the backbone network. The difference between the traditional U-Net and Pocket U-Net is illustrated in Fig. 1, wherein Pocket U-Net maintains a consistent number of feature channels across all scales, thereby ensuring optimal GPU utilization.

ROI Segmentation Network. Owing to the localization of major abdominal organs within a specific region, known as the ROI, voxels outside the ROI introduce additional complexity during both model training and inference. Thus, the first part of the cascaded network is designed with an ROI segmentation network to identify the ROI where abdominal organs are present, thereby reducing computational overhead. Specifically, all organ and tumor regions are set as foreground regions of the same labels (all labels are set to 1 in our method), and a pocket U-Net is employed to identify all foreground regions. Considering the relatively straightforward nature of this task and its low precision requirements, a light pocket U-Net was trained using only fully labeled data.

Herein, a light Pocket U-Net implies smaller target spacing (i.e., reduced image dimensions), small patch sizes, shallow depth, and multiple downsampling operations in z-axis.

Detail Segmentation Network. Once the ROI has been delineated by the ROI segmentation network, the image is cropped based on the ROI. Subsequently, the cropped image is then input to the detail segmentation network.

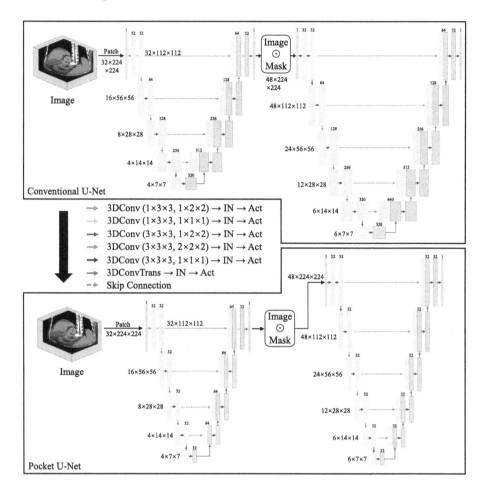

Fig. 1. Network Architecture. In contrast to the conventional U-Net, Pocket U-Net primarily modifies the number of channels, resulting in a substantial reduction of model parameters.

In contrast to the ROI segmentation network, the detail segmentation network utilizes a larger target spacing to retain finer details in the image. Furthermore, the detail segmentation network employs larger patch sizes and reduces the frequency of downsampling operations, facilitating the network in capturing both fine-grained details and contextual information. Another notable difference from the ROI segmentation network is that while the ROI segmentation network is trained once using fully labeled data, the detail segmentation network engages in semi-supervised learning and undergoes multiple iterations of training utilizing all available data.

Semi-supervised Learning. Semi-supervised learning plays a pivotal role in effectively harnessing partially labeled and unlabeled data [18,19]. The specific implementation of semi-supervised learning can be illustrated by the detail segmentation network, which involves a five-step process. First, the detail segmentation network undergoes initial training using fully labeled images. Following this initial training phase, the network is then deployed to generate initial pseudo labels for both partially labeled and unlabeled data. Second, in the second round of training for the detail segmentation network, in addition to the fully labeled data, partial labeling and unlabeled data are incorporated. Notably, a additional process is applied to the partially labeled data in this round. Specifically, the unlabeled portions within the partially labeled data are supplemented with the generated initial pseudo labels, whereas the labeled portions remain unaltered to ensure label accuracy. Meanwhile, the unlabeled data are entirely assigned pseudo labels. Similarly, the detail segmentation network trained in the second round is utilized to generate new pseudo labels. Third, building upon the pseudo labels generated in the second round, the procedure described in the second step is reiterated to conduct a third round of training. Furthermore, the detail segmentation network obtained from the third round of training can likewise be employed for pseudo label generation. Fourth, relying on the pseudo labels derived from the first three rounds of training, partially labeled and unlabeled data with pseudo labels for the final training are selected based on computed uncertainty scores [8]. Specifically, uncertainty scores are calculated by measuring the average overlap between the pseudo labels obtained in the first and second rounds and between the pseudo labels obtained in the second and third rounds. A higher degree of overlap corresponds to a lower uncertainty score, and the mathematical formula for calculating these scores is expressed as follows:

$$us = \frac{1}{3} \sum_{i=1}^{3} \frac{\mathbf{SUM}(\mathbf{v}_i^{\mathbf{x,y,z}} \neq \mathbf{v}_{\mathbf{i-1}}^{\mathbf{x,y,z}})}{\mathbf{SUM}(\mathbf{v}_{\mathbf{i}}^{\mathbf{x,y,z}} > \mathbf{0})} \tag{1}$$

where us denotes the uncertainty scores, $v_i^{x,y,z}$ denotes the value of voxels with coordinates (x, y, z) in the pseudo label obtained through ith round of training, and $\mathbf{SUM}(\cdot)$ denotes the sum of the number of voxels that meet the condition. Based on a pre-defined uncertainty score threshold, a selection was made to include partially labeled and unlabeled data for the final training. Additionally, the pseudo labels generated in the third round are utilized as labels for the unlabeled portions of these data, thus converting them into fully labeled data. Fifth and finally, the selected partially labeled and unlabeled data, now equipped with pseudo labels, are used in conjunction with fully labeled data for the final training of the detail segmentation network. The final trained detail segmentation network is seamlessly integrated with the ROI segmentation network to form the ultimate model.

Loss Function. Given the iterative training strategy used in semi-supervised learning, there is no requirement to introduce an additional loss specifically for semi-supervised learning purposes. Herein, a combination of the cross-entropy loss and Dice loss was utilized. This loss functions are presently well-established and extensively applied in the field of medical image segmentation [9,11].

2.3   Post-processing

To prevent isolated errors in the foreground regions, a connected component analysis was employed for segmentation result of each organ. Specifically, only the largest connected component was retained to improve performance. Additionally, since the images are cropped between the ROI segmentation network and the detail segmentation network, it is necessary to reconstruct the images in post-processing based on the cropping coordinates.

3   Experiments

3.1   Dataset and Evaluation Measures

The FLARE 2023 challenge is an extension of the FLARE 2021–2022 [13,14], aiming to aim to promote the development of foundation models in abdominal disease analysis. The segmentation targets cover 13 organs and various abdominal lesions. The training dataset is curated from more than 30 medical centers under the license permission, including TCIA [4], LiTS [1], MSD [17], KiTS [6,7], and AbdomenCT-1K [15]. The training set includes 4000 abdomen CT scans where 2200 CT scans with partial labels and 1800 CT scans without labels. Among them, the 2200 partially labeled CT scans contain partially labeled data for all organs and tumors, i.e., fully labeled data. The validation and testing sets include 100 and 400 CT scans, respectively, which cover various abdominal cancer types, such as liver cancer, kidney cancer, pancreas cancer, colon cancer, gastric cancer, and so on. The organ annotation process used ITK-SNAP [20], nnU-Net [9], and MedSAM [12].

The evaluation metrics encompass two accuracy measures-Dice Similarity Coefficient (DSC) and Normalized Surface Dice (NSD)-alongside two efficiency measures-running time and area under the GPU memory-time curve. These metrics collectively contribute to the ranking computation. Furthermore, the running time and GPU memory consumption are considered within tolerances of 15 s and 4 GB, respectively.

3.2   Implementation Details

Environment Settings. The development environments and requirements are presented in Table 1.

Table 1. Development environments and requirements.

System	Ubuntu 20.04.6 LTS
CPU	Intel(R) Xeon(R) Gold 5120 CPU @ 2.20 GHz
RAM	16 × 4 GB; 2.67MT/s
GPU (number and type)	One GeForce RTX 2080 Ti 11G
CUDA version	11.7
Programming language	Python 3.9
Deep learning framework	torch 2.0.1
Code	https://github.com/wt812549723/FLARE2023_solution

Training Protocols. The handling of unlabeled images and partially labeled data has been comprehensively explained in Sect. 2.3. Additionally, the data augmentation techniques employed in our proposed method align with the default settings utilized in nnU-Net [9], encompassing rotations, scaling, Gaussian noise, Gaussian blur, adjustments in brightness and contrast, simulation of low resolution, gamma correction, and mirroring. Furthermore, both the patch sampling strategy and the criteria for optimal model selection are entirely in accordance with the guidelines established by nnU-Net [9]. To further enhance segmentation efficiency, testtime augmentation (TTA) has been disabled during inference, and the step size for sliding window prediction has been set to 1 (Tables 2 and 3).

Table 2. Training protocols of ROI segmentation network.

Network initialization	"He" normal initialization
Batch size	2
Patch size	32 × 224 × 224
Total epochs	1000
Optimizer	SGD with nesterov momentum ($\mu = 0.99$)
Initial learning rate (lr)	0.01
Lr decay schedule	halved by 200 epochs
Training time	35.3 h
Loss function	Cross-Entropy loss + Dice loss
Number of model parameters	5.76M[a]
Number of flops	485.17G[b]

[a] https://github.com/sksq96/pytorch-summary
[b] https://github.com/Lyken17/pytorch-OpCounter

Table 3. Training protocols for detail segmentation network.

Network initialization	"He" normal initialization
Batch size	2
Patch size	$48 \times 224 \times 224$
Total epochs	1000
Optimizer	SGD with nesterov momentum ($\mu = 0.99$)
Initial learning rate (lr)	0.01
Lr decay schedule	halved by 200 epochs
Loss function	Cross-Entropy loss + Dice loss
Training time	44.0 h
Number of model parameters	7.97M[a]
Number of flops	2.77T[b]

[a] https://github.com/sksq96/pytorch-summary
[b] https://github.com/Lyken17/pytorch-OpCounter

4   Results and Discussion

4.1   Quantitative Results on Validation Set

Based on the results presented in Table 4, our method achieved notable performance in organ segmentation on the publicly available validation dataset. Specifically, it attained an average DSC of 88.76% and an average NSD of 93.16%.

Table 4. Quantitative evaluation results.

Target	Public Validation		Online Validation		Testing	
	DSC (%)	NSD (%)	DSC(%)	NSD (%)	DSC (%)	NSD (%)
Liver	98.12 ± 0.83	98.71 ± 1.82	97.97	98.38	75.37	75.40
Right Kidney	88.94 ± 21.75	89.54 ± 21.63	90.42	90.78	73.35	73.59
Spleen	94.38 ± 11.86	94.96 ± 11.89	93.91	94.84	72.70	73.34
Pancreas	85.72 ± 5.73	95.84 ± 3.21	84.17	94.65	68.77	74.35
Aorta	96.69 ± 3.19	98.46 ± 3.87	96.91	98.67	76.67	77.95
Inferior vena cava	92.32 ± 4.67	93.03 ± 5.44	91.90	92.46	72.51	73.35
Right adrenal gland	88.64 ± 4.71	97.34 ± 2.64	88.22	97.07	66.57	73.17
Left adrenal gland	84.69 ± 9.32	93.82 ± 8.03	84.31	93.22	66.47	72.77
Gallbladder	81.20 ± 26.12	81.33 ± 27.32	82.53	82.65	62.37	63.07
Esophagus	80.21 ± 16.40	89.39 ± 15.51	81.71	91.19	68.28	74.51
Stomach	92.12 ± 6.40	94.61 ± 7.12	92.43	94.75	72.16	73.62
Duodenum	80.58 ± 8.53	92.68 ± 6.22	80.54	92.52	65.21	73.27
Left kidney	90.27 ± 16.67	91.42 ± 15.77	91.26	91.82	72.47	73.00
Tumor	16.27 ± 21.01	8.87 ± 17.54	15.92	8.16	15.67	0.06
Average	88.76 ± 15.77	93.16 ± 15.77	88.94	93.31	70.22	73.18

Table 5. Comparison results on the public validation set, where "w/o" denotes "without".

Target	The Proposed Method		Pocket U-Net (w/o unlabeled data)	
	DSC (%)	NSD (%)	DSC (%)	NSD (%)
Liver	98.12 ± 0.83	98.71 ± 1.82	96.14 ± 4.87	95.78 ± 5.89
Right Kidney	88.94 ± 21.75	89.54 ± 21.63	90.24 ± 19.63	89.64 ± 20.27
Spleen	94.38 ± 11.86	94.96 ± 11.89	80.42 ± 24.33	78.94 ± 23.35
Pancreas	85.72 ± 5.73	95.84 ± 3.21	84.32 ± 8.80	94.91 ± 6.92
Aorta	96.69 ± 3.19	98.46 ± 3.87	96.41 ± 3.79	97.89 ± 4.80
Inferior vena cava	92.32 ± 4.67	93.03 ± 5.44	90.93 ± 7.29	91.03 ± 8.60
Right adrenal gland	88.64 ± 4.71	97.34 ± 2.64	86.44 ± 7.05	95.79 ± 5.32
Left adrenal gland	84.69 ± 9.32	93.82 ± 8.03	85.10 ± 8.30	94.03 ± 6.73
Gallbladder	81.20 ± 26.12	81.33 ± 27.32	73.26 ± 27.15	72.43 ± 27.92
Esophagus	80.21 ± 16.40	89.39 ± 15.51	80.56 ± 17.45	90.11 ± 16.71
Stomach	92.12 ± 6.40	94.61 ± 7.12	87.13 ± 13.60	89.64 ± 14.32
Duodenum	80.58 ± 8.53	92.68 ± 6.22	79.76 ± 10.87	92.90 ± 7.28
Left kidney	90.27 ± 16.67	91.42 ± 15.77	88.67 ± 19.06	87.46 ± 20.53
Tumor	16.27 ± 21.01	8.87 ± 17.54	39.26 ± 29.31	26.77 ± 22.11
Average	88.76 ± 15.77	93.16 ± 15.77	86.11 ± 6.37	90.04 ± 6.89

However, for tumor segmentation on the same dataset, our method achieved a comparatively lower average DSC of 16.27% and a moderate average NSD of 8.87%. Furthermore, on the online validation dataset, our method consistently demonstrated strong performance in organ segmentation, with an average DSC of 88.76% and an average NSD of 93.16%. However, in the challenging task of tumor segmentation on this dataset, our method achieved an average DSC of 15.92 and an average NSD of 8.16%. In addition, the post-processing method based on the largest connected analysis method brought an improvement of 1.21% to the model.

Analyzing these results reveals valuable insights. Our proposed method excels in segmenting larger organs, such as the liver, spleen, and stomach, as well as in delineating major blood vessels like the aorta and inferior vena cava. In contrast, its performance appears less robust when applied to smaller organs such as the gallbladder, esophagus, and duodenum. Notably, our method faces challenges in tumor segmentation, likely attributed to the diverse nature of tumors, their widespread distribution, and the absence of distinct concentration zones.

The comparison results indicate that the inclusion of unlabeled data has yielded a favorable impact on organ segmentation. Surprisingly, however, unlabeled data has adversely affected tumor segmentation, resulting in a significant decline in tumor segmentation metrics. This phenomenon may be attributed to the relatively low accuracy of tumor pseudo-labels, which introduced additional noise into the model (Table 6).

Table 6. Quantitative evaluation of segmentation efficiency in terms of the running them and GPU memory consumption. Total GPU denotes the area under GPU Memory-Time curve. Evaluation GPU platform: NVIDIA QUADRO RTX5000 (16G).

Case ID	Image Size	Running Time (s)	Max GPU (MB)	Total GPU (MB)
0001	(512, 512, 55)	54.24	3410	72616
0051	(512, 512, 100)	66.54	3710	94022
0017	(512, 512, 150)	92.46	3776	141352
0019	(512, 512, 215)	100.37	3546	148469
0099	(512, 512, 334)	117.00	3706	169899
0063	(512, 512, 448)	150.09	3770	224764
0048	(512, 512, 499)	169.41	3746	263733
0029	(512, 512, 554)	221.69	3960	392044

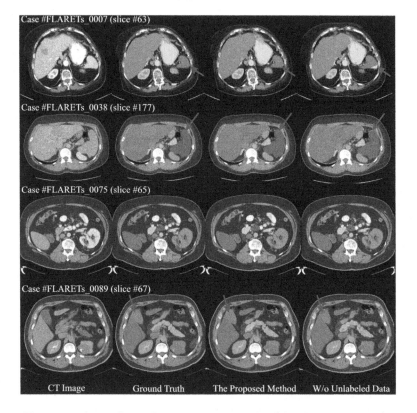

Fig. 2. Two examples with good segmentation results (the above two rows) and two examples with bad segmentation results (the following two rows) in the validation set. Among these, the first column represents the original images, the second column shows the gold standard, the third column displays the results of our proposed method, and the fourth column demonstrates the outcomes of the method that does not utilize unlabeled data. The red arrow indicates the improvement of semi-supervised training. (Color figure online)

4.2   Qualitative Results on Validation Set

Based on the results shown in Fig. 2, we have observed that our approach is not particularly sensitive to low-contrast tumor segmentation. The proposed method tends to classify low-contrast tumors as normal regions or background. Furthermore, while models that do not utilize unlabeled data perform significantly better than the proposed method in terms of tumor segmentation metrics, they also exhibit inaccuracies in tumor segmentation. In organ segmentation, the introduction of unlabeled data has led to performance improvements. It can be observed that our method performs better in spleen segmentation for Case #FLARETs_0007 and Case #FLARETs_0038, as well as gallbladder segmentation for Case #FLARETs_0089. Hence, the primary limitation of our approach lies in tumor segmentation.

4.3   Segmentation Efficiency Results on Validation Set

The segmentation efficiency results for the validation dataset are presented in Table 5. These primarily include running time, GPU memory consumption, and the area under the GPU Memory-Time curve. The shortest running time was 43.53 s, the longest was 221.69 s, with an average of 82.61 s. GPU memory consumption ranged from a minimum of 3200 MB to a maximum of 4388 MB, averaging at 3560 MB. The area under the GPU Memory-Time curve varied from a minimum of 53508 MB to a maximum of 392044 MB, with an average of 120090 MB. Compared to traditional U-Net, our approach offers significant advantages in terms of parameter size. In the ROI segmentation network, the parameter size for the traditional U-Net constructed by nnU-Net is 123.61M, whereas the parameter size of our method is only 5.76M. As for detail segmentation network, the parameter sizes of traditional U-Net and our method are 235.60M and 7.97M, respectively.

4.4   Results on Final Testing Set

As shown in Table 4, our method consistently demonstrated perform an average DSC of 88.76% and an average NSD of 93.16% in organ segmentation. In the challenging task of tumor segmentation on this dataset, our method achieved an average DSC of 15.92% and an average NSD of 8.16%.

4.5   Limitation and Future Work

The current method exhibits notable limitations in tumor segmentation, particularly in the identification of widely distributed and variably-sized abdominal tumors. In essence, the challenge of pan-cancer segmentation persists. Moreover, there is ample room for enhancing the model's efficiency. Despite the significant advantage in terms of model parameters, several areas can still be fine-tuned to further reduce inference time. Furthermore, there is a pressing need to explore novel semi-supervised learning approaches to fully exploit the potential of unlabeled data in tumor segmentation.

5   Conclusion

While our proposed method has demonstrated promising results in organ segmentation, it encounters substantial challenges in the realm of tumor segmentation. Surprisingly, the integration of unlabeled data had a detrimental impact on tumor segmentation. Furthermore, despite the minimal parameter count of our method, there is potential for further enhancement in segmentation efficiency across various aspects.

Acknowledgements. The authors of this paper declare that the segmentation method they implemented for participation in the FLARE 2023 challenge has not used any pre-trained models nor additional datasets other than those provided by the organizers. The proposed solution is fully automatic without any manual intervention. We thank all the data owners for making the CT scans publicly available and CodaLab [16] for hosting the challenge platform.

References

1. Bilic, P., et al.: The liver tumor segmentation benchmark (lits). Med. Image Anal. **84**, 102680 (2023)
2. Celaya, A., et al.: Pocketnet: a smaller neural network for medical image analysis. IEEE Trans. Med. Imaging **42**(4), 1172–1184 (2023)
3. Chen, X., Yuan, Y., Zeng, G., Wang, J.: Semi-supervised semantic segmentation with cross pseudo supervision. In: Proceedings of the IEEE/CVF Conference on Computer Vision and Pattern Recognition (CVPR), pp. 2613–2622 (2021)
4. Clark, K., et al.: The cancer imaging archive (TCIA): maintaining and operating a public information repository. J. Digit. Imaging **26**(6), 1045–1057 (2013)
5. He, R., Yang, J., Qi, X.: Re-distributing biased pseudo labels for semi-supervised semantic segmentation: A baseline investigation. In: Proceedings of the IEEE/CVF International Conference on Computer Vision (ICCV), pp. 6930–6940 (2021)
6. Heller, N., et al.: The state of the art in kidney and kidney tumor segmentation in contrast-enhanced CT imaging: results of the kits19 challenge. Med. Image Anal. **67**, 101821 (2021)
7. Heller, N., et al.: An international challenge to use artificial intelligence to define the state-of-the-art in kidney and kidney tumor segmentation in CT imaging. Proc. Am. Soc. Clin. Oncol. **38**(6), 626–626 (2020)
8. Huang, Z., et al.: Revisiting nnU-net for iterative pseudo labeling and efficient sliding window inference. In: Ma, J., Wang, B. (eds.) FLARE 2022. LNCS, vol. 13816, pp. 178–189. Springer, Cham (2022). https://doi.org/10.1007/978-3-031-23911-3_16
9. Isensee, F., Jaeger, P.F., Kohl, S.A., Petersen, J., Maier-Hein, K.H.: nnU-net: a self-configuring method for deep learning-based biomedical image segmentation. Nat. Methods **18**(2), 203–211 (2021)
10. Li, Y., Chen, J., Xie, X., Ma, K., Zheng, Y.: Self-loop uncertainty: a novel pseudo-label for semi-supervised medical image segmentation. In: Martel, A.L., et al. (eds.) MICCAI 2020 Part I. LNCS, vol. 12261, pp. 614–623. Springer, Cham (2020). https://doi.org/10.1007/978-3-030-59710-8_60
11. Ma, J., et al.: Loss odyssey in medical image segmentation. Med. Image Anal. **71**, 102035 (2021)

12. Ma, J., He, Y., Li, F., Han, L., You, C., Wang, B.: Segment anything in medical images. Nat. Commun. **15**, 654 (2024)
13. Ma, J., et al.: Fast and low-GPU-memory abdomen CT organ segmentation: the flare challenge. Med. Image Anal. **82**, 102616 (2022)
14. Ma, J., et al.: Unleashing the strengths of unlabeled data in pan-cancer abdominal organ quantification: the flare22 challenge. arXiv preprint arXiv:2308.05862 (2023)
15. Ma, J., et al.: Abdomenct-1k: Is abdominal organ segmentation a solved problem? IEEE Trans. Pattern Anal. Mach. Intell. **44**(10), 6695–6714 (2022)
16. Pavao, A., et al.: Codalab competitions: an open source platform to organize scientific challenges. J. Mach. Learn. Res. **24**(198), 1–6 (2023)
17. Simpson, A.L.,et al.: A large annotated medical image dataset for the development and evaluation of segmentation algorithms. arXiv preprint arXiv:1902.09063 (2019)
18. Wang, E., Zhao, Y., Wu, Y.: Cascade dual-decoders network for abdominal organs segmentation. In: Ma, J., Wang, B. (eds.) FLARE 2022. LNCS, vol. 13816, pp. 202–213. Springer, Cham (2022). https://doi.org/10.1007/978-3-031-23911-3_18
19. Yang, X., Song, Z., King, I., Xu, Z.: A survey on deep semi-supervised learning. IEEE Trans. Knowl. Data Eng. (2022)
20. Yushkevich, P.A., Gao, Y., Gerig, G.: Itk-snap: an interactive tool for semi-automatic segmentation of multi-modality biomedical images. In: Annual International Conference of the IEEE Engineering in Medicine and Biology Society, pp. 3342–3345 (2016)

A Lightweight nnU-Net Combined with Target Adaptive Loss for Organs and Tumors Segmentation

Tao Liu⬤, Xukun Zhang⬤, Minghao Han⬤, and Lihua Zhang$^{(\boxtimes)}$⬤

Fudan University, Shanghai 200082, China
lihuazhang@fudan.edu.cn

Abstract. Accurate and automated abdominal organs and tumors segmentation is of great importance in clinical practice. Due to the high time- and labor-consumption of manual annotating datasets, especially in the highly specialized medical domain, partially annotated datasets and unlabeled datasets are more common in practical applications, compared to fully labeled datasets. CNNs based methods have contributed to the development of medical image segmentation. However, previous CNN models were mostly trained on fully labeled datasets. So it is more vital to develop a method based on partially labeled datasets. In FLARE23, we design a model combining a lightweight nnU-Net and target adaptive loss (TAL) to obtain the segmentation results efficiently and make full use of partially labeled dataset. Our method achieved an average DSC score of 86.40% and 19.41% for the organs and lesions on the validation set and the average running time and area under GPU memory-time cure are 25.34 s and 23018 MB, respectively.

Keywords: abdominal organs and tumors segmentation · lightweight nnU-Net · target adaptive loss

1 Introduction

A precise pixel-level understanding of abdominal anatomy image is of vital importance for computer-aided clinical practice such as disease diagnosis, surgery navigation, radiation therapy and so on. Specifically, accurate abdominal organs and lesions segmentation plays a fundamental role in supporting clinical workflows, including diagnostic interventions and treatment planning, which can be essential steps for preoperative diagnosis.

Thanks to the significant development of deep learning, many abdominal organ segmentation methods have been designed based on deep CNNs, such as nn-UNet and 3D-UNet, which achieve great performance on different abdominal organ datasets. However, most models typically require all organs of interest to be annotated. But, it is unrealistic to get a dataset with all organs annotated because of the time- and labor-consuming labeling process. Hence, it is still an

J. Ma and B. Wang (Eds.): FLARE 2023, LNCS 14544, pp. 168–178, 2024.
https://doi.org/10.1007/978-3-031-58776-4_14

important task to segment multi-organs based on a partially labeled dataset. Currently, there exist also numerous studies dedicated to solving the problem of abdominal organ and tumor segmentation. But these methods all have a common limitation, which is that the models they developed are limited to the segmentation of a certain organ and its lesions. When it comes to migrating these models to another organ segmentation task, it does not work. There are still no general models for universal abdominal organ and tumor segmentation at present. As a result, it remains a challenging task to segment multi-organs and all tumors with one model.

FLARE2023 is a competition which aims to promote the development of universal organ and tumor segmentation in abdominal CT scans. The competition organizer provided a training set including 4000 3D CT scans from over 30 medical centers, of which 2200 cases are partial labeled and 1800 cases don't have labels, and a validation set including 100 cases. In addition to precise segmentation of the 13 abdominal organs, the algorithm provided by the contestants also requires the recognition and segmentation of all the tumors on different organs in abdominal CT images, which is a challenging task. This is the first challenge which focuses on pan-cancer segmentation in CT scans. In addition, the competition also imposes limitations on inference speed, memory, and GPU consumption. Each test sample needs to spend less than 28 GB of memory within 60 s of prediction time to obtain inference result. And the peak GPU memory overhead should preferably be below 4 GB, which further increases the difficulty of the competition.

We extensively investigated image segmentation methods based on partially annotated datasets, especially in medical domain. During the past several years, many studies have been devoted to solving the problem of abdominal multi-organ segmentation in partially annotated datasets, but this problem remains challenging. A straightforward strategy is to train as many networks as partially labeled datasets, but suffers from several shortcomings including: (1) less training data for each single network, (2) longer inference time and longer training time.

Also, much more attention have been paid on training one model with several partially labeled datasets. Intuitively speaking, this strategy has many advantages, including but not limited to fully utilizing different datasets to improve robustness of model. The methods can be generally grouped into two categories. The first category is to design new network to handle this problem. Chen et al. [2] designed a network with a task-shared encoder and as many task-specific decoders as partially labeled datasets. But this kind of network has been proven to be memory-consuming. Zhang et al. [21] proposed a dynamic on-demand network (DoDNet) by catenating a one-hot vector of equal length to the number of organs with the features of images as task-specific prompt to generate weights for dynamic convolution filters. The second type of methods attempt to design adaptive loss functions that can be directly applied to partially labeled data. Fang et al. [4] proposed a target adaptive loss (TAL) to train a network on several partially labeled datasets by treating the organs with unknown labels as background. Additionally, Shi et al. [17] merged unlabeled organs with the background by imposing an constraint on each voxel of images and then propose a marginal and exclusive loss to train a model based on a fully labeled dataset and several partially labeled datasets. Furthermore, Liu et al. [11] studied the existing approaches and identified three distinct types of supervision signals, including two signals derived from the ground truth and one from pseudo label and then they proposed a training framework called COSST, which combined comprehensive supervision signals and self-training with pseudo labels, which has been demonstrated consistent great performance.

After reviewing existing methods for abdominal multi-organ segmentation based on partially labeled datasets, inspired by Fang et al., we plan to follow their design in their work, treating unlabeled organs as background and using the target adaptive loss (TAL) function proposed in [4]. Specifically, we merge the output channels of unlabeled organs and the original background channel into a new one. The reason for doing this is because there are always unlabeled organs in most images of the FLARE23 dataset, resulting in the inapplicability of common segmentation losses, such as dice loss. By utilizing the TAL loss, the problem can be effectively handled. What's more, due to the official requirements for segmentation efficiency and memory consumption in the competition, existing default CNNs or transformers are not competent for this task. We retrospected the top methods in FLARE22 and FLARE21, and we found that the lightweight nnU-Net designed by the top method [9] in FLARE22 achieved remarkable efficiency without significantly reducing segmentation performance. Hence, we attempt to extend the lightweight nnU-Net proposed in FLARE22 with the target adaptive loss, to handle the segmentation of the partially labeled dataset in an efficient and effective manner.

All in all, our proposed method can be summarized as combining the lightweight nnU-Net with target adaptive loss function to achieve efficient and accurate segmentation. We will provide a detailed introduction to our proposed method in the following section.

2   Method

In this section, we will give a detailed description of our proposed method. As illustrated in Fig. 1, our proposed method is mainly based on a lightweight nnU-Net and a target adaptive loss, which is used to handle with the partially labeled dataset.

2.1   Preprocessing

It is vital to perform data preprocessing before training. In our proposed scheme, data preprocessing can be divided into five parts, which is:

(1) Statistical analysis: We conducted statistical analysis on the distribution of labels in the dataset and concluded that tumor labels are distributed across different organs and are unevenly distributed, making tumor segmentation tasks very difficult.

(2) Make sure the geometry of label file match with the geometry of image file. Some cases in the dataset doesn't meet this requirement, which will influence the subsequent operation.
(3) Cropping: Cropping out voxels with a value of zero in the image, which don't have useful information and don't affect the subsequent learning process. Instead, it can significantly reduce the image size and computational complexity.
(4) Resampling: Resampling is a crucial step to avoid the problem of inconsistent actual spatial sizes represented by individual voxels in different images. By default setting of nnU-Net, in anisotropic datasets, for dimension with particularly large spacing, take the 10% quantile of the spacing of that dimension in the dataset as the actual spatial size for that dimension.
(5) Normalization: The purpose of normalization is to ensure that the grayscale values of each image in the training set have the same distribution. The normalization operation in our method is the same as what standard nnU-Net does.

2.2   Proposed Method

Figure 1 shows the framework of our proposed method. As illustrated in Fig. 1, our proposed method mainly composes of two parts, a lightweight nnU-Net and a target adaptive loss (TAL), of which, the lightweight nnU-Net is adapted from the top method in FLARE22 and the TAL is used for training with partial labels.

Specifically, the lightweight nnU-Net is modified based on the default nnU-Net to improve inference speed and reduce resource consumption, and the main focus is to change channels in the first stage into 16, and change convolution number per stage into 2. Additionally, it performs downsampling only twice during inference stage, and the input patch size is reduced, the input spacing is increased to obtain a low resolution of image. We don't apply any extra strategy to improve inference speed and reduce resource consumption, except for following what the top method [9] did to their small nnU-Net.

Furthermore, the target adaptive loss we use can be formulated as follow:

$$L_{TAL} = \sum_{c \in B} y_v^c \log \hat{y_v^c} + \mathbf{1}_{[\sum_{c \in B} y_v^c = 0]} \log(1 - \sum_{c \in B} \hat{y_v^c})$$

where B denotes the organs labeled in the dataset, $\hat{y_v^c}$ is the predicted probability of voxel v labeled as class c and y_v^c is from ground truth, which indicates whether voxel v labeled as class c or not.

We treat the unlabeled organs in images as background by merging the output channels of unlabeled organs and original background channel into a new one. And then the network can be trained with supervision by TAL.

We used the pseudo labels of the 1800 unlabeled images, generated by the FLARE22 winning algorithm [9].

2.3   Post-processing

We didn't use any post-processing in our method.

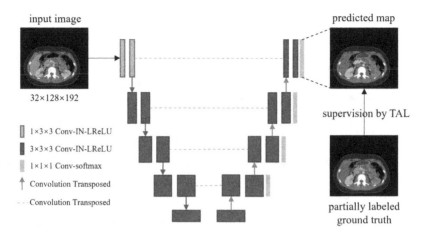

Fig. 1. Network architecture, which includes a lightweight nnU-Net to segment images efficiently and TAL to train model based on partially labeled dataset.

3   Experiments

3.1   Dataset and Evaluation Measures

The FLARE 2023 challenge is an extension of the FLARE 2021–2022 [13,14], aiming to aim to promote the development of foundation models in abdominal disease analysis. The segmentation targets cover 13 organs and various abdominal lesions. The training dataset is curated from more than 30 medical centers under the license permission, including TCIA [3], LiTS [1], MSD [18], KiTS [7,8], autoPET [5,6], TotalSegmentator [19], and AbdomenCT-1K [15]. The training set includes 4000 abdomen CT scans where 2200 CT scans with partial labels and 1800 CT scans without labels. The validation and testing sets include 100 and 400 CT scans, respectively, which cover various abdominal cancer types, such as liver cancer, kidney cancer, pancreas cancer, colon cancer, gastric cancer, and so on. The organ annotation process used ITK-SNAP [20], nnU-Net [10], and MedSAM [12].

The evaluation metrics encompass two accuracy measures-Dice Similarity Coefficient (DSC) and Normalized Surface Dice (NSD)-alongside two efficiency measures-running time and area under the GPU memory-time curve. These metrics collectively contribute to the ranking computation. Furthermore, the running time and GPU memory consumption are considered within tolerances of 15 s and 4 GB, respectively.

3.2   Implementation Details

Environment Settings. The development environments and requirements are presented in Table 1.

Table 1. Development environments and requirements.

System	Ubuntu 20.04.1 LTS
CPU	Intel(R) Xeon(R) CPU E5-2680 v4 @ 2.40 GHz
RAM	4 × 32 GB; 2400MT/s
GPU (number and type)	Two NVIDIA Quadro RTX 8000 48G
CUDA version	12.0
Programming language	Python 3.7
Deep learning framework	torch 1.12.0, torchvision 0.13.0
Specific dependencies	None
Code	

Training Protocols. We used the pseudo labels of the 1800 unlabeled images, generated by the FLARE22 winning algorithm [9]. As for the partial labels, We treated the unlabeled organs in images as background by merging the output channels of unlabeled organs and original background channel into a new one. Furthermore, we applied the same data augmentation, patch sampling strategy and optimal model selection criteria as the default settings of nnU-Net.

Table 2. Training protocols.

Network initialization	
Batch size	2
Patch size	32 × 128 × 192
Total epochs	1500
Optimizer	SGD
Initial learning rate (lr)	0.01
Lr decay schedule	$(1 - epoch/1000)^{0.9}$
Training time	36 h
Loss function	TAL (detailed in Sect. 2.2)
Number of model parameters	5.64M [a]
Number of flops	8.13G [b]
CO_2eq	5.3 Kg [c]

[a] https://github.com/sksq96/pytorch-summary
[b] https://github.com/facebookresearch/fvcore
[c] https://github.com/lfwa/carbontracker/

4 Results and Discussion

4.1 Quantitative Results on Validation Set

The Dice and NSD scores of organs and tumors on the validation set is given in Table 3.

Table 3. Quantitative evaluation results.

Target	Public Validation		Online Validation		Testing	
	DSC (%)	NSD (%)	DSC (%)	NSD (%)	DSC (%)	NSD (%)
Liver	95.59 ± 6.67	90.31 ± 8.44	95.87	96.51	94.03	94.50
Right Kidney	91.25 ± 10.14	88.74 ± 10.13	90.41	91.93	93.36	94.60
Spleen	95.68 ± 3.71	94.70 ± 6.32	95.62	96.96	95.37	96.96
Pancreas	83.57 ± 7.76	80.23 ± 11.67	82.13	94.21	86.13	95.39
Aorta	92.78 ± 5.08	91.27 ± 8.07	94.19	96.96	91.62	95.19
Inferior vena cava	89.33 ± 6.68	83.14 ± 9.38	89.99	91.75	86.68	89.25
Right adrenal gland	82.36 ± 3.50	93.16 ± 3.90	80.97	94.04	76.45	89.20
Left adrenal gland	79.58 ± 9.55	89.94 ± 10.07	79.16	91.27	76.72	88.45
Gallbladder	83.47 ± 13.53	83.47 ± 13.53	78.99	78.26	76.09	77.53
Esophagus	75.82 ± 17.90	77.64 ± 16.59	79.04	90.48	84.27	94.60
Stomach	89.23 ± 9.50	83.12 ± 15.55	88.78	92.23	84.53	87.90
Duodenum	77.51 ± 10.38	73.11 ± 11.33	77.36	91.75	78.39	91.77
Left kidney	89.68 ± 14.61	87.21 ± 15.70	90.69	91.88	94.16	95.63
Tumor	23.36 ± 25.43	18.83 ± 21.51	19.41	12.25	25.03	15.14
Average	82.09 ± 17.42	81.06 ± 11.59	81.62	86.46	81.63	86.18

We have done ablation studies to analyze the effect of unlabeled data. We trained another same network as mentioned above, but we only used labeled data to train this network. We divided 2200 labeled data into two equal parts, with the first 50% using official labels provided by the competition and the last 50% using pseudo labels generated by the FLARE22 winning algorithm [9]. Not surprisingly, the network model using unlabeled data performs better than the one that doesn't use. Network trained with both labeled and unlabeled data is exposed to more data during the training phase, result in stronger generalization ability. The validation results of the model trained without unlabeled data are given in Table 4.

4.2   Qualitative Results on Validation Set

Figure 2 shows four examples of segmentation results in the validation set, with two good ones and two bad ones. It can be easily seen that our method outperforms out ablation study results, which is due to the better generalization of model trained with more data. Case 0007 performed well in tumor segmentation tasks, but poorly in organ segmentation tasks. Our analysis suggests that the model may have focused more on tumors but neglected organs, and in this example, the tumor is completely located on the surface of the liver, making it difficult for the model to recognize the liver. Furthermore, we think the reason why case 0035 performed badly is that tumors spread all over left kidney, which is a hard case, causing the model to be unable to recognize left kidney and tumor. As for the two good ones, we think it may be because the position of the tumor is easier to recognize and the image is clearer.

Table 4. Quantitative evaluation results of the model trained without unlabeled data.

Target	Public Validation		Online Validation	
	DSC (%)	NSD (%)	DSC (%)	NSD (%)
Liver	95.62 ± 2.32	87.53 ± 7.79	95.71	94.21
Right Kidney	91.64 ± 7.42	86.56 ± 10.75	89.93	89.99
Spleen	90.01 ± 11.75	86.46 ± 11.41	89.07	87.38
Pancreas	80.75 ± 6.11	75.89 ± 11.14	78.74	90.38
Aorta	91.19 ± 6.41	86.65 ± 10.95	93.10	95.77
Inferior vena cava	85.28 ± 6.67	74.10 ± 9.62	87.86	88.84
Right adrenal gland	77.26 ± 6.15	87.09 ± 6.49	75.28	88.97
Left adrenal gland	72.97 ± 12.22	89.94 ± 10.07	71.41	84.42
Gallbladder	77.52 ± 19.74	74.22 ± 21.76	73.76	71.39
Esophagus	71.32 ± 17.38	71.31 ± 15.57	74.86	86.97
Stomach	86.01 ± 10.75	76.32 ± 17.93	85.69	87.01
Duodenum	68.93 ± 11.93	61.00 ± 13.61	69.55	88.03
Left kidney	84.45 ± 20.49	79.58 ± 18.90	85.51	85.07
Tumor	12.49 ± 18.64	11.51 ± 15.44	11.83	6.69
Average	77.53 ± 11.28	74.87 ± 12.96	77.30	81.79

Table 5. Quantitative evaluation of segmentation efficiency in terms of the running them and GPU memory consumption.

Case ID	Image Size	Running Time (s)	Max GPU (MB)	Total GPU (MB)
0001	(512, 512, 55)	23.46	1694	17257
0051	(512, 512, 100)	19.13	1978	17698
0017	(512, 512, 150)	35.94	2562	28826
0019	(512, 512, 215)	23.33	1694	21224
0099	(512, 512, 334)	29.93	2564	26540
0063	(512, 512, 448)	37.86	1694	33508
0048	(512, 512, 499)	41.66	1978	37977
0029	(512, 512, 554)	52.81	1694	46037

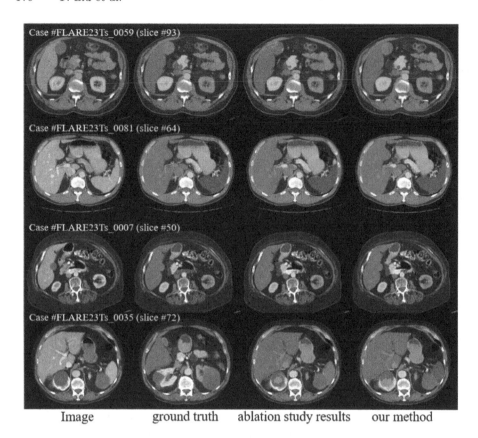

| Image | ground truth | ablation study results | our method |

Fig. 2. The top two lines are good results, while the bottom two lines are bad results. Only labeled data are used in the ablation study.

4.3 Segmentation Efficiency Results on Validation Set

The segmentation efficiency results of eight cases in the validation set under the hardware environment provided by the organizer are shown in Table 5. Also, we calculated the average segmentation efficiency of all the cases, with the mean running time of 25.34 s, the mean max GPU memory of 2317 MB and the mean total GPU memory of 23018 MB. This is actually a good memory and time consumption, which can be attributed to the lower computational complexity of lightweight nnU-Net.

4.4 Results on Final Testing Set

The results on the final testing set are given in Table 3.

4.5 Limitation and Future Work

As you can see, the evaluation metrics of our method are not very high, especially in tumor segmentation scenarios. The reason for this may be that we have not fully utilized unlabeled data and have not fully utilized tumor information in unlabeled data. In the future, we will further study segmentation based on partially labeled datasets on this basis.

5 Conclusion

In FLARE23 contest, we designed a model combining a lightweight nnU-Net and target adaptive loss, to segment all the organs and tumors in CT volumes and get a model trained based on the partially labeled dataset. Although the results we obtain are not that satisfying, this is the foundation of our future work and inspire us to pay more attention to making full use of unlabeled data and partially labeled dataset.

Acknowledgements. This project was funded by the National Natural Science Foundation of China 82090052. The authors of this paper declare that the segmentation method they implemented for participation in the FLARE 2023 challenge has not used any pre-trained models nor additional datasets other than those provided by the organizers. The proposed solution is fully automatic without any manual intervention. We thank all the data owners for making the CT scans publicly available and CodaLab [16] for hosting the challenge platform.

References

1. Bilic, P., et al.: The liver tumor segmentation benchmark (lits). Med. Image Anal. **84**, 102680 (2023)
2. Chen, S., Ma, K., Zheng, Y.: Med3d: transfer learning for 3d medical image analysis. arXiv preprint arXiv:1904.00625 (2019)
3. Clark, K., et al.: The cancer imaging archive (TCIA): maintaining and operating a public information repository. J. Digit. Imaging **26**(6), 1045–1057 (2013)
4. Fang, X., Yan, P.: Multi-organ segmentation over partially labeled datasets with multi-scale feature abstraction. IEEE Trans. Med. Imaging **39**(11), 3619–3629 (2020)
5. Gatidis, S., et al.: The autoPET challenge: towards fully automated lesion segmentation in oncologic PET/CT imaging. preprint at Research Square (Nature Portfolio) (2023). https://doi.org/10.21203/rs.3.rs-2572595/v1
6. Gatidis, S., et al.: A whole-body FDG-PET/CT dataset with manually annotated tumor lesions. Sci. Data **9**(1), 601 (2022)
7. Heller, N., et al.: The state of the art in kidney and kidney tumor segmentation in contrast-enhanced CT imaging: results of the kits19 challenge. Med. Image Anal. **67**, 101821 (2021)
8. Heller, N., et al.: An international challenge to use artificial intelligence to define the state-of-the-art in kidney and kidney tumor segmentation in ct imaging. Proc. Am. Soc. Clin. Oncol. **38**(6), 626–626 (2020)

9. Huang, Z., et al.: Revisiting nnU-Net for iterative pseudo labeling and efficient sliding window inference. In: Ma, J., Wang, B. (eds.) FLARE 2022. LNCS, vol. 13816, pp. 178–189. Springer, Cham (2022). https://doi.org/10.1007/978-3-031-23911-3_16

10. Isensee, F., Jaeger, P.F., Kohl, S.A., Petersen, J., Maier-Hein, K.H.: nnU-Net: a self-configuring method for deep learning-based biomedical image segmentation. Nat. Methods **18**(2), 203–211 (2021)

11. Liu, H., et al.: Cosst: Multi-organ segmentation with partially labeled datasets using comprehensive supervisions and self-training. IEEE Trans. Med. Imaging (2024)

12. Ma, J., He, Y., Li, F., Han, L., You, C., Wang, B.: Segment anything in medical images. Nat. Commun. **15**(1), 654 (2024)

13. Ma, J., et al.: Fast and low-GPU-memory abdomen CT organ segmentation: the flare challenge. Med. Image Anal. **82**, 102616 (2022)

14. Ma, J., et al.: Unleashing the strengths of unlabeled data in pan-cancer abdominal organ quantification: the flare22 challenge. arXiv preprint arXiv:2308.05862 (2023)

15. Ma, J., et al.: Abdomenct-1k: Is abdominal organ segmentation a solved problem? IEEE Trans. Pattern Anal. Mach. Intell. **44**(10), 6695–6714 (2022)

16. Pavao, A., et al.: Codalab competitions: an open source platform to organize scientific challenges. J. Mach. Learn. Res. **24**(198), 1–6 (2023)

17. Shi, G., Xiao, L., Chen, Y., Zhou, S.K.: Marginal loss and exclusion loss for partially supervised multi-organ segmentation. Med. Image Anal. **70**, 101979 (2021)

18. Simpson, A.L., et al.: A large annotated medical image dataset for the development and evaluation of segmentation algorithms. arXiv preprint arXiv:1902.09063 (2019)

19. Wasserthal, J., et al.: Totalsegmentator: robust segmentation of 104 anatomic structures in CT images. Radiol. Artif. Intell. **5**(5), e230024 (2023)

20. Yushkevich, P.A., Gao, Y., Gerig, G.: Itk-snap: an interactive tool for semi-automatic segmentation of multi-modality biomedical images. In: Annual International Conference of the IEEE Engineering in Medicine and Biology Society, pp. 3342–3345 (2016)

21. Zhang, J., Xie, Y., Xia, Y., Shen, C.: Dodnet: learning to segment multi-organ and tumors from multiple partially labeled datasets. In: Proceedings of the IEEE/CVF Conference on Computer Vision and Pattern Recognition, pp. 1195–1204 (2021)

AdaptNet: Adaptive Learning from Partially Labeled Data for Abdomen Multi-organ and Tumor Segmentation

JiChao Luo[1,2], Zhihong Chen[1,2], Wenbin Liu[1], Zaiyi Liu[2,4],
Bingjiang Qiu[2,3,4(✉)], and Gang Fang[1(✉)]

[1] Institute of Computing Science and Technology, Guangzhou University,
Guangzhou 510006, China
gangf@gzhu.edu.cn
[2] Department of Radiology, Guangdong Provincial People's Hospital
(Guangdong Academy of Medical Sciences), Southern Medical University,
Guangzhou 510080, China
[3] Guangdong Provincial People's Hospital, Guangdong Academy of Sciences,
Guangdong Cardiovascular Institute, Guangzhou 510080, China
[4] Guangdong Provincial Key Laboratory of Artificial Intelligence in Medical Image
Analysis and Application, Guangzhou 510080, China
qiubingjiang@gdph.org.cn

Abstract. Due to the high costs associated with the labor and expertise required for annotating 3D medical images at the voxel level, most public and in-house datasets only include annotations of a single (or a few) organ or tumor. This limitation results in what is commonly referred to as the 'partial labeling/annotation problem'. In order to tackle this issue, we introduce an adaptive learning network, AdaptNet, to effectively segment multiple organs and tumors within partially labeled data from abdomen CT images. AdaptNet comprises three key components: a segmentation network, a pseudo-label generation network, and an adaptive controller responsible for generating dynamic weights. AdaptNet generates adaptive weights dynamically through the controller, which takes into account the balance of the partial labels and the corresponding pseudo-labels. This approach enables AdaptNet to efficiently and flexibly learn multiple organ and tumor information from the partial labeling/annotation dataset, which is typically performed by multiple or multi-head networks. We conduct validation on a large-scale partially annotated dataset under MICCAI FLARE 2023 challenge and demonstrate that the proposed AdaptNet outperforms the baseline method across the 13 different organ and tumor segmentation tasks. Our method achieves a mean organ Dice Similarity Coefficient (DSC) of 89.61% and a Normalized Surface Dice (NSD) of 94.94%, and a tumor DSC and NSD of 39.16% and 30.52% on the FLARE 2023 online validation. Additionally, in the Final Testing dataset, our method achieves a mean organ DSC and NSD of 89.34% and 95.26% and a tumor DSC and NSD of 54.59% and 40.78%, and the area under GPU memory-time curve is 33.35 s and 84276 MB. The code is available at https://github.com/Prech-start/FLARE23_AdaptNet.

© The Author(s), under exclusive license to Springer Nature Switzerland AG 2024
J. Ma and B. Wang (Eds.): FLARE 2023, LNCS 14544, pp. 179–193, 2024.
https://doi.org/10.1007/978-3-031-58776-4_15

Keywords: Adaptive learning · partial labeling/annotation · Abdomen organ segmentation

1 Introduction

Abdominal organs are quite common cancer sites, such as colon and rectum cancer, and pancreas cancer, which are the 2nd and 3rd most common cause of cancer death [20]. Computed tomography (CT) provides doctors with valuable prognostic information. During the diagnosis process, the doctor evaluates the lesion or organ by manual annotation in two dimensions plane on the CT, which leads to a tedious procedure in the clinical practice. Moreover, the structural complexity of abdominal organs and their cancers make the annotation process challenging [12]. Currently, there are many high-quality publicly available tumor datasets, such as liver cancer segmentation [2], lung nodule segmentation [1], etc. However, they are all for one single type of tumor. In terms of organ segmentation, several multi-organ segmentation datasets with all the organ labels have been released, e.g., BTCV [14], AMOS [11], etc. However, this kind of dataset with all organs or tumors annotated is almost unachievable in real clinical workflow. Utilizing these datasets inevitably creates partial labeling/annotation problems. Furthermore, there is still no general and publicly available dataset with 'partial labeling/annotation problems' for universal abdominal organs and pan-cancer segmentation nowadays. FLARE2023 challenge, an extension of FLARE2021 and FLARE2022 challenges, provides such an opportunity, which aims to promote the development of universal organ and tumor segmentation in abdominal CT scans. FLARE2023 showcases a rich variety of tumor types and a combination of multiple different organ annotations, as shown in Fig. 1. This imbalanced labeling could potentially lead to the failure of the segmentation methods.

Formerly, researchers have proposed some traditional segmentation methods gray-level based methods [13], Live wire segmentation approaches [22], and mathematical fitting procedure [4] for segmentation tasks which are more efficiently than manual segmentation methods. However, the traditional methods need manual design features. Compared with the traditional methods, Deep Learning (DL) methods demonstrate enhanced accuracy and much better generalization capacity. In recent years, regardless of various works based on fully supervision learning method [15] achieve State-of-the-Art (SOTA) performance in single data centers, many of which are small and single data center [19]. Furthermore, most of the SOTA methods cannot be easily verified and generalized in other datasets with imbalanced annotations.

To address the problem, this study intends to use the core concept of semi-supervised learning to effectively use unlabeled organ samples to improve model performance. Semi-supervised learning potentially learns wrong information from incorrect pseudo-labels, which would lead to performance degradation. Normally, selecting high-confidence predictions can fix the problem of performance degradation. However, this way would exclude a large amount of unlabeled data from the training process, resulting in insufficient model training.

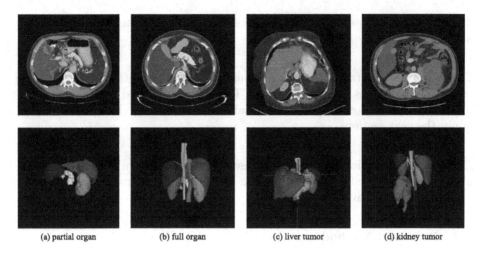

(a) partial organ   (b) full organ   (c) liver tumor   (d) kidney tumor

Fig. 1. Samples of imbalanced annotations in FLARE2023. Partial organ annotations are observed in some cases, as depicted in case (a). In other cases, all organs are annotated, but tumors are absent, as shown in case (b). There are also cases with annotations covering both tumors and organs, as demonstrated in cases (c) and (d).

Furthermore, this way leads to the low-quality pseudo-labels not being utilized in training. Therefore, based on that, we propose an adaptive learning segmentation method to efficiently utilize and learn pseudo-labels.

In this paper, we propose an automatic segmentation method, AdaptNet, for abdominal organs and cancers based on FLARE2023 dataset with imbalanced partial labeling. The proposed framework AdaptNet mainly contains three components: a pseudo-label generation network that creates the class-wise annotations which not exist in the true labels, a controller responsible for generating dynamic weights, and a segmentation network that segments lesions and organs based on adaptive weights generated by dynamic weights controller. The main contributions of this work are summarized as follows: (1) Through the proposed AdaptNet, pseudo-labels have been effectively utilized and learned, which introduces the unlabeled organ information, while also avoiding the misleading from incorrect pseudo-labels. (2) To balance the pseudo-labels and the original label, dynamic weights are generated automatically by a controller. (3) To mitigate the misleading of incorrect pseudo-labels, an adaptive loss approach is employed to train the segmentation model. Experiments show the effectiveness of the proposed AdaptNet for the partial labeling problem.

2   Method

2.1   Preprocessing

Resample and Normalization. We resample the pixel spacing to (2.2838, 1.8709, 1.8709) for all cases, and clip the pixel value based on the Hounsfield units to $[-160, 240]$, and normalize all the cases in $[0, 1]$ to ensure data stability and consistency.

Cropping the Data. To reduce redundant or irrelevant information and save computing resources, all the original CT matrix is cropped according to the foreground markers generated by original labels and pseudo-labels (the details are in the next section).

Data Augmentation. In order to prevent the model from over-fitting, data augmentation is used in this study. The augmentation approaches of nnU-Net methodology [10] have been utilized.

2.2   Proposed Method

Specifically, the proposed AdaptNet contains a pseudo-label generator network which is followed by a label filling module, a baseline network which is to make a segmentation prediction, and a dynamic weights controller which is mainly made up of an adaptive weight calculation (AWC) module, as shown in Fig. 2.

Pseudo-Label Generator. Pseudo-labels contain valuable information about the location and boundary of target organs and tumors during training, which enhances the model's discriminative ability. By incorporating pseudo-labels, pseudo-label generator arguments the datasets and promotes the model to learn more boundary information from unlabeled organs in true labels. Here, we apply the segmentation network from [9] as the pseudo-label generator network, which has achieved remarkable results in the FLARE2022 challenge.

Segmentation Network. The baseline network is built upon nnU-Net [10], utilizing parameters generated using the nnU-Net methodology.

Label Filling Module. To incorporate pseudo-labels into the true labels, Label Filling Module is used after pseudo-labels were generated. The details are illustrated in Fig. 2. In general, the Label Filling Module can be expressed in the following equation:

$$ML = R(PL, U_{TL} \cap U_{PL}, 0) + TL \tag{1}$$

where the U_{TL} and U_{PL} denote the list of classes for true label (TL) and pseudo-label (PL). The expression $R(S, I, 0)$ signifies the substitution of the intersection I with the value 0 within the set S, and then combining TL and PL to form a mixed-label (ML).

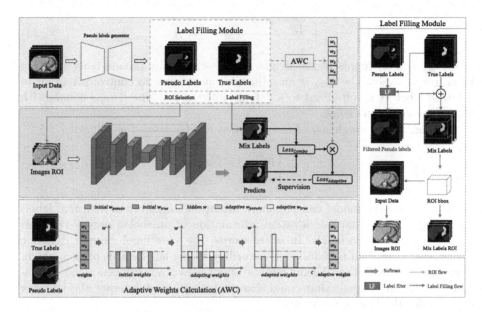

Fig. 2. Overview of our proposed AdaptNet. Green block: Generate the mix label and ROI bounding box by Label Filling Module, and weight of adaptive loss calculation by AWC. Pink block: Baseline segmentation network. Blue block: Adaptive weight calculation (AWC) module: calculate the weight according to the unique object class between the pseudo-label and the true label. Yellow Block: Label Filling Module filters the interfering information and combines the pseudo-label and true label into a mix-label. (Color figure online)

Adaptive Weight Calculation. Considering the potentially misleading effects of pseudo-labels during training, we introduce an adaptive loss to impose constraints. The main idea of adaptive loss is to automatically weaken learning efficiency from pseudo-labels while amplifying the guiding capability of true labels during training. For the purpose of this paper, we define symbol C_O as $[1, class\_count]$, where the $class\_count$ means the total class counts for the segmentation task, and suppose C_{pseudo} represents the unique indexes collection of pseudo-label. Its definition is

$$C_{pseudo} = \{c_i \mid c_i \in C_O, c_i \text{ is pseudo label}\},$$

where i is the i-th class index. Then, indexes collection of true label C_{true} is

$$C_{true} = \{c_i \mid c_i \in C_O, c_i \text{ is true label}\}.$$

Then, the updated steps of loss weight for each target class are as follows:

$$w_i^o = \frac{1}{class\_count}, i \in C_O, \qquad (2)$$

$$w_i^p = \xi_{ada} * w_i^o, i \in C_{pseudo}, \qquad (3)$$

$$w_i^t = w_i^o + \frac{\sum^{c \in C_{pseudo}}(w_c^o - w_c^p)}{|C_{true}|}, i \in C_{true}, \tag{4}$$

where w_i^p and w_i^t represent the weight of the i-th class in pseudo-label and true label, respectively. The ξ_{ada} is an adjustable parameter to control attention to the true label. It is initialized to a default value of 0.5. The $|C_{true}|$ equals with class number in true label.

In general, the weight w_i of the i-th class can be defined as follows:

$$w_i = \begin{cases} w_i^p, & i \in C_{pseudo} \\ w_i^t, & i \in C_{true} \end{cases} \tag{5}$$

In this way, the model can pay more attention to the organ with real labels and also learn the shape or location information of unlabeled organs via their corresponding pseudo-labels. In other words, the true label gains a dynamic higher loss score than pseudo-labels according to the label status of each patch. Therefore, the Adaptive Weight module suppresses gradients generated by features in the filled labels that could disrupt training and enhance the learning capacity for the true annotations.

Then, we combine the adaptive weight and *ComboLoss* function which is combined with *DiceLoss* and *CELoss*. The *ComboLoss* converges considerably faster than cross-entropy loss during training [24]. It is defined as:

$$L_{CE}(y, \hat{y}, w) = \sum_i^{C_O} w_i(-\frac{1}{N}\sum_{j=1}^{N} y_j^i log(\hat{y}_j^i) + (1 - y_j^i)log(1 - \hat{y}_j^i)), \tag{6}$$

$$L_{Dice}(y, \hat{y}, w) = \sum_i^{C_O} w_i(1 - \frac{2\sum_{j=1}^{N} y_j^i \hat{y}_j^i}{\sum_{j=1}^{N} y_j^i + \hat{y}_j^i}), \tag{7}$$

$$loss(y, \hat{y}, w) = \alpha_{ce} * L_{CE}(y, \hat{y}, w) + \alpha_{dc} * L_{Dice}(y, \hat{y}, w), \tag{8}$$

where the y_j^i and $\hat{y}_j^i$ mean the ground truth and the predicted probability of pixel j, respectively, and N is the number of pixels. α_{ce} and α_{dc} are the hyper-parameters to balance the contribution of *DiceLoss* and *CELoss*. α_{ce} and α_{dc} are set to 0.5 in this study.

Training Strategies. One of the obstacles to training 3D networks is the problem of "insufficient memory". A common solution is to train a 3D network from smaller sub-volumes (3D patches) and test it by sliding window. We set the step of the sliding window and use multithreaded preprocessing of CT image to reduce our inference time. The shape of the sliding window is consistent with the patch as shown in Table 3. Here, to reduce the inference time, the length of the step is $[5/6, 7/8, 9/10]$ times the window width for each axis instead of the default parameter $[1/2, 1/2, 1/2]$ of nnU-Net. Consequently, the inference time significantly decreases, e.g., from 72 s to 48 s for case 0048 in the environment of this study.

2.3   Post-processing

In the post-processing stage, we employ a connected component-based method after the segmentation prediction. Particularly in organ image segmentation, it helps remove the disconnected voxels, consequently, reducing false positives. In the study, the largest connected component of each segmented organ volume is simply selected.

3   Experiments

3.1   Dataset and Evaluation Measures

The FLARE 2023 challenge is an extension of the FLARE 2021–2022 [17] [18], aiming to promote the development of foundation models in abdominal disease analysis. The segmentation targets cover 13 organs (liver, spleen, pancreas, right kidney (RK), left kidney (LK), stomach, gallbladder, esophagus, aorta, inferior vena cava (IVC), right adrenal gland (RAG), left adrenal gland (LAG), and duodenum) and various abdominal lesions, which cover various abdominal cancer types, such as liver cancer, kidney cancer, pancreas cancer, colon cancer, gastric cancer, and so on. The organ annotation process used ITK-SNAP [26], nnU-Net [10], and MedSAM [16]. The training dataset is curated from more than 30 medical centers under the license permission, including TCIA [3], LiTS [2], MSD [23], KiTS [7,8], autoPET [5,6], TotalSegmentator [25], and AbdomenCT-1K [19]. The training set includes 4000 abdomen CT scans where 2200 CT scans with partial labels and 1800 CT scans without labels. The validation and testing sets include 100 and 400 CT scans. In this study, unlabeled images were not used. Only 2200 scans with partial labels have been used due to the computational resource limitation, and the 1800 unlabled images are not used. The frequency statistics about the 2200 cases regarding organ and tumor annotations are provided in Table 1. 5-fold cross-validation has been performed, in which 1760 cases are chosen as the training dataset, and the rest 440 cases are as the internal validation dataset in each fold.

Table 1. Organ annotation occurrence frequency(%) summary

Target	Liver	RK	Spleen	Pancreas	Aorta	IVC	RAG
Frequency	59.6	59.1	59.4	59.6	11.3	11.3	11.3

Target	LAG	Gallbladder	Esophagus	Stomach	Duodenum	LK	Tumor
Frequency	11.2	10.2	11.3	11.3	11.3	59.0	68.0

The evaluation metrics encompass two accuracy measures-Dice Similarity Coefficient (DSC) and Normalized Surface Dice (NSD)-alongside two efficiency measures-running time and area under the GPU memory-time curve. These metrics collectively contribute to the ranking computation. Furthermore, the running time and GPU memory consumption are considered within tolerances of 15 s and 4 GB, respectively.

3.2   Implementation Details

Environment Settings. The development environments and requirements are presented in Table 2.

Table 2. Development environments and requirements.

System	Ubuntu 23.04
CPU	Intel(R) Core(TM) i9-10900X CPU@3.70 GHz
RAM	4 × 32 GB; 2933MT/s
GPU	NVIDIA GeForce RTX^{TM}3090 24G
CUDA version	12.0
Programming language	Python 3.9.16
Deep learning framework	Pytorch (Torch 2.0.1)
Code	https://github.com/Prech-start/FLARE23_AdaptNet

Training Protocols. During the training phase, we set the batch size to 2 and randomly select all samples within each epoch. For each sample, we perform random patch cropping with patch sizes of $(96, 128, 160)$. As for the optimizer, we utilize AdamW with a learning rate of $1e-3$ and a weight decay of $1e-5$. The learning rate updating follows the default mechanism of AdamW. Additional details are presented in Table 3.

Table 3. Training protocols.

Network initialization	"he" normal initialization
Batch size	2
Patch size	96 × 128 × 160
Total epochs	120
Optimizer	AdamW with weight decay($\mu = 1e-5$)
Initial learning rate (lr)	0.001
Lr decay schedule	halved by 200 epochs
Training time	11 h per fold
Loss function	Adaptive Loss
Number of model parameters	30.8M
Number of flops	838.6116 G
CO_2eq	3.91908 Kg

[a] https://github.com/sksq96/pytorch-summary
[b] https://github.com/facebookresearch/fvcore
https://github.com/lfwa/carbontracker/

4   Results and Discussion

The best fold was selected via the results in the Public validation, as shown in
Table 4. The result of Public Validation is calculated with the 50 open cases from
100 Validation set. The result for Online Validation is collected from FLARE2023
website. It is worth noting that in the metrics for public validation, we have
included the standard deviation, represented as evaluation score±std. The std
of the online validation is not available since it is not reported online. The results
for the validation are listed in Table 5.

Table 4. Segmentation DSC(%) of five fold from Public Validation.

Target	baseline		label filling		proposed	
	Organ	Tumor	Organ	Tumor	Organ	Tumor
fold0	34.84	36.89	89.25	40.94	88.96	45.12
fold1	36.18	37.20	89.30	40.75	88.97	43.24
fold2	35.79	34.15	89.05	42.02	89.02	45.35
fold3	35.57	40.17	89.20	44.19	89.09	43.75
fold4	35.07	39.61	89.22	41.73	88.94	45.04
mean	35.49	37.60	89.20	41.92	88.96	44.50

Table 5. Result in Public Validation, Online Validation and Final Testing.

Target	Public Validation		Online Validation		Testing	
	DSC(%)	NSD(%)	DSC(%)	NSD(%)	DSC(%)	NSD (%)
Liver	97.74 ± 0.44	99.28 ± 0.73	97.60	99.07	96.68	98.05
RK	94.44 ± 7.76	95.92 ± 8.61	93.83	95.36	94.56	95.82
Spleen	96.88 ± 0.94	99.12 ± 1.75	96.94	99.19	96.42	98.90
Pancreas	86.06 ± 5.58	97.06 ± 4.01	84.70	96.18	88.40	96.84
Aorta	94.74 ± 1.25	98.78 ± 2.29	94.74	98.72	94.95	99.54
IVC	88.62 ± 7.60	91.26 ± 7.90	88.30	90.60	88.60	91.88
RAG	81.41 ± 12.23	94.97 ± 13.68	81.43	95.51	81.39	95.15
LAG	82.64 ± 5.66	95.96 ± 4.34	80.86	94.37	81.78	94.68
Gallbladder	86.53 ± 18.94	88.38 ± 20.43	84.11	85.80	82.69	85.65
Esophagus	79.95 ± 16.67	90.77 ± 16.92	81.14	92.53	86.48	96.91
Stomach	93.14 ± 3.20	97.25 ± 4.10	93.67	97.59	93.39	97.01
Duodenum	81.51 ± 7.90	94.80 ± 5.91	81.43	94.54	83.55	93.90
LK	93.45 ± 6.72	94.73 ± 8.90	93.18	94.81	94.69	96.37
Organ Average	89.01 ± 6.13	95.25 ± 3.23	88.61	94.94	89.51	95.44
Tumor	43.75 ± 35.21	35.46 ± 29.93	39.16	30.52	54.65	41.01

4.1   Quantitative Results on Validation Set

As shown in Table 6, the quantitative experiments have been carried out for more comprehensive ablation studies on the Pseudo-label filling and Adapting weight calculation. For the tumor segmentation, the proposed method performs better than the baseline model and the label-filling-based model, with an improvement of at least 0.0258 and 0.0295 in DSC and NSD scores, respectively. For the organ segmentation, the segmentation result of our proposed method is slightly worse (with a decline of only 0.0027 in DSC score) than the model that used pseudo-label filling. Specifically, comparisons with Quantitative evaluation in Table 6 and annotation statistics in Table 1 illustrate that the baseline model is invalid in segmenting the organs with low frequency, i.e., aorta (0.113), IVC (0.113), RAG (0.113), LAG (0.112), gallbladder (0.102), esophagus (0.113), stomach (0.113), and duodenum (0.113). The model's ability is strengthened in tumors and organs with high frequency (e.g., liver, spleen, etc.). It also demonstrates the effectiveness of pseudo-label filling in the segmentation task with imbalance annotations. The proposed AdaptNet approach improves segmentation of the part of objects with high frequency (i.e., RK (0.591), LK (0.590), and tumor (0.680)), while the segmentation results from AdaptNet are not as promising as the model used pseudo-label filling for the organs with low frequency. According to the weight calculation algorithm and the frequency of organ annotation occurrence, it can be inferred that this situation is reasonable in that the lower the labeling frequency, the less guided by the real annotation.

Table 6. Overview of Ablation Experiment Results. Note: Label filling: baseline + Label filling module. Proposed: baseline + Label filling module + Adaptive weight calculation.

Target	Baseline		Label filling		Proposed	
	DSC(%)	NSD(%)	DSC(%)	NSD(%)	DSC(%)	NSD(%)
Liver	90.78	91.85	97.76	99.26	97.72	99.22
RK	89.08	90.35	93.84	95.25	94.02	95.39
Spleen	91.71	93.57	96.90	99.22	96.85	99.10
Pancreas	80.25	91.39	85.87	96.93	85.85	96.90
Aorta	1.73	1.59	94.78	98.90	94.68	98.69
IVC	2.29	2.12	89.32	92.12	88.62	91.25
RAG	6.96	7.61	81.24	94.86	81.26	94.87
LAG	6.23	7.26	82.33	95.73	81.85	95.35
Gallbladder	10.24	10.03	85.08	87.02	83.96	85.74
Esophagus	3.78	4.50	80.54	91.37	80.25	91.13
Stomach	3.54	3.85	93.80	97.70	93.40	97.69
Duodenum	0.46	0.59	82.06	94.88	81.31	94.68
LK	88.64	89.76	93.15	94.19	93.37	94.59
Organ Average	36.60	38.04	88.97	95.19	88.70	94.97
Tumor	37.60	27.68	41.93	32.34	44.51	35.29

4.2   Qualitative Results on Validation Set

In this section, we show the two good segmentation cases and two bad segmentation cases.

Good Segmentation Cases. As shown in case-0087 of Fig. 3, the baseline method is not available to segment the IVC, aorta, stomach, duodenum and RAG. Meanwhile, the baseline method misclassifies part of LK as spleen. The label filling method can only segment part of the duodenum. Compared to the under-segmentation of the baseline method and the label filling method in the kidney, our method performs much better in the tumor. In case-0057 of Fig. 3, the tumor in RK, stomach, aorta, LK and IVC are not segmented in the baseline method. The part of LK is misclassified as part of the tumor and the lesion in LK is under-segmentation by the label filling method, while the proposed AdaptNet can almost segment the tumor in LK, however, the small part of LK is misclassified as pancreas. Compared to the label filling method, our approach exhibits a better ability to highlight tumor segmentation. It demonstrates improved tumor segmentation performance.

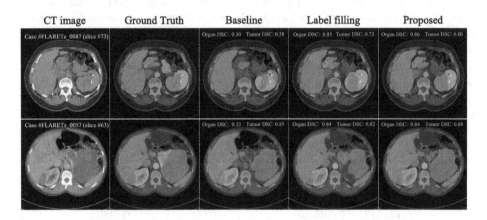

Fig. 3. Good segmentation cases from 50 validation set.

Bad Segmentation Cases. In case-0067 of Fig. 4, the baseline has trouble in segmenting the IVC and aorta. And all three methods fail to segment the esophagus. It can be explained that the location of the esophagus makes all the methods confusing. In case-0095, as shown in Fig. 4, the baseline model does not segment the duodenum, IVC, gallbladder and aorta. The three methods misclassify the LK as the tumor. The duodenum and pancreas are similar in gray scale so the boundary of these organs is not clear in the predictive segmentation.

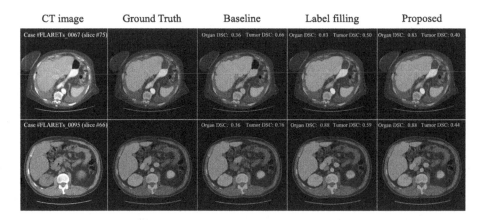

Fig. 4. Bad segmentation cases from 50 validation set.

4.3 Segmentation Efficiency Results on Validation Set

We have submitted our Docker container encapsulating our model to the official challenge. We have tested it on 20 cases, and the efficiency metrics were as follows: an average execution time of 40.673 s, an average maximum GPU memory usage of 4499.8MB, and an average area under the CPU curve of 124628 s. There are 8 cases with efficiency as shown in Table 7.

Table 7. Quantitative evaluation of segmentation efficiency in terms of the running them and GPU memory consumption. Total GPU denotes the area under GPU Memory-Time curve. Evaluation GPU platform: NVIDIA QUADRO RTX5000 (16G).

Case ID	Image Size	Running Time (s)	Max GPU (MB)	Total GPU (MB)
0001	(512, 512, 55)	33.39	4088	75893
0051	(512, 512, 100)	43.83	4850	154144
0017	(512, 512, 150)	46.19	4938	161893
0019	(512, 512, 215)	41.23	4394	122667
0099	(512, 512, 334)	51.92	4686	155622
0063	(512, 512, 448)	53.18	4674	154248
0048	(512, 512, 499)	59.8	4658	175999
0029	(512, 512, 554)	75.38	5202	231308

4.4 Results on Final Testing Set

The testing results from the docker of our solution were evaluated by the challenge officially on the Final Testing, and are shown in Table 5.

4.5   Limitation and Future Work

Upon reflecting on our study, it becomes evident that we encounter certain limitations in the following aspects.

Calculation of Adaptive Weights: The computation of adaptive weights did not take into consideration the issue of small organ volumes, resulting in a lack of differentiation in loss weights between small organs. Moreover, we find the phenomenon that the lower occurrence of label frequency resulted in a loss of segmentation accuracy, as evidenced by the fact that in our approach, while there was an improvement in tumor DSC, the mean DSC for organs experienced a slight decrease.

Effect of Different Preprocessing Strategies: Different preprocessing strategies were found to impact the contrast of the images. Future work may involve training on a fusion of images processed using various preprocessing methods.

Frequency is Not Fully Taken into Account in Modeling: The frequency of each object is different in the dataset. Considering the frequency of each object would improve the segmentation performance of the model.

5   Conclusion

In order to tackle 'partial labeling/annotation problem', we develop an adaptive learning network, AdaptNet, to effectively segment multiple organs and tumors within partially labeled datasets from abdomen CT images. The quantitative and qualitative results show that AdaptNet can efficiently and flexibly learn multiple organ and tumor information from the partial labeling/annotation dataset, which is typically performed by multiple or multi-head networks. We conducted validation on a large-scale partially annotated dataset under MICCAI FLARE 2023 challenge and demonstrated that the proposed AdaptNet outperforms baseline segmentation methods across the 13 different organ and tumor segmentation tasks.

Acknowledgements. The authors of this paper declare that the segmentation method they implemented for participation in the FLARE 2023 challenge has not used any pre-trained models nor additional datasets other than those provided by the organizers. The proposed solution is fully automatic without any manual intervention. We thank all the data owners for making the CT scans publicly available and CodaLab [21] for hosting the challenge platform. We also acknowledge Dr. Zheng Yunlin for kindly sharing the clinical knowledge and supporting some analysis for the segmentation results. This research was supported by the National Natural Science Foundation of China[No. 61972107]; Regional Innovation and Development Joint Fund of National Natural Science Foundation of China [No. U22A20345]. National Science Foundation for Young Scientists of China [No. 82202142]; China Postdoctoral Science Foundation [No. 2022M720857];Guangdong Provincial Key Laboratory of Artificial Intelligence in Medical Image Analysis and Application [No. 2022B1212010011]; High-level Hospital

Construction Project [No. DFJHBF202105]; Open Project of Guangdong Provincial Key Laboratory of Artificial Intelligence in Medical Image Analysis and Application [No. 2022B1212010011].

References

1. Armato III, S.G., et al.: The lung image database consortium (LIDC) and image database resource initiative (IDRI): a completed reference database of lung nodules on CT scans. Med. Phys. **38**(2), 915–931 (2011)
2. Bilic, P., et al.: The liver tumor segmentation benchmark (LITS). Med. Image Anal. **84**, 102680 (2023)
3. Clark, K., et al.: The cancer imaging archive (TCIA): maintaining and operating a public information repository. J. Digit. Imaging **26**(6), 1045–1057 (2013)
4. Gao, L., Heath, D.G., Fishman, E.K.: Abdominal image segmentation using three-dimensional deformable models. Invest. Radiol. **33**(6), 348–355 (1998)
5. Gatidis, S., et al.: The autopet challenge: Towards fully automated lesion segmentation in oncologic pet/CT imaging. preprint at Research Square (Nature Portfolio) (2023). https://doi.org/10.21203/rs.3.rs-2572595/v1
6. Gatidis, S., et al.: A whole-body FDG-PET/CT dataset with manually annotated tumor lesions. Scientific Data **9**(1), 601 (2022)
7. Heller, N., et al.: The state of the art in kidney and kidney tumor segmentation in contrast-enhanced CT imaging: results of the kits19 challenge. Med. Image Anal. **67**, 101821 (2021)
8. Heller, N., et al.: An international challenge to use artificial intelligence to define the state-of-the-art in kidney and kidney tumor segmentation in ct imaging. Proc. Am. Soc. Clin. Oncol. **38**(6), 626–626 (2020)
9. Huang, Z., et al.: Revisiting nnU-net for iterative pseudo labeling and efficient sliding window inference. In: Ma, J., Wang, B. (eds.) FLARE 2022. LNCS, vol. 13816, pp. 178–189. Springer, Cham (2022)
10. Isensee, F., Jaeger, P.F., Kohl, S.A., Petersen, J., Maier-Hein, K.H.: nnU-net: a self-configuring method for deep learning-based biomedical image segmentation. Nat. Methods **18**(2), 203–211 (2021)
11. Ji, Y., et al.: Amos: a large-scale abdominal multi-organ benchmark for versatile medical image segmentation. Adv. Neural. Inf. Process. Syst. **35**, 36722–36732 (2022)
12. Joskowicz, L., Cohen, D., Caplan, N., Sosna, J.: Inter-observer variability of manual contour delineation of structures in CT. Eur. Radiol. **29**, 1391–1399 (2019)
13. Kobashi, M., Shapiro, L.G.: Knowledge-based organ identification from CT images. Pattern Recogn. **28**(4), 475–491 (1995)
14. Landman, B., Xu, Z., Igelsias, J., Styner, M., Langerak, T., Klein, A.: Miccai multi-atlas labeling beyond the cranial vault-workshop and challenge (2015). https://doi.org/10.7303/syn3193805 (2015)
15. Li, Z., et al.: Lvit: language meets vision transformer in medical image segmentation. IEEE Trans. Med. Imaging (2023)
16. Ma, J., He, Y., Li, F., Han, L., You, C., Wang, B.: Segment anything in medical images. Nat. Commun. **15**(1), 654 (2024)
17. Ma, J., et al.: Fast and low-GPU-memory abdomen CT organ segmentation: the flare challenge. Med. Image Anal. **82**, 102616 (2022)
18. Ma, J., et al.: Unleashing the strengths of unlabeled data in pan-cancer abdominal organ quantification: the flare22 challenge. arXiv preprint arXiv:2308.05862 (2023)

19. Ma, J.: Abdomenct-1k: Is abdominal organ segmentation a solved problem? IEEE Trans. Pattern Anal. Mach. Intell. **44**(10), 6695–6714 (2021)
20. National Cancer Institute. Bethesda, M.: https://seer.cancer.gov/statfacts/html/common.html
21. Pavao, A., et al.: Codalab competitions: an open source platform to organize scientific challenges. Ph.D. thesis, Université Paris-Saclay, FRA (2022)
22. Schenk, A., Prause, G., Peitgen, H.-O.: Efficient semiautomatic segmentation of 3D objects in medical images. In: Delp, S.L., DiGoia, A.M., Jaramaz, B. (eds.) MICCAI 2000. LNCS, vol. 1935, pp. 186–195. Springer, Heidelberg (2000). https://doi.org/10.1007/978-3-540-40899-4_19
23. Simpson, A.L., et al.: A large annotated medical image dataset for the development and evaluation of segmentation algorithms. arXiv preprint arXiv:1902.09063 (2019)
24. Taghanaki, S.A., et al.: Combo loss: handling input and output imbalance in multi-organ segmentation. Comput. Med. Imaging Graph. **75**, 24–33 (2019)
25. Wasserthal, J., et al.: Totalsegmentator: robust segmentation of 104 anatomic structures in CT images. Radiol. Artif. Intell. **5**(5), e230024 (2023)
26. Yushkevich, P.A., Gao, Y., Gerig, G.: Itk-snap: an interactive tool for semi-automatic segmentation of multi-modality biomedical images. In: Annual International Conference of the IEEE Engineering in Medicine and Biology Society, pp. 3342–3345 (2016)

Two-Stage Training for Abdominal Pan-Cancer Segmentation in Weak Label

Hanwen Zhang[1,2] , Yongzhi Huang[1,2,3] , and Bingding Huang[1(✉)]

[1] College of Big Data and Internet, Shenzhen Technology University, Shenzhen 518188, China
huangbingding@sztu.edu.cn
[2] College of Applied Sciences, Shenzhen University, Shenzhen 518060, China
[3] School of Artificial Intelligence, Beijing University of Posts and Telecommunications, Beijing 100876, China

Abstract. Constructing comprehensive labeled datasets for medical image segmentation tasks is time-consuming, requiring intensive masks annotated carefully by experienced radiologists. Existing benchmark datasets provide the necessary masks to train the supervised-based segmentation models, including single-organ datasets and multiple-organ datasets. However, it is still challenging when deploying large-scale models with a union of multiple datasets due to annotation conflicts. For example, some organ or tumor annotations are missing in most cases (weak label) in the FLARE23 challenge dataset. To overcome the limitation of segmentation models in this situation, we propose a two-stage training method to train an efficient segmentation model with weak label. In the first stage, only strong labels (complete organ labels) are used to train models by the nnU-Net, while the weak labels (incomplete organ labels) are filled by generating pseudo labels using nnU-Net. Then the lightweight coarse-to-fine network is trained using the supplemented data in the second stage. Experiments on the FLARE23 challenge (MICCAI FLARE23) demonstrate that coarse-to-fine networks can reduce computational complexity and resource consumption during the inference stage while maintaining high performance, in the case of pseudo labeled supplementary data. With a speed of 12.6 s per case, our proposed method achieves an average DSC of 0.8920 and an average NSD of 0.9482 on the FLARE23 validation set.

Keywords: Weak label · Pseudo label · Two-stage training

1 Introduction

Abdominal organ segmentation is a crucial step in the clinical diagnosis of abdominal diseases. Deep learning-based segmentation methods have demonstrated the ability to efficiently and accurately identify organ boundaries, sizes, and locations, aiding doctors in rapidly identifying potential lesions and disease areas [1]. The family of U-Net [2] architectures is the most mainstream

© The Author(s), under exclusive license to Springer Nature Switzerland AG 2024
J. Ma and B. Wang (Eds.): FLARE 2023, LNCS 14544, pp. 194–208, 2024.
https://doi.org/10.1007/978-3-031-58776-4_16

in deep supervised learning methods for medical image segmentation tasks. Subsequently, various CNN-based segmentation networks based on the U-Net architecture emerged, such as ResU-Net [3] and U-Net++ [4]. Meanwhile, the transformer-based models are also naturally compatible with U-Net architecture, and excellent networks such as Trans U-Net [5], Swin U-Net [6], and so on have emerged for medical image segmentation. Additionally, some works focus on improving segmentation performance by using multi-view, multi-task, and multi-scale techniques, trying complex data augmentation methods, or other tricks like multi-level feature fusion and deep supervision. The most representative framework is nnU-Net [7], which is a milestone work that achieves SOTA performance using U-Net architecture with a series of heuristic rules that can deploy and train segmentation models on any dataset automatically, demonstrating the high adaptability and robustness of its framework.

However, even such a comprehensive framework, nnU-Net, cannot be used directly for annotations with different labels in multiple datasets, which is caused by the problem of annotation conflicts. Figure 1 gives a specific example to illustrate this problem. Specifically, weak label case (2) contains only tumor, case (3) contains tumor and some organs, and (4) includes all organs without tumor. Therefore, some organs are incorrectly annotated as background, and overlapping annotation conflicts over cases. Although partly labeled data has additional annotation information and also inherits semantic information like unlabeled data, due to annotation conflicts, the performance of models trained by multiple datasets will probably not improve or even degrade compared with models using a single dataset.

To address this issue, many attempts have been made to explore multiple weak label datasets in a more efficient manner. Fang et al. proposed a new network named Pyramid Input Pyramid Output Feature Abstraction Network (PIPO-FAN) using multi-scale features to exploit weak label proportion information [8]. Enlightened by multi-branch networks and dynamic filter learning, Zhang et al. considered multiple datasets as independent tasks and designed a single shared model, a dynamic on-demand network (DoDNet), receiving task-specific signals to avoid label conflicts [9]. A similar approach is conditional nnU-Net proposed by Zhang et al. [10], which also used special signals to control segmentation models dynamically. Different from the design of segmentation architectures, some works tried to reconsider the point of loss functions to solve label conflicts. For instance, Shi et al. proposed marginal loss and exclusion loss for weak label supervised multi-organ segmentation [11]. Furthermore, Liu et al. merged weak labeled datasets using incremental learning methods, introducing a light memory module mechanism based on marginal loss and exclusion loss to further improve and stabilize the model performance with continuously incremental datasets [12]. These methods fully used weak label datasets, enabling the deployment of a comprehensive segmentation model trained by multiple datasets simultaneously.

In the FLARE23 challenge, the dataset consists of labeled, weakly labeled, and unlabeled CT image data. As shown in Fig. 2, only 222 images have complete annotations for all organs, and the remaining 1978 cases only have annotations for specific organs. To achieve higher segmentation performance than baseline supervised learning methods, fully utilizing unlabeled data and resolving annotation conflicts caused by weak label data is a key breakthrough in this competition. To this end, we attempt to merge weak labeled data with completely labeled data and propose an efficient strategy that breaks down the barriers between weak label datasets, even existing conflicts overlapping and further alleviates the problem of developing vanilla segmentation methods combining several different benchmark datasets. We also follow the trend of the FLARE competition series, and pay attention to optimizing the resource consumption and speed in the inference phase. Based on the experience of the Flare22 challenge [13] (2022-MICCAI-FLARE), using either the nnU-Net [7] adaptive framework or the EfficientSeg [14] coarse-to-fine framework combined with a semi-supervised algorithm can effectively handle unlabeled data. We will use the two networks mentioned above to design a training framework that can use weak labels to address the abovementioned challenges.

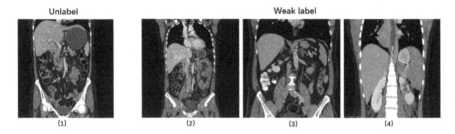

Fig. 1. Image(1) shows a CT without any annotation. Images (2), (3), and (4) show the weak label, where (2) has only tumor labeling, (3) contains tumor labeling and labeling of some organs, and (4) includes labeling all organs without tumors.

2   Method

To address the challenges posed by weak labels and imbalanced data in abdominal organ segmentation, we propose a novel training framework that utilizes statistical analysis to divide the data into different categories.

The main objective of our approach is to select relatively well-annotated strong labels from weak labels for the first round of training. We then use the model obtained from the first round of training to supplement the weak label data according to specific rules, enabling iterative training to obtain the final model.

In Sect. 2.2, we provide further details on our proposed approach, including the specific rules used to supplement the weak label data and the iterative training process. Our approach leverages the strengths of both the nnU-Net adaptive framework and the two-stage EfficientSeg framework, combined with semi-supervised learning algorithms, to improve the accuracy and efficiency of abdominal organ segmentation.

2.1 Preprocessing

Our proposed approach leverages the strengths of two networks, nnU-Net and EfficientSeg, each with its own preprocessing techniques.

nnU-Net provides a self-configuration pre-training pipeline depending on statistics information in specific datasets. To ensure the high performance of nnU-Net, we utilized this automatic preprocessing method for the FLARE23 dataset, including adjusting the target spacing and then resampling, voxel intensity normalization, and data augmentation techniques.

As for EfficientSeg, the network is a two-stage segmentation network that accepts an interpolated overall image as input, eliminating the need to adjust the image spacing. During the coarse segmentation stage, the image is interpolated and scaled to a size of [160, 160, 160]. During the fine segmentation stage, images are cropped so that only foreground regions remain and then padded to a size of [192, 192, 192] before being interpolated and scaled. The foreground information in the training process is provided by ground truths, while the one in the inference process is from masks generated from the coarse segmentation stage. The image intensity is clipped to a range of [–325, 325]. Additionally, a series of data augmentations are used in the fine segmentation stage, shown in Table 1.

Table 1. Data augmentation details in the fine segmentation stage.

RandFlipd-x	prob=0.5
RandFlipd-y	prob=0.5
RandFlipd-z	prob=0.5
RandZoomd	min-zoom=0.9, max-zoom=1.2, prob=0.15
RandGaussianNoised	std=0.01, prob=0.15
RandGaussianSmoothd	sigma=(0.5, 1.15), prob=0.15
RandScaleIntensityd	factors=0.3, prob=0.15
RandAdjustContrastd	prob=0.15

2.2 Proposed Method

As shown in Fig. 2, statistical analysis is conducted on 2200 annotated data samples in this dataset, revealing a ubiquitous lack or omission of organ or tumor segmentation. To address the challenges of weak labels and imbalanced data, we further analyze the distribution of annotations and propose a framework that can effectively train segmentation models with weak labels. It is worth mentioning that all unlabeled images are not used in our proposed method.

After checking category information in annotations, we found that annotations with a single category (excluding background) were mainly for the pancancer region segmentation. In contrast, annotations with thirteen categories mainly include regions of abdomen organs. Therefore, we split the dataset into two categories: cases with complete organ annotations (strong label) and cases with partial organ annotations (weak label).

Based on the condition of the FLARE23 dataset, our motivation is to distill knowledge from cases with strong labels, then use it to guide models to segment organs annotated wrongly as background in the weak label, and finally re-train the segmentation model with the whole annotated data. Specifically, our proposed framework consists of three stages: strong label training, weak label supplement, and retraining, as shown in Fig. 3. Each stage's network architecture is configured separately based on specific objectives and requirements. First, the strong label training stage automatically applies the self-configured framework nnU-Net to learn from the well-annotated strong label data. Second, the weak label supplement stage utilizes the EfficientSeg coarse-to-fine framework combined with semi-supervised learning algorithms to supplement the weak label data. Third, the retraining stage combines the two networks to iteratively refine the segmentation model using the supplement weak label data.

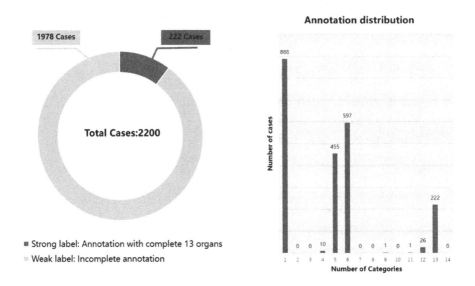

Fig. 2. Distribution of label counts: one important finding from our statistical analysis of the 2200 annotated data samples was that 888 of them contained only one label, which was mainly for pan-cancer region segmentation. On the other hand, the 222 samples that contained thirteen labels were primarily used for abdominal multi-organ segmentation.

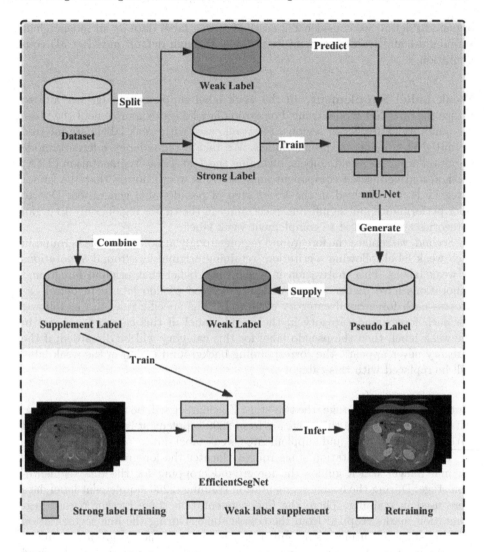

Fig. 3. This framework consists of three parts. Strong label training: Strong labels are selected from weak labels to be trained individually using nnU-Net. Weak label supplement: The remaining weak label is complemented using nnU-Net-generated labels. Retraining: The coarse-to-fine EfficientSegNet is trained using all the supplement labels to obtain the inference model.

Strong Label Training. In this stage, all annotated training data is split into two parts: weak label data and strong label data. Weak label data are not used due to annotation conflicts caused by missing organ annotations, resulting in degeneration and even not convergence during the training stage. To solve this problem, the strong label is selected to train nnU-Net as a teacher model that can generate credible pseudo labels for complementing annotations on missing organs. In detail, we consider 222 cases of strong label data as an independent training set and train a segmentation model through default nnU-Net 3D configuration.

Weak Label Supplement. In the weak label supplement stage, we aim to utilize the nnU-Net model trained on strong label data to complement the missing annotations for organ regions. First, all cases with weak labels are inferred by nnU-Net to generate pseudo labels. We take a redundancy inference mode to obtain accurate pseudo labels, including the Test-Time Augmentation (TTA) method and connected component analysis. It is worth noting that the tumor category is not involved in the above step of pseudo-label generation. Due to poor performance and significant uncertainty in the tumor region, only 13 organ categories are predicted to complement weak labels.

Second, we replace the foreground region wrongly annotated as background in each weak label following a criterion: retaining original foreground annotations in weak labels. This motivation is based on a belief that original foreground annotations have higher accuracy than predicted pseudo labels. In detail, we process each foreground category separately. The specific rules are as follows: For each foreground category in the pseudo label, if this category appears in the weak label, then the pseudo label for this category will be discarded; if the category never appears, the corresponding background region in the weak label will be replaced with this category.

Retraining. At this stage, the two-stage EfficientSeg will be used for retraining. All annotations used in this stage are from 2200 supplement label data combined with strong label data and supplemented weak label data.

The coarse segmentation stage roughly locates the foreground region in the original image, which guides the foreground cropping for the fine segmentation stage. During the coarse segmentation training, 2200 supplement label data were used in training. Then, the fine segmentation stage further refined segmentation masks cropped from the coarse stage. During the fine segmentation training stage, we utilized supplement labels to locate the foreground as input. By utilizing the supplement labels for fine segmentation training, we achieved significantly improved segmentation accuracy and robustness in EfficientSeg.

Inference Speed and Resources Consumption Trade-Offs. We use a coarse-to-fine segmentation network in the inference stage to optimize the inference speed and resource usage and to avoid using a time-consuming sliding window technique. Any size image can be segmented through two inference stages by using the coarse-to-fine network. Therefore, the inference speed is improved significantly compared with one-stage segmentation models with the sliding window technique. Following the EfficientSeg implementation, anisotropic convolution, anisotropic pooling, and FP16 are also used to reduce GPU memory usage, which is discussed in detail in [14].

2.3 Post-processing

We employed TTA to improve the final segmentation results during the strong label training stage. Additionally, final segmentation will adaptively keep the largest connected region to reduce false positives. Meanwhile, the coarse and fine segmentation results are also refined by the connected region analysis.

3 Experiments

3.1 Dataset and Evaluation Measures

The FLARE 2023 challenge is an extension of the FLARE 2021–2022 [15,16], aiming to promote the development of foundation models in abdominal disease analysis. The segmentation targets cover 13 organs and various abdominal lesions. The training dataset is curated from more than 30 medical centers under the license permission, including TCIA [17], LiTS [18], MSD [19], KiTS [20,21], and AbdomenCT-1K [22]. The training set includes 4000 abdomen CT scans where 2200 CT scans with weak label and 1800 CT scans without label. The validation and testing sets include 100 and 400 CT scans, respectively, which cover various abdominal cancer types, such as liver cancer, kidney cancer, pancreas cancer, colon cancer, gastric cancer, and so on. The organ annotation process used ITK-SNAP [23], nnU-Net [7], and MedSAM [24].

The evaluation metrics encompass two accuracy measures-Dice Similarity Coefficient (DSC) and Normalized Surface Dice (NSD)-alongside two efficiency measures-running time and area under the GPU memory-time curve. These metrics collectively contribute to the ranking computation. Furthermore, the running time and GPU memory consumption are considered within tolerances of 15 s and 4 GB, respectively.

3.2 Implementation Details

Environment Settings. The development environments and requirements are presented in Table 2.

Dataset Split. There is no multiple cross-validation for the training of nn-Unet and EfficientSegNet. For the nnU-net, 20% of 222 cases was randomly selected as the validation set. For the EfficientSegNet, 100 cases in 2200 cases were randomly selected as the validation set.

Training Protocols. In both the strong label training stage and retraining process of our proposed framework, we utilized three different models with different configurations to improve segmentation accuracy. The protocols of these models are shown in Table 3. In the training stage of nnU-Net, relevant hyperparameters are automatically generated according to its adaptive rules. Patch size is fixed as 32 * 128 * 192 (D * W * H) and network training using SGD

Table 2. Development environments and requirements.

System	Ubuntu 20.04.1 LTS
CPU	AMD EPYC 7742 64-Core Processor
RAM	1.8TB
GPU	8 NVIDIA A100 (40G)
CUDA version	11.7
Programming language	Python 3.10
Deep learning framework	torch 1.10, monai 1.0
Code	https://github.com/XIANYUNYEHE-DEL/two-stage-retraining-seg

with a learning rate of 0.01 for 1000 epochs. As for EfficientSegNet, training will be divided into coarse model training and fine model training. In the coarse model training stage, batch size is set to 2 and patch size is fixed as 160 * 160 * 160 (W * H * D). Optimizer in the training is used AdamW with 0.01 learning rate and 0.00001 weight decay. First 50 epochs used as warm-up and using 500 epochs for the training with Cosine Annealing strategy. Loss function is selected to Dice and Cross-Entropy. In the fine model training stage, Most of the settings have not been modified. Patch size is fixed as 192 * 192 * 192 (W * H * D) and training epochs reduced to 300 for saving training time.

Table 3. Training and Inference protocols.

Stage	Pseudo labeling	Coarse model	Fine model
Mode	nnU-Net 3D	3D U-Net	EfficientSegNet
Network initialization	"he" normal initialization	"he" normal initialization	"he" normal initialization
Batch size	2	2	2
Patch size	48 × 192 × 192	160 × 160 × 160	192 × 192 × 192
Total epochs	1000	500	300
Optimizer	SGD	AdamW	AdamW
Weight decay	3e−5	1e−5	1e−5
Initial learning rate (lr)	0.01	0.01	0.01
Lr scheduler	ReduceLROnPlateau	Warmup and Cosine Annealing	Warmup and Cosine Annealing
Training time	72 h	24 h	36 h
Loss function	Dice and Cross-Entropy	Dice and Cross-Entropy	Dice and Cross-Entropy

4   Results and Discussion

4.1   Quantitative Results on Validation Set

We used EfficientSegNet, which was trained directly using 2200 cases of labeled data as the baseline. nnU-Net, which was trained using 222 cases (strong label) containing all organ segmentations, and EfficientSegNet, which was trained using our weak label training framework, were compared with baseline on public validation, respectively. The quantitative results are shown in Table 4.

Table 4. Quantitative evaluation results for ablation study on online validation.

Target	baseline		nnU-net(222)		EfficientSegNet	
	DSC (%)	NSD (%)	DSC (%)	NSD (%)	DSC (%)	NSD (%)
Liver	94.72	93.03	96.58	98.34	97.45	98.63
Right Kidney	87.81	85.23	93.12	94.29	93.36	94.11
Spleen	91.55	91.51	96.04	97.35	96.71	98.29
Pancreas	02.08	02.37	84.69	96.29	84.67	95.19
Aorta	85.36	84.95	96.28	98.62	95.85	98.68
Inferior vena cava	71.92	63.29	94.47	96.24	93.78	96.17
Right adrenal gland	02.00	02.00	83.08	95.39	81.18	94.64
Left adrenal gland	01.00	01.00	80.59	93.18	78.55	92.03
Gallbladder	10.00	10.00	82.93	82.01	85.38	85.87
Esophagus	00.00	00.00	83.17	93.47	82.79	93.53
Stomach	04.73	03.55	92.71	96.65	92.67	96.66
Duodenum	31.19	55.92	84.84	95.97	83.76	95.27
Left kidney	87.84	91.34	84.95	92.29	93.13	93.55
Tumor	05.48	01.68	00.00	00.00	29.98	20.49
Average	43.83	44.47	89.22	94.62	89.20	94.82

We observed that using weak labels for direct training often resulted in poor labeling quality, which can negatively impact the training process and lead to eventual failure. We decomposed the task into three stages to address this issue: strong label training, weak label supplement, and retraining.

For strong label training, we utilized nnU-Net, a well-established segmentation model trained on a dataset of 222 cases containing all organ segmentations with strong labels. Our experiments showed that nnU-Net achieved a Dice similarity coefficient (DSC) of 0.892, indicating that it is effective in organ segmentation. We then used the organ segmentation results obtained from nnU-Net as a generative network for organ pseudo-label.

We used EfficientSegNet to train on the 2200 cases with pseudo-label for retraining. Our experiments showed that EfficientSegNet achieved an average DSC of 0.892 for all organs and a tumor DSC of 0.299.

4.2   Qualitative Results on Validation Set

Figure 4 shows the segmentation results for the baseline and our method. Among the results in case#0047 and case#0070, our method can accurately segment organs and identify tumor regions and make precise judgments even for segmentation at the boundaries of some small organs. However, in case#0029 and case#0035, our method shows some false-negative determinations of the tumor region. The locations marked in the red box in the diagram show some false-negative situations. The blue area in the box is the pan-cancer area label. It can be observed that our method always wrongly classified tumor regions as nor-

Table 5. Quantitative evaluation results.

Target	Public Validation		Online Validation		Testing	
	DSC (%)	NSD (%)	DSC (%)	NSD (%)	DSC (%)	NSD (%)
Liver	97.46 ± 1.03	94.61 ± 5.13	97.45	98.63	96.11	96.77
Right Kidney	90.46 ± 19.95	87.09 ± 20.45	93.36	94.11	94.70	94.53
Spleen	95.83 ± 8.02	96.87 ± 7.34	96.71	98.29	96.01	97.39
Pancreas	86.09 ± 7.24	83.09 ± 11.89	84.67	95.19	88.62	96.44
Aorta	95.03 ± 2.98	95.42 ± 5.30	95.85	98.68	96.14	99.15
Inferior vena cava	92.70 ± 3.84	89.18 ± 6.59	93.78	96.17	94.18	96.92
Right adrenal gland	77.31 ± 20.09	89.80 ± 19.19	81.18	94.64	80.48	94.15
Left adrenal gland	77.35 ± 16.86	88.95 ± 19.38	78.55	92.03	79.75	93.32
Gallbladder	79.84 ± 28.03	79.85 ± 29.78	85.38	85.87	81.34	83.69
Esophagus	81.58 ± 16.65	83.45 ± 17.22	82.79	93.53	88.10	97.69
Stomach	93.21 ± 3.89	90.62 ± 10.57	92.67	96.66	92.00	96.00
Duodenum	83.49 ± 6.38	79.70 ± 9.00	83.76	95.27	85.91	96.02
Left kidney	91.43 ± 14.96	87.72 ± 17.00	93.13	93.55	94.86	95.46
Tumor	35.39 ± 34.80	24.97 ± 28.54	29.98	20.49	39.73	26.71
Organ average	84.08 ± 22.19	83.67 ± 23.83	89.20	94.82	89.86	95.19

mal organs. The reason may be that there is tumor regions in the supplemented organ label area, but our method has no suitable strategy to correct it.

4.3 Segmentation Efficiency Results on Validation Set

The efficiency test results are shown in Table 6. Using less than 4GB of GPU Memory, our method can also infer larger images in less than 20 s.

Table 6. Quantitative evaluation of segmentation efficiency in terms of the running them and GPU memory consumption. Total GPU denotes the area under the GPU Memory-Time curve. Evaluation GPU platform: NVIDIA QUADRO RTX5000 (16G).

Case ID	Image Size	Running Time (s)	Max GPU (MB)	Total GPU (MB)
0001	(512, 512, 55)	12.6	3032	10455
0051	(512, 512, 100)	9.04	2956	9044
0017	(512, 512, 150)	9.64	2970	10245
0019	(512, 512, 215)	11.39	2994	13420
0099	(512, 512, 334)	11.33	3172	13395
0063	(512, 512, 448)	14.58	3400	20043
0048	(512, 512, 499)	14.6	3254	19642
0029	(512, 512, 554)	16.87	3938	24931

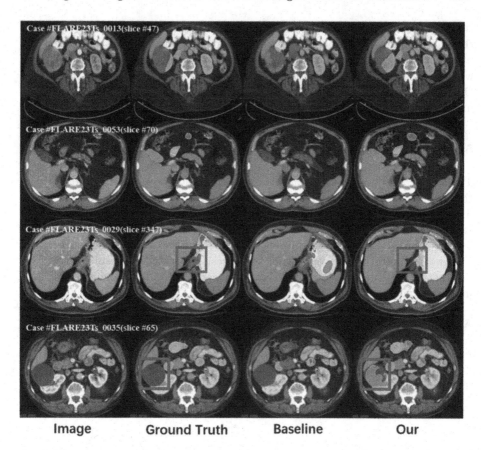

Image   Ground Truth   Baseline   Our

Fig. 4. Qualitative results of on good (#0047 and #0070) and bad (#0029 and #0035) cases. The first column is the image, the second is the ground truth, the third is the Baseline results, and the fourth is the predicted results by our method.

4.4 Results on Final Testing Set

The test results are shown in Table 5. In the test dataset, we achieved an average DSC of 0.8969 and NSD of 0.9502 for all organs. This is reliable for organ segmentation. At the same time, the average inference time of our method is less than 10 s with few resources. However, there are great limitations on the segmentation effect of tumors.

4.5 Limitation and Future Work

The two-stage coarse-to-fine model used in our proposed framework maintains high inference speed while achieving a high level of segmentation performance. However, we found that the performance of tumor segmentation was worse than that of abdominal organs. After an elaborate analysis of bad cases, we found that tumors are annotated as irregular regions with non-smooth edges. In contrast, the predicted ones are probably smoothed into sphere-like regions after the resizing operation, resulting in an unnegligible error in the edge. In future work, we will further investigate segmentation models with high performance on tumors. One solution is to replace the traditional resizing operation with learning-based methods like correlation interpolation.

5   Conclusion

This paper proposed a two-stage training approach to overcome the problem that weak label data cannot be used for training general segmentation models directly. A pseudo-label generating network is trained using those cases with strong labels in the first training. After supplementing all weak label data using pseudo labels, the coarse-to-fine network is retrained for the inference stage. Under the limitation of computing resources, experimental results show that our method fully uses weak label data and performs well in segmentation and inference speed.

Acknowledgements. We would like to thank the School-Enterprise Graduate Student Cooperation Fund of Shenzhen Technology University. The authors of this paper declare that the segmentation method they implemented for participation in the FLARE 2023 challenge has not used any pre-trained models nor additional datasets other than those provided by the organizers. The proposed solution is fully automatic without any manual intervention. We thank all the data owners for making the CT scans publicly available and CodaLab [25] for hosting the challenge platform.

References

1. Shen, D., Guorong, W., Suk, H.-I.: Deep learning in medical image analysis. Annu. Rev. Biomed. Eng. **19**, 221 (2017)
2. Ronneberger, O., Fischer, P., Brox, T.: U-net: convolutional networks for biomedical image segmentation. In: Navab, N., Hornegger, J., Wells, W.M., Frangi, A.F. (eds.) MICCAI 2015. LNCS, vol. 9351, pp. 234–241. Springer, Cham (2015). https://doi.org/10.1007/978-3-319-24574-4_28
3. Xiao, X., Lian, S., Luo, Z., Li, S.: Weighted res-unet for high-quality retina vessel segmentation. In: 2018 9th International Conference on Information Technology in Medicine and Education (ITME), pp. 327–331. IEEE (2018)
4. Zhou, Z., Rahman Siddiquee, M.M., Tajbakhsh, N., Liang, J.: UNet++: a nested u-net architecture for medical image segmentation. In: Stoyanov, D., et al. (eds.) DLMIA/ML-CDS-2018. LNCS, vol. 11045, pp. 3–11. Springer, Cham (2018). https://doi.org/10.1007/978-3-030-00889-5_1
5. Chen, J., et al.: Transunet: transformers make strong encoders for medical image segmentation. *arXiv preprint*arXiv:2102.04306 (2021)

6. Cao, H. et al.: Swin-Unet: unet-like pure transformer for medical image segmentation. In: Karlinsky, L., Michaeli, T., Nishino, K. (eds.) Computer Vision – ECCV 2022 Workshops, ECCV 2022, LNCS, vol. 13803, pp. 205–218. Springer, Cham (2023). https://doi.org/10.1007/978-3-031-25066-8_9

7. Isensee, F., Jaeger, P.F., Kohl, S.A., Petersen, J., Maier-Hein, K.H.: nnU-net: a self-configuring method for deep learning-based biomedical image segmentation. Nat. Methods 18(2), 203–211 (2021)

8. Fang, X., Yan, P.: Multi-organ segmentation over partially labeled datasets with multi-scale feature abstraction. IEEE Trans. Med. Imaging 39(11), 3619–3629 (2020)

9. Zhang, J., Xie, Y., Xia, Y., Shen, C.: Dodnet: learning to segment multi-organ and tumors from multiple partially labeled datasets. In: Proceedings of the IEEE/CVF Conference on Computer Vision and Pattern Recognition, pp. 1195–1204 (2021)

10. Zhang, G., Yang, Z., Huo, B., Chai, S., Jiang, S.: Multiorgan segmentation from partially labeled datasets with conditional nnu-net. Comput. Biol. Med. 136, 104658 (2021)

11. Shi, G., Xiao, L., Chen, Y., Zhou, S.K.: Marginal loss and exclusion loss for partially supervised multi-organ segmentation. Med. Image Anal 70, 101979 (2021)

12. Liu, P., et al.: Learning incrementally to segment multiple organs in a CT image. In: Wang, L., Dou, Q., Fletcher, P.T., Speidel, S., Li, S. (eds.) Medical Image Computing and Computer Assisted Intervention – MICCAI 2022, MICCAI 2022, LNCS, vol. 13434, pp. 714–724. Springer, Cham (2022). https://doi.org/10.1007/978-3-031-16440-8_68

13. Ma, J., Wang, B.: Fast and Low-Resource Semi-supervised Abdominal Organ Segmentation: MICCAI 2022 Challenge, FLARE 2022, Held in Conjunction with MICCAI 2022, Singapore, September 22, 2022, Proceedings, vol. 13816. Springer Nature (2023)

14. Zhang, F., Wang, Y., Yang H.: Efficient context-aware network for abdominal multi-organ segmentation. *arXiv preprint*arXiv:2109.10601 (2021)

15. Ma, J., et al.; Fast and low-GPU-memory abdomen CT organ segmentation: the flare challenge. Med. Image Anal. 82, 102616 (2022)

16. Ma, J., et al.: Unleashing the strengths of unlabeled data in pan-cancer abdominal organ quantification: the flare22 challenge. *arXiv preprint*arXiv:2308.05862 (2023)

17. Clark, K., et al.: The cancer imaging archive (TCIA): maintaining and operating a public information repository. J. Digit. Imaging 26(6), 1045–1057 (2013)

18. Bilic, P., et al.: The liver tumor segmentation benchmark (lits). Med. Image Anal 84, 102680 (2023)

19. Simpson, A.L., et al.: A large annotated medical image dataset for the development and evaluation of segmentation algorithms. *arXiv preprint*arXiv:1902.09063 (2019)

20. Heller, N., et al.: The state of the art in kidney and kidney tumor segmentation in contrast-enhanced CT imaging: results of the kits19 challenge. Med. Image Anal. 67, 101821 (2021)

21. Heller, N., et al.: An international challenge to use artificial intelligence to define the state-of-the-art in kidney and kidney tumor segmentation in CT imaging. Am. Soc. Clin. Oncol. 38(6), 626–626 (2020)

22. Ma, J., Zhang, Y., Song, G., Zhu, C., Ge, C., Zhang, Y., An, X., Wang, C., Wang, Q., Liu, X., Cao, S., Zhang, Q., Liu, S., Wang, Y., Li, Y., He, J., Yang, X.: Abdomenct-1k: Is abdominal organ segmentation a solved problem? IEEE Trans. Pattern Anal. Mach. Intell. 44(10), 6695–6714 (2022)

23. Yushkevich, P.A., Gao, Y., Gerig, G.: Itk-snap: An interactive tool for semi-automatic segmentation of multi-modality biomedical images. In: Annual International Conference of the IEEE Engineering in Medicine and Biology Society, pp. 3342–3345 (2016)
24. Ma, J., He, Y., Li, F., Han, L., You, C., Wang, B.: Segment anything in medical images. Nat. Commun. **15**(1), 654 (2024)
25. Pavao, A., et al.: Codalab competitions: an open source platform to organize scientific challenges. J. Mach. Learn. Res. **24**(198), 1–6 (2023)

Selected Partially Labeled Learning for Abdominal Organ and Pan-Cancer Segmentation

Yuntao Zhu[✉][iD], Liwen Zou[iD], Linyao Li[iD], and Pengxu Wen[iD]

Department of Mathematics, Nanjing University, Nanjing, China
YuntaoZhu7@smail.nju.edu.cn

Abstract. Obtaining labeled data from medical images is very expensive and labor intensive. At the same time, the large number of existing publicly available medical image datasets are usually labeled with only some of the organs as target regions, while other organs in the image are ignored. It is a challenge to train a neural network to segment all labeled categories using only partially labeled data. We design a compound loss, the selected partially cross entropy and dice loss, that allows the neural network to learn specific categories from partially labeled data. In addition, we improve the inference and training process of nnU-Net to reduce computational resources and accelerate inference. Experiments demonstrate that our method achieves the average Dice Similarity Coefficient of 0.8514 and 0.1514 on 13 abdominal organ and tumor segmentation tasks, and enables the network to efficiently segment specific categories from partially labeled data. Moreover, it significantly improves the inference speed, with an average running time of 21.8 s, and uses only an average of 2531 MB of maximum GPU memory.

Keywords: Partially labeled learning · Accelerate inference · Lightweight network

1 Introduction

Medical image segmentation aims to extract and quantify regions of interest in biological tissue or organ images. The results of target organ segmentation have many important clinical applications, such as organ quantification, surgical planning, and disease diagnosis. In recent years, deep learning-based methods have been widely used to automatically segment abdominal organs. Among these methods, nnU-Net [11] is a popular and robust framework that has won a number of organ segmentation challenges. Although it is convenient for fully supervised organ segmentation tasks and provides a solid baseline result by automatically setting network hyperparameters, this approach does not support weakly supervised segmentation and the inference process is computationally expensive and time consuming. Numerous studies have shown that the methodological performance of deep neural networks often relies heavily on the availability of large,

J. Ma and B. Wang (Eds.): FLARE 2023, LNCS 14544, pp. 209–221, 2024.
https://doi.org/10.1007/978-3-031-58776-4_17

high-quality labeled datasets for organ segmentation tasks. In order to learn robust data representations for robust and efficient medical image segmentation, we need large datasets with thousands of labeled or unlabeled data for supervised, weakly supervised, and self-supervised learning. But, the annotation of 3D medical images is a difficult and laborious task. Thus, depending on the task, only a bare minimum of images and target structures is usually annotated. This results in a situation where a zoo of partially labeled datasets is available to the community. In this context, the organizer of FLARE2023 build a large-scale and diverse abdomen CT dataset, including 4000 CT scans from servel medical datasets. There are 2200 labeled data and 1800 unlabeled data available. Compared with FLARE 2021–2022 [17,18], the challenge for FLARE 2023 is how to leverage the large amount of partial labels and unlabeled data to improve the segmentation performance while taking into account efficient inference.

In recent years, there has been a rapid evolution of semi-supervised and self-supervised learning methods [24,31]. These techniques typically learn better representations by utilizing unlabeled data, ultimately improving segmentation performance. On the one hand, one frequently employed approach in semi-supervised learning is pseudo-labeling. This method pairs the segmentation results of the network on unlabeled data as pseudo-labels, adds them to the training set, and repeats the process over several iterations. On the other hand, integrating potentially valuable additional information from different datasets, which are partially labeled, can provide more information about different anatomical target structures or related details, as well as different types of pathology. Therefore, recent advances in weak supervision explore how partially annotated datasets can train a model to segment all annotated categories [12]. Early methods considered unlabeled organs as background [4,21] and imposed penalties for overlapping predictions based on mutual exclusivity of organs [5,22]. [26] transforms the cross-entropy loss and dice loss by assigning unlabeled data from partially labeled data to the background class. [3,13,30] predict just one structure of concern per forward pass through the integration of category information at various network stages. [14] use of partial cross entropy and intraclass gray regular terms allows segmentation under weak supervision. [25] ignores the channels where unlabeled categories are located, designs a loss function that mixes binary cross-entropy and dice loss, and can handle the task of category overlap in partial labeling learning. However, there is a lack of methods that utilize both pseudo-labeled data and partially labeled learning techniques to handle organ, tumor segmentation tasks like FLARE23 that contain partially labeled and unlabeled data.

In this paper, we present a framework that utilizes both pseudo-labeled and partially labeled learning by designing a selected partially loss. We also improve nnU-Net for efficient inference and less computational resource respectively. Specifically, we choose to merge 13 organ classes of pseudo-labels and partial labels, while leaving the remaining classes unchanged, resulting in a partial labeling of the tumor. The selected partially loss, which is a combination of cross-entropy loss and dice loss, introduces a selected class mask to determine whether the class loss will compute and backward gradient. Otherwise, we find that the resampling process in the inference is time-consuming. To address this issue, we have rewritten the implementation of the resampling method and utilized a smaller network and lower resolution to minimize the computational requirements during inference.

Our main contributions are summarized as follows:

- We present a new approach, selected partially loss, which enables the use of both pseudo label and partial label data, thereby expanding the potential applications of current segmentation models.
- We optimize the time-consuming components of the resampling code in nnU-Net.
- The experiment shows that our method improves the detectability of the segmentation network for the selected class. This outperforms the baseline by 5% points for the Dice Similarity Coefficient (DSC).

2 Method

2.1 Preprocessing

For image prepossessing, all of our settings follow the default nnU-NetV2.

- Statistical analysis is conducted on data pertaining to volume spacing and foreground intensity.
- CT images are clipped at the 0.5 and 99.5 percentiles of foreground voxels.
- All images are normalized through the subtraction of the mean and division by the standard deviation.
- The volume is then resampled to a target spacing of (2.42,1.95,1.95).

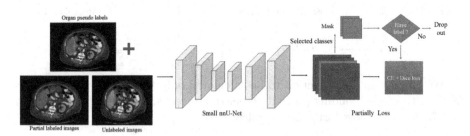

Fig. 1. Overview of our framework. Our framework consists of three parts. Firstly, we construct a training set by combining pseudo-labels. Secondly, we reduce computation costs by using a small nnU-Net. Lastly, we train nnU-Net by a selected-partially-loss so that it can learn from both unlabeled and partially-labeled data.

2.2 Proposed Method

In Fig. 1 we present an overview of our framework, which consists of three components. We filter the data by pseudo and select 300 cases as the training set. We then train a small nnU-Net using a compound partially loss on lower resolution. And our compound partially loss main refer to [14,25,26].

Fusion of Pseudo-labels and Partial-Labels. We use two pseudo-labels generated by [10,27], consisting of 13 organ categories for all 4000 cases. First, We calculate the DSC of the two pseudo-labels, evaluate their differences, and filter out the samples with DSC greater than 0.85. we sort them by their ID numbers. Subsequently, we select first 200 cases from partially labeled CT volumes and first 100 cases from unlabeled CT volumes to construct the training set. Then, the pseudo-labels are merged with the selected cases that do not contain the ground truth annotation of the class. Therefore, for the 300 cases, there are 13 organ labels (ground truth or pseudo) and tumor is partially labeled. All of our results use the pseudo-labels generated by the two FLARE 2022 methods.

Problem Definition. We begin with a dataset D, with N image and label pairs $D = \{(x,y)_1, ..., (x,y)_N\}$. In the dataset, every image voxel $x_i, i \in [1,I]$, is assigned to one class $c \in C$, where C is the label set associated to dataset D. Since the tumor is included in some organs commonly, but the pseudo label does not annotate the tumor. This implies that the network must predict multiple classes for one voxel to account for the inconsistent class definitions. To resolve the issue of label inconsistency, we separate the segmentation results for each class by applying a sigmoid activation function to replace the softmax activation function on the dataset.

Partially Loss for Selected Categories. We employ the binary cross-entropy (BCE) loss and the dice loss for each class over all $B, b \in [1, B]$, images in a batch:

$$L_c = \frac{1}{B \times I} \sum_{b,i} BCE(\hat{y}_{i,b,c},\ y_{i,b,c}) - \frac{2\sum_{b,i}\hat{y}_{i,b,c}\,y_{i,b,c}}{\sum_{b,i}\hat{y}_{i,b,c} + \sum_{b,i}y_{i,b,c}} \tag{1}$$

We modify the loss function to be calculated only for classes that are annotated in the corresponding partially labeled dataset [4,21].

This partially loss formalize as follow:

$$L = \frac{1}{\sum_{b,c}\mathbb{I}_{b,c}^{(h)}} \sum_{b,c} \left(\frac{\mathbb{I}_{b,c}^{(h)}}{I} \sum_{i} BCE(\hat{y}_{i,b,c},\ y_{i,b,c}) - \frac{2\sum_i \mathbb{I}_{b,c}^{(h)}\,\hat{y}_{i,b,c}\,y_{i,b,c}}{\sum_i \mathbb{I}_{b,c}^{(h)}\,\hat{y}_{i,b,c} + \sum_i \mathbb{I}_{b,c}^{(h)}\,y_{i,b,c}} \right) \tag{2}$$

$$\mathbb{I}_{b,c}^{(h)} = \begin{cases} 0,\ if\ c \in S\ \text{and}\ h = False, \\ 1,\ otherwise, \end{cases}$$

where $c \in S$ is the selected class set, we set $S = \{tumor\}$, h is false if the ground truth data does not include the class c, otherwise it is true. The loss use the summation between dice loss and binary cross entropy loss because compound loss functions have been proved to be robust in various medical image segmentation tasks [15].

Table 1. Network architecture and inference process.

Channels in the first stage	16
Convolution number per stage	2
Patch size	$128 \times 128 \times 128$
Downsampling times	4
inference process	(Sigmoid, Threshold, Resample)
Deep supervision	True

Speeding Inference. In order to improve inference speed and reduce resource consumption, we use a small-size network structure in reference [10]. And we change the default resampling function and order, which effectively speeds up the inference. The setup of network architecture and inference process are presented in Table 1. Comparison of different strategy settings in Table 2 . The default is full resolution setting of nnU-Net and the small is low resolution modified. The tiny is the first stage of the cascade network that we design to have a lower resolution. However, we do not use the cascade network as the final docker submission because it does not improve the accuracy and speed of the segmentation results.

Table 2. Comparison of different strategy settings. The order of axes of input patch size and spacing is (z,y,x).

Settings	Default	Small	Tiny
Channels in the first stage	32	16	8
Convolution number per stage	2	2	2
Patch size	$56 \times 192 \times 160$	$128 \times 128 \times 128$	$80 \times 96 \times 96$
Downsampling times	5	4	4
Input spacing	(2.5, 0.8, 0.8)	(2.42, 1.95, 1.95)	(5, 3.9, 3.9)

2.3 Post-processing

We do not perform any post-processing, such as connected component analysis or testing time augmentation, during our inference.

3   Experiments

3.1   Dataset and Evaluation Measures

The FLARE 2023 challenge is an extension of the FLARE 2021–2022 [17] [18], aiming to aim to promote the development of foundation models in abdominal disease analysis. The segmentation targets cover 13 organs and various abdominal lesions. The training dataset is curated from more than 30 medical centers under the license permission, including TCIA [2], LiTS [1], MSD [23], KiTS [8,9], autoPET [6,7], TotalSegmentator [28], and AbdomenCT-1K [19]. The training set includes 4000 abdomen CT scans where 2200 CT scans with partial labels and 1800 CT scans without labels. The validation and testing sets include 100 and 400 CT scans, respectively, which cover various abdominal cancer types, such as liver cancer, kidney cancer, pancreas cancer, colon cancer, gastric cancer, and so on. The organ annotation process used ITK-SNAP [29], nnU-Net [11], and MedSAM [16].

The evaluation metrics encompass two accuracy measures-Dice Similarity Coefficient (DSC) and Normalized Surface Dice (NSD)-alongside two efficiency measures-running time and area under the GPU memory-time curve. These metrics collectively contribute to the ranking computation. Furthermore, the running time and GPU memory consumption are considered within tolerances of 15 s and 4 GB, respectively.

3.2   Implementation Details

Environment Settings. The development environments and requirements are presented in Table 3.

Table 3. Development environments and requirements.

System	Ubuntu 20.04.5 LTS
CPU	Intel(R) Xeon(R) Gold 6354 CPU @ 3.00 GHz
RAM	16 ×4 GB; 1600 MT/s
GPU (number and type)	1 × NVIDIA A100 40 G
CUDA version	11.7
Programming language	Python 3.10.11
Deep learning framework	Pytorch 2.0.0, torchvision 0.2.2
Specific dependencies	nnU-Net 2.0
Code	https://github.com/orangeqqq/FLARE23

Training Protocols. The training protocols of the small nnU-Net are listed in Table 4. For the unlabeled images, we select 100 cases with the pseudo label to train the network. For partial labels, we use the partial cross-entropy and dice loss in the training stage. the pseudo labels generated by the FLARE22 winning algorithm [10] and the best-accuracy-algorithm [27]. We employ the same

Table 4. Training protocols.

Network initialization	"He" normal initialization
Batch size	4
Patch size	$128 \times 128 \times 128$
Total epochs	1000
Optimizer	SGD with nesterov momentum (μ =0.99)
Initial learning rate (lr)	0.01
Lr decay schedule	Poly learning rate policy: $(1 - epoch/1000)^{0.9}$
Training time	10 h
Loss function	Cross entropy loss and dice loss
Number of model parameters	5.22 M[a]
Number of flops	121 G[b]
CO$_2$eq	11.2 Kg[c]

[a] https://github.com/sksq96/pytorch-summary
[b] https://github.com/facebookresearch/fvcore
[c] https://github.com/lfwa/carbontracker/

data augmentation as the default setting of nnU-Net, which includes additive brightness, gamma, rotation, scaling, and elastic deformation on the fly during training. During inference, the model does not perform test time augmentation (TTA) of flipping. The patch sampling strategy is foreground over-sampling. Finally, we choose the model that obtains the fast and best accuracy on the online validation.

4   Results and Discussion

Table 5. Quantitative evaluation results in terms of DSC(%) and NSD(%).

Target	Public Validation		Online Validation		Testing	
	DSC	NSD	DSC	NSD	DSC	NSD
Liver	95.54 ± 2.53	96.86 ± 5.34	95.62	97.12	93.65	95.47
Right Kidney	87.89 ± 19.54	88.35 ± 20.41	89.35	90.01	91.63	91.62
Spleen	93.06 ± 3.77	93.55 ± 8.12	93.18	93.86	92.49	93.09
Pancreas	82.05 ± 5.93	95.41 ± 4.86	80.72	94.5	82.06	95.09
Aorta	93.05 ± 2.06	97.64 ± 3.19	93.35	97.98	93.04	98.29
Inferior vena cava	88.05 ± 5.56	90.98 ± 6.52	88.06	90.7	88.69	92.17
Right adrenal gland	74.67 ± 12.86	91.33 ± 13.74	75.24	92.12	72.23	90.71
Left adrenal gland	71.41 ± 13.29	88.43 ± 14.0	72.83	89.22	71.06	88.45
Gallbladder	82.06 ± 19.92	81.27 ± 21.06	82.52	81.86	74.11	74.13
Esophagus	78.46 ± 14.01	91.15 ± 14.41	79.12	92.15	81.85	94.98
Stomach	90.23 ± 6.08	95.25 ± 6.71	90.6	95.07	89.48	94.36
Duodenum	78.06 ± 8.28	93.96 ± 5.57	78.25	93.53	78.86	94.19
Left kidney	86.96 ± 16.61	87.77 ± 17.72	87.96	88.78	91.23	91.43
Tumor	18.21 ± 23.28	10.27 ± 15.24	15.14	8.72	17.62	8.37
Average	79.98 ± 10.98	85.87 ± 11.21	80.14	86.12	79.86	85.88

4.1   Quantitative Results on Validation Set

In Table 5, we report the DSC and NSD of the final docker commit results. The average of the 50 public validation and the 100 online validation are the same, both achieving a DSC of about 0.80 and an NSD of 0.86. In general, large organs like the liver, spleen, kidney, and stomach have high accuracy. However, accurate identification of small and complex objects, such as tumors, adrenal glands, and the duodenum, presents significant challenges. It requires more attention, especially when dealing with extremely small and indistinct boundaries.

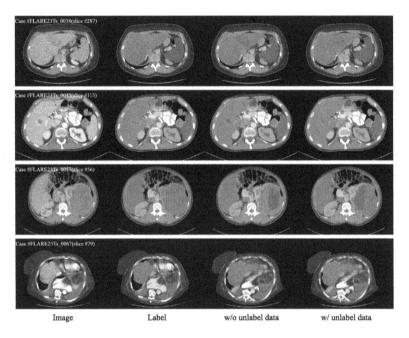

Image   Label   w/o unlabel data   w/ unlabel data

Fig. 2. Qualitative results on two easy cases (Case #FLARE23Ts_0038 with DSC of 0.89 and Case #FLARE23Ts_0043 with DSC of 0.84) and two hard cases (Case #FLARE23Ts_0057 with DSC of 0.66 and Case #FLARE23Ts_0067 with DSC of 0.74).

We report the online validation results of the model without unlabelled data, normal inference processes, and cascade networks in Table 7. The model using unlabelled data resulted in an increase of the DSC from 0.7925 to 0.8013. Specifically, in tumor regions, it increased the DSC by 0.045. Additionally, normal inference alone increased the DSC by approximately 0.04. However, the cascade network, P-Cascade and N-Cascade, which added a network training in a lower resolution setup with twice the spacing of the original, did not achieve higher DSC and NSD results. P-Cascade is the results of partially compound loss and N-Cascade is the results of normal compound loss. Comparing the two, we find that the model trained by partially labeled loss has better results for tumor segmentation, with an improvement in DSC value of 0.05.

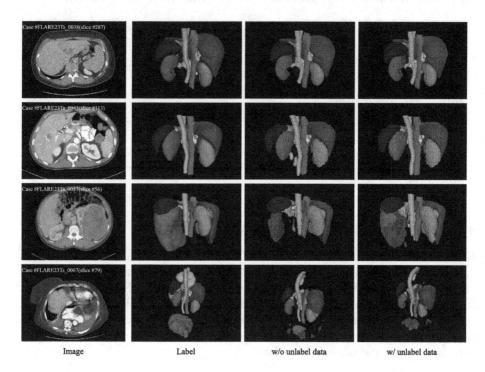

Fig. 3. 3D visualization on two easy cases (Case #FLARE23Ts_0038 with DSC of 0.89 and Case #FLARE23Ts_0043 with DSC of 0.84) and two hard cases (Case #FLARE23Ts_0057 with DSC of 0.66 and Case #FLARE23Ts_0067 with DSC of 0.74).

4.2 Qualitative Results on Validation Set

Figure 2 presents easy and difficult validation set examples for segmentation, along with a 3D visualization in Fig. 3. Promising results were observed for Case #FLARE23Ts_0038 and Case #FLARE23Ts_0043, but the segmentation of Case #FLARE23Ts_0057 and Case #FLARE23Ts_0067 was poor due to a large tumor that caused the network to make classification errors.

4.3 Segmentation Efficiency Results on Validation Set

In Table 6, we observe a set of cases that increase in size from (512, 512, 55) to (512, 512, 554). The efficiency evaluation results are reported from official tests. It is seen that the average max GPU is 2531MB, and run time increase twice for the biggest case #0029 than the smallest case #0001. This demonstrates the effectiveness of our inference strategy.

Table 6. Quantitative evaluation of segmentation efficiency in terms of the running time and GPU memory consumption. Total GPU denotes the area under GPU Memory-Time curve. Evaluation GPU platform: NVIDIA QUADRO RTX5000 (16 G).

Case ID	Image Size	Running Time (s)	Max GPU (MB)	Total GPU (MB)
0001	(512, 512, 55)	19.61	2426	10028
0051	(512, 512, 100)	17.83	2590	12296
0017	(512, 512, 150)	30.86	2634	15949
0019	(512, 512, 215)	22.72	2486	12401
0099	(512, 512, 334)	27.94	2586	15394
0063	(512, 512, 448)	33.50	2630	17508
0048	(512, 512, 499)	35.22	2614	18610
0029	(512, 512, 554)	42.53	2744	22299

4.4   Results on Final Testing Set

In Table 5, we report the DSC and NSD of the final testing set. The average values are comparable to those of the 50 public validations and the 100 online validations, with both achieving a DSC of about 0.80 and a NSD of about 0.86. In general, the low accuracy of segmenting small and complex shaped objects such as tumors, adrenal glands and duodenums Their accurate segmentation still faces great challenges and needs more attention, especially when dealing with extremely small and unclear boundaries.

4.5   Limitation and Future Work

There are many ways to improve the network inference process, such as a more efficient sliding window. The challenge provided 4000 CT cases, but we only utilized 300 cases and did not adequately utilize the data. For the challenging task of tumor segmentation, pseudo-labeling is a simple and effective way to improve model performance, and we will continue to explore methods that utilize both pseudo-labeling and partial labeling learning in the future.

Table 7. Ablation studies of online validation quantitative evaluation results in terms of DSC(%) and NSD(%). P-Cascade is the results of partially compound loss and N-Cascade is the results of normal compound loss.

Target	w/o unlabeled data		Normal inference		N-Cascade		P-Cascade	
	DSC	NSD	DSC	NSD	DSC	NSD	DSC	NSD
Liver	95.77	97.09	97.34	97.46	95.63	97.63	95.9	97.5
Right Kidney	89.93	90.49	92.18	91.46	90.27	91.27	89.9	91.28
Spleen	93.57	94.46	97	97.58	91.34	92.01	92.68	93.44
Pancreas	79.66	93.5	84.22	94.82	79.74	93.78	79.79	93.6
Aorta	92.29	96.86	96.57	99.03	92.59	97.42	93.23	97.79
Inferior vena cava	87.24	89.84	91.06	91.43	86.38	88.25	87.06	89.12
Right adrenal gland	74.24	91.78	85.51	95.48	72.75	90.19	73.35	90.59
Left adrenal gland	71.19	87.59	83.27	93.27	72.47	89.09	72.33	88.76
Gallbladder	80.34	79.38	86.09	86.55	77.9	77.05	80.54	79.83
Esophagus	78.13	90.88	83.09	93.4	78.57	91.89	79.05	92.26
Stomach	90.52	94.52	93.12	95.51	89.95	94.58	90.37	94.91
Duodenum	77.31	93.19	81.45	93.43	78.42	94.19	78.25	93.97
Left kidney	88.69	88.97	91.06	90.65	88.23	89.43	87.67	86.93
Tumor	10.64	5.92	15.17	8.42	10.25	6.99	15.88	10.43
Average	79.25	85.32	84.08	87.75	78.89	85.27	79.71	85.74

5 Conclusion

In this paper, we present a framework that combines partial labeling learning and pseudo-labeling, which is effective and flexible for a variety of situations. In addition, we use a small nnU-Net and improve the inference process, effectively reducing its required computational resources and inference time. Because the amount of data used in training is small, performance on the full data will be explored in the future. The approach in this paper will be a good baseline result for exploring partial labeling learning and pseudo-labeling.

Acknowledgements. The authors of this paper declare that the segmentation method they implemented for participation in the FLARE 2023 challenge has not used any pre-trained models nor additional datasets other than those provided by the organizers. The proposed solution is fully automatic without any manual intervention. We thank all the data owners for making the CT scans publicly available and CodaLab [20] for hosting the challenge platform.

References

1. Bilic, P., et al.: The liver tumor segmentation benchmark (lits). Med. Image Anal. **84**, 102680 (2023)
2. Clark, K., et al.: The cancer imaging archive (TCIA): maintaining and operating a public information repository. J. Digit. Imaging **26**(6), 1045–1057 (2013)
3. Dmitriev, K., Kaufman, A.E.: Learning multi-class segmentations from single-class datasets. In: Conference on Computer Vision and Pattern Recognition (CVPR) (2019)

4. Fang, X., Yan, P.: Multi-organ segmentation over partially labeled datasets with multi-scale feature abstraction. IEEE Trans. Med. Imaging **39**(11), 3619–3629 (2020)
5. Fidon, L., et al.: Label-set loss functions for partial supervision: application to fetal brain 3d MRI parcellation. In: Medical Image Computing and Computer Assisted Intervention (2021)
6. Gatidis, S., et al.: The autopet challenge: towards fully automated lesion segmentation in oncologic pet/ct imaging. preprint at Research Square (Nature Portfolio) (2023). https://doi.org/10.21203/rs.3.rs-2572595/v1
7. Gatidis, S., et al.: A whole-body FDG-pet/CT dataset with manually annotated tumor lesions. Sci. Data **9**(1), 601 (2022)
8. Heller, N., et al.: The state of the art in kidney and kidney tumor segmentation in contrast-enhanced CT imaging: results of the kits19 challenge. Med. Image Anal. **67**, 101821 (2021)
9. Heller, N., et al.: An international challenge to use artificial intelligence to define the state-of-the-art in kidney and kidney tumor segmentation in ct imaging. Proc. Am. Soc. Clin. Oncol. **38**(6), 626–626 (2020)
10. Huang, Z., et al.: Revisiting nnU-net for iterative pseudo labeling and efficient sliding window inference. In: Ma, J., Wang, B. (eds.) Fast and Low-Resource Semi-supervised Abdominal Organ Segmentation, FLARE 2022, LNCS, vol. 13816, pp. 178–189. Springer, Cham (2022). https://doi.org/10.1007/978-3-031-23911-3_16
11. Isensee, F., Jaeger, P.F., Kohl, S.A., Petersen, J., Maier-Hein, K.H.: nnU-net: a self-configuring method for deep learning-based biomedical image segmentation. Nat. Methods **18**(2), 203–211 (2021)
12. Li, S., Wang, H., Meng, Y., Zhang, C., Song, Z.: Multi-organ segmentation: a progressive exploration of learning paradigms under scarce annotation. arXiv preprint arXiv:2302.03296 (2023)
13. Liu, J., et al.: Clip-driven universal model for organ segmentation and tumor detection. In: Proceedings of the IEEE/CVF International Conference on Computer Vision, pp. 21152–21164 (2023)
14. Luo, X., et al.: Word: a large scale dataset, benchmark and clinical applicable study for abdominal organ segmentation from CT image. Med. Image Anal. **82**, 102642 (2022)
15. Ma, J., et al.: Loss odyssey in medical image segmentation. Med. Image Anal. **71**, 102035 (2021)
16. Ma, J., He, Y., Li, F., Han, L., You, C., Wang, B.: Segment anything in medical images. Nat. Commun. **15**(1), 654 (2024)
17. Ma, J., et al.: Fast and low-GPU-memory abdomen CT organ segmentation: the flare challenge. Med. Image Anal. **82**, 102616 (2022)
18. Ma, J., et al.: Unleashing the strengths of unlabeled data in pan-cancer abdominal organ quantification: the flare22 challenge. arXiv preprint arXiv:2308.05862 (2023)
19. Ma, J., et al.: Abdomenct-1k: Is abdominal organ segmentation a solved problem? IEEE Trans. Pattern Anal. Mach. Intell. **44**(10), 6695–6714 (2022)
20. Pavao, A., et al.: Codalab competitions: an open source platform to organize scientific challenges. J. Mach. Learn. Res. **24**(198), 1–6 (2023)
21. Roulet, N., Slezak, D.F., Ferrante, E.: Joint learning of brain lesion and anatomy segmentation from heterogeneous datasets. In: Proceedings of The 2nd International Conference on Medical Imaging with Deep Learning (2019)
22. Shi, G., Xiao, L., Chen, Y., Zhou, S.K.: Marginal loss and exclusion loss for partially supervised multi-organ segmentation. Med. Image Anal. **70**, 101979 (2021)

23. Simpson, A.L., et al.: A large annotated medical image dataset for the development and evaluation of segmentation algorithms. arXiv preprint arXiv:1902.09063 (2019)

24. Tang, Y., et al.: Self-supervised pre-training of swin transformers for 3d medical image analysis. In: Conference on Computer Vision and Pattern Recognition (CVPR) (2022)

25. Ulrich, C., Isensee, F., Wald, T., Zenk, M., Baumgartner, M., Maier-Hein, K.H.: Multitalent: a multi-dataset approach to medical image segmentation. arXiv preprint arXiv:2303.14444 (2023)

26. Wang, C., Cui, Z., Yang, J., Han, M., Carneiro, G., Shen, D.: Bowelnet: joint semantic-geometric ensemble learning for bowel segmentation from both partially and fully labeled CT images. IEEE Trans. Med. Imaging **42**(4), 1225–1236 (2023)

27. Wang, E., Zhao, Y., Wu, Y.: Cascade dual-decoders network for abdominal organs segmentation. In: Ma, J., Wang, B. (eds.) Fast and Low-Resource Semi-supervised Abdominal Organ Segmentation, FLARE 2022, LNCS, vol. 13816, pp. 202–213. Springer, Cham (2022). https://doi.org/10.1007/978-3-031-23911-3_18

28. Wasserthal, J., et al.: Totalsegmentator: robust segmentation of 104 anatomic structures in CT images. Radiol. Artif. Intell. **5**(5), e230024 (2023)

29. Yushkevich, P.A., Gao, Y., Gerig, G.: Itk-snap: an interactive tool for semi-automatic segmentation of multi-modality biomedical images. In: Annual International Conference of the IEEE Engineering in Medicine and Biology Society, pp. 3342–3345 (2016)

30. Zhang, J., Xie, Y., Xia, Y., Shen, C.: Dodnet: learning to segment multi-organ and tumors from multiple partially labeled datasets. In: Proceedings of the IEEE/CVF Conference on Computer Vision and Pattern Recognition (CVPR), June 2021

31. Zhou, Z., Sodha, V., Pang, J., Gotway, M.B., Liang, J.: Models genesis. Med. Image Anal. **67**, 101840 (2021)

3D Swin Transformer for Partial Medical Auto Segmentation

Aneesh Rangnekar(✉) ⓘ, Jue Jiang, and Harini Veeraraghavan

Memorial Sloan Kettering Cancer Center, New York, USA
rangnea@mskcc.org

Abstract. Transformers are the highest accuracy segmentation frameworks in computer vision for natural imagery from the past few years. In contrast, medical imaging approaches, except a select few (for example, SwinUNETR and SMIT), are still dominated by the nnU-Net architecture family. In this paper, we investigate the application of a hierarchical vision transformer to the FLARE-23 challenge.

Specifically, we benchmark our results using a relatively lightweight architecture, Swin-X Seg. We use multi-model self-training, wherein we use nnU-Net for predicting pseudo labels on partially labeled cases and then optimize the transformer architecture for memory requirements. Our network achieved the average DSC scores of 83.13 % and 35.19 % on the open validation set (50 cases) for organs and tumors, respectively, while staying under a max GPU memory utilization of 4GB at evaluation runtime. Our results show that there is potential for the transformer architecture to perform at par or better than conventional convolutional approaches, and we hope our findings encourage more research in the area.

Keywords: Auto Segmentation · Self-training · Swin Transformer

1 Introduction

Accurate, fast, and automated volumetric segmentation of organs and tumors is essential for radiotherapy treatment planning. It often constitutes one of the time-consuming parts of radiation treatment planning workflows [37]. Abdominal organs are particularly time-consuming to segment owing to the presence of a large number of organs as well as due to the random and large variation in the appearance and shape of gastrointestinal organs and limited soft-tissue contrast on clinically used computed tomography (CT) images. Hence, deep learning methods to generate segmentation are under active development [2,20].

Deep learning methods have shown the capability to generate multi-organ segmentation for abdomen [1,16,18,34] and other disease sites. The availability of well-curated public challenge datasets [2,20] has enabled the evaluation of various methods using the same reference benchmark with well-defined metrics. However, a fundamental prerequisite of well-curated pixel-wise annotations

J. Ma and B. Wang (Eds.): FLARE 2023, LNCS 14544, pp. 222–235, 2024.
https://doi.org/10.1007/978-3-031-58776-4_18

or volumetric segmentations of the various organs for training these networks must be more expensive and time-consuming to generate on large datasets. One recent promising approach to alleviate the need for large, curated datasets is the self-supervised pretraining followed by a fine-tuning approach that has demonstrated success in medical image analysis, mainly when using transformer-based architectures [18,34]. Swin UNETR [34] and SMIT [18] have shown that using self-supervised learning (SSL) improves the performance of transformer-based networks on semantic segmentation, as compared to training the networks from scratch. Our approach builds on these methods and utilizes a transformer architecture [21] for segmentation with a pretraining step (self-supervised learning) using labeled and unlabeled examples followed by fine-tuning.

We also follow the FLARE-23 rules, whereby, unlike prior works [18,34], which used a large number of CT scans from various disease sites for pretraining, we used only the 4,000 example scans provided as part of the training set for self-supervised pretraining. Furthermore, keeping with the requirements for using a relatively small architecture with limited memory requirements, we also constructed a lightweight transformer architecture.

Our learning framework uses multi-model self-training [32,41,42], where the teacher is an fine-tuned nnU-Net [15] that generates pseudo labels for the various categories. The student network uses a Swin transformer backbone [21] segmentation network (here on referred to as Swin-X Seg) that accepts a combination of FLARE-23 and pseudo labeled examples for fine-tuning (Fig. 1). Our initial studies show that naively using the partially labeled dataset, with a transformer backbone to obtain pseudo labels, results in poor performance across multiple categories [5,36,40]. Hence, we resort to this combination of semi-supervised learning, wherein the teacher is an nnU-Net and the student is Swin-X Seg.

Our approach allows us to fully utilize the partially-labeled training dataset to its fullest extent, while leveraging fundamental augmentation techniques shown to be effective in natural image analysis. This mitigates the need for requiring complex approaches like the CutMix [43] or ClassMix [29], wherein extensive registration would be required before mixing two 3D scans so that the networks do not lose understanding of organ placements, especially with architectures that rely heavily on positional information.

Our key contributions are (a) a lightweight 3D vision transformer applied to multi-organ and tumor segmentation, (b) the SSL approach extending prior works by learning the downstream task using partial labels, and the application of this approach on an open-source FLARE-23 dataset.

2   Method

2.1   Overview

We studied the performance of hierarchical vision transformer-based U-Net architecture on the FLARE-23 challenge. Vision transformers require large amounts of data [5,19,36,40] to achieve high generalization performance. Hence, FLARE-23, which consists of 4,000 training images, provides a nice test bed for

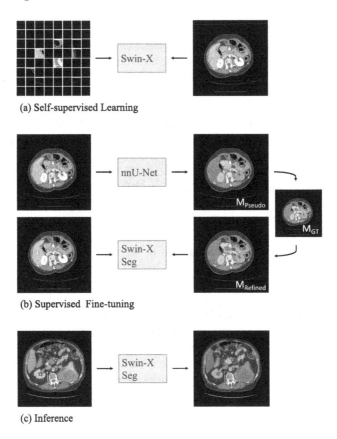

Fig. 1. Our three-stage pipeline: (a) self-supervised training of the backbone network [17], (b) uses a combination of pseudo labels (M_{Pseudo}) [15] and FLARE-23 provided annotations (M_{GT}) to obtain refined labels ($M_{Refined}$) for learning segmentation, and (c) inference on a new unseen volumetric scan.

evaluating vision transformer architectures. However, 1800 CTs in FLARE-23 are unlabeled with the remaining 2200 CTs provided with partial labels, wherein some but not all the 14 different organs and tumors were segmented, which makes supervised training challenging. Therefore, we used a two-step training approach consisting of: (i) self-supervised pretraining performed on the entire dataset of 4,000 CTs without using any segmentations for supervised training, and (ii) supervised fine-tuning that combined fully labeled CTs together with CTs with pseudo labels created using a different model. We discuss each part of our approach in detail, and the specificities involved in our final implementation.

2.2   Preprocessing

We used the following preprocessing steps in all our experiments:

– Reorient the scans to the right-anterior-superior (RAS) view.

- Clip the intensities based on the Hounsfield units to $[-250, 250]$.
- We resize all scans to x, y, z volumetric spacings of $1.0, 1.0, 1.0$ during training and inference.
- In addition, we randomly sample 4 scans of $96 \times 96 \times 96$ size from each scan as training examples, representing 2 positive and 2 negative samples for the network at every instance.

2.3 Proposed Method

Choice of Transformer:
Hierarchical Vision Transformers [8,21] are pyramid-shaped architectures that rely on gradual down-sampling, similar to convolutional neural networks, while maintaining a global look-out with their multi-scale designs. We use the Swin-Transformer backbone for our approach as it has been widely adopted for 3D medical auto segmentation [18,34] and shown to be more accurate than the vanilla vision transformer [7].

Swin UNETR [34] and SMIT [18] have over 60 million (M) parameters. Whereas Swin UNETR processes data at $96 \times 96 \times 96$, SMIT processes data at $128 \times 128 \times 128$ resolution. Both methods use sliding windows for generating final inference. The FLARE-23 constraints require memory efficient inference. A straightforward memory efficient approach to reduce the total number of flops used for inference would be to utilize CT scans reduced to $96 \times 96 \times 96$ pixels, at the risk of decreasing the image resolution, which can impact accuracy for smaller organs. Hence, we reduced the number of parameters used in the network by decreasing the total number of blocks per depth to the final $2 - 2 - 2 - 2$ configuration as well as reduced the total number of channels through the UNETR architecture using 1×1 convolutions. This reduced the network size from 60M parameters to 31M parameters, a relatively lightweight architecture compared to current state-of-the-art methods. This is also crucial towards keeping the GPU requirements under 4GB as stipulated under FLARE-23 rules.

Self-supervised Learning: The SSL approach made use of the self-distillation based pretext tasks used in the SMIT [18], including namely Masked Image Modeling (MIM), Masked Patch self-Distillation (MPD) and Image Token self-Distillation (ITD). SMIT performs self distillation by concurrently maintaining an online teacher model (NET_T) with the same network architecture as the student model (NET_S) [35]. The loss functions used to optimize the network are briefly discussed here and we refer interested details to the original paper [18] for more details.

Suppose $\{x_1, x_2\}$ are two augmented views of a 3D image x. N image patches are extracted from the images to create a sequence of image tokens [7]. The image tokens are then corrupted by randomly masking image tokens based on a binary vector, with a probability p, and then replacing with mask token [3]. The second augmented view v is also corrupted but using a different mask vector instance. In this order, the three losses deal with the views in the following manner:

- **Masked Image Prediction (MIP)** $\rightarrow x_1$, NET_S, involves dense pixel regression of image intensities within masked patches using the context of unmasked patches [12].
- **Masked patch token self-distillation (MPD):** $\rightarrow x_1$, NET_S, NET_T, trains the student network to predicts the tokens of the teacher network (distillation).
- **Global image token self-distillation (ITD):** $\rightarrow x_1, x_2$, NET_S, NET_T, learns to match the global image embedding of the view-scan seen by the student network to the view-scan seen by the teacher network.

SSL training is performed by optimizing the network using all three aforementioned losses. FLARE-23 rules dictate that no external data be used. Hence, following the rules, SSL used the same 4,000 CTs provided as part of the training set. No segmentations provided with the data was used for network optimization in this step.

Supervised Fine-tuning:
In order to fully utilize all available training data to improve accuracy, we used the best performing nnU-Net model, the winner from FLARE22 [15] to provide pseudo labels for the partially labeled and unlabeled datasets the FLARE 23 training sets. We only use 735 examples from the 2200 images that contain a labeled instance of tumor, with the combination of FLARE-23 and nnU-Net pseudo labels (Fig. 1). We trained our network sing a combination of Dice loss and cross-entropy loss following previous approaches [16,18,24,34].

2.4 Post-processing

No data specific post processing was used following pixel-level classifications generated by the segmentation methods. Sliding window inference with 50% overlap was used for generating segmentations for the whole 3D image volumes.

3 Experiments

3.1 Dataset and Evaluation Measures

The FLARE-23 challenge is an extension of the FLARE 2021–2022 [26] [27], aiming to promote the development of foundation models in abdominal disease analysis. The segmentation targets cover 13 organs and various abdominal lesions around the organs. The dataset comprises scans from more than 30 medical centers, including TCIA [6], LiTS [4], MSD [33], KiTS [13,14], autoPET [9,10], TotalSegmentator [39], and AbdomenCT-1K [28], with appropriate licensing. The training set includes 4,000 abdomen CT scans, 2,200 CT scans with partial segmentation labels for some of them, and 1,800 CT scans without any segmentation labels. The validation and testing sets include 100 and 400 CT scans, respectively, covering various abdominal cancer types, such as liver, kidney, pancreas, colon, and gastric, to name a few. The organ annotation process used ITK-SNAP [44], nnU-Net [16], and MedSAM [25].

Table 1. Development environments and requirements.

System	Ubuntu 18.04.5 LTS
CPU	AMD EPYC 7543P 32-Core Processor @ 2.8 Ghz
RAM	128 GB
GPU (number and type)	NVIDIA A100 80 GB × 4
CUDA version	11.8
Programming language	Python 3.8
Deep learning framework	Pytorch 1.13 ± CUDA 11.7 [30]
Specific dependencies	MONAI, SimpleITK, Nibabel
Code	https://github.com/The-Veeraraghavan-Lab/FLARE23

Table 2. Training protocols.

Network initialization	SSL-FLARE-23 [18]
Batch size	4
Patch size	96 × 96 × 96
Total epochs	100
Optimizer	AdamW [23]
Initial learning rate (lr)	$2e-4$
Lr decay schedule	Linear Warmup with Cosine Annealing [11,22]
Training time	33 h
Loss function	Cross-Entropy Loss /w Dice Loss

The evaluation metrics encompass two accuracy measures-Dice Similarity Coefficient (DSC) and Normalized Surface Dice (NSD)-alongside two efficiency measures-running time and instantaneous GPU maximum memory consumption.

3.2 Implementation Details

Environment Settings. The development environments and requirements are presented in Table 1. We provide all the requirements in our released codebase on GitHub.

Training Protocols. The model training protocols are shown in Table 2. An image patch size of 96 × 96 × 96 with random 3D flips performed on the data to provide augmented samples was used for network training.

Table 3. Quantitative evaluation results. Segmentation accuracy results (DSC and NSD with mean and standard deviation) are reported on the publicly provided 50 validation cases made available by the FLARE-23 organizers.

Target	Public Validation	
	DSC (%)	NSD (%)
Liver	96.08 ± 4.230	93.58 ± 10.66
Right Kidney	87.00 ± 20.81	83.37 ± 21.81
Spleen	93.24 ± 9.730	90.92 ± 14.23
Pancreas	80.47 ± 7.860	89.99 ± 7.020
Aorta	90.55 ± 14.80	91.61 ± 16.30
Inferior vena cava	87.88 ± 6.800	86.97 ± 9.300
Right adrenal gland	77.35 ± 17.46	87.78 ± 19.00
Left adrenal gland	72.44 ± 15.83	82.03 ± 16.59
Gallbladder	75.61 ± 28.21	71.61 ± 30.06
Esophagus	74.81 ± 16.56	84.85 ± 15.99
Stomach	89.17 ± 9.110	87.60 ± 11.85
Duodenum	70.78 ± 10.77	84.21 ± 9.240
Left kidney	85.65 ± 21.81	82.33 ± 23.22
Tumor	35.19 ± 30.17	22.99 ± 22.10
Average (Organ)	83.13 ± 8.440	85.55 ± 12.58
Average	79.70 ± 11.43	81.08 ± 14.93

4   Results and Discussion

4.1   Quantitative Results on Validation Set

Table 3 shows our Swin-X Seg's performance on the 50 validation cases provided by the FLARE-23 organizers. The network was slightly less accurate (<80% DSC) for organs such as the adrenal glands, gallbladder, esophagus, duodenum, as well as for tumors compared to larger organs like the liver, spleen, left and right kidneys, and the stomach. The tumor segmentation accuracy was low because of the larger variability in the types of tumors analyzed and the relatively few examples with complete labels. Overall, the network accuracy was lower for smaller organs like the adrenal glands and gallbladder when compared to larger organs like the liver. Poor accuracy for organs also resulted when they were adjacent to the tumors.

Table 4 shows that inference requirements of under 4 GB GPU memory consumption were satisfied for all cases. However, all except two cases (0001, 0019) did not satisfy the running time requirement under 60 secs owing to sliding window-based inference, with 50% overlap. A natural option is to use sliding window inference without any overlap (0%). However, this results in a poor overall score (77% DSC average on organ, 27% DSC on tumor); hence, we did

Table 4. Quantitative evaluation of segmentation efficiency of the reported cases using running time and maximum GPU memory consumption (<4096 MB). Evaluation GPU platform: A100 (80GB).

Case ID	Image Size	Running Time (s)	Max GPU (MB)
0001	(512, 512, 55)	28.01	3464
0051	(512, 512, 100)	65.86	3850
0017	(512, 512, 150)	73.94	3896
0019	(512, 512, 215)	48.00	3616
0099	(512, 512, 334)	69.28	3756
0063	(512, 512, 448)	84.76	3776
0048	(512, 512, 499)	74.73	3748
0029	(512, 512, 554)	102.5	4032

not pursue it. In addition, we optimized for test-time efficiency by performing foreground thresholding to use only the body regions for analysis by ignoring the surrounding air for inference. Our analysis showed that in cases with larger field of view, wherein the body occupied higher volume the inference time utilization increased (e.g. 0017 > 0019, 0063 > 0048).

4.2 Qualitative Results on Validation Set

Figures 2 and 3 show the segmentations generated by our network on representative examples taken from the validation set of FLARE-23. As shown in Fig. 2, whereas the model tends to consistently segment the normal tissues with high accuracy, misclassifications occur within tumor regions, tumor voxels classified as the kidney, despite achieving a relatively high DSC accuracy for the tumors. The higher DSC accuracy for tumors is not surprising given the larger tumor volumes. On the other hand, as shown in Fig. 3 for really large tumors such as #0057 and #0095, the algorithm generated highly inaccurate segmentation, misclassifying the tumors occurring on the left side of anatomy as liver. #0027 shows an example where the kidney tumor was correctly segmented together with the kidney adjacent to the tumor, although the esophagus occurring distally to the pancreatic head was misclassified as pancreas. Similarly, in #0089, the pancreas is oversegmented by the model, whereas the kidney tumor encased within the kidney is undersegmented, highlighting the challenges, particularly when the tumor and the healthy tissues are adjacent to each other.

4.3 Segmentation Efficiency Results on Validation Set

We optimized for segmentation inference efficiency by extracting the foreground or the body as a preprocessing step using standard image thresholding. No additional optimization was performed in terms of training or testing. Even this simple approach showed that it is possible to improve inference efficiency as seen in Table 4.

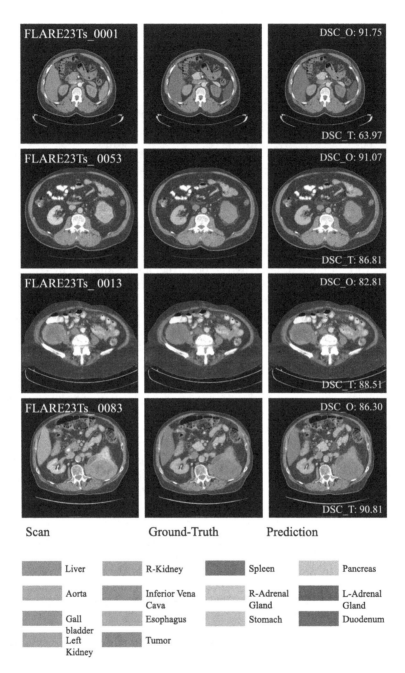

Fig. 2. Example scans showing relatively good performance in terms of misclassifications by the trained Swin-X Seg model. DSC_T refers to tumor DSC and DSC_O refers to average multi-organs DSC.

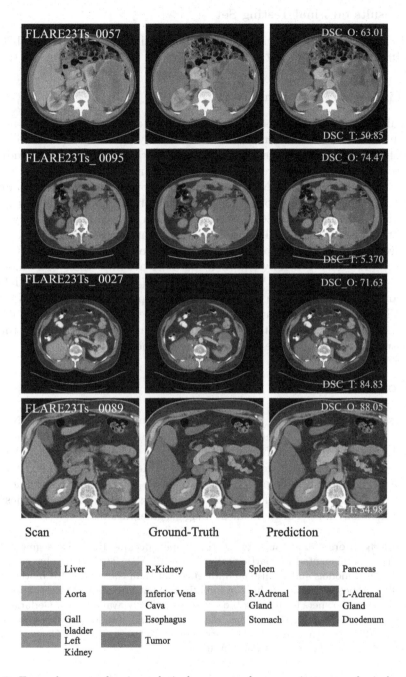

Fig. 3. Example scans showing relatively poor performance in terms of misclassifications by the trained Swin-X Seg network. DSC_T refers to tumor DSC and DSC_O refers to average multi-organs DSC.

4.4   Results on Final Testing Set

This is a placeholder. We will send you the testing results during MICCAI (2023.10.8). (This is to be left as is.)

4.5   Limitation and Future Work

Our goal was to evaluate the capability of transformer-based approach for multi-organ and tumor segmentation. We used a relatively lightweight (31M) in order to satisfy the memory requirements of the competition as well as to study to what extent such methods are successful in comparison to convolutional-based approaches such as the nnU-Net used in the previous iteration of the competition [15,38]. Our approach to use nnU-Net generated pseudo labels was motivated by prior results using Semiformer [40], which showed poor accuracy with vision transformer with small labeled training samples can be improved when combined with pseudo labels produced by convolutional neural networks (CNN). However, VITs have generally shown to be more accurate than CNN models. Hence, one approach is to use VIT instead of a CNN for providing pseudo labels. its important to note that the approach combining pseudo labels with CNN and larger VIT models becomes impractical due to increasing memory needs. Another limitation of our approach is the poor segmentations we observed on the tumor and tissue interface, which we plan to address in the future.

5   Conclusion

We presented our approach, multi-model self-training, that used nnU-Net to generate pseudo labels and then Swin transformer to establish a foundation for research into auto segmentation with pseudo labels. In addition, we also identify limitations and discuss research approaches to mitigate them, including knowledge distillation and semi-supervised learning. We believe that our framework serves as a good foundation for further research into efficient network designs and methodology for accurate medical image segmentation.

Acknowledgements. The authors of this paper declare that the segmentation method they implemented for participation in the FLARE-23 challenge has not used any pre-trained models and additional datasets other than those provided by the organizers. The proposed solution is fully automatic without any manual intervention. We thank all the data owners for making the CT scans publicly available and CodaLab [31] for hosting the challenge platform. This research was partly funded through grant from NCI R01CA258821-01A1 and the Memorial Sloan Kettering (MSK) Cancer Center Support Grant/Core Grant NCI P30 CA008748.

References

1. Amjad, A., et al.: General and custom deep learning autosegmentation models for organs in head and neck, abdomen, and male pelvis. Med. Phys. **49**(3), 1686–1700 (2022)
2. Antonelli, M., et al.: The medical segmentation decathlon. Nat. Commun. **13**(1), 4128 (2022)
3. Bao, H., Dong, L., Piao, S., Wei, F.: BEiT: BERT pre-training of image transformers. arXiv preprint arXiv:2106.08254 (2021)
4. Bilic, P., et al.: The liver tumor segmentation benchmark (LiTS). Med. Image Anal. **84**, 102680 (2023)
5. Cao, Y.H., Yu, H., Wu, J.: Training vision transformers with only 2040 images. In: Avidan, S., Brostow, G., Cisse, M., Farinella, G.M., Hassner, T. (eds.) ECCV 2022. LNCS, vol. 13685, pp. 220–237. Springer, Cham (2022). https://doi.org/10.1007/978-3-031-19806-9_13
6. Clark, K., et al.: The cancer imaging archive (TCIA): maintaining and operating a public information repository. J. Digit. Imaging **26**(6), 1045–1057 (2013)
7. Dosovitskiy, A., et al.: An image is worth 16×16 words: transformers for image recognition at scale. arXiv preprint arXiv:2010.11929 (2020)
8. Fan, H., et al.: Multiscale vision transformers. In: Proceedings of the IEEE/CVF International Conference on Computer Vision, pp. 6824–6835 (2021)
9. Gatidis, S., et al.: The autopet challenge: towards fully automated lesion segmentation in oncologic PET/CT imaging. Preprint at Research Square (Nature Portfolio) (2023). https://doi.org/10.21203/rs.3.rs-2572595/v1
10. Gatidis, S., et al.: A whole-body FDG-PET/CT dataset with manually annotated tumor lesions. Sci. Data **9**(1), 601 (2022)
11. Goyal, P., et al.: Accurate, large minibatch SGD: training imagenet in 1 hour. arXiv preprint arXiv:1706.02677 (2017)
12. He, K., Chen, X., Xie, S., Li, Y., Dollár, P., Girshick, R.: Masked autoencoders are scalable vision learners. In: Proceedings of the IEEE/CVF Conference on Computer Vision and Pattern Recognition, pp. 16000–16009 (2022)
13. Heller, N., et al.: The state of the art in kidney and kidney tumor segmentation in contrast-enhanced CT imaging: results of the KiTS19 challenge. Med. Image Anal. **67**, 101821 (2021)
14. Heller, N., et al.: An international challenge to use artificial intelligence to define the state-of-the-art in kidney and kidney tumor segmentation in CT imaging. Proc. Am. Soc. Clin. Oncol. **38**(6), 626 (2020)
15. Huang, Z., et al.: Revisiting nnU-net for iterative pseudo labeling and efficient sliding window inference. In: Ma, J., Wang, B. (eds.) FLARE 2022. LNCS, vol. 13816, pp. 178–189. Springer, Cham (2022). https://doi.org/10.1007/978-3-031-23911-3_16
16. Isensee, F., Jaeger, P.F., Kohl, S.A., Petersen, J., Maier-Hein, K.H.: nnU-Net: a self-configuring method for deep learning-based biomedical image segmentation. Nat. Methods **18**(2), 203–211 (2021)
17. Jiang, J., et al.: Nested block self-attention multiple resolution residual network for multiorgan segmentation from CT. Med. Phys. **49**(8), 5244–5257 (2022)
18. Jiang, J., Tyagi, N., Tringale, K., Crane, C., Veeraraghavan, H.: Self-supervised 3D anatomy segmentation using self-distilled masked image transformer (SMIT). In: Wang, L., Dou, Q., Fletcher, P.T., Speidel, S., Li, S. (eds.) MICCAI 2022. LNCS, vol. 13434, pp. 556–566. Springer, Cham (2022). https://doi.org/10.1007/978-3-031-16440-8_53

19. Kirillov, A., et al.: Segment anything. arXiv preprint arXiv:2304.02643 (2023)
20. Landman, B., Xu, Z., Igelsias, J., Styner, M., Langerak, T., Klein, A.: MICCAI multi-atlas labeling beyond the cranial vault–workshop and challenge. In: Proceedings of the MICCAI Multi-Atlas Labeling Beyond Cranial Vault-Workshop Challenge, vol. 5, p. 12 (2015)
21. Liu, Z., et al.: Swin transformer: hierarchical vision transformer using shifted windows. In: Proceedings of the IEEE/CVF International Conference on Computer Vision, pp. 10012–10022 (2021)
22. Loshchilov, I., Hutter, F.: SGDR: stochastic gradient descent with warm restarts. arXiv preprint arXiv:1608.03983 (2016)
23. Loshchilov, I., Hutter, F.: Decoupled weight decay regularization. arXiv preprint arXiv:1711.05101 (2017)
24. Ma, J., et al.: Loss odyssey in medical image segmentation. Med. Image Anal. **71**, 102035 (2021)
25. Ma, J., He, Y., Li, F., Han, L., You, C., Wang, B.: Segment anything in medical images. Nat. Commun. **15**, 654 (2024)
26. Ma, J., et al.: Fast and low-GPU-memory abdomen CT organ segmentation: the flare challenge. Med. Image Anal. **82**, 102616 (2022)
27. Ma, J., et al.: Unleashing the strengths of unlabeled data in pan-cancer abdominal organ quantification: the flare22 challenge. arXiv preprint arXiv:2308.05862 (2023)
28. Ma, J., et al.: AbdomenCT-1K: is abdominal organ segmentation a solved problem? IEEE Trans. Pattern Anal. Mach. Intell. **44**(10), 6695–6714 (2022)
29. Olsson, V., Tranheden, W., Pinto, J., Svensson, L.: Classmix: segmentation-based data augmentation for semi-supervised learning. In: Proceedings of the IEEE/CVF Winter Conference on Applications of Computer Vision (WACV), pp. 1369–1378 (2021)
30. Paszke, A., et al.: Pytorch: an imperative style, high-performance deep learning library. In: Wallach, H., Larochelle, H., Beygelzimer, A., d' Alché-Buc, F., Fox, E., Garnett, R. (eds.) Advances in Neural Information Processing Systems 32, pp. 8024–8035. Curran Associates, Inc. (2019). http://papers.neurips.cc/paper/9015-pytorch-an-imperative-style-high-performance-deep-learning-library.pdf
31. Pavao, A., et al.: CodaLab competitions: an open source platform to organize scientific challenges. J. Mach. Learn. Res. **24**(198), 1–6 (2023)
32. Rangnekar, A., Kanan, C., Hoffman, M.: Semantic segmentation with active semi-supervised representation learning. arXiv preprint arXiv:2210.08403 (2022)
33. Simpson, A.L., et al.: A large annotated medical image dataset for the development and evaluation of segmentation algorithms. arXiv preprint arXiv:1902.09063 (2019)
34. Tang, Y., et al.: Self-supervised pre-training of swin transformers for 3D medical image analysis. In: Proceedings of the IEEE/CVF Conference on Computer Vision and Pattern Recognition, pp. 20730–20740 (2022)
35. Tarvainen, A., Valpola, H.: Mean teachers are better role models: weight-averaged consistency targets improve semi-supervised deep learning results. In: Proceedings of the 31st International Conference on Neural Information Processing Systems, NIPS 2017, pp. 1195–1204. Curran Associates Inc., Red Hook (2017)
36. Touvron, H., Cord, M., Douze, M., Massa, F., Sablayrolles, A., Jégou, H.: Training data-efficient image transformers & distillation through attention. In: International Conference on Machine Learning, pp. 10347–10357. PMLR (2021)
37. Vandewinckele, L., et al.: Overview of artificial intelligence-based applications in radiotherapy: recommendations for implementation and quality assurance. Radiother. Oncol. **153**, 55–66 (2020)

38. Wang, E., Zhao, Y., Wu, Y.: Cascade dual-decoders network for abdominal organs segmentation. In: Ma, J., Wang, B. (eds.) FLARE 2022. LNCS, vol. 13816, pp. 202–213. Springer, Cham (2022). https://doi.org/10.1007/978-3-031-23911-3_18
39. Wasserthal, J., et al.: TotalSegmentator: robust segmentation of 104 anatomic structures in CT images. Radiol. Artif. Intelli. 5(5), e230024 (2023)
40. Weng, Z., Yang, X., Li, A., Wu, Z., Jiang, Y.G.: Semi-supervised vision transformers. In: Avidan, S., Brostow, G., Cissé, M., Farinella, G.M., Hassner, T. (eds.) ECCV 2022. LNCS, vol. 13690, pp. 605–620. Springer, Cham (2022). https://doi.org/10.1007/978-3-031-20056-4_35
41. Xie, Q., Luong, M.T., Hovy, E., Le, Q.V.: Self-training with noisy student improves imagenet classification. In: Proceedings of the IEEE/CVF Conference on Computer Vision and Pattern Recognition, pp. 10687–10698 (2020)
42. Yang, L., Zhuo, W., Qi, L., Shi, Y., Gao, Y.: ST++: make self-training work better for semi-supervised semantic segmentation. In: Proceedings of the IEEE/CVF International Conference on Computer Vision and Pattern Recognition (CVPR) (2022)
43. Yun, S., Han, D., Oh, S.J., Chun, S., Choe, J., Yoo, Y.: CutMix: regularization strategy to train strong classifiers with localizable features. In: Proceedings of the IEEE/CVF International Conference on Computer Vision, pp. 6023–6032 (2019)
44. Yushkevich, P.A., Gao, Y., Gerig, G.: ITK-snap: an interactive tool for semi-automatic segmentation of multi-modality biomedical images. In: Annual International Conference of the IEEE Engineering in Medicine and Biology Society, pp. 3342–3345 (2016)

Partial-Labeled Abdominal Organ and Cancer Segmentation via Cascaded Dual-Decoding U-Net

Zhiyu Ye[1,2,3], Hairong Zheng[1,3], and Tong Zhang[2(✉)]

[1] Shenzhen Institute of Advanced Technology, Shenzhen, China
[2] Peng Cheng Laboratory, Shenzhen, China
zhangt02@pcl.ac.cn
[3] University of Chinese Academy of Sciences, Beijing, China

Abstract. In the FLARE2023 challenge, we developed a cascaded dual-decoding U-Net framework to address the complex task of partial-labeled abdominal organ and cancer segmentation. Initially, we explored the potential of 3D transformer-based models but transitioned to 2D U-Net solutions due to computational resource and inference time constraints. We first trained separate 3D models for cancer and full-organ segmentation using data that included labels for both cancer and full organs. Subsequently, we generated pseudo labels for unlabeled and partially labeled data based on these initial models. To enable a single model to effectively learn and infer both organ and cancer labels within images, we designed a dual-decoding structure based on the 2D U-Net architecture. Our training process involved several steps with various subsets of the training data. By comparing our model trained without unlabeled data, we discussed the impact of unlabeled data and its pseudo labels on the experimental results. Our method, the version trained without unlabeled data, achieved an average DSC score of 83.22% for organs and 33.22% for lesions on the validation set. The average running time and area under the GPU memory-time curve were 33.8 s and 50066.25 MB, respectively. The codes has been open-sourced to https://openi.pcl.ac.cn/OpenMedIA/pclmedia_FLARE23.

Keywords: FLARE2023 · Partial-labeled abdominal organ and cancer segmentation · U-Net

1 Introduction

The segmentation of abdominal organs and lesions has always been a classic research task in medical image analysis and also plays a fundamental role in facilitating medical practitioners in areas such as diagnosis, surgical planning, and various clinical applications. In open datasets and challenges focused on individual organs, such as LiTS [2] and KiTS [11,12], the developed models have consistently achieved impressive results, with state-of-the-art Dice Similarity

J. Ma and B. Wang (Eds.): FLARE 2023, LNCS 14544, pp. 236–252, 2024.
https://doi.org/10.1007/978-3-031-58776-4_19

Coefficient (DSC) scores consistently surpassing 0.95. Furthermore, researchers are also working towards the development of models with the capacity to concurrently segment multiple organs and lesions, ultimately augmenting the utility of automated segmentation in medical practice. However, the existing open datasets for multiple abdominal organs often fall short of meeting the demands for training comprehensive segmentation models encompassing all abdominal organs and lesions. To illustrate, the AbdomenCT-1K dataset [21] covers only four abdominal organs, while the BTCV dataset [15], though has thirteen organ labels, comprises only 50 images, and none of these two datasets includes lesion segmentation.

Addressing the time-consuming and labour-intensive nature of labelling targets for segmentation in extensive medical images is a significant challenge that must be tackled in the development of medical image segmentation algorithms. A viable solution is trying to make the most of labeled data for certain organs and lesions, or even leveraging unlabeled data. From this perspective, FLARE2023 offers a dataset comprising 1800 unlabeled and 2200 partially labelled CT images, with the aim of encouraging participants to develop solutions that can effectively perform simultaneous segmentation of thirteen abdominal organs and cancer.

In recent years, extensive research has been conducted to address the problem of partial-label segmentation for abdominal organs and cancer. Several methods have emerged as promising solutions for this task. One approach is to achieve dynamic and diverse object segmentation by incorporating with adaptive filters during the decoding or output stages within a unified encoding-decoding architecture. Notable examples of this approach include DoDNet [31] and the conditional nnU-Net [30]. Another prevalent architectural design tailored to this domain is the implementation of a multi-head decoder. For instance, models like MFUnetr [8] incorporate separate segmentation heads for both full and partial organ segmentation. In terms of learning strategies, researchers have explored various methods to utilize the unlabeled data. These strategies encompass multi-stage training, model distillation and integration, semi-supervised learning method such as pseudo label generation, sometimes even combining multiple strategies. It is noteworthy that the FLARE2022 conference proceedings [18] feature an extensive array of solutions that exemplify the practical application of these methods.

Moreover, self-supervised learning methods offer a practical approach to this task. One widely used strategy is the pre-training and fine-tuning of transformer-based networks. During the pre-training stage, an abundance of unlabeled images can be leveraged to equip the transformer encoder with the ability to comprehend input images and extract meaningful features. An illustrative example is Swin UNETR [26], which achieved state-of-the-art results on BTCV [15] and MSD [1] datasets after pre-training on 5050 unlabeled data. Similarly, UNETR [9], which also employs a vision transformer as the encoder, can employ this self-supervised learning approach.

At the outset, we embarked on a self-supervised learning approach with 3D transformer-based networks, specifically Swin UNETR and UNETR. In parallel, we supervised trained a 3D U-Net model using a limited portion of labelled data for comparison. However, it became evident that the GPU memory consumption of 3D models far exceeded the specified 4 GB. As a result, we pivoted directly to a different strategy, opting for the classic 2D UNet architecture and embracing a semi-supervised training strategy. This involved initial training on unlabeled data with pseudo labels generated by 3D U-Net, and the model was sequentially trained on data with varying label patterns. Ultimately, this revised approach yielded a model that surpassed our initial 3D models in terms of both segmentation performance and inference efficiency. In this paper, we will discuss our solution and contributions from the following aspects:

- We adopted various strategies and trained multiple networks to address this task, including transformer-based Swin UNETR and UNETR, as well as CNN-based 3D and 2D U-Net models for this task. We conducted comprehensive comparisons and in-depth analyses of the results derived from these varied approaches.
- To facilitate training on partially-labeled data, we devised a dual decoding structure based on the 2D U-Net architecture. This design enables us to fix certain parameters while updating others during different training steps.
- In our comparison between 2D models trained with and without unlabeled data, we observed that even the model was trained with inaccurate pseudo labels of unlabeled data, it led to an improvement in the model's performance.

2   Method

Figure 1 presents an overview of our method. Given the evolution of our method, transitioning from a transformer-based to a CNN-based approach and from 3D to 2D, it is structured into two distinct stages: the 3D model training stage (Fig. 1(b)) and the 2D model training stage (Fig. 1(d)). Within each training stage, several steps were undertaken, and each step is trained on a subset as defined in Fig. 1(a) of the training data. Notably, the 3D models play a pivotal role in generating pseudo labels for the subsequent training of the 2D model, as illustrated in Fig. 1(c).

2.1   Data Partition

There are a total of fourteen classes to be segmented in the FLARE2023 task, where labels 1 to 13 correspond to thirteen abdominal organs, and label 14 corresponds to cancer. The training data can be categorized into different subsets based on their label patterns, as demonstrated in Fig. 1(a):

- D_u: 1800 unlabeled images.
- D_{l1}: 250 images with labels for all thirteen organs (labels 1 to 13).
- D_{l2}: 458 images with labels for only five organs (labels 1, 2, 3, 4, and 13), representing the liver, right kidney, spleen, pancreas, and left kidney, respectively.

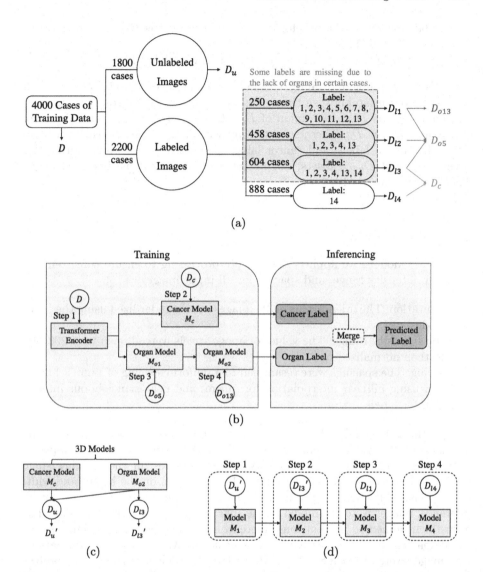

Fig. 1. Visualization of our data partitioning method and training strategy. (a) Data Partitioning. The entire training dataset D has been segmented into five distinct subsets D_u, D_{l1}, D_{l2}, D_{l3}, and D_{l4}. Specifically, D_{o13}, D_{o5}, and D_c represent data containing 13 organ labels, 5 organ labels, and cancer labels, respectively. (b) Training and Inference Process for 3D Models. Transformer-based models underwent four training steps, while the 3D U-Net skipped the first two steps. (c) Pseudo Label Generation with 3D Models. The trained 3D U-Net M_c and M_{o2} are employed to generate pseudo labels for cancer and organs in images from datasets D_u and D_{l3}. These images with pseudo labels are denoted as D_u' and D_{l3}'. (d) Training Process for 2D U-Net. In the first two training steps, all model parameters were updated, while in steps 3 and 4, only some of the model parameters were updated.

- D_{l3}: 604 images with labels for the same five organs as D_{l2}, as well as cancer (label 1, 2, 3, 4, 13 and 14).
- D_{l4}: 888 images with label exclusively for cancer (label 14).

Therefore, the complete training dataset D is the union of D_u, D_{l1}, D_{l2}, D_{l3}, and D_{l4}, with no overlap between these subsets. Additionally, for training purposes, we denote D_{l1} as D_{o13}, the union of D_{l1}, D_{l2}, and D_{l3} as D_{o5}, and the union of D_{l3} and D_{l4} as D_c. These subsets represent data containing thirteen organ labels, five organ labels, and cancer labels, respectively. It's worth noting that within D_{o5} and D_{o13} subsets, not all images have labels as described above. There are instances where certain organs are missing, resulting in some images lacking one or several labels corresponding to the absent organs.

2.2   Pre-processing

For the 3D models, we applied uniform pre-processing to ensure consistent orientation, intensity range, and spacing for all input images:

- Orientation: The orientations of 3D images were standardized using the 'RAS' axcodes.
- Scale Intensity Range: The values of image voxels were clipped to $[-200, 300]$ and then normalized to $[0, 1]$.
- Spacing: The spacings were resampled to a uniform spacing of $1\,\text{mm} \times 1\,\text{mm} \times 1\,\text{mm}$ using bilinear interpolation for images and nearest neighbour interpolation for labels.

For the 2D models, the pre-processing steps were similar but with some parameter differences. Specifically, the values of image voxels were clipped to $[-200, 300]$ when scaling the intensity ranges. Besides, in the training stage, images were resampled to the spacing of $1\,\text{mm} \times 1\,\text{mm}$ on the height and width dimensions, while the depth dimension remained unchanged. However, during inference, images were resampled to the spacing of $1\,\text{mm} \times 1\,\text{mm} \times 2.5\,\text{mm}$. This adjustment aimed to prevent long inference times caused by some images with small spacing and an excessive number of slices. After these transformations, the images were sliced into 2D samples along the depth dimension to prepare for training.

2.3   Proposed Method

Our approach comprises two primary stages: 3D model training and 2D model training. Initially, we aimed to develop our model based on state-of-the-art architectures like Swin UNETR [26] or UNETR [9]. Unfortunately, the performance of these 3D transformer-based models did not meet our expectations and even underperformed in comparison to 3D U-Net [4], as detailed in Sect. 4.1. Furthermore, these 3D transformer-based models need excessive GPU memory consumption and long running times, making them cost-ineffective to optimize.

Consequently, we made the decision to pivot towards solutions rooted in the conventional 2D U-Net [24] architecture. To maximize the utilization of the unlabeled data, we leveraged the trained 3D models to generate pseudo labels for 2D model training.

3D Training Stage. The training process of our 3D models is illustrated in Fig. 1(b). For transformer-based networks, specifically Swin UNETR and UNETR, we initiated the training by pre-training their transformer encoders using the MAE method, as described in [3,10], on the complete training dataset D, then we fixed the parameters of the transformer encoders throughout the subsequent steps.

Given that our image data was partially labeled, we pursued the training of two separate models-one for predicting cancer labels and the other for organ labels. These two training processes occurred in parallel. Building upon the pre-trained encoder, one model underwent fine-tuning solely on the dataset D_c to yield the cancer model M_c. Concurrently, another model was initially fine-tuned on the dataset D_{o5} to obtain model M_{o1}, which was designed to predict labels for five specific organs. Subsequently, model M_{o1} underwent continuous fine-tuning on the dataset D_{o13}, ultimately yielding the comprehensive organ model M_{o2}, which is capable of predicting labels for all organs.

In contrast, the 3D U-Net did not undergo a pre-training phase or training on dataset D_{o5}. Instead, we directly trained two distinct models, M_c and M_{o2}, for the segmentation of cancer and organs by utilizing the datasets D_c and D_{o13}, respectively.

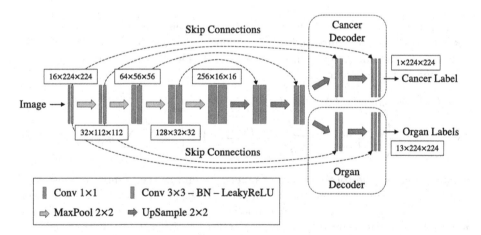

Fig. 2. The network architecture of our proposed dual-decoding U-Net. In this configuration, the decoder comprises two branches in the final two upsampling stages, enabling the network to simultaneously train on data labeled for both organs and cancers, and generate corresponding labels for both.

2D Training Stage. In light of the insights gained from the training of our 3D models and with the aim of further enhancing efficiency, we have transitioned away from training separate models for cancer and organs. Instead, we have devised a network featuring a dual-decoding structure based on the 2D U-Net architecture. This design enables the model to produce labels for both cancer and organs concurrently. We refer to the two decoders responsible for generating these labels as the 'cancer decoder' and the 'organ decoder'. A schematic representation of this network is illustrate in Fig. 2. Furthermore, we have ensured that the network's parameters remain unaffected during training on different types of data. This network structure provides the capability to simultaneously extract features related to both cancer and organs from images, while also allowing us to leverage unlabeled data.

To made the use of models M_c and M_{o1} from the 3D U-Net version, we utilized them to predict pseudo labels for all images within D_{l3} and unlabeled images in D_u (Fig. 1(c)). It is important to note that within D_{l3}, only pseudo labels for the eight remaining organs were used, as the other five organs already had ground truth labels. For clarity, we denote datasets D_u and D_{l3} with pseudo labels as D'_u and D'_{l3}, respectively.

The training process for this 2D model consists of four steps. In the first and second steps, the entire network was trained using datasets D'_u and D'_{l3}, respectively. Moving to the third step, training was conducted on dataset D_{l1}, which includes thirteen organ labels. The parameters of the network were fixed in this step, except for those of organ decoder. The fourth step is similar to the third step, but dataset D_{l4} was used. In this case, the parameters of the cancer decoder updated, while keeping the other parameters fixed.

Loss Function. We used the summation between Dice loss [22] and cross-entropy loss because compound loss functions have been proven to be robust in various medical image segmentation tasks [16]. The loss function is calculated according to the following formula:

$$L\left(G, P\right) = L_{dice}\left(G, P\right) + L_{ce}\left(G, P\right)$$
$$= \left(1 - \frac{2}{J} \sum_{j=1}^{J} \frac{\sum_{i=1}^{I} g_{i,j} p_{i,j}}{\sum_{i=1}^{I} g_{i,j}^2 + \sum_{i=1}^{I} p_{i,j}^2}\right) + \left(-\frac{1}{I} \sum_{i=1}^{I} \sum_{j=1}^{J} g_{i,j} \log p_{i,j}\right) \quad (1)$$

where I denotes the total number of pixels, J denotes the number of classes. G and P respectively represent the sets of pixels in the ground truth and prediction. For any pixel $g_{i,j} \in G$ and its corresponding prediction $p_{i,j} \in P$, $g_{i,j} = 1$ if the i-th pixel is classified into the j-th class and $g_{i,j} = 0$ if not, $p_{i,j}$ is the predicted probability of the i-th pixel belonging to class j.

2.4   Post-processing

In our method, whether 3D or 2D models, the initial model outputs provide either cancer labels or organ labels which do not encompass all fourteen labels.

The comprehensive predicted results, including all fourteen labels, were achieved by overlaying the cancer labels onto the organ labels.

To ensure that the final prediction results align with the original input image, the inverse transforms of the orientation and spacing during the pre-processing were performed on the final outputs. Besides, no additional post-processing was applied.

3   Experiments

3.1   Dataset and Evaluation Measures

The FLARE 2023 challenge is an extension of the FLARE 2021–2022 [19] [20], aiming to aim to promote the development of foundation models in abdominal disease analysis. The segmentation targets cover 13 organs and various abdominal lesions. The training dataset is curated from more than 30 medical centers under the license permission, including TCIA [5], LiTS [2], MSD [25], KiTS [11,12], autoPET [6,7], TotalSegmentator [28], and AbdomenCT-1K [21]. The training set includes 4000 abdomen CT scans where 2200 CT scans with partial labels and 1800 CT scans without labels. The validation and testing sets include 100 and 400 CT scans, respectively, which cover various abdominal cancer types, such as liver cancer, kidney cancer, pancreas cancer, colon cancer, gastric cancer, and so on. The organ annotation process used ITK-SNAP [29], nnU-Net [14], and MedSAM [17].

The evaluation metrics encompass two accuracy measures-Dice Similarity Coefficient (DSC) and Normalized Surface Dice (NSD)-alongside two efficiency measures—running time and area under the GPU memory-time curve. These metrics collectively contribute to the ranking computation. Furthermore, the running time and GPU memory consumption are considered within tolerances of 15 s and 4 GB, respectively.

Table 1. Development environments and requirements.

System	Ubuntu 20.04.5 LTS
CPU	Intel(R) Xeon(R) Platinum 8260 CPU @ 2.40 GHz
RAM	4 × 16 DDR4 2933 MHz
GPU (number and type)	Two NVIDIA V100 32G
CUDA version	12.0
Programming language	Python 3.8.13
Deep learning framework	torch 1.13.0, monai 1.1.0
Specific dependencies	NA
Code	NA

3.2   Implementation Details

Details regarding the development environments and requirements are presented in Table 1. Our method was implemented using PyTorch[1] and MONAI[2]. We leveraged modules and functions from MONAI for pre-processing and post-processing during both training and inference.

The non-random preprocessing, as introduced in Sect. 2.2, was consistently applied during both training and inference. Additionally, for the purpose of data augmentation during training, several other transforms were employed:

- Crop Foreground: All input images underwent cropping based on their image intensity. Only the largest bounding box containing voxel values greater than 0 within the image was retained.
- Randomly Crop Samples: For 3D models, input images were randomly cropped into two patches of size $128 \times 128 \times 128$. For 2D models, input images were randomly cropped into samples of size 224×224.
- Gaussian Noise: Gaussian noise with a standard deviation of 0.05 was randomly added with a probability of 0.5.
- Intensity Scaling and Shifting: Image intensities were randomly scaled by a factor of 0.1 and shifted with randomly selected offsets from the range $[-0.1, 0.1]$. Both of these operations occurred with a probability of 0.5.

The training protocols for 3D and 2D U-Net models are outlined in Table 2 and Table 3, respectively. In the case of the 3D U-Net, we selected the model with the lowest Dice loss as the optimal model. As for the 2D U-Net, approximately 20% of the slices were designated as validation data, ensuring that slices from the same image were either included in the validation set or the training set. The optimal model for the 2D U-Net was chosen based on the Dice score achieved on the validation data.

Table 2. Training protocols for 3D U-Net.

Training Model	cancer model M_c	organ model M_{o2}
Network initialization	random	
Batch size	4	
Patch size	$128 \times 128 \times 128$	
Number of data (cases)	1492	250
Total epochs	60	250
Optimizer	AdamW, weight decay 10^{-5}	
Initial learning rate (lr)	5×10^{-4}	
Lr schedule	warm up of 5 epochs	warm up of 10 epochs
Training time	88 h	32 h
Loss function	Dice loss and cross-entropy loss	
Number of model parameters	1.439 M	
Number of flops	21.9 G	

---

[1] https://pytorch.org/.
[2] https://monai.io/.

Table 3. The training protocols for the 2D U-Net models M_1 to M_4 correspond to the four steps outlined in Fig. 1(d).

Training Model	M_1	M_2	M_3	M_4
Network initialization	random	M_1	M_2	M_3
Batch size	128			
Patch size	224×224			
Number of data (slices)	330828	123698	64121	349701
Total epochs	20	30	60	20
Optimizer	AdamW, weight decay 10^{-5}			
Initial learning rate (lr)	10^{-4}	5×10^{-4}	5×10^{-4}	10^{-4}
Lr schedule	polynomial decay with power 0.9			
Training time	24.5 h	9 h	9.5 h	26 h
Loss function	Dice loss and cross-entropy loss			
Number of model parameters	2.388 M			
Number of flops	26 G			

4   Results and Discussion

4.1   Quantitative Results on Validation Set

Results of the Submitted Solution. The validation results of our submitted solution can be found in Table 4. Regrettably, we did not discover that we had accidentally included the 50 validation cases with ground truth in our training data until writing this paper, despite our initial intent to use this data solely for selecting the optimal model. As a result, the submitted model's performance was unfairly influenced. Consequently, we retrained our models entirely from scratch. The results of the retraining models are presented in subsequent ablation studies, and these results are truly noteworthy and thought-provoking.

Ablation Studies. In this part, we present a comparative analysis of the performance of our 3D and 2D models on validation data.

Table 5 displays the online validation results for the 3D models Swin UNETR, UNETR, and U-Net. Despite Swin UNETR and UNETR being pre-trained on the entire training dataset, their performance falls significantly short of that achieved by the 3D U-Net model. From the table, it is evident that the average DSC and NSD)scores for the 3D U-Net across all fourteen classes are approximately 4–6% higher compared to the other two models. Regarding cancer segmentation specifically, the DSC score of 3D U-Net surpasses that of Swin UNETR by 0.14% and UNETR by 6.8%, respectively. Furthermore, while Swin UNETR outperforms UNETR marginally in terms of the results, Swin UNETR

Table 4. Quantitative evaluation results of our submitted solution. The public validation denotes the performance on the 50 validation cases with ground truth. The online validation denotes the leaderboard results. The Testing results will be released during MICCAI.

Target	Public Validation		Online Validation		Testing	
	DSC(%)	NSD(%)	DSC(%)	NSD(%)	DSC(%)	NSD (%)
Liver	98.45 ± 0.42	99.58 ± 0.50	97.90	98.19	95.18	94.80
Right Kidney	97.12 ± 1.74	98.67 ± 2.28	94.08	94.80	93.73	93.36
Spleen	97.78 ± 0.62	99.13 ± 1.26	95.48	95.58	93.78	92.19
Pancreas	88.32 ± 3.67	98.41 ± 1.33	79.33	91.52	72.62	85.53
Aorta	95.87 ± 3.77	98.38 ± 2.69	94.85	96.80	94.82	96.97
Inferior vena cava	92.37 ± 3.77	94.91 ± 4.35	89.61	90.58	87.69	87.89
Right adrenal gland	82.98 ± 10.86	94.70 ± 8.19	78.43	91.12	67.65	80.24
Left adrenal gland	81.62 ± 10.29	93.86 ± 7.59	73.28	84.33	64.39	75.28
Gallbladder	91.80 ± 13.78	94.10 ± 14.02	83.78	84.37	69.53	68.30
Esophagus	86.09 ± 5.16	96.46 ± 3.64	81.50	92.84	79.85	90.66
Stomach	95.38 ± 1.87	98.60 ± 1.66	91.38	92.75	84.09	83.74
Duodenum	87.06 ± 5.94	99.05 ± 1.20	76.00	92.31	64.31	84.02
Left kidney	96.53 ± 2.27	97.64 ± 3.89	93.23	93.79	93.69	93.22
Tumor	87.19 ± 8.30	86.22 ± 10.03	57.66	52.38	17.58	9.64
Average	91.33 ± 2.74	96.41 ± 3.56	84.75	89.38	77.06	81.13

Table 5. Online validation results of Swin UNETR, UNETR and 3D U-Net.

Target	Swin UNETR		UNETR		3D U-Net	
	DSC(%)	NSD(%)	DSC(%)	NSD(%)	DSC(%)	NSD (%)
Liver	94.24	94.55	94.22	94.68	94.59	96.25
Right Kidney	83.78	84.95	88.89	90.57	87.71	89.85
Spleen	91.63	92.36	89.33	89.32	90.51	91.20
Pancreas	70.15	85.08	69.05	85.28	75.58	91.09
Aorta	86.79	88.84	86.74	86.29	92.81	95.61
Inferior vena cava	85.13	86.81	81.54	79.08	89.34	91.21
Right adrenal gland	70.23	87.18	65.12	82.13	71.46	88.48
Left adrenal gland	61.88	77.92	60.36	75.11	68.17	85.26
Gallbladder	69.90	66.73	64.68	57.81	70.44	66.65
Esophagus	69.07	83.32	67.26	83.35	76.59	90.10
Stomach	82.65	84.99	78.77	80.90	86.51	90.09
Duodenum	66.96	84.94	58.51	81.98	73.42	89.93
Left kidney	78.41	79.65	84.72	86.27	86.68	88.79
Tumor	11.34	5.99	14.67	6.18	21.47	11.65
Average	73.01	78.81	71.70	77.07	77.52	83.30

Table 6. Comparison of quantitative evaluation results in online validation between models trained with and without unlabeled data.

Model trained	w/o unlabeled data		with unlabeled data	
Target	DSC(%)	NSD(%)	DSC(%)	NSD(%)
Liver	96.67	95.62	96.88	95.19
Right Kidney	89.24	88.3	88.72	87.69
Spleen	93.15	91.24	93.06	91.1
Pancreas	78.54	90.39	74.63	85.99
Aorta	94.45	96.66	91.97	94.3
Inferior vena cava	90.41	91.65	87.46	88.05
Right adrenal gland	69.89	84.98	68.23	80.64
Left adrenal gland	67.68	79.08	59.73	72.85
Gallbladder	74.79	72.45	74.06	70.73
Esophagus	79.05	91.35	76.07	89.01
Stomach	87.59	87.17	85.19	85.89
Duodenum	72.72	87.95	65.12	86.24
Left kidney	87.64	86.87	83.86	83.44
Tumor	33.22	23.32	33.31	23.1
Average	79.65	83.36	77.02	81.02

consumes significantly more GPU memory and takes longer running times during both training and inference when compared to UNETR.

For 2D models, our primary focus was to assess the influence of utilizing unlabeled data on model performance, and the results are presented in Table 6. The model that excluded unlabeled data was trained following the steps outlined in Fig. 1(d), omitting step 1. From the table, it is evident that the model's performance, when trained with unlabeled data, does not surpass that of the model trained without unlabeled data. In fact, the overall DSC score has decreased by 2.63%. Notably, the inclusion of unlabeled data resulted in a significant decrease in DSC scores for all organs, except for the liver. This decrease was particularly pronounced in the left adrenal gland and duodenum. However, it is worth mentioning that unlabeled data did lead to a slight improvement in cancer segmentation, with online validation DSC scores 0.11% higher than those achieved by models trained exclusively on labeled data. This performance disparity may be attributed to the absence of filtering or restrictions applied to the pseudo labels generated from unlabeled data. It is worth noting that the 3D U-Net model used for generating these pseudo labels demonstrated limited reliability, as evidenced by its average DSC score, which is only 77.52% in online validation. Consequently, during the final training steps with labeled data, where most model parameters were fixed and only certain parameters in decoder were updated, the model's performance was significantly influenced by the data quality used in the initial training steps. Additionally, the unlabeled data comprises a portion of full-body CT scans, while the validation set exclusively consists of abdominal CT scans. This divergence in data distribution can also contribute to the decline in model performance when unlabeled data was utilized. In the context of cancer segmentation, the considerable variation in the number, size, and location of cancer lesions compared to organs is critical. Therefore, even if the pseudo labels for unlabeled data are not highly accurate, a substantial volume of anisotropic data may still contribute to improving the model's ability to segment cancer to some extent.

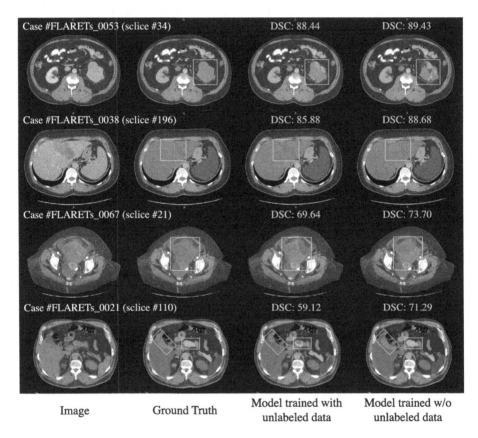

| Image | Ground Truth | Model trained with unlabeled data | Model trained w/o unlabeled data |

Fig. 3. Visualizations of segmentation results. The top two rows showcase two examples with good segmentation results, while the bottom two rows display two instances with bad segmentation results in the validation set. The DSC scores (%) are calculated for cases, not for slices. Areas with notable differences between the model's segmentation and ground truth have been highlighted within yellow boxes. (Color figure online)

4.2   Qualitative Results on Validation Set

Figure 3 presents four segmentation results from the validation set. Specifically, Case ♮00053 and ♮0038 have relatively high DSC scores, while Case ♮0067 and

Table 7. Quantitative evaluation of segmentation efficiency in terms of the running time and GPU memory consumption. Total GPU denotes the area under GPU Memory-Time curve. Evaluation GPU platform: NVIDIA QUADRO RTX5000 (16G).

Case ID	Image Size	Running Time (s)	Max GPU (MB)	Total GPU (MB)
0001	(512, 512, 55)	50.82	3012	41724
0051	(512, 512, 100)	34.39	3860	53855
0017	(512, 512, 150)	48.45	4642	56855
0019	(512, 512, 215)	42.4	5360	42851
0099	(512, 512, 334)	38.16	7152	73287
0063	(512, 512, 448)	33.82	8796	72601
0048	(512, 512, 499)	35.92	9492	78669
0029	(512, 512, 554)	52.49	10424	121664

♮0021 have relatively low DSC scores. The yellow boxes in the first three lines signify that the trained model encounters difficulties in cancer segmentation. When cancer lesions are large or significantly alter the original organ shape, achieving accurate segmentation becomes a challenging task. In addition, these four examples collectively illustrate that models trained with unlabeled data exhibit greater stability in organ segmentation compared to models trained without unlabeled data. This finding aligns with the conclusion presented in Table 6.

4.3 Segmentation Efficiency Results on Validation Set

Though our submitted model did not achieve fairness in validation results, it is essential to note that its network structure remained unchanged in the retrained model, ensuring the validity and consistency of segmentation efficiency results.

Table 7 presents the segmentation efficiency for eight validation cases, arranged in order of increasing image depths from top to bottom. Notably, GPU and total memory consumption increased as the number of image layers increased, with only Case ♮0001 and Case ♮0051 utilizing the maximum GPU memory within the recommended 4 GB limit. Additionally, the running times do not exhibit consistent changes with varying image sizes. This discrepancy arises because all images were reshaped to have identical spacing before prediction, resulting in inconsistent numbers of slices to be inferred compared to the original images.

It's important to mention that in post-processing, our initial approach was to resize the predicted labels using nearest-neighbor interpolation, an operation suitable for CPU. However, we faced a challenge that the orientations of images were not consistently aligned. We had uniformly applied MONAI modules to adjust the orientation during pre-processing, and only MONAI's inverse modules were capable of reversing this transformation. Since both pre- and post-processing operations in MONAI rely on GPU, this approach resulted in nearly doubling the GPU memory consumption.

4.4   Results on Final Testing Set

This is a placeholder. We will send you the testing results during MICCAI (2023.10.8).

4.5   Limitation and Future Work

Cancer segmentation remains a persistent challenge in our research, with results that continue to fall short of expectations. The intricacies of training high-performing models on datasets characterized by inconsistent annotations and anisotropic images represent a compelling and enduring topic in the field of medical image analysis. Further exploration and innovation in this domain are warranted to advance the state-of-the-art and improve the accuracy of cancer segmentation together with organ segmentation.

In the analysis in Sect. 4.1, we observed that the quality of pseudo labels from unlabeled data could influence model performance in our approach. Although we were provided with pseudo labels generated by the FLARE22 winning algorithm [13] and the best-accuracy-algorithm [27], we did not incorporate them into our work. Additionally, our method comprises multiple training steps, yet our ablation analysis solely focused on the utilization of unlabeled data. Furthermore, we did not conduct ablation experiments to assess the impact of our designed dual-decoding network framework. As a result, future research can also explore the effects of varying pseudo label quality on model performance. Moreover, investigations can be extended to evaluate the influence of different methodological steps and network structures on model performance. This comprehensive analysis can provide a deeper understanding of the factors contributing to model effectiveness.

5   Conclusion

In the FLARE2023 challenge, we presented a cascaded dual-decoding U-Net solution for this partial-labeled abdominal organ and cancer segmentation. Throughout our research, we explored various model architectures, including both transformer-based and CNN-based models, as well as 3D and 2D models. Through continuous analysis of results and strategy adjustments, we ultimately adopted a designed 2D dual-coding U-Net, utilizing 3D U-Net for pseudo label generation and conducting multi-step iterative training. We also conducted an in-depth analysis of the influence of unlabeled data on model performance. Interestingly, our findings demonstrated that pseudo labels of low quality may not only fail to improve model performance but can even degrade the model's organ segmentation performance, as indicated by the results of online validation. In conclusion, our model trained without the use of unlabeled data achieved average DSC and NSD scores of 79.65% and 83.36%, respectively, in online validation.

Acknowledgements. The authors of this paper declare that the segmentation method they implemented for participation in the FLARE 2023 challenge has not used any pre-trained models nor additional datasets other than those provided by the organizers. The proposed solution is fully automatic without any manual intervention. We thank all the data owners for making the CT scans publicly available and CodaLab [23] for hosting the challenge platform. This work is supported in part by the Major Key Project of PCL (grant No. PCL2023AS7-1) and the National Natural Science Foundation of China (grant No. U21A20523). The computing resources of Pengcheng Cloudbrain are used in this research. We acknowledge the support provided by OpenI Community (https://git.openi.org.cn).

References

1. Antonelli, M., et al.: The medical segmentation decathlon. Nat. Commun. **13**(1), 4128 (2022)
2. Bilic, P., et al.: The liver tumor segmentation benchmark (LiTS). Med. Image Anal. **84**, 102680 (2023)
3. Chen, Z., Agarwal, D., Aggarwal, K., Safta, W., Balan, M.M., Brown, K.: Masked image modeling advances 3D medical image analysis. In: Proceedings of the IEEE/CVF Winter Conference on Applications of Computer Vision, pp. 1970–1980 (2023)
4. Çiçek, Ö., Abdulkadir, A., Lienkamp, S.S., Brox, T., Ronneberger, O.: 3D U-Net: learning dense volumetric segmentation from sparse annotation. In: Ourselin, S., Joskowicz, L., Sabuncu, M.R., Unal, G., Wells, W. (eds.) MICCAI 2016. LNCS, vol. 9901, pp. 424–432. Springer, Cham (2016). https://doi.org/10.1007/978-3-319-46723-8_49
5. Clark, K., et al.: The cancer imaging archive (TCIA): maintaining and operating a public information repository. J. Digit. Imaging **26**(6), 1045–1057 (2013)
6. Gatidis, S., et al.: The autopet challenge: towards fully automated lesion segmentation in oncologic PET/CT imaging. Preprint at Research Square (Nature Portfolio) (2023). https://doi.org/10.21203/rs.3.rs-2572595/v1
7. Gatidis, S., et al.: A whole-body FDG-PET/CT dataset with manually annotated tumor lesions. Sci. Data **9**(1), 601 (2022)
8. Hao, Q., Tian, S., Yu, L., Wang, J.: MFUnetr: a transformer-based multi-task learning network for multi-organ segmentation from partially labeled datasets. Biomed. Signal Process. Control **85**, 105081 (2023)
9. Hatamizadeh, A., et al.: UNETR: transformers for 3D medical image segmentation. In: Proceedings of the IEEE/CVF Winter Conference on Applications of Computer Vision, pp. 574–584 (2022)
10. He, K., Chen, X., Xie, S., Li, Y., Dollár, P., Girshick, R.: Masked autoencoders are scalable vision learners. In: Proceedings of the IEEE/CVF Conference on Computer Vision and Pattern Recognition, pp. 16000–16009 (2022)
11. Heller, N., et al.: The state of the art in kidney and kidney tumor segmentation in contrast-enhanced CT imaging: results of the KiTS19 challenge. Med. Image Anal. **67**, 101821 (2021)
12. Heller, N., et al.: An international challenge to use artificial intelligence to define the state-of-the-art in kidney and kidney tumor segmentation in CT imaging. Proc. Am. Soc. Clin. Oncol. **38**(6), 626 (2020)
13. Huang, Z., et al.: Revisiting nnU-Net for iterative pseudo labeling and efficient sliding window inference. In: Ma, J., Wang, B. (eds.) FLARE 2022. LNCS, vol. 13816, pp. 178–189. Springer, Cham (2022). https://doi.org/10.1007/978-3-031-23911-3_16

14. Isensee, F., Jaeger, P.F., Kohl, S.A., Petersen, J., Maier-Hein, K.H.: nnU-Net: a self-configuring method for deep learning-based biomedical image segmentation. Nat. Methods **18**(2), 203–211 (2021)
15. Landman, B., Xu, Z., Igelsias, J., Styner, M., Langerak, T., Klein, A.: MICCAI multi-atlas labeling beyond the cranial vault–workshop and challenge. In: Proceedings of the MICCAI Multi-Atlas Labeling Beyond Cranial Vault-Workshop Challenge, vol. 5, p. 12 (2015)
16. Ma, J., et al.: Loss odyssey in medical image segmentation. Med. Image Anal. **71**, 102035 (2021)
17. Ma, J., He, Y., Li, F., Han, L., You, C., Wang, B.: Segment anything in medical images. Nat. Commun. **15**(1), 654 (2024)
18. Ma, J., Wang, B. (eds.): MICCAI 2022. LNCS, vol. 13816. Springer, Cham (2022). https://doi.org/10.1007/978-3-031-23911-3
19. Ma, J., et al.: Fast and low-GPU-memory abdomen CT organ segmentation: the flare challenge. Med. Image Anal. **82**, 102616 (2022)
20. Ma, J., et al.: Unleashing the strengths of unlabeled data in pan-cancer abdominal organ quantification: the flare22 challenge. arXiv preprint arXiv:2308.05862 (2023)
21. Ma, J., et al.: AbdomenCT-1K: is abdominal organ segmentation a solved problem? IEEE Trans. Pattern Anal. Mach. Intell. **44**(10), 6695–6714 (2022)
22. Milletari, F., Navab, N., Ahmadi, S.A.: V-net: fully convolutional neural networks for volumetric medical image segmentation. In: 2016 Fourth International Conference on 3D Vision (3DV), pp. 565–571. IEEE (2016)
23. Pavao, A., et al.: CodaLab competitions: an open source platform to organize scientific challenges. J. Mach. Learn. Res. **24**(198), 1–6 (2023)
24. Ronneberger, O., Fischer, P., Brox, T.: U-net: convolutional networks for biomedical image segmentation. In: International Conference on Medical Image Computing and Computer-Assisted Intervention, pp. 234–241 (2015)
25. Simpson, A.L., et al.: A large annotated medical image dataset for the development and evaluation of segmentation algorithms. arXiv preprint arXiv:1902.09063 (2019)
26. Tang, Y., et al.: Self-supervised pre-training of swin transformers for 3D medical image analysis. In: Proceedings of the IEEE/CVF Conference on Computer Vision and Pattern Recognition, pp. 20730–20740 (2022)
27. Wang, E., Zhao, Y., Wu, Y.: Cascade dual-decoders network for abdominal organs segmentation. In: Ma, J., Wang, B. (eds.) FLARE 2022. LNCS, vol. 13816, pp. 202–213. Springer, Cham (2022). https://doi.org/10.1007/978-3-031-23911-3_18
28. Wasserthal, J., et al.: TotalSegmentator: robust segmentation of 104 anatomic structures in CT images. Radiol. Artif. Intell. **5**(5), e230024 (2023)
29. Yushkevich, P.A., Gao, Y., Gerig, G.: ITK-snap: an interactive tool for semi-automatic segmentation of multi-modality biomedical images. In: Annual International Conference of the IEEE Engineering in Medicine and Biology Society, pp. 3342–3345 (2016)
30. Zhang, G., Yang, Z., Huo, B., Chai, S., Jiang, S.: Multiorgan segmentation from partially labeled datasets with conditional nnU-Net. Comput. Biol. Med. **136**, 104658 (2021)
31. Zhang, J., Xie, Y., Xia, Y., Shen, C.: DoDNet: learning to segment multi-organ and tumors from multiple partially labeled datasets. In: Proceedings of the IEEE/CVF Conference on Computer Vision and Pattern Recognition, pp. 1195–1204 (2021)

Conformer: A Parallel Segmentation Network Combining Swin Transformer and Convolutional Neutral Network

Yanbin Chen⬡, Zhicheng Wu⬡, Hao Chen⬡, and Mingjing Yang(✉)

College of Physics and Information Engineering, Fuzhou University, Fuzhou, China
yangmj5@fzu.edu.cn

Abstract. Abdominal organ segmentation can help doctors to have a more intuitive observation of the abdominal organ structure and tissue lesion structure, thereby improving the accuracy of disease diagnosis. Accurate segmentation results can provide valuable information for clinical diagnosis and follow-up, such as organ size, location, boundary status, and spatial relationship of multiple organs. Manual labels are precious and difficult to obtain in medical segmentation, so the use of pseudo-labels is an irresistible trend. In this paper, we demonstrate that pseudo-labels are beneficial to enrich the learning samples and enhance the feature learning ability of the model for abdominal organs and tumors. In this paper, we propose a semi-supervised parallel segmentation model that simultaneously aggregates local and global information using parallel modules of CNNS and transformers at high scales. The two-stage strategy and lightweight network make our model extremely efficient. Our method achieved an average DSC score of 89.75% and 3.78% for the organs and tumors, respectively, on the testing set. The average NSD scores were 93.51% and 1.82% for the organs and tumors, respectively. The average running time and area under GPU memory-time curve are 14.85 s and 15963 MB.

Keywords: Abdominal organ and tumor segmentation · Hybrid architecture · Pseudo-label

1 Introduction

The CT scan is a standard diagnostic method for abdominal-related diseases in clinical practice. Through CT scans, doctors can obtain a more intuitive observation of the abdominal organ structures and pathological changes, thereby improving the accuracy of disease diagnosis. Accurate segmentation results can provide valuable information for clinical diagnosis and follow-up, such as organ size, lesion position, boundary status, and spatial relationships of multiple organs [1]. In clinical practice, doctors often have to manually annotate organ segmentation, which is both time-consuming and prone to subjective opinions. Developing an automated multi-organ segmentation model using deep learning can improve

J. Ma and B. Wang (Eds.): FLARE 2023, LNCS 14544, pp. 253–266, 2024.
https://doi.org/10.1007/978-3-031-58776-4_20

the efficiency of clinical workflows, including disease diagnosis, prognosis analysis, and treatment planning.

It is known from previous work [2–4]that the combination of Transformer and CNN has achieved remarkable results in the field of multi-object segmentation. Our proposed model leverages the capabilities of Convolutional Neural Networks (CNN) in conjunction with the state-of-the-art **Swin Transformer** [5] to employ parallel modules at deep stages. These modules are adept at concurrently aggregating both local and global information, thereby enabling more effective segmentation. To optimize computational efficiency, we employ standard convolutional blocks exclusively in the shallow layers of our network, mitigating excessive computational demands. In addition, our network adopts a two-stage cascade framework, with the first stage for organ region localization and the second stage for whole-organ and tumor-refined segmentation. We believe that simultaneous learning of tumors and organs facilitates the acquisition of tumor information. To further augment our dataset and bolster tumor labeling, we employ a trained fine organ segmentation model to generate pseudo-labels for organs from data that is only annotated for tumors. This strategy not only expands the available tumor data but also leverages the interplay between organ and tumor structures, leading to more comprehensive and accurate segmentation results.

The main contributions of this work are summarized as follows:

(1) Proposing a Parallel CNN and Transformer hybrid modules for information aggregation which effectively aggregates local and global information.
(2) The two-stage cascade framework from coarse to fine can effectively reduce the redundancy of image information and alleviate the computational load.

2   Method

We propose a two-stage strategy as shown in Fig. 1. In the first stage, coarse segmentation is performed on the binary classification to obtain the region of interest (ROI) for the entire organ. In the second stage, fine segmentation is performed on the cropped ROI.

2.1   Preprocessing

All the training images are uniformly preprocessed as follows:

– Referring to Liu et al. [2], all the data were resampled to the same size. The image data and the segmentation were interpolated using bi-cubic interpolation and nearest neighbor methods. The images used for coarse segmentation training in the first stage were resampled to $64 \times 64 \times 64$ size, and the images used for fine segmentation training in the second stage were resampled to $96 \times 192 \times 192$ size.
– The data was standardized by Z-Score.

2.2   Proposed Method

Figure 2 shows the encoder-decoder architecture of our model. There are four stages in this configuration. In the first two stages, convolutional blocks are used, while the subsequent two stages employ parallel blocks. Within the first two scales, the skip-connection linking the pure convolutional blocks is implemented using a concatenation operation. In the last two stages, the skip-connection that connects the convolutional blocks uses the same concatenation operation, while the addition operation is applied between the transformers. The two-stage strategy and the utilization of parallel hybrid convolution at the deep stages effectively reduce the complexity of the model while still maintaining segmentation accuracy.

We employ two models in the fine segmentation part to correspond to organ segmentation and tumor segmentation. Both models have the same network framework. During training, we utilize the summation of Dice loss and cross-entropy loss as the loss function. When it comes to training the organ model, a noteworthy concern arises when using partial labels directly from the dataset. This approach has the potential to cause confusion within the organ model, resulting in incomplete organ segmentation outcomes. Specifically, this manifests as the segmentation of fewer than the expected 13 organ classes. To mitigate this issue, we adopt a different strategy. We utilize both the complete set of organ labels and an additional 1800 pseudo labels generated through the FLARE22 winning algorithm [6] and the best accuracy algorithm [7] to facilitate the training of the organ model. Subsequently, we employ the trained organ model to generate pseudo labels specifically for unlabeled organs when dealing with partially labeled data. These pseudo-labels are then integrated into the training process of the tumor model. The resulting dataset, which consists of a combination of labeled and pseudo-labeled data, is used to train the tumor model. Importantly, the predictions generated by the tumor model are limited to only retaining the tumor segmentation results. Notably, our empirical observations indicate improved performance when training both the tumor and organ models simultaneously.

Parallel Block. The Conv Block consists of $3 \times 3 \times 3$ conv layer, IN layer and GELU layer. The composition of Swin Block 3D [5] is shown in Fig. 3. It consists of two basic units, W-MSA and SW-MSA. The former computes the similarity between tokens in the same window. This segmentation strategy is helpful to deal with large-size images, so that the model can effectively deal with large-scale data. The latter moves the input token in each dimension by s units, and then calculates the similarity within the window, which is beneficial to capture the information between different blocks and obtain global image information. The first unit consists of a norm layer(LN), a Window Multi-head Self-attention 3D(W-MSA-3D) module, a norm layer, and an MLP module, in order. The second unit uses the Window Shifting Multi-head Self-Attention 3D (SW-MSA-3D) module to replace the W-MSA-3D module in the first unit, and the rest of the structure is the same as the first unit. We need to convert voxels to tokens before performing Swin Block, flattening a block of voxels of dimension $[H \times W \times D]$ into a one-dimensional token of length $H \times W \times D$ by matrix dimension transformation. Similarly, after the self-attention calculation is completed, the tokens are converted into voxels.

Loss Function. We utilize a combination of the Dice loss and cross-entropy loss. The overall loss of our Conformer is defined as:

$$L_S = L_{WCE}(G, S) + L_{dice}(G, S), \tag{1}$$

L_{WCE} is formulated as:

$$L_{WCE}(G, S) = \frac{\sum_{c \in C} \| - w_c \cdot S_c \cdot log(G_c) \|}{H \cdot W \cdot D}, \tag{2}$$

where $\|\cdot\|$ denotes the L1 norm, w_c is the weight for c-th class. L_{dice} is formulated as:

$$L_{dice}(G, S) = 1 - \sum_{c \in C} \frac{2 \sum_{i=1}^{N} G_c^i S_c^i}{\sum_{i=1}^{N} G_c^i G_c^i + S_c^i S_c^i}, \tag{3}$$

where G_c^i, S_c^i respectively denote the ground truth and output of voxel i for class c.

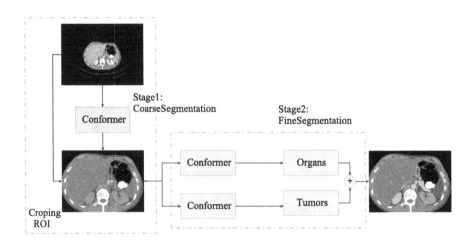

Fig. 1. Overview of our two-stage segmentation frame

2.3   Post-processing

In post-processing, the largest connected component is employed to refine the segmentation results. It is noteworthy that segmentation algorithms occasionally generate diminutive, extraneous segmented regions, which can be attributed

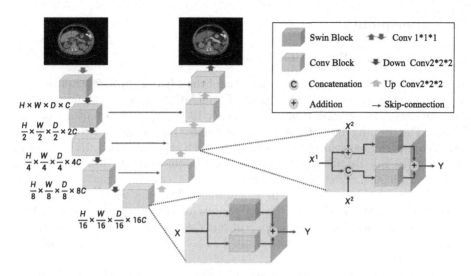

Fig. 2. Network architecture: Our network framework follows the encoder-decoder architecture, using Conv Blocks in the shallow layers and Parallel Blocks consisting of Convolutional Blocks and Swin Block in the deep layers.

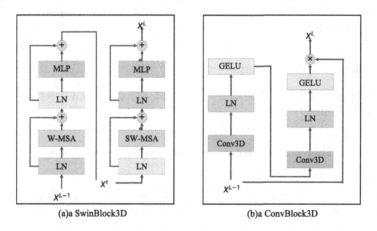

(a)a SwinBlock3D   (b)a ConvBlock3D

Fig. 3. Overview of the structure of Swin Block and Conv Block.

to inherent noise or algorithmic inaccuracies. Through the application of the largest connected component, the extraneous segments can be effectively discarded, thereby mitigating the likelihood of incorrect segmentation outcomes. Additionally, certain instances may arise where segmentation algorithms partition a single anatomical organ into multiple disjointed segments. By utilizing the concept of the largest connected component, fragmented segments can be merged into a continuous anatomical region. This process improves the comprehensibility and visual consistency of the segmentation results.

3   Experiments

3.1   Dataset and Evaluation Measures

The FLARE 2023 challenge is an extension of the FLARE 2021–2022 [8,9], aiming to aim to promote the development of foundation models in abdominal disease analysis. The segmentation targets cover 13 organs and various abdominal lesions. The training dataset is curated from more than 30 medical centers under the license permission, including TCIA [10], LiTS [11], MSD [12], KiTS [13,14], autoPET [15,16], TotalSegmentator [17], and AbdomenCT-1K [18]. The training set includes 4000 abdomen CT scans where 2200 CT scans with partial labels and 1800 CT scans without labels. The validation and testing sets include 100 and 400 CT scans, respectively, which cover various abdominal cancer types, such as liver cancer, kidney cancer, pancreas cancer, colon cancer, gastric cancer, and so on. The organ annotation process used ITK-SNAP [19], nnU-Net [20], and MedSAM [21].

The evaluation metrics encompass two accuracy measures-Dice Similarity Coefficient (DSC) and Normalized Surface Dice (NSD)-alongside two efficiency measures-running time and area under the GPU memory-time curve. These metrics collectively contribute to the ranking computation. Furthermore, the running time and GPU memory consumption are considered within tolerances of 15 s and 4 GB, respectively.

3.2   Implementation Details

Environment Settings. The development environments and requirements are presented in Table 1.

Table 1. Development environments and requirements.

System	Ubuntu 20.04.4 LTS
CPU	12th Gen Intel(R) Core(TM) i9-12900K CPU@3.20 GHz
RAM	42 GB
GPU (number and type)	One GeForce RTX 3080 12 GB
CUDA version	12.0
Programming language	Python 3.8
Deep learning framework	torch 1.12.1, torchvision 0.13.1
Specific dependencies	
Code	

Training Protocols. We applied two models in the fine segmentation part to correspond to organ segmentation and tumor segmentation. We divided the data provided by FLARE 2023 into four types: (1) The cases without tumors but with whole organ labels. (2) The cases with partial organ labels, some of which included tumor labels. (3) The cases with only tumor labels. (4) The 1800 organ pseudo-label without tumors labels generated by the top teams last year [6]. In the training phase, the first type of data is used to train the coarse segmentation model, while the first and fourth types of data are used to train the organ fine segmentation model. When training the tumor model, we discovered that only the fourth data label had a minimal impact. When the third type of data was utilized, the effect was enhanced. We convinced that learning about both organs and tumors simultaneously can enhance the understanding of tumor information. We applied the trained fine organ segmentation model to the organ pseudo-labels generated from the third type of data to obtain labels that encompass entire organs and tumors. We therefore adopted the new third data to train the tumor model, setting it to 15 classifications, but leaving only the final tumor segmentation output.

We apply the following augmentation methods to the training data: random rotation, scaling, addition of Gaussian white noise, Gaussian blur, gamma transformation, and elastic deformation. Each Swin Block contains a multi-head attention mechanism layer. According to the design of **Swin Unet** [4], the number of multi-head attention mechanisms in the encoder is 3, 6, and 9, respectively. Similarly, the number of multi-head attention mechanisms used in the decoder is 6,3 respectively. In the two-stage cascade network, the input data for coarse segmentation is $64 \times 64 \times 64$, and its attention window size is set to $4 \times 4 \times 4$. On the other hand, the input for fine segmentation is $96 \times 192 \times 192$, and the attention window size is set to $4 \times 3 \times 3$. The base number of channels is set to 16. Batch size is set to 1.

4   Results and Discussion

4.1   Quantitative Results on Validation Set

The quantitative results of the validation set are shown in Table 4. Our method achieves an average DSC of 83.88% $\pm$ 11.12% and an average NSD of 87.50% $\pm$ 11.00%. Table 7 shows the effectiveness of utilizing unlabeled data. Controlled experiments were performed using the same training configuration described in Sect. 3.2. Compared to using only labeled data to train the organ segmentation model, the utilization of pseudo-labeled data significantly enhanced the accuracy of organ segmentation. The average organ DSC score increased from 74.75% to 89.12%, and the organ NSD increased from 80.71% to 93.18%. We attempted to exclusively utilize the tumor label data for training the tumor model as a binary classification, but the results were nearly negligible. When we used the data with both organ and tumor labels for training, we observed an improvement

Table 2. Training protocols for coarse model.

Network initialization	
Batch size	1
Patch size	$64 \times 64 \times 64$
Total epochs	500
Optimizer	AdamW
Initial learning rate (lr)	0.01
Lr decay schedule	Cosine Annealing LR
Training time	3.05 h
Loss function	Dice + Cross entropy
Number of model parameters	6.66M[a]
Number of flops	20146.29M[b]

[a] https://github.com/sksq96/pytorch-summary
[b] https://github.com/facebookresearch/fvcore

Table 3. Training protocols for the refine model.

Network initialization	organ/tumor
Batch size	1
Patch size	$96 \times 192 \times 192$
Total epochs	500
Optimizer	AdamW
Initial learning rate (lr)	0.01
Lr decay schedule	Cosine Annealing LR
Training time	21.43 h/23.56 h
Loss function	Dice + Cross entropy
Number of model parameters	6.66M[a]
Number of flops	272606.26M/272662.88M[b]

[a] https://github.com/sksq96/pytorch-summary
[b] https://github.com/facebookresearch/fvcore

in the effectiveness of the tumor. Therefore, we employed the trained organ segmentation model to generate pseudo-organ labels. Subsequently, the data containing both organ and tumor labels was used to train the tumor model. The results showed an increase in both tumor metrics. Tumor NSD is 5.51% and Tumor DSC is 8.91% (Tables 2 and 3).

Table 4. Segmentation DSC of abdominal organs and tumors.

Target	Public Validation		Online Validation		Testing	
	DSC(%)	NSD(%)	DSC(%)	NSD(%)	DSC(%)	NSD (%)
Liver	98.03 ± 1.02	98.63 ± 1.83	97.73	98.18	95.81	96.47
Right Kidney	93.20 ± 15.10	92.28 ± 15.46	92.34	91.19	95.24	93.98
Spleen	97.24 ± 3.43	97.23 ± 6.42	96.70	96.88	96.10	96.85
Pancreas	85.37 ± 7.60	95.31 ± 7.18	82.06	92.18	84.74	92.90
Aorta	96.99 ± 1.86	98.86 ± 2.62	97.05	98.90	97.69	99.17
Inferior vena cava	91.89 ±6.66	92.74 ±7.00	91.29	98.90	90.98	91.75
Right adrenal gland	85.28 ± 13.59	94.76 ± 14.10	85.14	98.90	86.38	95.40
Left adrenal gland	84.88 ± 7.52	95.02 ± 5.34	83.65	93.15	85.60	94.17
Gallbladder	80.29 ±28.45	79.95 ±29.45	81.41	81.59	78.88	80.48
Esophagus	82.65 ± 15.69	91.55 ± 15.94	84.00	93.16	89.49	97.50
Stomach	92.94 ± 6.67	95.69 ± 7.13	94.91	92.59	90.89	92.98
Duodenum	82.53 ± 8.05	94.13 ± 6.15	92.59	92.79	79.81	89.52
Left kidney	92.28 ± 14.28	91.10 ± 16.08	82.03	92.79	95.11	94.40
Tumor	10.63 ±25.72	7.81 ± 1.34	8.91	5.51	3.78	1.82
Average	83.88 ± 11.12	87.50 ± 11.00	89.12	93.18	83.61	86.96

Table 5. Quantitative evaluation of segmentation efficiency in terms of the running them and GPU memory consumption.

Case ID	Image Size	Running Time (s)	Max GPU (MB)	Total GPU (MB)
0001	(512, 512, 55)	12.87	2778	13249
0051	(512, 512, 100)	12.82	2772	13652
0017	(512, 512, 150)	13.81	2778	14127
0019	(512, 512, 215)	17.44	2660	19189
0099	(512, 512, 334)	17.07	2660	18226
0063	(512, 512, 448)	21.63	2660	22592
0048	(512, 512, 499)	22.03	2772	23147
0029	(512, 512, 554)	27.84	3018	30459

Table 6. Ablation study on the architecture.

Method	Params (M)	FLOPs(G)
Conformer -1,2,3,4	7.35	353.78
Conformer -2,3,4	6.79	285.28
Conformer -3,4	6.66	266.21

Table 7. The effect of using unlabeled data.

Target	Without unlabeled		With unlabeled	
	DSC(%)	NSD(%)	DSC(%)	NSD(%)
Liver	94.45	94.98	97.73	98.18
Right Kidney	88.06	89.44	92.34	91.19
Spleen	58.76	59.63	96.70	96.88
Pancreas	67.00	79.16	82.06	92.18
Aorta	89.51	90.95	97.05	98.90
Inferior vena cava	85.58	85.52	91.29	98.90
Right adrenal gland	74.45	90.54	85.14	98.90
Left adrenal gland	63.36	78.31	83.65	93.15
Gallbladder	67.28	67.44	81.41	81.59
Esophagus	70.47	80.47	84.00	93.16
Stomach	78.90	82.29	94.91	92.59
Duodenum	67.51	81.97	92.59	92.79
Left kidney	66.43	68.48	82.03	92.79
Tumor	6.58	3.44	8.91	5.51
Average	74.75	80.71	89.12	93.18

4.2 Qualitative Results on Validation Set

Figure 4 shows our visualization results. Specifically, we present three examples of effective segmentation and three examples of poor segmentation. In cases where segmentation is successful, the results obtained closely align with the ground truth labels, demonstrating a high level of accuracy in our segmentation method. However, in FLARE23Ts 11 subject, the segmentation of the duodenum is notably poor. This discrepancy can be attributed to the presence of substantial deformations and blurred boundaries within the duodenum region. Furthermore, in FLARE23Ts 28 subject, our model incorrectly identifies the tumor as a part of the stomach, indicating a misclassification issue. Additionally, in FLARE23Ts 48 subject, the tumor is not successfully identified, highlighting the model's limitations in addressing certain tumor characteristics. This poor performance can be attributed to various factors. Firstly, the non-uniform sizes of tumors and their distribution across multiple organs pose a significant challenge to our segmentation model. Additionally, the limited availability of tumor samples hinders the model's learning capabilities. Therefore, enhancing the dataset with alternative methods to strengthen the representation of tumor samples may be a crucial approach for improvement.

4.3 Segmentation Efficiency Results on Validation Set

The segmentation efficiency is shown in Table 5. We compared the number of parameters and FLOPs using hybrid modules at different stages in Table 6. "-

3,4" represents the use of hybrid modules in the third and fourth layers, and pure convolutional modules in the remaining layers. "-2.3,4" represents the utilization of hybrid modules in the second, third, and fourth layers. "-1,2.3,4" represents the utilization of hybrid modules at each stage. The proposed method is significantly faster than other methods in terms of inference time. This is due to our two-stage strategy and the use of Conv Blocks at shallow layers and Parallel Blocks exclusively at deep layers.

4.4   Results on Final Testing Set

The effects of the test set evaluated by the official are shown in Table 8.

Table 8. The testing results from the official evaluation.

Organ DSC	Organ NSD	Lesion DSC	Lesion NSD	Time	GPU Memory
89.75%	93.51%	3.78%	1.82%	14.85 s	15963 MB

4.5   Limitation and Future Work

The current state of tumor segmentation is characterized by a notable degree of inefficiency. To improve the accuracy of tumor segmentation, it is crucial to develop strategies that focus on improving the quality of tumor samples. Notably, there is inherent heterogeneity in the tumor features exhibited across different anatomical organs. It is conceivable that one potential approach to addressing this heterogeneity involves dividing tumor segmentation into distinct segments that are specific to each organ. This approach seeks to acquire a refined understanding of the tumor characteristics associated with each organ. However, it is imperative to acknowledge that this level of detail inherently increases the computational workload associated with the segmentation process.

An additional strategy under consideration involves utilizing prior knowledge of the relative positions of organs. Such an approach is intended to reduce the occurrence of incorrect segmentation. Nevertheless, the variability observed in the relative positions of organs across different cases presents a significant challenge in determining a fair and appropriate range of positions.

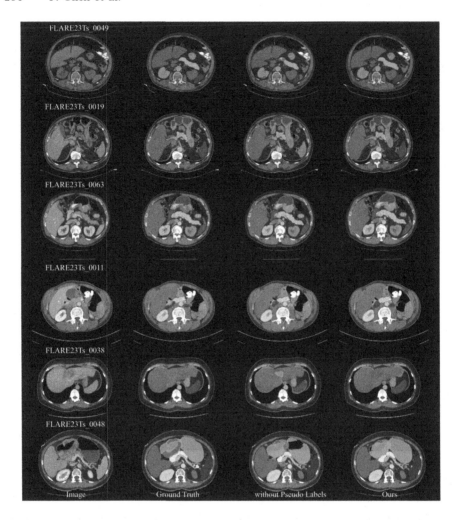

Fig. 4. Visualization of segmentation results of abdominal organs and tumors.

5   Conclusion

We propose a two-stage segmentation network for the FLARE 2023 abdominal
organ segmentation task. The network combining CNN and **Swin Transformer**
effectively aggregates local features and global information. The use of pseudo-
labels effectively enhances the accuracy of organ and tumor segmentation. In
addition, our two-stage and lightweight network framework achieves high efficiency. Our method achieves an average organ DSC of 89.75% and an average
organ NSD of 93.51%. In our environment configuration, the average running
time for each example during testing cases is 14.85 s, the average maximum
GPU memory is 15963 MB.

Acknowledgements. The authors of this paper declare that the segmentation method they implemented for participation in the FLARE 2023 challenge has not used any pre-trained models nor additional datasets other than those provided by the organizers. The proposed solution is fully automatic without any manual intervention. We thank all the data owners for making the CT scans publicly available and CodaLab [22] for hosting the challenge platform.

This work was supported by National Natural Science Foundation of China (62271149), Fujian Provincial Natural Science Foundation project(2021J02019, 2021J01578).

References

1. Tang, Y., et al.: High-resolution 3D abdominal segmentation with random patch network fusion. Med. Image Anal. **69**, 101894 (2021)
2. Liu, W., Xu, W., Yan, S., Wang, L., Li, H., Yang, H.: Combining self-training and hybrid architecture for semi-supervised abdominal organ segmentation. In: Ma, J., Wang, B. (eds.) FLARE 2022. LNCS, vol. 13816, pp. 281–292. Springer, Cham (2022). https://doi.org/10.1007/978-3-031-23911-3_25
3. Liu, W., et al.: PHTrans: parallelly aggregating global and local representations for medical image segmentation. In: Wang, L., Dou, Q., Fletcher, P.T., Speidel, S., Li, S. (eds.) MICCAI 2022. LNCS, vol. 13435, pp. 235–244. Springer, Cham (2022). https://doi.org/10.1007/978-3-031-16443-9_23
4. Cao, H., et al.: Swin-Unet: Unet-like pure transformer for medical image segmentation. In: Karlinsky, L., Michaeli, T., Nishino, K. (eds.) ECCV 2022. LNCS, vol. 13803, pp. 205–218. Springer, Cham (2023). https://doi.org/10.1007/978-3-031-25066-8_9
5. Liu, Z., et al.: Swin transformer: hierarchical vision transformer using shifted windows. In: Proceedings of the IEEE/CVF International Conference on Computer Vision, pp. 10012–10022 (2021)
6. Huang, Z., et al.: Revisiting nnU-net for iterative pseudo labeling and efficient sliding window inference. In: Ma, J., Wang, B. (eds.) FLARE 2022. LNCS, vol. 13816, pp. 178–189. Springer, Cham (2022). https://doi.org/10.1007/978-3-031-23911-3_16
7. Wang, E., Zhao, Y., Wu, Y.: Cascade dual-decoders network for abdominal organs segmentation. In: Ma, J., Wang, B. (eds.) FLARE 2022. LNCS, vol. 13816, pp. 202–213. Springer, Cham (2022). https://doi.org/10.1007/978-3-031-23911-3_18
8. Ma, J., et al.: Fast and low-GPU-memory abdomen CT organ segmentation: the flare challenge. Med. Image Anal. **82**, 102616 (2022)
9. Ma, J., et al.: Unleashing the strengths of unlabeled data in pan-cancer abdominal organ quantification: the flare22 challenge. arXiv preprint arXiv:2308.05862 (2023)
10. Clark, K., et al.: The cancer imaging archive (TCIA): maintaining and operating a public information repository. J. Digit. Imaging **26**(6), 1045–1057 (2013)
11. Bilic, P., et al.: The liver tumor segmentation benchmark (LiTS). Med. Image Anal. **84**, 102680 (2023)
12. Simpson, A.L., et al.: A large annotated medical image dataset for the development and evaluation of segmentation algorithms. arXiv preprint arXiv:1902.09063 (2019)
13. Heller, N., et al.: The state of the art in kidney and kidney tumor segmentation in contrast-enhanced CT imaging: results of the KiTS19 challenge. Med. Image Anal. **67**, 101821 (2021)

14. Heller, N., et al.: An international challenge to use artificial intelligence to define the state-of-the-art in kidney and kidney tumor segmentation in CT imaging. Am. Soc. Clin. Oncol. **38**(6), 626 (2020)
15. Gatidis, S., et al.: A whole-body FDG-PET/CT dataset with manually annotated tumor lesions. Sci. Data **9**(1), 601 (2022)
16. Gatidis, S., et al.: The autopet challenge: towards fully automated lesion segmentation in oncologic PET/CT imaging. Preprint at Research Square (Nature Portfolio) (2023)
17. Wasserthal, J., et al.: TotalSegmentator: robust segmentation of 104 anatomic structures in CT images. Radiol. Artif. Intell. **5**(5), e230024 (2023)
18. Ma, J., et al.: AbdomenCT-1K: is abdominal organ segmentation a solved problem? IEEE Trans. Pattern Anal. Mach. Intell. **44**(10), 6695–6714 (2022)
19. Yushkevich, P.A., Gao, Y., Gerig, G.: ITK-snap: an interactive tool for semi-automatic segmentation of multi-modality biomedical images. In: Annual International Conference of the IEEE Engineering in Medicine and Biology Society, pp. 3342–3345 (2016)
20. Isensee, F., Jaeger, P.F., Kohl, S.A.A., Petersen, J., Maier-Hein, K.H.: nnU-Net: a self-configuring method for deep learning-based biomedical image segmentation. Nat. Methods **18**(2), 203–211 (2021)
21. Ma, J., He, Y., Li, F., Han, L., You, C., Wang, B.: Segment anything in medical images. Nat. Commun. **15**, 654 (2024)
22. Pavao, A., et al.: CodaLab competitions: an open source platform to organize scientific challenges. J. Mach. Learn. Res. **24**(198), 1–6 (2023)

Multi-Organ and Pan-Cancer Segmentation Framework from Partially Labeled Abdominal CT Datasets: Fine and Swift nnU-Nets with Label Fusion

Youngbin Kong[1,2] , Kwangtai Kim[2] , Seoi Jeong[2] , Kyu Eun Lee[3,4] ,
and Hyoun-Joong Kong[2,3,5(✉)]

[1] Interdisciplinary Program in Bioengineering, Graduate School,
Seoul National University, Seoul, Republic of Korea
[2] Department of Transdisciplinary Medicine, Seoul National University Hospital,
Seoul, Republic of Korea
[3] Medical Big Data Research Center, Seoul National University College of Medicine,
Seoul, Republic of Korea
[4] Department of Surgery, Seoul National University Hospital and College
of Medicine, Seoul, Republic of Korea
[5] Department of Medicine, Seoul National University College of Medicine, Seoul,
Republic of Korea
gongcop7@snu.ac.kr

Abstract. Segmentation of organs and tumors from abdominal computed tomography (CT) scans is crucial for cancer diagnosis and surgical planning. Since traditional segmentation methods are subjective and labor-intensive, deep learning-based approaches have been introduced recently which incur high computational costs. This study proposes an accurate and efficient segmentation method for abdominal organs and tumors in CT images utilizing a partially-labeled abdominal CT dataset. Fine nnU-Net was used for the pseudo-labeling of unlabeled images. And the Label Fusion Algorithm combined the benefits of the provided datasets to build an optimal training dataset, using Swift nnU-Net for efficient inference. In online validation using Swift nnU-Net, the dice similarity coefficient (DSC) values for organs and tumors segmentation were 89.56% and 35.70%, respectively, and the normalized surface distance (NSD) values were 94.67% and 25.52%. In our own efficiency experiments, the inference time was an average of 10.7 s and the area under the GPU memory time curve was an average of 20316.72 MB. Our method enables accurate and efficient segmentation of abdominal organs and tumors using partially labeled data, unlabeled data, and pseudo-labels. This method could be applied to multi-organ and pan-cancer segmentation in abdominal CT images under low-resource environments.

Keywords: Label Fusion · Abdominal CT · Segmentation · Partially Labeled Dataset · Deep Learning

J. Ma and B. Wang (Eds.): FLARE 2023, LNCS 14544, pp. 267–282, 2024.
https://doi.org/10.1007/978-3-031-58776-4_21

1   Introduction

In the medical field, the precise segmentation of organs and tumors in abdominal images from medical imaging modalities, such as computed tomography (CT), magnetic resonance imaging (MRI), constitutes a pivotal and indispensable undertaking. This crucial process plays a pivotal role in the diagnosis and management of cancer, encompassing both treatment planning and execution, as well as ongoing patient monitoring [8]. Patient-specific anatomical models based on segmentation are used in the surgical planning phase and during surgical procedures. Especially CT should accurately segment multiple organs and tumors in the abdominal region within a CT image, owing to its critical use in many medical diagnoses. However, due to low-contrast binary CT images [25], traditional manual segmentation can be subjective when outlining soft tissues, such as organs [5], resulting in inconsistent results and significant labor and expertise. Based on these limitations, recent research trends have focused on deep-learning-based methods, such as nnU-Net [14], UNETR [10], EfficientSeg [26], V-Net [20], and Med3D [2], to segment multiple organs and tumors in the abdominal region of CT images. Furthermore, to intricately segment the complex structures of the abdomen and tumors, models based on convolutional neural networks are equipped with sophisticated architectures designed. However, these findings are limited to specific organs and their associated tumors, including liver and kidney tumors [9, 11]. Comprehensive studies addressing the segmentation of multiple organs and tumors throughout the abdomen are limited. Furthermore, producing fully labeled datasets still relies on traditional annotation techniques, focusing on expensive supervised and semi-supervised learning [15]. Consequently, studies based on partial labels, in which only some images are annotated, are becoming increasingly important [28].

Most deep-learning-based medical image analysis tasks focusing on high-resolution, large-capacity three-dimensional image data and high-performance models require considerable computational time and graphical processing unit (GPU) resources [3]. However, owing to the possibility of an urgent surgery, hospitals should promptly provide accurate segmentation results.

Thus, FLARE22 focused on a semi-supervised segmentation task that required a fully labeled dataset for multiple organs, whereas FLARE23 extended the topic to a partial-label segmentation task for multiple organs and tumors. Additionally, it provides partially labeled and unlabeled images. Moreover, pseudo-labels generated by models from FLARE22, which had demonstrated superior accuracy for the entire image set, are also being offered.

In this study, we propose a method to perform fast and accurate segmentation of abdominal organs and tumors based on the nnU-Net, which has attracted attention for overall medical image segmentation problems. Compared to conventional U-Net, nnU-Net is a model with wider scalability in medical image analysis, which has an encoder-decoder structure similar to U-Net and applies techniques such as skip connections. Variables in this nnU-Net that impact accuracy and efficiency were identified and adjusted to construct our model. Our methodology consists of a 'Fine nnU-Net' designed to make precise predictions for high-quality pseudo-labeling of unlabeled images, a 'Label Fusion Algorithm' that combines different types of labels to create meaningful labels, and a "Swift nnU-Net" that is lightly optimized for fast inference. For efficient prediction, we adopted methods proposed in FLARE22 such as the efficient sliding window technique [13].

Our contributions are as follows:

- **Utilization and Advancement of nnU-Net:** We propose an enhanced-accuracy segmentation method for abdominal organs and tumors based on the pivotal nnU-Net in the medical image segmentation field.
- **Effective Label Processing Methodology:** To effectively combine various labels, we propose Fine nnU-Net for high-quality pseudo-labeling for unlabeled images by leveraging partially annotated images and Label Fusion Algorithm.
- **Optimization in Low-Resource Environment:** Using the optimized "Swift nnU-Net," we enable fast inference and suggest model optimizations to function efficiently even in limited computational resource environment.

2   Method

In this study, we designed two 3D nnU-Nets for effective training and inference. Our framework consists of three steps, as depicted in Fig. 1. (a) using the Fine nnU-Net to perform pseudo-labeling on unlabeled images; (b) applying the Label Fusion Algorithm to build the training dataset of the final model; and (c) training the Swift nnU-Net based on the final dataset and performing an efficient inference. Each nnU-Net model has adjustable hyperparameters to improve its accuracy and efficiency.

We used three labels provided by FLARE23. (1) Partial Labels, which were partially labeled out of 14 classes consisting of 13 organs and 1 tumor; (2) Pseudo-labels A, based on the model of Team Aladdin5 [23], which had the highest dice similarity coefficient (DSC) in FLARE22; and (3) Pseudo-labels B, based on the model of Team Blackbean [13], which had the highest normalized surface distance (NSD). Example images and descriptions of each label are shown in Fig. 2.

2.1   Preprocessing

Preprocessing was performed using similar techniques as those for nnU-Net. The preprocessing cropped the image to include crucial regions or regions of interest, resampling to ensure that all image pixels were equally spaced according to the target spacing, and normalization to ensure consistency in the intensity range of pixels in the image. On the other hand, we didn't conduct any postprocessing in our settings.

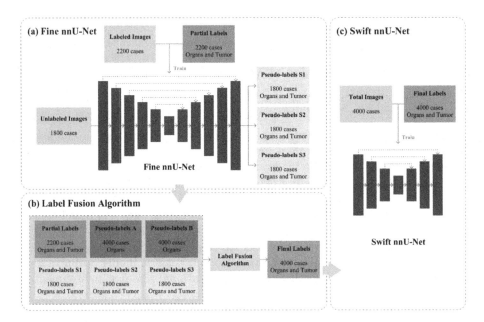

Fig. 1. Overall framework of the proposed method (a) Pseudo-label unlabeled images with Fine nnU-Net, which is designed to perform fine segmentation, and the pseudo-labels created by our Team Snuhmedisc are called Pseudo-labels S1, S2, and S3, respectively. (b) Create Final Labels to be used in the final model based on the algorithm designed by our team using the provided or generated labels. (c) Train Swift nnU-Net, a final model designed to make efficient inference based on the Final Labels created for all images, including unlabeled images.

2.2   Proposed Method

Fine nnU-Net. The Fine nnU-Net is a model designed to generate high-quality pseudo-labels S1, S2, and S3 for unlabeled images and is trained with Partial Labels. Precise segmentation is crucial because the generated pseudo-labels are used as training data for the final model through the Label Fusion Algorithm. The hyperparameters of nnU-Net was tuned to effectively perform the segmentation of abdominal organs and tumors in abdominal CT scans. The values used in the Fine nnU-Net are listed in Table 1.

Label Fusion Algorithm. The Label Fusion Algorithm presented in this study was designed to collect the benefits of the provided datasets to form a complete dataset suitable for final training. The label data used were partial labels, which contain the tumor class, compared to other labels, such as pseudo-labels A and B, which ensure high performance for 13 organs, and pseudo-labels S1, S2, and S3, which were generated by our team from the three latest models of Fine nnU-Net. They are the models saved after 1000, 950, and 900 epochs. All algorithmic

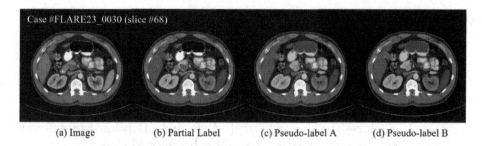

(a) Image   (b) Partial Label   (c) Pseudo-label A   (d) Pseudo-label B

Fig. 2. Examples of the three types of labels provided for the training dataset: (a) Slice #68 image from Case #FLARE23_0030, (b) Partial Labels, which are only partially annotated for 14 classes, (c) Pseudo-labels A for 13 organs generated from Team Aladdin5's model with the best DSC on FLARE22, and (d) Pseudo-labels B for 13 organs generated from Team Blackbean's model with the best NSD on FLARE22.

Table 1. Fine nnU-Net Hyperparameters

Base number of features	32
Patch size	[56, 224, 224]
Target spacing	[2.50, 0.80, 0.80]
Number of stages	6
Convolution kernel sizes	[[3,3,3], [3,3,3], [3,3,3], [3,3,3], [3,3,3], [3,3,3]]
Pooling operation kernel sizes	[[1,2,2], [2,2,2], [2,2,2], [2,2,2], [1,2,2]]

processing was centered on the nonzero mask regions of the provided pseudo-labels, allowing precise analysis of the abdominal region.

The Label Fusion Algorithm is designed as a different algorithm for each provided label of labeled and unlabeled images, which is divided into two parts as follows; the detailed flowchart is shown in Fig. 3.

(a) Algorithm for Labeled Images
- Organs (class 1–13)
    1. Pseudo-labels A and B was used because of their proven performance for organs. The organ labels are fused using a union operation, and the union operation is chosen because both pseudo-labels are generated from the models with the best DSC and NSD.
    2. If pseudo-labels A and B mark different organs in a particular pixel, majority voting is performed by referring to the corresponding pixel values of the partial labels.
    3. If all three labels (pseudo-labels A and B, and partial labels) point to different organs, the pixel is assigned to the background class.
- Tumors (class 14)
    1. Overlay the tumor labels with partial labels over the organ labels generated in the previous step.

(b) Algorithm for Unlabeled Images
- Organs (class 1–13)
    1. Perform a union operation on classes 1–13 of pseudo-labels A and B in the same manner as in labeled image processing.
    2. If pseudo-labels A and B represent different organs in a particular pixel, majority voting is performed by referring to the corresponding pixel value in pseudo-label S1.
    3. If all three labels (pseudo-labels A, B, and S1) pointed to different organs, the pixel was assigned to the background class.

- Tumors (class 14)
    1. Perform majority voting based on the tumor labels in pseudo-labels S1, S2, and S3.
    2. Overlay the resulting tumor labels over the organ labels generated in the previous step.

Swift nnU-Net. In this study, the Swift nnU-Net was proposed to achieve fast inference speed and efficient computation in a low-resource environment by modifying the existing nnU-Net structure and hyperparameters. Training was performed using the final labels for the entire image generated by the Label Fusion Algorithm. The detailed values of the model are listed in Table 2.

Table 2. Swift nnU-Net Hyperparameters

Base number of features	24
Patch size	[32, 128, 192]
Target spacing	[3.00, 1.50, 1.50]
Number of stages	4
Convolution kernel sizes	[[3,3,3], [3,3,3], [3,3,3], [3,3,3]]
Pooling operation kernel sizes	[[1,2,2], [2,2,2], [2,2,2]]

3   Experiments

3.1   Dataset and Evaluation Measures

The FLARE23 is an advanced challenge from FLARE21-22 [17,18] and the dataset including TCIA [4], LiTS [1], MSD [22], KiTS [11,12], autoPET [6,7], TotalSegmentator [24], and AbdomenCT-1K [19] comprises multiracial, multi-center, multidisease, multiphase, and multivendor CT images collected from over 30 medical centers under the license permission. The training dataset consisted of 4,000 images, of which 2,200 were labeled images with partial labels, and the remaining 1,800 were unlabeled images.

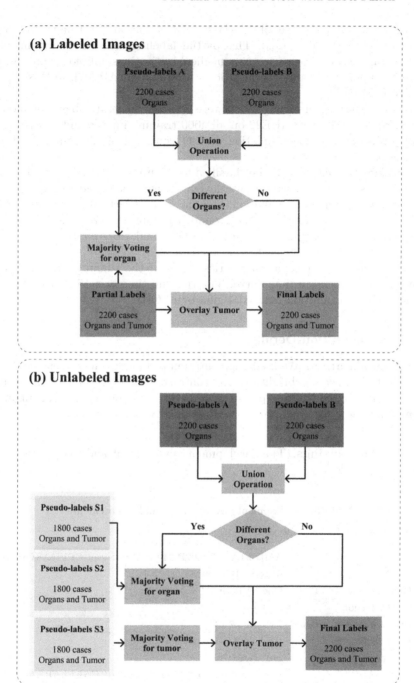

Fig. 3. Overall flowchart of Label Fusion Algorithm. (a) For labeled images, majority voting for organs is performed; (b) for unlabeled images, majority voting for organs and tumor is performed.

The partial labels consisted of 14 classes, 13 organs and 1 tumor, but only limited targets were annotated. This partial labeling setup is consistent with real-world applications because many medical institutions only focus on specific organs or tumors. The annotation process used ITK-SNAP [27], nnU-Net [14], and MedSAM [16].

In addition, two types of pseudo-labels were provided, generated based on models that performed well in FLARE22 on all 4000 training images and consisting of classes for 13 organs. The validation dataset consisted of 100 images and 400 test datasets.

These evaluation measures can be classified as accuracy and efficiency. The evaluation metrics related to accuracy are the DSC, which shows the overlap between the ground truth and the prediction, and the NSD, which shows the similarity between the outer boundaries of the ground truth and the prediction. The DSC and NSD for the 13 organ classes and the DSC and NSD for the tumor class were separated and used as evaluation metrics.

The efficiency-related evaluation metrics included the running time and area under the GPU memory-time curve. The running time was 15 s for each case, and the GPU consumption reached 4 giga byte (GB).

3.2 Implementation Details

Data Augmentation. We used augmentation techniques such as elastic deformation, rotation, scaling, brightness and contrast adjustment, and gamma transformation during the training process. Moreover, we applied test time augmentation (TTA) only for inference in the Fine nnU-Net.

Environment Settings. The development environment and requirements are presented in Table 3.

Table 3. Development environments and requirements

System	Ubuntu 18.04.6 LTS
CPU	AMD EPYC 7402 2P 24-Core Processor CPU@2.8 GHz
RAM	64 × 8 GB; 3200 MT/s
GPU (number and type)	One NVIDIA RTX A6000 D6 48 GB
CUDA version	11.3
Programming language	Python 3.7.13
Deep learning framework	torch 1.12.0, torchvision 0.13.0
Specific dependencies	nnU-Net 1.7.0
Code	https://github.com/YoungKong/MICCAI-FLARE23

Training Protocols. The training protocols of Fine nnU-Net and Swift nnU-Net are listed in Table 4 and 5 respectively.

Table 4. Training protocols for Fine nnU-Net

Network initialization	"He" normal initialization
Batch size	2
Patch size	$56 \times 224 \times 224$
Total epochs	1000
Optimizer	SGD with nesterov momentum ($\mu = 0.99$)
Initial learning rate (lr)	0.01
Lr decay schedule	reduced by 10% every 200 epochs
Training time	40 h
Number of model parameters	87.22M
Number of flops	497T
CO_2eq	5.7 kg

Table 5. Training protocols for Swift nnU-Net

Network initialization	"He" normal initialization
Batch size	2
Patch size	$32 \times 128 \times 192$
Total epochs	1500
Optimizer	SGD with nesterov momentum ($\mu = 0.99$)
Initial learning rate (lr)	0.01
Lr decay schedule	reduced by 17.81% every 200 epochs
Training time	15.43 h
Number of model parameters	3.15M
Number of flops	62.17G
CO_2eq	2.20 kg

4 Results and Discussion

4.1 Quantitative Results on Validation Set

In this study, an experiment was conducted to verify the effectiveness of using unlabeled images with the proposed Label Fusion Algorithm. Based on our baseline model, we compared the training results with the Label Fusion Algorithm on

2200 labeled images with those on all 4000 images, including unlabeled images. Furthermore, when using the entire image, the performance improved by 0.56% in DSC and 0.22% in NSD for organs, and 9.85% in DSC and 6.57% in NSD for tumors. The results are presented in Table 6.

Table 6. Unlabeled images ablation study

Target	Labeled Only		With Unlabeled	
	DSC (%)	NSD (%)	DSC (%)	NSD (%)
Liver	97.20	98.33	97.27	98.70
Right Kidney	93.11	94.67	93.14	93.65
Spleen	96.49	98.11	95.71	97.66
Pancreas	83.85	95.57	84.17	95.84
Aorta	95.34	98.35	95.36	98.81
Inferior vena cava	90.43	92.33	91.66	93.71
Right adrenal gland	82.48	95.39	83.74	95.80
Left adrenal gland	81.73	94.08	83.78	95.15
Gallbladder	83.10	83.59	82.83	83.48
Esophagus	80.96	92.10	81.64	93.00
Stomach	92.66	96.42	93.06	96.31
Duodenum	80.83	94.29	82.86	95.32
Left kidney	92.20	93.83	92.46	92.47
Tumor	26.15	19.46	36.00	26.03
Organs Average	88.49	94.39	89.05	94.61
Total Average	84.04	89.04	85.26	89.71

After verifying the effectiveness of using unlabeled images, we conducted experiments on hyperparameters that could balance the efficiency and accuracy for all 4000 images. The experimental results, based on the determined hyperparameters, are listed in Table 7 and Table 8.

Table 7. Final DSC, NSD results for validation set

Target	Public Validation		Online Validation	
	DSC (%)	NSD (%)	DSC (%)	NSD (%)
Liver	97.42 ± 0.68	98.63 ± 1.67	97.23	98.28
Right Kidney	94.16 ± 6.89	93.81 ± 8.89	93.39	92.82
Spleen	96.37 ± 2.21	97.42 ± 5.09	95.99	97.37
Pancreas	85.74 ± 5.42	96.84 ± 4.77	84.26	95.82
Aorta	94.96 ± 3.05	98.63 ± 3.21	95.31	98.95
Inferior vena cava	91.84 ± 4.06	94.39 ± 4.58	91.55	93.98
Right adrenal gland	88.05 ± 4.04	98.60 ± 1.54	87.20	98.25
Left adrenal gland	87.94 ± 3.45	98.00 ± 2.33	86.65	96.69
Gallbladder	83.12 ± 24.77	84.58 ± 26.01	82.02	83.18
Esophagus	80.76 ± 16.32	91.47 ± 15.71	81.54	92.50
Stomach	92.83 ± 4.78	95.32 ± 6.71	93.23	95.92
Duodenum	82.31 ± 7.41	94.65 ± 5.33	82.90	94.93
Left kidney	92.45 ± 9.56	91.48 ± 11.93	92.96	92.06
Tumor	38.38 ± 32.01	27.61 ± 25.53	35.70	25.52
Organs Average	89.84 ± 8.70	94.90 ± 7.60	89.56	94.67
Total Average	86.17 ± 17.65	90.10 ± 20.61	85.71	89.73

Table 8. Quantitative evaluation of segmentation efficiency in terms of the running time and GPU memory consumption. Total GPU denotes the area under GPU Memory-Time curve. Evaluation GPU platform: NVIDIA QUADRO RTX5000 (16G)

Case ID	Image Size	Running Time (s)	Max GPU (MB)	Total GPU (MB)
0001	(512, 512, 55)	27.41	2626	20535
0051	(512, 512, 100)	18.13	2060	21754
0017	(512, 512, 150)	20.39	2060	21826
0019	(512, 512, 215)	32.95	2060	23259
0099	(512, 512, 334)	20.82	2060	22904
0063	(512, 512, 448)	24.9	2060	27210
0048	(512, 512, 499)	26.48	2060	29680
0029	(512, 512, 554)	30.57	2060	32723

4.2   Qualitative Results on Validation Set

Examples of the segmentation results based on the Swift nnU-Net are shown in Fig. 4. These are the final segmentation results after training with 4000 datasets using the Label Fusion Algorithm and applying strategies for fast inference. In Cases 7 and 77, all large and small organs and tumors were well segmented. However, for Case 13, insignificant tumors were not well predicted, and for Case 67, predicting tumors in organs that do not belong to the 13 organs being segmented is challenging.

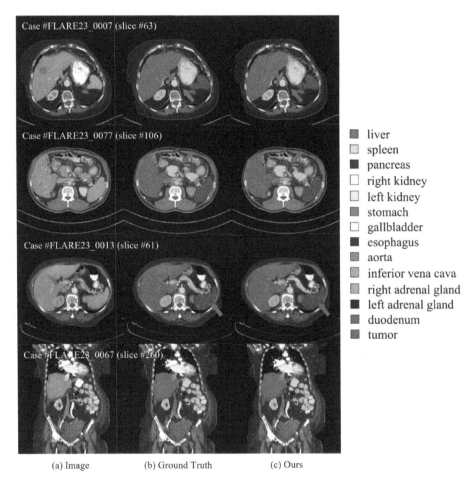

liver
spleen
pancreas
right kidney
left kidney
stomach
gallbladder
esophagus
aorta
inferior vena cava
right adrenal gland
left adrenal gland
duodenum
tumor

(a) Image   (b) Ground Truth   (c) Ours

Fig. 4. Qualitative results of our Swift nnU-Net. Examples of good segmentation of organs and tumors were Case #FLARE23_0007 and Case #FLARE23_0077, whereas challenging cases were Case #FLARE23_0013 and Case #FLARE23_0067.

4.3 Segmentation Efficiency Results on Validation Set

Efficiency experiments on the final submitted Docker were conducted using a GPU: One NVIDIA GeForce RTX 3070 8G, CPU: AMD Ryzen 7 5800X 8-Core Processor CPU@3.80 GHz, RAM:16 × 4 GB; 3200 MT/s. Segmentation efficiency was measured using the official evaluation code for 100 validation cases, and the results are listed in Table 9.

Table 9. Efficiency evaluation results of our submitted docker. All metrics reported are the average values on 100 validation cases

Time	Max GPU Memory	AUC GPU Time
10.7 s	3344.9 MB	20316.72 MB

4.4 Results on Final Testing Set

Based on our methodology, experiments were conducted on 400 final testing sets. In terms of efficiency, the inference time was an average of 14.03 s and the AUC GPU Time was 15400 MB. In terms of accuracy, the DSC values for organs and tumors segmentation were 89.83% and 37.36%, respectively, and the NSD values were 95.00% and 24.53%. Table 10 and Table 11 show the detailed results.

Table 10. Final DSC, NSD results for testing set

Target	Testing	
	DSC (%)	NSD (%)
Liver	96.27	96.95
Right Kidney	93.94	93.09
Spleen	96.05	97.61
Pancreas	87.93	96.83
Aorta	95.37	99.52
Inferior vena cava	92.10	95.14
Right adrenal gland	83.41	96.18
Left adrenal gland	84.06	95.60
Gallbladder	80.91	83.76
Esophagus	86.32	96.46
Stomach	93.19	95.84
Duodenum	85.38	95.84
Left kidney	92.81	92.15
Tumor	37.36	24.53
Organs Average	89.83	95.00
Total Average	86.08	89.96

4.5 Limitation and Future Work

The main limitation of this study was the low performance of tumor segmentation compared to that of organs. Because the features of tumors were obtained using only partially labeled data than fully labeled data, this limited the ability to achieve high performance for tumor segmentation. In future work, we will investigate techniques for improving the performance of tumor segmentation, particularly for abdominal organ and tumor segmentation problems in a partially labeled environment.

Table 11. Final efficiency for testing set

Time	AUC GPU Time
14.03 s	15400 MB

5 Conclusion

This study aimed to address the problem of abdominal organ and pan-cancer segmentation in CT images using partially labeled datasets, unlabeled images, and pseudo-labels in medical imaging, where generating fully labeled datasets is challenging. The Fine nnU-Net and Label Fusion Algorithm for the precise pseudo-labeling of unlabeled images and the Swift nnU-Net for efficient inference were proposed. Experiments for accuracy and efficiency verified the effectiveness of the proposed method, its utilization of partial labels, unlabeled images, and efficient inference strategies. Our proposed methodology with innovative framework will be a crucial step towards more precise and efficient approaches for medical imaging environment with low computational resource.

Acknowledgements. We declare that the segmentation method we implemented for participation in the FLARE 2023 challenge has not used any pre-trained models nor additional datasets other than those provided by the organizers. The proposed solution is fully automatic without any manual intervention. We thank all the data owners for making the CT scans publicly available and CodaLab [21] for hosting the challenge platform.

This work was supported by Institute of Information & communications Technology Planning & Evaluation (IITP) grant funded by the Korea government (MSIT) (No. 2021-0-0052, Cloud-based XR content conversion and service technology development that changes according to device performance) and Institute of Information and Communications Technology Planning and Evaluation (IITP) grant funded by the Korea Government (MSIT) (No. 2021-0-00312, development of non-face-to-face patient infection activity prediction and protection management SW technology at home and community treatment centers for effective response to infectious disease).

References

1. Bilic, P., et al.: The liver tumor segmentation benchmark (LiTs). Med. Image Anal. **84**, 102680 (2023)
2. Chen, S., Ma, K., Zheng, Y.: Med3d: transfer learning for 3D medical image analysis. arXiv preprint arXiv:1904.00625 (2019)
3. Chetty, G., Yamin, M., White, M.: A low resource 3D U-net based deep learning model for medical image analysis. Int. J. Inf. Technol. **14**(1), 95–103 (2022)
4. Clark, K., et al.: The cancer imaging archive (TCIA): maintaining and operating a public information repository. J. Digit. Imaging **26**(6), 1045–1057 (2013)
5. Fu, Y., Lei, Y., Wang, T., Curran, W.J., Liu, T., Yang, X.: A review of deep learning based methods for medical image multi-organ segmentation. Physica Med. **85**, 107–122 (2021)
6. Gatidis, S., et al.: The autoPET challenge: towards fully automated lesion segmentation in oncologic PET/CT imaging (2023)
7. Gatidis, S.: A whole-body FDG-PET/CT dataset with manually annotated tumor lesions. Sci. Data **9**(1), 601 (2022)
8. Gibson, E., et al.: Automatic multi-organ segmentation on abdominal CT with dense V-networks. IEEE Trans. Med. Imaging **37**(8), 1822–1834 (2018)
9. Gul, S., Khan, M.S., Bibi, A., Khandakar, A., Ayari, M.A., Chowdhury, M.E.: Deep learning techniques for liver and liver tumor segmentation: a review. Comput. Biol. Med. **147**, 105620 (2022)
10. Hatamizadeh, A., et al.: UNETR: transformers for 3D medical image segmentation. In: Proceedings of the IEEE/CVF Winter Conference on Applications of Computer Vision, pp. 574–584 (2022)
11. Heller, N., et al.: The state of the art in kidney and kidney tumor segmentation in contrast-enhanced CT imaging: results of the kits19 challenge. Med. Image Anal. **67**, 101821 (2021)
12. Heller, N., et al.: An international challenge to use artificial intelligence to define the state-of-the-art in kidney and kidney tumor segmentation in CT imaging. Proc. Am. Soc. Clin. Oncol. **38**(6), 626 (2020)
13. Huang, Z., et al,.: Revisiting nnU-Net for iterative pseudo labeling and efficient sliding window inference. In: Ma, J., Wang, B. (eds.) Fast and Low-Resource Semi-supervised Abdominal Organ Segmentation. FLARE 2022. LNCS, vol. 13816, pp. 178–189. Springer, Cham (2022). https://doi.org/10.1007/978-3-031-23911-3_16
14. Isensee, F., Jaeger, P.F., Kohl, S.A., Petersen, J., Maier-Hein, K.H.: nnU-Net: a self-configuring method for deep learning-based biomedical image segmentation. Nat. Methods **18**(2), 203–211 (2021)
15. Ji, Y., et al.: AMOS: a large-scale abdominal multi-organ benchmark for versatile medical image segmentation. In: Advances in Neural Information Processing Systems, vol. 35, pp. 36722–36732 (2022)
16. Ma, J., He, Y., Li, F., Han, L., You, C., Wang, B.: Segment anything in medical images. Nat. Commun. **15**(1), 654 (2024)
17. Ma, J., et al.: Fast and low-GPU-memory abdomen CT organ segmentation: the flare challenge. Med. Image Anal. **82**, 102616 (2022)
18. Ma, J., et al.: Unleashing the strengths of unlabeled data in pan-cancer abdominal organ quantification: the flare22 challenge. arXiv preprint arXiv:2308.05862 (2023)
19. Ma, J., et al.: Abdomenct-1k: is abdominal organ segmentation a solved problem? IEEE Trans. Pattern Anal. Mach. Intell. **44**(10), 6695–6714 (2022)

20. Milletari, F., Navab, N., Ahmadi, S.A.: V-Net: fully convolutional neural networks for volumetric medical image segmentation. In: 2016 Fourth International Conference on 3D Vision (3DV), pp. 565–571. IEEE (2016)

21. Pavao, A., et al.: Codalab competitions: an open source platform to organize scientific challenges. J. Mach. Learn. Res. **24**(198), 1–6 (2023)

22. Simpson, A.L., et al.: A large annotated medical image dataset for the development and evaluation of segmentation algorithms. arXiv preprint arXiv:1902.09063 (2019)

23. Wang, E., Zhao, Y., Wu, Y.: Cascade dual-decoders network for abdominal organs segmentation. In: Ma, J., Wang, B. (eds.) Fast and Low-Resource Semi-supervised Abdominal Organ Segmentation. FLARE 2022. LNCS, vol. 13816, pp. 202–213. Springer, Cham (2022). https://doi.org/10.1007/978-3-031-23911-3_18

24. Wasserthal, J., et al.: Totalsegmentator: robust segmentation of 104 anatomic structures in CT images. Radiol. Artif. Intell. **5**(5), e230024 (2023)

25. Xia, H., Sun, W., Song, S., Mou, X.: MD-Net: multi-scale dilated convolution network for CT images segmentation. Neural Process. Lett. **51**, 2915–2927 (2020)

26. Yesilkaynak, V.B., Sahin, Y.H., Unal, G.: EfficientSeg: an efficient semantic segmentation network. arXiv preprint arXiv:2009.06469 (2020)

27. Yushkevich, P.A., Gao, Y., Gerig, G.: ITK-SNAP: an interactive tool for semi-automatic segmentation of multi-modality biomedical images. In: Annual International Conference of the IEEE Engineering in Medicine and Biology Society, pp. 3342–3345 (2016)

28. Zhang, J., Xie, Y., Xia, Y., Shen, C.: DoDNet: learning to segment multi-organ and tumors from multiple partially labeled datasets. In: Proceedings of the IEEE/CVF Conference on Computer Vision and Pattern Recognition, pp. 1195–1204 (2021)

From Whole-Body to Abdomen: Streamlined Segmentation of Organs and Tumors via Semi-Supervised Learning and Efficient Coarse-to-Fine Inference

Shoujin Huang[iD], Huaishui Yang[iD], Lifeng Mei[iD], Tan Zhang[iD], Shaojun Liu[iD], and Mengye Lyu[✉][iD]

Shenzhen Technology University, Shenzhen, China
lvmengye@sztu.edu.cn

Abstract. Precise and automated segmentation of abdominal organs and tumors is an important research area of medical image analysis. This domain faces three key challenges: the presence of partially labeled training data that can mislead model training, the variable morphologies of tumors complicating the segmentation process, and the computationally demanding nature of inference in whole/half-body CT scans. In our study, we leverage advanced techniques to generate pseudo-labels, thereby adequately addressing the limitations of partially annotated datasets in a semi-supervised manner. Furthermore, we introduce a novel perspective that allows the segmentation of whole/half-body CT scans to be streamlined into focused abdominal segmentation. To achieve this, we re-engineered the nnU-Net V2 inference engine to incorporate a coarse-to-fine strategy, leading to a remarkable 15× speed-up by eliminating extraneous regions. The mean under the GPU memory-time curve is 7918 Mb. Our approach yields a mean Dice Similarity Coefficient (DSC) of 90.75/47.95 and a Normalized Surface Dice (NSD) of 95.54/40.16 for organ and tumor segmentation, respectively, in the FLARE 2023 validation dataset. Importantly, our method accomplishes these results with an average processing time of only 27.47 s per case.

Keywords: FLARE 2023 · Segmentation

1 Introduction

Automated and precise segmentation of abdominal organs and tumors is crucial for a wide range of medical applications, including computer-assisted diagnosis and biomarker measurement systems. The growing need for automated segmentation in abdominal medical imaging highlights its essential role in facilitating accurate diagnoses, surgical planning, and disease localization. This area faces three key challenges. First, the existence of partially labeled training data complicates model learning. Second, the varied morphologies of tumors present difficulties for accurate segmentation. Third, the high voxel count in whole or half-body CT scans requires significant computational resources, leading to prolonged inference times.

J. Ma and B. Wang (Eds.): FLARE 2023, LNCS 14544, pp. 283–292, 2024.
https://doi.org/10.1007/978-3-031-58776-4_22

Previously, Z. Huang et al. employed big nnU-Net models to generate effective pseudo-labels, which were then provided to small nnU-Net models for learning [8]. F. Zhang et al. utilized model distillation techniques along with unlabeled data [19], achieving significant improvement on segmentation accuracy compared to full-supervised models. Both of their approaches underscore the potential of semi-supervised pseudo-labeling methods in enhancing model robustness. On the other hand, S. Huang et al. focused on optimizing processing time through GPU-based re-implementation of several frequent operations, leading to a substantial increase in inference speed [7].

In this paper, we utilize the FLARE 2022 winner model [8] to generate a large set of pseudo-labels for the issues of partially labeled training data. These pseudo-labels play a crucial role in augmenting annotations within both the partially labeled and unlabeled datasets. Subsequently, they are employed for training nnU-Net models. Furthermore, we introduce a new approach wherein mask calculations, performed via patch slide window prediction for whole/half-body CT scans, can be essentially refocused solely on abdominal region segmentation. This refocus is justified by the fact that only the abdominal regions containing the target organs require high-precision inference; all other regions may be selectively excluded or omitted entirely. As a result, we have modified the nnU-Net V2 inference engine to include a coarse-to-fine strategy. This adaptation dramatically reduces the need for processing extraneous regions (such as the head and feet), thereby achieving precise abdominal segmentation along with an impressive 15-fold increase in processing speed.

Our main contributions are summarized as follows:

- We introduce a novel perspective that allows the segmentation of whole/half-body CT scans to be streamlined into focused abdominal segmentation. This refines the computational scope and significantly alleviates the need for extensive computational resources.
- By incorporating a coarse-to-fine strategy into the nnU-Net V2 inference engine, we achieve a remarkable 15-fold acceleration in processing speed without compromising on segmentation accuracy.
- Through rigorous experimentation, we validate the superior performance and efficiency of our innovative framework, establishing it as a robust method for precise segmentation of both organs and tumors in abdominal CT scans.

2 Method

2.1 Preprocessing

Following [9], we implement the following preprocessing steps:

- Crop individual scans to the non-zero region.
- Apply global dataset intensity percentile clipping and z-score normalization using global foreground mean and standard deviation.
- Train the coarse model using data with a spacing of $(2.5, 0.79, 0.79)$, and the fine model with a spacing of $(0.5, 0.79, 0.79)$.

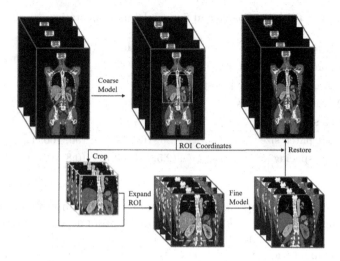

Fig. 1. The proposed coarse-to-fine segmentation streamline. The inference from the coarse model is used for the fine model to focus on the abdominal ROI. Crop means cutting the approximate position of the organs/tumors from the original image, and Restore means placing the prediction back to the position before cropping.

We utilize intensity percentile clipping and normalization based on the global foreground mean and standard deviation. These preprocessing steps are essential, as CT scan values represent physical properties that must be preserved in the processed data.

2.2 Streamline

In terms of inference stage, as a core part of this study, we introduce a segmentation streamline as illustrated in Fig. 1. Initially, we employ the coarse model with a step size of 1 to obtain approximate segmentation results from the input CT scan. Subsequently, we extract the coordinates of the abdomen region of interest (ROI) based on the coarse segmentation. The ROI box is then expanded by 20 mm in every direction to ensure that the organ is fully encompassed within it. Following this, we crop the corresponding area and perform inference using the fine model with a step value of 0.5. Finally, we restore the inference results to their original cropped area using the ROI coordinates. Note that we perform all interpolation operations using GPU device instead of CPU device.

2.3 Coarse and Fine Models

The configuration details of our coarse and fine segmentation models are outlined in Table 1. Both models are built upon the U-Net architecture [15] from nnU-Net V2 [9] and include downsampling and upsampling layers. The downsampling layers are responsible for reducing the scale of features and expanding feature

Table 1. Coarse and fine model implementation

Settings	Coarse Model	Fine Model
Channels in the first stage	24	32
Convolution number per stage	2	3
Downsampling times	5	5
Step size	1	0.5
Input patch size	(96, 160, 128)	(96, 160, 128)
Input spacing	(2.5, 0.79, 0.79)	(0.8, 0.79, 0.79)

channels, while the upsampling layers upscale the downsampled features. These are then concatenated with skip connections before undergoing convolution to obtain the final feature maps. It is noteworthy that the primary objective of the coarse segmentation model is to swiftly identify ROI with less emphasis on segmentation accuracy. Consequently, we have reduced the parameters of the coarse model and optimized step sizes to enhance speed for ROI extraction. In contrast, the fine segmentation model demands higher precision. Additionally, we employed a loss function that combines Dice Loss and Cross-Entropy Loss.

3 Experiments

3.1 Dataset and Evaluation Measures

The FLARE 2023 challenge extends previous FLARE 2021–2022 [11,12], aiming to promote the development of foundation models for abdominal disease analysis. The segmentation targets encompass 13 organs and various abdominal lesions. The training dataset has been curated from more than 30 medical centers, with licensing permissions, and includes sources such as TCIA [2], LiTS [1], MSD [16], KiTS [5,6], autoPET [3,4], TotalSegmentator [17], and AbdomenCT-1K [13]. The training set comprises 4,000 abdominal CT scans, of which 2,200 have partial labels and 1,800 lack labels. The validation and testing sets include 100 and 400 CT scans, respectively, covering various types of abdominal cancer such as liver, kidney, pancreas, colon, and gastric cancer. Organ annotations were performed using ITK-SNAP [18], nnU-Net [9], and MedSAM [10].

The evaluation metrics include two accuracy measures: the Dice Similarity Coefficient (DSC) and the Normalized Surface Dice (NSD), as well as two efficiency measures: running time and area under the GPU memory-time curve. These metrics collectively contribute to the overall ranking computation. Additionally, the running time and GPU memory consumption are evaluated within tolerances of 15 s and 4 GB, respectively.

3.2 Implementation Details

Environment Settings. The development environments and requirements are presented in Table 2.

Table 2. Development environments and requirements.

System	Ubuntu 22.04
CPU	AMD Ryzen 9 5900X 12-Core Processor
RAM	4 × 32 GB
GPU (number and type)	Two NVIDIA GeForce RTX 3090 24G
CUDA version	12.2
Programming language	Python 3.9.7
Deep learning framework	torch 2.0, torchvision 0.2.2
Code	

Training Protocols. Regarding the coarse model, it is unnecessary distinguish tumor segmentation results. Hence, we exclusively utilized the 13 available organ labels in the dataset to train this model. In contrast, for the fine model, we also utilized the partially labeled data with pseudo-labels generated by Z. Huang [8]. Subsequently, we trained the fine model through the nnU-Net V2 framework. During the initial training phase, 80% of the labels were used for training, while the remaining 20% were reserved for validation. In the final training phase, we selected the fine model with the lowest validation loss and performed a fine-tuning process using the entire pseudo-label dataset. Additionally, we adjusted the initial learning rate to 1e-4 and disabled data augmentation during this fine-tuning procedure.

4   Results and Discussion

4.1   Quantitative Results on Validation Set

The public validation represents the performance on the 50 validation cases with ground truth. The online validation corresponds to the leaderboard results. The testing results will be released during MICCAI 2023. As shown in Table 3, we provide both the mean scores and standard deviations.

4.2   Qualitative Results on Validation Set

Figure 2 displays two examples with good segmentation results and two examples with poor segmentation results in the validation set. In the case of Case#43 and Case#77, our method successfully segments all organs, achieving high DSC scores. In the case of Case#32 and Case#87, our method also performs well on large organs with clear boundaries (e.g., liver and stomach) but struggles with tumor segmentation. Furthermore, after the utilization of pseudo-labels, kidney and spleen segmentation significantly improves. The experimental results underscore the capacity of pseudo-labels to enhance the accuracy of our algorithm.

4.3   Segmentation Efficiency on Validation Set

Table 4 presents the efficiency measures of inference for various samples. Notably, as the number of slices increases, the time required for some of our samples

Table 3. Quantitative evaluation results.

Target	Public Validation		Online Validation		Testing	
	DSC (%)	NSD (%)	DSC (%)	NSD (%)	DSC (%)	NSD (%)
Liver	98.22 ± 1.32	98.41 ± 3.47	98.29	98.59	96.04	96.19
Right Kidney	95.51 ± 7.70	95.45± 8.87	94.45	94.71	95.14	95.82
Spleen	98.00 ± 1.17	99.03 ± 1.80	98.15	99.20	96.54	97.68
Pancreas	87.56 ± 6.48	97.08 ± 4.22	86.72	96.40	89.38	95.85
Aorta	96.62 ± 2.40	98.56 ± 3.02	96.66	98.56	96.58	98.81
Inferior vena cava	94.56 ± 3.05	96.37 ± 3.82	94.06	95.48	93.75	95.78
Right adrenal gland	85.56 ± 5.36	96.88 ± 2.63	84.39	96.23	81.83	94.00
Left adrenal gland	83.46 ± 6.38	95.60 ± 3.74	82.38	94.35	81.33	93.46
Gallbladder	85.47 ± 18.99	86.17 ± 20.20	85.26	85.68	81.39	83.95
Esophagus	83.71 ± 15.83	92.76 ± 15.23	84.40	94.10	90.35	98.01
Stomach	93.79 ± 3.66	96.90 ± 4.77	94.22	97.46	93.35	96.92
Duodenum	83.34 ± 7.03	95.00 ± 5.05	83.73	95.45	86.01	96.59
Left kidney	93.95 ± 11.13	93.81 ± 12.15	93.80	94.07	95.13	96.08
Tumor	47.95 ± 34.47	40.16 ± 32.39	43.12	36.87	40.31	31.02
Average	90.75 ± 6.96	95.54 ± 6.84	90.50	95.41	90.53	95.32

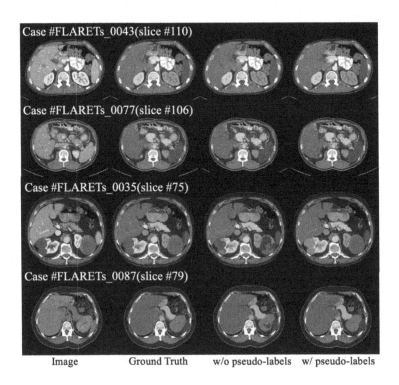

Fig. 2. Two examples with good segmentation and two examples with poor segmentation in the validation. The first column displays the image, the second column shows the ground truth, the third column presents the prediction by the model trained with labeled data but without tumor annotations, and the fourth column shows the prediction by the model trained with pseudo-labels.

does not increase proportionally. For instance, when comparing Case#0048 and Case#0063, it becomes evident that Case#0048 requires less time despite having a greater number of slices. This discrepancy is primarily due to the incorrect computation of the excessively large ROI box in Case#0063, resulting in an extended duration for the second step involving the fine model. In response to time constraints during the competition, we opted not to implement post-processing steps aimed at enhancing the quality of the coarse segmentation to maintain robustness in the coarse process. However, the successful handling of high-slice samples like Case#0099 and Case#0048 demonstrates that we can effectively treat large-slice samples as if they were smaller ones during the inference process. This further underscores the effectiveness and superiority of our proposed coarse-to-fine segmentation streamline.

4.4 Ablation Study

In this section, we conducted experiments to investigate the improvement in robustness resulting from the utilization of pseudo-labels, as well as the time reduction achieved through our proposed coarse-to-fine acceleration strategy. Please note that our ablation study experiments were conducted within the environments and requirements presented in Table 2, using the public validation dataset.

Table 4. Quantitative evaluation of segmentation efficiency in terms of the running time and GPU memory consumption. Total GPU denotes the area under GPU memory-time curve. Evaluation GPU platform: NVIDIA QUADRO RTX5000 (16G).

Case ID	Image Size	Running Time (s)	Max GPU (MB)	Total GPU (MB)
0001	(512, 512, 55)	22.75	5596	53528
0051	(512, 512, 100)	33.25	11448	152572
0017	(512, 512, 150)	35.91	11420	146076
0019	(512, 512, 215)	29.89	5472	52459
0099	(512, 512, 334)	24.75	5868	66231
0063	(512, 512, 448)	34.87	11396	133175
0048	(512, 512, 499)	30.03	7328	85168
0029	(512, 512, 554)	50.34	16170	255586

Effect of Pseudo-Labels. In this experiment, labeled data refers to 597 samples that possess organ annotations but lack tumor annotations, and pseudo-labels denote annotations generated using Z. Huang et al.'s method [8] to complete and rectify the partially labeled data. Table 5 illustrates the impact of incorporating pseudo-labels alongside labeled data during the training of the organ segmentation model. It is evident that the inclusion of pseudo-labels results in a noticeable improvement in model accuracy.

Table 5. Ablation study on pseudo-labels data effection.

Variant	Organ		Tumor	
	DSC (%)	NSD (%)	DSC (%)	NSD (%)
nnU-Net V2+labeled data	88.66	94.09	-	-
nnU-Net V2+pseudo-labels data	90.20	95.15	48.10	40.21
ours+labeled data	89.67	94.92	-	-
ours+pseudo-labels data	90.75	95.54	47.95	40.16

Effect of Coarse-to-Fine Design. Table 6 provides an overview of the time consumption achieved by our proposed method in various variants. *nnU-Net V2* refers to the original inference engine of nnU-Net V2 without any modifications, and *w/o coarse model* indicates using our proposed method but without the coarse model for ROI area computation yet with the GPU-based interpolation. From the experimental results, it becomes evident that when tested with identical model weights, our proposed engine framework significantly outperforms plain *nnU-Net V2* in terms of accuracy, exhibiting a notable improvement of 0.55/0.39 in organ segmentation. In terms of time efficiency, our method also surpasses the original inference of nnU-Net V2, achieving an impressive 15× acceleration.

Table 6. Ablation study on time analysis.

Variant	Organ		Tumor		Consume time
	DSC (%)	NSD (%)	DSC (%)	NSD (%)	seconds
nnU-Net V2	90.20	95.15	48.10	40.21	6959.82
w/o coarse model	89.22	93.78	47.52	39.37	1090.46
ours	90.75	95.54	47.95	40.16	467.96

4.5   Results on Final Testing Set

Our approach demonstrates a mean Dice Similarity Coefficient (DSC) of 90.53/95.32 and a Normalized Surface Dice (NSD) of 40.31/31.02 for organ and tumor segmentation, respectively, in the FLARE 2023 final testing set. Furthermore, the average processing time is 20.26 s, with GPU memory utilization at 54,842 MB.

4.6   Limitation and Future Work

The current study has a few limitations. Firstly, we were unable to introduce post-processing analysis after coarse and fine segmentation to enhance the algorithm's robustness due to competition time constraints. Secondly, we struggled to strike a balance between model accuracy and efficiency, prolonging inference times even with the utilization of proposed framework. Finally, directly performing image interpolation on the GPU could potentially lead to insufficient GPU memory, thereby causing program crashes. In our future work, we will incorporate GPU-based post-processing after segmentation. Additionally, we aim to implement image interpolation efficiently on the GPU platform with low resource consumption.

5   Conclusion

Our proposed novel perspective and inference framework have proven effective, and the incorporation of pseudo-labels has been shown to enhance model robustness. Initially, we introduced the concept of simplifying the segmentation of whole/half-body CT scans into abdominal segmentation. Building upon this concept, we restructured the inference framework based on nnU-Net V2 and employed a coarse-to-fine segmentation approach. Experimental results demonstrate that our novel approach achieves a remarkable 15× speedup in segmentation compared to the original nnU-Net V2 inference engine while preserving tumor segmentation accuracy to a significant extent. Furthermore, there is a noticeable improvement in organ segmentation accuracy.

Acknowledgements. The authors of this paper declare that the segmentation method they implemented for participation in the FLARE 2023 challenge has not used any pre-trained models nor additional datasets other than those provided by the organizers. The proposed solution is fully automatic without any manual intervention. We thank all the data owners for making the CT scans publicly available and CodaLab [14] for hosting the challenge platform. This work was supported in part by the National Natural Science Foundation of China under Grant 62101348, the Shenzhen Higher Education Stable Support Program under Grant 20220716111838002, and the Natural Science Foundation of Top Talent of Shenzhen Technology University under Grants 20200208 and GDRC202117.

References

1. Bilic, P., et al.: The liver tumor segmentation benchmark (LiTS). Med. Image Anal. **84**, 102680 (2023)
2. Clark, K., et al.: The cancer imaging archive (TCIA): maintaining and operating a public information repository. J. Digit. Imaging **26**(6), 1045–1057 (2013)
3. Gatidis, S., et al.: The autoPET challenge: towards fully automated lesion segmentation in oncologic PET/CT imaging. preprint at Research Square (Nature Portfolio) (2023). https://doi.org/10.21203/rs.3.rs-2572595/v1
4. Gatidis, S., et al.: A whole-body FDG-PET/CT dataset with manually annotated tumor lesions. Sci. Data **9**(1), 601 (2022)
5. Heller, N., et al.: The state of the art in kidney and kidney tumor segmentation in contrast-enhanced CT imaging: results of the kits19 challenge. Med. Image Anal. **67**, 101821 (2021)

6. Heller, N., et al.: An international challenge to use artificial intelligence to define the state-of-the-art in kidney and kidney tumor segmentation in CT imaging. Proc. Am. Soc. Clin. Oncol. **38**(6), 626 (2020)

7. Huang, S., et al.: Abdominal CT organ segmentation by accelerated nnU-Net with a coarse to fine strategy. In: Ma, J., Wang, B. (eds.) Fast and Low-Resource Semi-supervised Abdominal Organ Segmentation. FLARE 2022. LNCS, vol. 13816, pp. 23–34. Springer, Cham (2022). https://doi.org/10.1007/978-3-031-23911-3_3

8. Huang, Z., et al.: Revisiting nnU-Net for iterative pseudo labeling and efficient sliding window inference. In: Ma, J., Wang, B. (eds.) Fast and Low-Resource Semi-supervised Abdominal Organ Segmentation. FLARE 2022. LNCS, vol. 13816, pp. 178–189. Springer, Cham (2022). https://doi.org/10.1007/978-3-031-23911-3_16

9. Isensee, F., Jaeger, P.F., Kohl, S.A., Petersen, J., Maier-Hein, K.H.: nnU-Net: a self-configuring method for deep learning-based biomedical image segmentation. Nat. Methods **18**(2), 203–211 (2021)

10. Ma, J., He, Y., Li, F., Han, L., You, C., Wang, B.: Segment anything in medical images. Nat. Commun. **15**, 654 (2024)

11. Ma, J., et al.: Fast and low-GPU-memory abdomen CT organ segmentation: the flare challenge. Med. Image Anal. **82**, 102616 (2022)

12. Ma, J., et al.: Unleashing the strengths of unlabeled data in pan-cancer abdominal organ quantification: the flare22 challenge. arXiv preprint arXiv:2308.05862 (2023)

13. Ma, J.: Abdomenct-1k: is abdominal organ segmentation a solved problem? IEEE Trans. Pattern Anal. Mach. Intell. **44**(10), 6695–6714 (2022)

14. Pavao, A., et al.: CodaLab competitions: an open source platform to organize scientific challenges. J. Mach. Learn. Res. **24**(198), 1–6 (2023)

15. Ronneberger, O., Fischer, P., Brox, T.: U-net: convolutional networks for biomedical image segmentation. In: International Conference on Medical Image Computing and Computer-assisted Intervention, pp. 234–241 (2015)

16. Simpson, A.L., et al.: A large annotated medical image dataset for the development and evaluation of segmentation algorithms. arXiv preprint arXiv:1902.09063 (2019)

17. Wasserthal, J., et al.: TotalSegmentator: robust segmentation of 104 anatomic structures in CT images. Radiol. Artif. Intell. **5**(5), e230024 (2023)

18. Yushkevich, P.A., Gao, Y., Gerig, G.: ITK-SNAP: an interactive tool for semi-automatic segmentation of multi-modality biomedical images. In: Annual International Conference of the IEEE Engineering in Medicine and Biology Society, pp. 3342–3345 (2016)

19. Zhang, F., Wang, M., Yang, H.: Self-training with selective re-training improves abdominal organ segmentation in CT image. In: Ma, J., Wang, B. (eds.) Fast and Low-Resource Semi-supervised Abdominal Organ Segmentation. FLARE 2022. LNCS, vol. 13816, pp. 1–10. Springer, Cham (2022). https://doi.org/10.1007/978-3-031-23911-3_1

Semi-supervised Abdominal Organ and Pan-Cancer Segmentation with Efficient nnU-Net

Ziran Chen[1,3], Taiyu Han[2,3], Xueqiang Zeng[2,3], Guangtao Huang[2,3], Huihui Yang[2,3], and Yan Kang[1,2,3(✉)]

[1] College of Medicine and Biological Information Engineering, Northeastern University, Shenyang, China
[2] College of Applied Sciences, Shenzhen University, Shenzhen, China
[3] College of Health Science and Environmental Engineering, Shenzhen Technology University, Shenzhen, China
kangyan@sztu.edu.cn

Abstract. Abdominal organs serve as frequent sites for the manifestation of cancer, however, a prevailing gap exists in the availability of a widely accessible and precise segmentation model tailored to these organs and associated tumors. While nnU-Net has become a powerful baseline for medical image segmentation in recent years, its default configuration lacks the ability to leverage unlabeled data and falls short in terms of inference efficiency. To surmount these inherent constraints, we propose an improved approach based on nnU-Net. Our proposed method incorporates a semi-supervised algorithm that utilizes pseudo-labeling to effectively process unlabeled data within the nnU-Net framework. We improve the utilization of unlabeled data by generating high quality pseudo-labels with the default nnU-Net. Additionally, we reduce the network complexity of 3D U-Net and train a lightweight student model using a combination of labeled and pseudo-labeled data. In terms of performance, our lightweight student model achieved promising results on the validation set. The method yielded the average DSC of 0.8856 and NSD of 0.9451 in the process of segmenting 13 abdominal organs. For tumor segmentation, the average DSC and NSD were computed as 0.4258 and 0.3513, respectively. The average running time per case is 29 s and the average GPU memory is 25411 MB. In conclusion, our approach effectively addresses the limitations of nnU-Net, improving both inference efficiency and the utilization of unlabeled data. The encouraging results obtained in the FLARE 2023 challenge underscore the potential of our method to advance practical clinical applications in the field of medical image segmentation.

Keywords: Segmentation · Semi-supervised learning · Pseudo-labels

1 Introduction

Accurate segmentation of abdominal organs is crucial for diagnosing and treating abdominal lesions [1], with CT imaging being widely used in clinical practice.

Manual segmentation is time-consuming, labor-intensive, and prone to variability among observers [2]. AI development presents an opportunity to automate this process, reducing the burden on clinicians and enabling applications like surgical planning. However, deep learning models have become increasingly complex, requiring large amounts of labeled data [3]. Medical image segmentation, especially for intricate abdominal organs or diseases, requires pixel-level labels that can only be provided by experts. The growing size and resolution of images exacerbate these challenges. In clinical settings, there is a significant amount of semi-labeled or unlabeled data that cannot be effectively utilized with fully supervised learning approaches.

In this context, the practicality of semi-supervised segmentation methods has seen a notable increase, primarily attributed to their ability to effectively exploit small, accurately labeled datasets while leveraging larger pools of unlabeled data, resulting in enhanced model accuracy [4]. In recent years, the field of medical image segmentation has witnessed widespread application of semi-supervised learning techniques. These approaches exploit the global characteristics of data by incorporating unlabeled samples and can be broadly categorized into three types [5]: first, utilizing model predictions on unlabeled images to generate pseudo-labels for subsequent model training; second, jointly training the model with both labeled and unlabeled data; third, incorporating unlabeled images with prior knowledge (such as shape and location) along with labeled images during model training. Initially, pseudo-labeling was employed in early semi-supervised methods [6], and many existing frameworks have integrated this concept [7–10]. Presently, the latest advancements in semi-supervised segmentation revolve around consistency learning, adversarial learning, and entropy minimization. Furthermore, hybrid semi-supervised learning [11–14] has gained significant attention and application, where diverse methods are integrated to optimize the model and enhance segmentation performance.

In recent years, the nnU-Net framework [15] has been widely adopted for medical image segmentation. While it excels in fully supervised scenarios, it lacks built-in support for semi-supervised training. In practical clinical settings, time constraints for inference and limited labeled data availability hinder optimal efficiency with the default nnU-Net. The first-place solution of Flare 2022 challenge developed a semi-supervised learning framework based on nnU-Net [16], demonstrating the efficacy of pseudo-labeling methods in leveraging unlabeled data to enhance model robustness.

In this work, we propose a semi-supervised framework based on nnU-Net for abdominal organ segmentation, aiming to meet the requirements of fast inference and low computational cost while making the most of a limited amount of labeled data. We introduce high-quality pseudo-labels by utilizing a resource-intensive nnU-Net trained on fully labeled CT scan data to generate them for the semi-labeled data. In a lightweight nnU-Net, we jointly train the labeled images with pseudo-labels and the unlabeled images to obtain a model capable of fast inference. Additionally, we have implemented a method proposed in the literature [16,17] that utilizes efficient sliding window strategies based on prior knowledge of abdominal organs to reduce the number of inference windows and leverages GPU for resizing data, leading to improved inference efficiency.

The principal contributions of our study can be outlined as follows:

– We propose a semi-supervised segmentation framework based on nnU-Net, which effectively utilizes unlabeled data to improve the segmentation accuracy of models.
– We performed compression optimization on the default nnU-Net. By reducing the input data size and using a narrower network width, we maintained high segmentation accuracy while minimizing GPU resource requirements, making it more suitable for practical applications and competition needs.

2 Method

To leverage unlabeled data, we initiate the process by training a teacher model using labeled data. We chose the default nnU-Net as the teacher model, which works well in most cases. Subsequently, we utilize the well-trained teacher model to generate predictions for the unlabeled data, thereby obtaining high-quality pseudo-labels that significantly enhance the training process. To optimize inference efficiency, we draw inspiration from the first-place solution of the previous Flare 2022 challenge [16] and downscale the default U-Net network of the nnU-Net framework to serve as a student model. The modified student model is trained by leveraging these pseudo-labeled data in combination with the labeled dataset. This approach ensures that the smaller student model achieves segmentation accuracy comparable to its larger teacher model while concurrently improving segmentation efficiency to meet the resource-constrained requirements. An overview of the framework we designed is shown in Fig. 1.

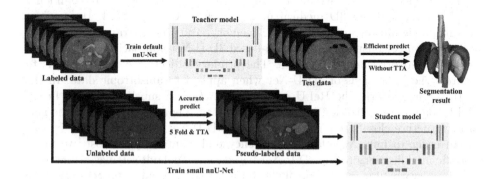

Fig. 1. Teacher-Student Semi-Supervised segmentation framework: During the model training, the teacher model infers on unlabeled data and utilizes high-quality pseudo-labeled data generated by the larger teacher model to train a more efficient student model.

2.1   Preprocessing

We divided our partially labeled dataset of 2,200 samples into two distinct train-ing sets based on the labeled content. The first set consisted of 222 samples, each labeled with all 13 organs, and was used to train a teacher model for organ seg-mentation. The second set encompassed a collection of 597 samples, each labeled to encompass tumors and six additional organs, thereby serving as the founda-tion for training dedicated tumor segmentation models. This approach allowed us to train independent models for organ segmentation and tumor segmentation, enabling us to focus on the specific features and characteristics of each segmen-tation type, resulting in improved accuracy and efficiency of our analysis.

Regarding image preprocessing, we applied several steps to the FLARE 2023 dataset using the default nnU-Net settings. First, we cropped each CT scan to remove non-zero regions. Subsequently, the CT images were subject to clipping, specifically aligned with the 0.5 and 99.5 percentiles of the foreground voxels, followed by the implementation of Z-score normalization utilizing the global foreground mean and standard deviation. Finally, we resampled each scan to a specific uniform spacing to ensure consistency in the dataset. We used third-order spline interpolation and nearest-neighbor interpolation methods for the data and segmentation mask, respectively. This step was crucial since CT scan values are directly related to physical properties, and keeping them in a preprocessing state was essential for accurate analysis. The resampling spacing for the teacher model is [2.5, 0.86, 0.86], whereas for the student model, it is [4.0, 1.2, 1.2]. Overall, these preprocessing steps ensured that the FLARE 2023 dataset was suitable for meaningful and accurate analysis of abdominal tumors and organs.

2.2   Proposed Method

Our backbone network utilizes the 3D U-Net structure, which is commonly employed for training 3D medical images such as CT and MRI. However, it requires a significant amount of GPU memory. To enhance training speed and reduce resource consumption, a patch-based 3D U-Net approach can be adopted to lower network computing costs. The primary objective of 3D U-Net is to address the limitations of 2D U-Net when applied to anisotropic data. In the nnU-Net framework, the ReLU activation function is substituted with Leaky ReLU, batch normalization is replaced by instance normalization, and the net-work structure closely resembles the default 3D U-Net architecture.

In order to improve inference efficiency and computational cost, we made specific modifications to the 3D U-Net based on the default settings of the nnU-Net framework. Our small-scale 3D U-Net network takes input patches of size 32 × 128 × 192, with a batch size of 2, and comprises four up-sampling and down-sampling layers. Each layer consists of 3D convolution, LReLU activation, and instance normalization. The initial layer of the 3D U-Net extracts 16 feature maps, while each downsampling process extracts a maximum of 256 feature maps. The structure of the 3D U-Net backbone network is depicted in Fig. 2.

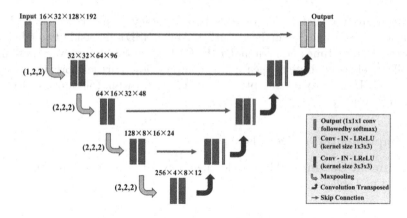

Fig. 2. The small 3D U-Net network architecture.

Loss function: We utilize the default composite loss function in nnU-Net, which combines the Dice loss and Cross-entropy loss. This composite loss function has been proven to exhibit robustness in various medical image segmentation tasks [18].

2.3 Post-processing

Due to meet time constraints, we opted not to employ complex post-processing techniques. To expedite the inference process, Test Time Augmentation (TTA) was disabled, resulting in a 2x reduction in inference time. Given that we have two segmentation models, it is necessary to integrate the results of the organ segmentation and tumor segmentation models. The tumor segmentation results are superimposed on the organ segmentation results, and if there are any conflicts, the tumor segmentation results are given priority.

3   Experiments

3.1 Dataset and Evaluation Measures

The FLARE 2023 challenge is an extension of the FLARE 2021–2022 [19,20], aiming to aim to promote the development of foundation models in abdominal disease analysis. The segmentation targets cover 13 organs and various abdominal lesions. The training dataset is curated from more than 30 medical centers under the license permission, including TCIA [21], LiTS [22], MSD [23], KiTS [24,25], and AbdomenCT-1K [26]. The training set includes 4000 abdomen CT scans where 2200 CT scans with partial labels and 1800 CT scans without labels. The validation and testing sets include 100 and 400 CT scans, respectively, which cover various abdominal cancer types, such as liver cancer, kidney cancer, pancreas cancer, colon cancer, gastric cancer, and so on. The organ annotation process used ITK-SNAP [27], nnU-Net [15], and MedSAM [28].

The evaluation metrics encompass two accuracy measures-Dice Similarity Coefficient (DSC) and Normalized Surface Dice (NSD)-alongside two efficiency measures-running time and area under the GPU memory-time curve. These metrics collectively contribute to the ranking computation. Furthermore, the running time and GPU memory consumption are considered within tolerances of 15 s and 4 GB, respectively.

3.2   Implementation Details

Environment Settings. The development environments and requirements are presented in Table 1.

Table 1. Development environments and requirements.

System	Ubuntu 18.04.4 LTS
CPU	Intel(R) Xeon(R) Gold 6146 CPU@3.20 GHz
RAM	256G
GPU	Two NVIDIA V100 16G
CUDA version	10.2
Programming language	Python 3.8
Deep learning framework	torch 1.11, torchvision 0.12.0
Specific dependencies	nnU-Net

Training Protocols. We employed nnU-Net's deep supervision loss, a methodology that incorporates the output layer into the loss calculation during each upsampling operation. To achieve this, different weights are assigned to the shallowest and deeper layers, with a weight of 1 for the shallowest layer and halved weights for each subsequent deeper layer. This combined approach integrates equally weighted dice and cross-entropy loss terms, facilitating comprehensive and effective training. To harness the benefits of ensemble learning, we trained five teacher models iteratively until reaching convergence. Subsequently, we utilized their collective predictions on the unlabeled samples to generate pseudo labels, which were then employed for training the student model. This teacher-student training paradigm with pseudo labels serves to leverage the information-rich unlabeled data effectively, enhancing the performance of the student model. For the specifics of our training procedure, including batch size, number of epochs, optimizer choice, and other relevant details, please refer to Tables 2 and 3 for comprehensive information. These tables present a clear and organized overview of the training protocols, ensuring reproducibility and facilitating comparison with other methodologies in the field.

Data Augmentation. During the training of the teacher model, several data augmentation techniques were employed, including the use of Gaussian noise, brightness adjustment, gamma correction, rotation, scaling, elastic deformation, and simulated low-resolution data. It is worth noting that for the training of the student model, only a subset of these techniques were utilized, specifically luminance adjustment, gamma correction, rotation, scaling, and elastic deformation.

Table 2. Training protocols for teacher model.

Network initialization	"HE" normal initialization
Batch size	2
Patch size	Stage0 [64,192,192], Stage1 [48,192,192]
Total epochs	1000
Optimizer	SGD with nesterov momentum ($\mu = 0.99$)
Initial learning rate (lr)	0.01
Lr decay schedule	Poly learning rate policy:$(1 - epoch/1000)^{0.9}$
Training time	72 h
Number of model parameters	31.2M
Number of flops	230G

Table 3. Training protocols for student model.

Network initialization	"HE" normal initialization
Batch size	2
Patch size	Stage0 [32,128,192], Stage1 [32,128,192]
Total epochs	1500
Optimizer	SGD with nesterov momentum ($\mu = 0.99$)
Initial learning rate (lr)	0.01
Lr decay schedule	Poly learning rate policy:$(1 - epoch/1500)^{0.9}$
Training time	24 h
Number of model parameters	6.1M
Number of flops	140G

4 Results and Discussion

The DSC and NSD results for all experiments were obtained through the online validation leaderboard in the MICCAI FLARE 2023 challenge. Additionally, the detailed results of the 50 public validation sets were processed privately. The challenge organizers provided an efficiency analysis based on the Docker containers we submitted.

4.1 Quantitative Results on Validation Set

Overall, the quantitative evaluation results on the provided validation and test sets are shown in Table 4. On the validation set, the average DSC for the 13 organs is 0.8856, with an average NSD of 0.9491. The DSC for tumor segmentation is 0.4258, with an NSD of 0.3513. On the test dataset, the average DSC for the 13 organs is 0.8856, with an average NSD of 0.9491. The DSC for tumor segmentation is 0.4258, with an NSD of 0.3513. Due to limitations in inference time and memory, our approach employed larger spacing for resampling the input data and used smaller patch sizes. This exacerbated the risk of losing contextual information when dealing with small targets. It can be observed that the segmentation performance for the right adrenal gland, left adrenal gland, and gallbladder, which are small-volume organs, is relatively poor.

Table 4. Quantitative evaluation results.

Target	Public Validation		Online Validation		Testing	
	DSC (%)	NSD (%)	DSC (%)	NSD (%)	DSC (%)	NSD (%)
Liver	97.37 ± 0.55	84.58 ± 4.46	97.30	98.76	95.72	96.90
Right Kidney	94.35 ± 7.38	93.98 ± 8.70	93.32	94.99	94.89	96.11
Spleen	96.46 ± 1.65	98.61 ± 2.84	95.67	97.96	95.81	97.87
Pancreas	85.70 ± 6.25	94.38 ± 6.12	84.53	95.77	88.34	96.92
Aorta	94.92 ± 2.11	99.49 ± 1.56	95.02	98.22	95.29	99.17
Inferior vena cava	93.61 ± 2.13	99.53 ± 0.96	93.21	96.45	93.33	96.91
Right adrenal gland	81.28 ± 6.24	99.95 ± 0.19	80.30	94.79	78.02	93.32
Left adrenal gland	78.52 ± 7.14	99.83 ± 0.39	78.08	92.59	77.49	92.44
Gallbladder	83.62 ± 18.8	93.93 ± 19.9	84.67	83.62	81.14	82.64
Esophagus	81.21 ± 15.2	96.85 ± 14.4	81.71	93.85	87.46	98.34
Stomach	92.11 ± 3.63	98.33 ± 3.69	92.63	97.34	92.32	97.28
Duodenum	81.67 ± 7.49	96.85 ± 3.76	82.27	95.18	85.07	96.80
Left kidney	92.26 ± 12.5	97.98 ± 7.72	92.53	94.28	94.70	96.52
Tumor	49.38 ± 33.0	64.71 ± 37.8	42.58	35.13	36.28	26.78
Organ Average	88.70 ± 6.52	96.48 ± 4.03	88.59	94.91	89.20	95.48

4.2 Qualitative Results on Validation Set

Figure 3 presents four representative segmentation results obtained from our final submission using the small nnU-Net. The top two rows depict case 17 and case 75, where the network successfully achieved high-accuracy identification of all organs. However, in the bottom two rows, specifically case 124 and case 94, noticeable segmentation deficiencies and over-segmentation errors are apparent. These issues may be attributed to the limited contextual information capturing capability of the small 3D nnU-Net and the loss of important details due to the large spacing of the resampled images, resulting in suboptimal segmentation of small-volume organs.

It is worth noting that compared to models trained solely on fully labeled data, the use of pseudo-labels in the semi-supervised approach improves segmentation accuracy. It can be observed that models employing pseudo-labels demonstrate higher generalization performance, highlighting the benefits of leveraging unlabeled data in these specific cases.

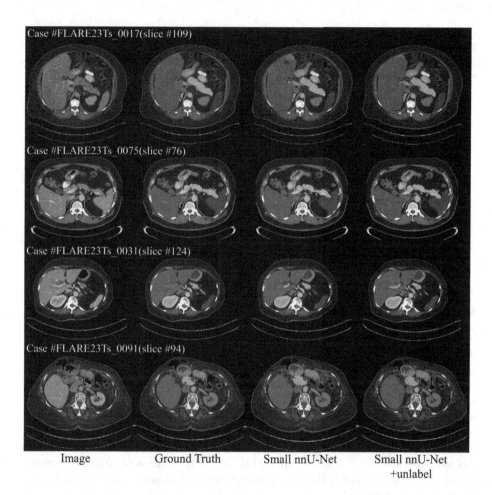

Fig. 3. Qualitative results of our small nnU-Net on two easy cases (case 17, case 75) and two challenging cases (case 124, case 94).

4.3 Segmentation Efficiency Results on Validation Set

Our validation Docker was submitted to an official evaluation platform with NVIDIA QUADRO RTX5000 (16G) and 28G RAM. The evaluation was performed on 100 validation sets, with an average running time of 29 s per case. The average maximum GPU memory utilization was 3077 MB, and the average area under the GPU memory time curve was 25411. We conducted an efficiency analysis by selecting validation set data of different sizes, and the results are presented in Table 5. Since our organ segmentation and tumor segmentation are separate models, we need to perform inference twice on the same sample, which contributes to longer run times. However, our GPU exhibits lower maximum memory usage.

Table 5. Quantitative evaluation of segmentation efficiency in terms of the running time and GPU memory consumption. (Total GPU denotes the area under GPU Memory-Time curve)

Case ID	Image Size	Running Time (s)	Max GPU (MB)	Total GPU (MB)
0001	(512, 512, 55)	27.73	2538	23063
0051	(512, 512, 100)	27.58	2538	25422
0017	(512, 512, 150)	31.46	3700	29963
0019	(512, 512, 215)	30.08	3700	25978
0099	(512, 512, 334)	34.74	1954	28417
0063	(512, 512, 448)	41.71	3700	34501
0048	(512, 512, 499)	46.18	3700	38808
0029	(512, 512, 554)	48.52	1690	39530

4.4   Effect of Unlabeled Data

In this study, we developed separate models for organ segmentation and tumor segmentation. Table 6 illustrates the impact of incorporating unlabeled data with labeled data during the training of the organ segmentation model. The results clearly demonstrate that this semi-supervised learning approach leads to enhanced performance compared to models trained solely on labeled data. It is worth noting that smaller models utilizing efficient inference strategies exhibit particularly significant performance improvements. Due to the time constraints of the competition, our tumor segmentation model was trained only on 597 fully labeled cases and did not utilize unlabeled data. Therefore, a comparative experiment between different training approaches for the tumor segmentation model could not be conducted.

Table 6. The segmentation accuracy of the default nnU-Net model and the small nnU-Net model in the validation set with or without the use of pseudo-labeled data.

Method	Val Organ DSC (%)	Val Organ NSD (%)	Running Time
Default nnU-Net	87.51	92.92	4 min
Default nnU-Net+unlabel	89.40	94.31	
Small nnU-Net	85.49	90.94	29 s
Small nnU-Net+unlabel	88.59	94.91	

4.5   Limitation and Future Work

Several limitations have been discerned within the scope of our investigation. Due to time constraints during inference, we had to make compromises and increase the resample spacing, which has impacted the performance of model for small-scale targets. Exploring alternative resample strategies and optimizing this process could enhance the segmentation accuracy. Additionally, we have not investigated more complex neural network structures, such as the cascade 3D U-Net, which could potentially improve the ability of model to handle small targets. Future work should also include exploring advanced data augmentation techniques, such as CutMix, and employing sophisticated post-processing methods to further enhance the model's performance and robustness. Furthermore, the segmentation of organs and tumors is currently performed by two separate models, leading to low inference efficiency. Moving forward, our focus should be directed towards the integration of these two distinct models, with the overarching objective of attaining a unified framework proficient in undertaking both tasks. Addressing these limitations will contribute to refining and improving the applicability of our model.

5   Conclusion

This paper presents a semi-supervised learning framework based on nnU-Net, which leverages unlabeled data to enhance model performance and generalization. Additionally, we have made improvements to nnU-Net and compressed it to improve model inference efficiency while maintaining high accuracy to meet the requirements of the competition. Experimental results on the FLARE 2023 validation dataset demonstrate that, with an average inference time of 29 s for the lightweight nnU-Net, incorporating unlabeled data leads to an increase of 0.0310 in the DSC metric and 0.0397 in the NSD metric for the organ segmentation model, compared to models trained solely on labeled data. Ultimately, we have successfully developed a low-resource, fast-processing model for abdominal CT organ and tumor segmentation.

Acknowledgement. The authors of this paper declare that the segmentation method they implemented for participation in the FLARE 2023 challenge has not used any pretrained models nor additional datasets other than those provided by the organizers. The proposed solution is fully automatic without any manual intervention. We thank all the data owners for making the CT scans publicly available and CodaLab [29] for hosting the challenge platform. This research was funded by the National Key Research and Development Program of China, grant number 2022YFF0710800; the National Key Research and Development Program of China, grant number 2022YFF0710802; the National Natural Science Foundation of China, grant number 62071311; the special program for key fields of colleges and universities in Guangdong Province (biomedicine and health) of China, grant number 2021ZDZX2008; and the Stable Support Plan for Colleges and Universities in Shenzhen of China, grant number SZWD2021010.

References

1. Wolz, R., Chu, C., Misawa, K., Fujiwara, M., Mori, K., Rueckert, D.: Automated abdominal multi-organ segmentation with subject-specific atlas generation. IEEE Trans. Med. Imaging **32**(9), 1723–1730 (2013)
2. Heimann, T., Meinzer, H.P.: Statistical shape models for 3D medical image segmentation: a review. Med. Image Anal. **13**(4), 543–563 (2009)
3. Manko, M.: Segmentation of organs at risk in chest cavity using 3D deep neural network. In: 2019 Signal Processing Symposium (SPSympo), pp. 287–290. IEEE (2019)
4. Chen, X., et al.: Recent advances and clinical applications of deep learning in medical image analysis. Med. Image Anal. **79**, 102444 (2022)
5. Jiao, R., et al.: Learning with limited annotations: a survey on deep semi-supervised learning for medical image segmentation. Comput. Biol. Med. 107840 (2023)
6. Zhu, X.J.: Semi-supervised learning literature survey. World (2005)
7. Rizve, M.N., Duarte, K., Rawat, Y.S., Shah, M.: In defense of pseudo-labeling: an uncertainty-aware pseudo-label selection framework for semi-supervised learning. arXiv preprint arXiv:2101.06329 (2021)
8. Shi, Y., Huang, Z., Feng, S., Zhong, H., Wang, W., Sun, Y.: Masked label prediction: unified message passing model for semi-supervised classification. arXiv preprint arXiv:2009.03509 (2020)
9. Zou, Y., et al.: PseudoSeg: designing pseudo labels for semantic segmentation. arXiv preprint arXiv:2010.09713 (2020)
10. Sohn, K., et al.: FixMatch: simplifying semi-supervised learning with consistency and confidence. In: Advances in Neural Information Processing Systems, vol. 33, pp. 596–608 (2020)
11. Hu, H., Wei, F., Hu, H., Ye, Q., Cui, J., Wang, L.: Semi-supervised semantic segmentation via adaptive equalization learning. In: Advances in Neural Information Processing Systems, vol. 34, pp. 22106–22118 (2021)
12. Lai, X., et al.: Semi-supervised semantic segmentation with directional context-aware consistency. In: Proceedings of the IEEE/CVF Conference on Computer Vision and Pattern Recognition, pp. 1205–1214 (2021)
13. Zhou, Y., Xu, H., Zhang, W., Gao, B., Heng, P.A.: C3-semiSeg: contrastive semi-supervised segmentation via cross-set learning and dynamic class-balancing. In: Proceedings of the IEEE/CVF International Conference on Computer Vision, pp. 7036–7045 (2021)
14. Huang, W., et al.: Semi-supervised neuron segmentation via reinforced consistency learning. IEEE Trans. Med. Imaging **41**(11), 3016–3028 (2022)
15. Isensee, F., Jaeger, P.F., Kohl, S.A., Petersen, J., Maier-Hein, K.H.: nnU-Net: a self-configuring method for deep learning-based biomedical image segmentation. Nat. Methods **18**(2), 203–211 (2021)
16. Huang, Z., et al.: Revisiting nnU-Net for iterative pseudo labeling and efficient sliding window inference. In: Ma, J., Wang, B. (eds.) Fast and Low-Resource Semi-supervised Abdominal Organ Segmentation. FLARE 2022. LNCS, vol. 13816, pp. 178–189. Springer, Cham (2022). https://doi.org/10.1007/978-3-031-23911-3_16
17. Huang, S., et al.: Abdominal CT organ segmentation by accelerated nnU-Net with a coarse to fine strategy. In: Ma, J., Wang, B. (eds.) Fast and Low-Resource Semi-supervised Abdominal Organ Segmentation. FLARE 2022. LNCS, vol. 13816, pp. 23–34. Springer, Cham (2022). https://doi.org/10.1007/978-3-031-23911-3_3

18. Ma, J., et al.: Loss odyssey in medical image segmentation. Med. Image Anal. **71**, 102035 (2021)
19. Ma, J., et al.: Fast and low-GPU-memory abdomen CT organ segmentation: the flare challenge. Med. Image Anal. **82**, 102616 (2022)
20. Ma, J., et al.: Unleashing the strengths of unlabeled data in pan-cancer abdominal organ quantification: the flare22 challenge. arXiv preprint arXiv:2308.05862 (2023)
21. Clark, K.: The cancer imaging archive (TCIA): maintaining and operating a public information repository. J. Digit. Imaging **26**(6), 1045–1057 (2013)
22. Bilic, P., et al.: The liver tumor segmentation benchmark (LiTS). Med. Image Anal. **84**, 102680 (2023)
23. Simpson, A.L., et al.: A large annotated medical image dataset for the development and evaluation of segmentation algorithms. arXiv preprint arXiv:1902.09063 (2019)
24. Heller, N., et al.: The state of the art in kidney and kidney tumor segmentation in contrast-enhanced CT imaging: results of the kits19 challenge. Med. Image Anal. **67**, 101821 (2021)
25. Heller, N., et al.: An international challenge to use artificial intelligence to define the state-of-the-art in kidney and kidney tumor segmentation in CT imaging. Proc. Am. Soc. Clin. Oncol. **38**(6), 626 (2020)
26. Ma, J., et al.: AbdomenCT-1K: is abdominal organ segmentation a solved problem? IEEE Trans. Pattern Anal. Mach. Intell. **44**(10), 6695–6714 (2022)
27. Yushkevich, P.A., Gao, Y., Gerig, G.: ITK-SNAP: an interactive tool for semi-automatic segmentation of multi-modality biomedical images. In: Annual International Conference of the IEEE Engineering in Medicine and Biology Society, pp. 3342–3345 (2016)
28. Ma, J., He, Y., Li, F., Han, L., You, C., Wang, B.: Segment anything in medical images. Nat. Commun. **15**(1), 654 (2024)
29. Pavao, A.: CodaLab competitions: an open source platform to organize scientific challenges. J. Mach. Learn. Res. **24**(198), 1–6 (2023)

Multi-task Learning with Iterative Training in Hybrid Labeling Dataset for Semi-supervised Abdominal Multi-organ and Tumor Segmentation

Zhiqiang Zhong[1], Rongxuan He[1,2], Deming Zhu[1], Mengqiu Tian[1], and Songfeng Li[1(✉)]

[1] Percept Vis Med Technol Co LTD., Guangzhou 510275, People's Republic of China
lisongfeng@pvmedtech.com
[2] Johns Hopkins University, Baltimore, MD 21218, USA

Abstract. Simultaneous segmentation of organs and tumors from abdominal CT images is challenging, and the task has many critical clinical applications such as disease diagnosis, lesion and organ measurements, and surgical planning. Based on nnU-Net, we develop a method for abdominal organ and whole-body pan-tumor segmentation for both abdominal and whole-body CT images. First, in a fully supervised setting, we train the base models of organs and tumors to generate initial pseudo-labels. Then, in a semi-supervised setting, a mixed-labeled dataset is used to iteratively train a higher-performance segmentation model to create higher-quality pseudo-labels. Due to the correlation between organs and tumors in the abdominal region, we leverage the idea of multi-task learning to train a single model to segment both organs and tumors to improve the performance of a single task. Finally, to trade off segmentation efficiency and accuracy, we design a sliding window strategy based on the body prior and a simplified version of test-time augmentation (TTA4). Our final model achieved 88.93% mean organ DSC and 45.76% tumor DSC on the FLARE23 online validation set. In addition, the average running time and area under GPU memory-time curve were 26.7 s and 49352.9MB, respectively. On the test set, we achieved mean organ and tumor DSC of 89.85% and 63.21%, respectively, NSD of 96.07% and 52.22%, respectively, and average inference time of 18.53 s. Our code is publicly available at https://github.com/LeoZhong997/FLARE23.

Keywords: Segmentation · Multi-task learning · Semi-supervised learning

1 Introduction

Simultaneous segmentation of organs and tumors from abdominal CT images is a formidable challenge that holds immense clinical significance. It plays a pivotal role in various critical clinical applications, such as disease diagnosis, precise

© The Author(s), under exclusive license to Springer Nature Switzerland AG 2024
J. Ma and B. Wang (Eds.): FLARE 2023, LNCS 14544, pp. 306–318, 2024.
https://doi.org/10.1007/978-3-031-58776-4_24

lesion and organ measurements, and the development of surgical plans. Nevertheless, manually labeling organs and lesion locations is a time-consuming task that demands a great deal of expertise from physicians. FLARE23 is a challenge aimed at fostering the development of fully automatic solutions for this task. Expanding upon the 13 abdominal organs segmentation task of FLARE22 [13], FLARE23 requires participants to simultaneously segment tumors, a more practical study given that the majority of real clinical data may contain lesions. Furthermore, the challenge restricts the inference time and GPU memory usage to mimic actual clinical conditions, implying that we cannot complete the task solely by increasing the model size or using more computational resources.

Semi-supervised learning is a crucial strategy employed in medical image segmentation tasks, due to the limited availability of medical data and the time-consuming annotation process. One of the most common approaches to semi-supervised segmentation is to use pseudo-labels [9] generated by a model trained on the labeled data. When training a model with a large amount of unlabeled data, the accuracy of the pseudo-labels becomes critical. Consequently, eliminating uncertain pseudo-labels is a vital step in the training procedure. The standard method for filtering out uncertain pseudo-labels involves applying a confidence threshold to determine whether the pseudo-labels are reliable. Furthermore, recent studies have demonstrated that these unreliable pseudo-labels can also be leveraged in the self-training process [17].

In this paper, we propose an iterative training framework based on nnU-net to perform organ and tumor segmentation tasks. We start from a single-task setting, where we iteratively train the organ segmentation model. Semi-supervised learning is employed to generate pseudo labels for the partially labeled data and unlabeled data. Subsequently, we transition to a multi-task setting, training a model to perform both organ and tumor segmentation tasks using the pseudo labels generated in the prior stage. Additionally, we incorporate unlabeled data into the training set. Furthermore, to enhance inference speed, we introduce a sliding window strategy and we utilize a simplified version of test-time augmentation (TTA4) to improve segmentation accuracy.

2 Method

2.1 Preprocessing

The preprocessing strategies we use are as follows:

- Data cleaning or statistical analysis:
  We perform label analysis to check label completeness. Out of 2200 labeled data, 222 cases include complete organ labels without tumors, and 1497 cases have tumor labels. These two subsets are utilized for training our single-task models.
- Reorientation:
  As we want the network to predict images regardless of orientation, we reorient the images to the standard RAS orientation during the training phase.

Later, we will apply mirroring operations in the later stages of data augmentation to enhance the network's orientation robustness.
- Resampling method for anisotropic data:
  In order to leverage the physical information within the CT data, all images are resampled to the same resolution of 4.0 mm × 1.2 mm × 1.2 mm.
- Intensity normalization method:
  Initially, we compute the 0.5 and 99.5 percentiles, as well as the mean and standard deviation of the data intensity. Subsequently, the data is clipped to the 0.5 and 99.5 percentiles, and z-score normalization is applied using the global mean and standard deviation.

2.2   Proposed Method

We introduce an iterative training framework for the task of multi-organ and tumor segmentation. Our networks are derived from the 3D nnU-Net [8]. However, we separate from the nnU-Net's auto-configuration and introduce two fixed network architectures: the medium and large nnU-Net, with their parameters detailed in the experiment part. Figure 1 illustrates the workflow of our proposed approach. Our approach comprises two stages: single-task training and multi-task training.

Single-Task Training. During the single-task stage, we train the nnU-Net separately for organ and tumor segmentation. To address the multi-organ segmentation task, we utilize the 222 labeled data that include complete organ labels.

Following the development of the organ segmentation model, we employ it to generate pseudo labels for the remaining 1978 labeled data lacking organ labels. Nevertheless, within these 1978 labeled data, we have part of ground truth labels. We propose combining these ground truth labels with the pseudo labels. Since this model only performs organ segmentation, we filter out organs that do not contain tumors in the true labels. Determining the organ to which the tumor belongs is accomplished through morphological analysis. We conduct a morphological dilation operation on the tumors and if an overlap exists between the tumor and an organ, the tumor is attributed to that organ. Subsequently, we replace the corresponding pseudo labels with the ground truth labels for organs without tumors, resulting in a hybrid labeled dataset.

The hybrid labeled dataset is employed for training the organ segmentation model, and we utilize the model to generate pseudo labels for the entire 2200 training set. Iterative training is then conducted to enhance the accuracy of our pseudo labels of organs.

In the context of the tumor segmentation task, we utilize the 1497 labeled data containing tumor labels. However, due to suboptimal Dice Similarity Coefficient (DSC) and Normalized Surface Dice (NSD) performance, we do not employ this model in our subsequent training procedures.

Multi-task Training. To reduce inference time costs and maximize the utilization of the correlation between organs and tumors, we suggest training a single model capable of accomplishing both organ and tumor segmentation tasks. The organ model trained in the previous stage is utilized to generate the pseudo labels for the 1497 labeled data. These pseudo labels are then combined with the ground truth, following the same procedure described earlier. Following the utilization of the hybrid labeled subset for training the multi-task model, we employ the model to generate the pseudo labels of the 2200 training set and retrain the model.

Once the multi-task model is trained using the 2200 labeled data, we employ the model to generate the pseudo labels of the 1800 unlabeled data. Subsequently, we straightforwardly add these data to the training set and conduct iterative training twice to obtain the final model.

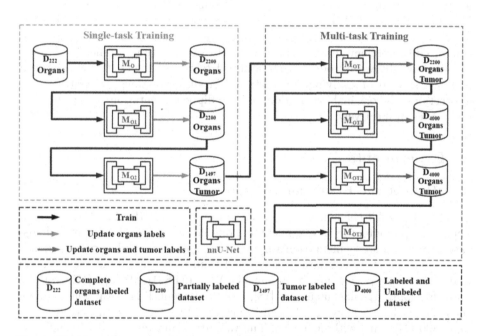

Fig. 1. Workflow of our proposed approach. The workflow comprises two stages: single-task training and multi-task training.

Loss Function. We use the summation between a weighted Dice loss and cross-entropy loss because compound loss functions have been proven to be robust in various medical image segmentation tasks [10]. What's more, deep supervision is used to fully utilize the feature information of the intermediate encoding and decoding layers.

Sliding Window Strategy. In order to improve inference speed and reduce resource consumption, we adopt the sliding window strategy to fuse the predictions of overlapping patches. We adapt the fast sliding window strategy initially proposed by the FLARE22 winning team [7] to align it with the requirements of the tumor segmentation task. Given that tumors can appear in various regions in the abdominal area, the absence of a label in the central patch does not necessarily imply the absence of tumors in the surrounding patches. Consequently, for every slice along the z-axis, after the acquisition of the central patch, we also retrieve all the surrounding patches to generate the final prediction.

2.3   Post-processing

To improve the performance of pseudo-labels, we employ connected component analysis on organs, retaining the largest 3D connected component. If the organ's Dice loss increases following connected component analysis, we opt to conduct the analysis for that specific organ. During the validation and testing phases, connected component analysis is deactivated to reduce time overhead.

Additionally, we introduce a streamlined test-time augmentation approach (TTA4). Instead of applying augmentation in all 8 directions, we restrict it to 4 directions: the original orientation and the flipped orientations along the x, y, and z axes, respectively.

3   Experiments

3.1   Dataset and Evaluation Measures

The FLARE 2023 challenge is an extension of the FLARE 2021–2022 [12,13], aiming to promote the development of foundation models in abdominal disease analysis. The segmentation targets cover 13 organs and various abdominal lesions. The training dataset is curated from more than 30 medical centers under the license permission, including TCIA [2], LiTS [1], MSD [16], KiTS [5,6], autoPET [3,4], TotalSegmentator [18], and AbdomenCT-1K [14]. The training set includes 4000 abdomen CT scans where 2200 CT scans with partial labels and 1800 CT scans without labels. The validation and testing sets include 100 and 400 CT scans, respectively, which cover various abdominal cancer types, such as liver cancer, kidney cancer, pancreas cancer, colon cancer, gastric cancer, and so on. The organ annotation process used ITK-SNAP [19], nnU-Net [8], and MedSAM [11].

The evaluation metrics encompass two accuracy measures—Dice Similarity Coefficient (DSC) and Normalized Surface Dice (NSD)—alongside two efficiency measures—running time and area under the GPU memory-time curve. These metrics collectively contribute to the ranking computation. Furthermore, the running time and GPU memory consumption are considered within tolerances of 15 s and 4 GB, respectively.

3.2 Implementation Details

Environment Settings. The development environments and requirements are presented in Table 1. The training protocols of medium nnU-Net and large nnU-Net are listed in Table 2 and Table 3 respectively. We adopt data augmentation of rotation, scaling, Gaussian noise and blur, brightness, contrast, gamma, elastic deformation, and mirror on the fly during training. Notably, we reduced the number of test time augmentation(TTA) flips to balance segmentation accuracy and inference time.

Table 1. Development environments and requirements.

System	Ubuntu 18.04.5 LTS
CPU	Intel(R) Xeon(R) Gold 6326 CPU @ 2.90 GHz
RAM	8×64 GB; 3200MT/s
GPU (number and type)	Four NVIDIA A4000 16G
CUDA version	11.6
Programming language	Python 3.8.13
Deep learning framework	torch 1.13, torchvision 0.14.0
Specific dependencies	nnU-Net 1.7.0
Code	https://github.com/LeoZhong997/FLARE23

Table 2. Training protocols for medium nnU-Net

Network initialization	"He" normal initialization
Batch size	2
Stage number	5
Convolution number per stage	2
Patch size	$32 \times 128 \times 192$
Total epochs	1500
Optimizer	SGD with nesterov momentum ($\mu = 0.99$)
Initial learning rate (lr)	0.01
Lr decay schedule	Poly learning rate policy: $(1 - epoch/1000)^{0.9}$
Training time	25 h
Loss function	Dice loss and cross-entropy loss
Number of model parameters	22M
Number of flops	253.90G
CO_2eq	8.14 Kg

Table 3. Training protocols for large nnU-Net

Network initialization	"He" normal initialization
Batch size	2
Stage number	6
Convolution number per stage	3
Patch size	$32 \times 128 \times 192$
Total epochs	1500
Optimizer	SGD with nesterov momentum ($\mu = 0.99$)
Initial learning rate (lr)	0.01
Lr decay schedule	Poly learning rate policy: $(1 - epoch/1000)^{0.9}$
Training time	33 h
Loss function	Dice loss and cross-entropy loss
Number of model parameters	85M
Number of flops	375.14G
CO_2eq	9.83 Kg

4   Results and Discussion

4.1   Quantitative Results on Validation Set

First, we train the single models M_O and M_T on the fully-labeled dataset of 222 cases of organ and 1497 cases of tumor, respectively. To obtain complete labels of organs, M_O first generates pseudo-labels on partially-labeled data of 2200 cases and combines them with ground true labels to produce a mixed-labeled organ dataset for training M_{O1}, and continues to iterate to generate a new dataset for training M_{O2}, to produce high-quality organ pseudo labels.

To validate the effectiveness of multi-task segmentation, we combine the mixed labels of organs with the ground true label of tumor on 1497 cases to train the model M_{OT}, which is able to segment all organs and tumor at once and achieves better segmentation performance than single-task segmentation.

Further, M_{OT} was utilized to generate new organs and tumor pseudo-labels on 2200 images and combined with ground true labels to form a hybrid-label dataset, wherein, due to the low accuracy of tumor segmentation, we utilized organs to constrain tumor pseudo-labels during label merging, and disregarded the results of tumor segmentation outside of organs. Using this dataset, we trained the model M_{OT1}.

In order to verify the effectiveness of unlabeled data on model segmentation performance improvement, we use M_{OT1} to generate segmentation results on 4000 cases, of which 2200 cases are regenerated as a mixed-labeled dataset on partially-labeled data. The remaining 1800 cases are directly used as pseudo-labels for unlabeled data. We train the model M_{OT2} on these 4000-cases dataset.

Finally, we utilize M_{OT2} to iterate on the 4000-cases to generate a new dataset and upgrade the medium model to large to extract more feature information, then train the final model M_{OT3}. In order to balance the inference speed and segmentation accuracy, we adopt the TTA4 strategy (by reducing the number of flips of TTA, i.e., flipping the input image over x, y, and z, respectively) to complete the final inference process.

We report the final results of DSC and NSD of organ and tumor on the validation set in Table 4. The results of ablation studies to analyze the effect of multi-task segmentation and unlabeled data can be obtained from Table 5.

Table 4. Quantitative evaluation results. The public validation denotes the performance on the 50 validation cases with ground truth. Please present both the mean score and standard deviation. The online validation denotes the leaderboard results. The Testing results will be released during MICCAI.

Target	Public Validation		Online Validation		Testing	
	DSC(%)	NSD(%)	DSC(%)	NSD(%)	DSC(%)	NSD (%)
Liver	97.46±0.48	99.26±1.32	97.44	99.15	96.59	98.21
Right kidney	94.35±8.27	97.4±7.01	93.56	95.61	94.74	95.99
Spleen	96.51±0.69	99.76±0.58	96.72	99.23	96.02	98.4
Pancreas	86.14±5.42	98.38±2.79	85.49	96.99	89.89	98.28
Aorta	94.68±1.67	98.09±2.37	95.38	98.94	95.56	99.43
Interior vena cava	92.94±1.66	96.69±2.69	93.94	97.27	94.43	98.32
Right adrenal gland	80.21±12.36	96.66±14.01	79.74	93.8	79.08	93.53
Left adrenal gland	80.48±5.9	97.54±2.89	79.62	93.67	79.18	93.67
Gallbladder	81.95±24.98	88.32±27.02	80.87	81.42	79.46	81.7
Esophagus	81.09±14.86	94.51±14.65	82.41	94.39	87.45	98.53
Stomach	92.69±3	98.37±3.27	93.37	98.45	93.08	98.35
Duodenum	83.46±6.07	96.49±4.48	84.38	96.33	87.95	97.98
Left kidney	93.99±6.21	96.33±8.33	93.22	95.24	94.64	96.48
Tumor	52.23±35.08	51.8±34.38	45.76	38.5	63.21	52.22
Average	86.30	93.54	85.85	91.36	87.95	92.94

4.2 Qualitative Results on Validation Set

Figure 2 shows four representative segmentation results of the final model M_{OT3} in the validation dataset. For Case #FLARETs_0083 and Case #FLARETs_0027, the model successfully identified all organs and accurately segmented the tumor boundaries. For Case #FLARETs_0051, although the model had identified all the correct organs, it failed to successfully segment the tumor, resulting in lower metrics for both the tumor and the organs. In Case #FLARETs_0091, the model even failed to determine the location of the prostate tumor. We believe that, on the one hand, there is no annotation information for prostate organs in the dataset, resulting in the failure to establish a

Table 5. DSC(%) and NSD(%) of organs and tumors on online validation set.

Model	Training images	Metrics	Liver	RK	Spleen	Pancreas	Aorta	IVC	RAG	LAG	Gallbladder	Esophagus	Stomach	Duodenum	LK	Tumor	organ Mean
M_O	222	DSC	95.72	90.75	94.14	82.41	94.79	92.65	78.73	77.09	78.00	80.14	91.00	81.55	89.88	-	86.68
		NSD	97.48	92.72	95.09	95.71	97.96	95.55	93.53	92.03	76.50	92.72	95.19	94.34	91.95	-	93.14
M_{O1}	2200	DSC	96.65	91.80	95.97	83.49	95.19	93.57	79.50	78.08	82.24	81.85	92.30	82.74	89.01	-	87.88
		NSD	98.14	93.91	98.03	96.13	98.73	96.75	93.67	92.34	81.92	93.97	96.91	95.20	91.23	-	94.38
M_{O2}	2200	DSC	97.08	92.03	96.63	84.90	95.43	94.06	79.97	79.53	81.43	82.57	92.79	84.12	88.41	-	88.38
		NSD	98.67	94.61	99.04	96.83	99.02	97.44	94.13	93.80	81.56	94.73	97.76	96.13	91.85	-	95.04
M_T	1497	DSC	-	-	-	-	-	-	-	-	-	-	-	-	-	34.34	-
		NSD	-	-	-	-	-	-	-	-	-	-	-	-	-	24.02	-
M_{OT}	1497	DSC	97.32	92.62	96.46	84.56	95.19	93.61	79.84	79.46	81.18	81.88	93.12	83.50	92.88	43.76	88.59
		NSD	99.00	94.68	98.85	96.62	98.64	96.72	93.89	93.62	81.38	93.94	98.13	95.86	94.86	36.22	95.09
M_{OT1}	2200	DSC	97.42	93.44	96.64	85.23	95.29	93.85	79.63	79.34	81.45	82.26	93.05	83.98	93.47	44.31	88.85
		NSD	99.17	95.48	99.09	96.88	98.80	97.21	93.95	93.63	81.82	94.52	98.03	96.13	95.41	37.49	95.39
M_{OT2}	4000	DSC	97.43	93.67	96.63	84.99	95.28	93.88	80.77	79.60	80.61	82.12	93.08	83.83	93.32	44.73	88.86
		NSD	99.22	95.84	99.02	96.77	98.79	97.24	94.79	93.64	80.92	94.18	98.09	96.03	95.27	37.41	95.37
M_{OT3}	4000	DSC	97.44	93.56	96.72	85.49	95.38	93.94	79.74	79.62	80.87	82.41	93.37	84.38	93.22	45.76	88.93
		NSD	99.15	95.61	99.23	96.99	98.94	97.27	93.80	93.67	81.42	94.39	98.45	96.33	95.24	38.50	95.42

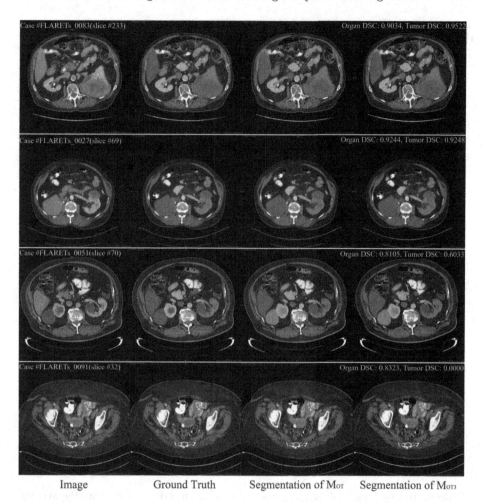

| Image | Ground Truth | Segmentation of M_{OT} | Segmentation of M_{OT3} |

Fig. 2. Qualitative results of our final model on two easy cases and two hard cases.

connection between organ and tumor; on the other hand, prostate tumors are a low percentage in the dataset, and the model lacks sufficient data to learn to segment this target.

4.3 Segmentation Efficiency Results on Validation Set

We applied a sliding window strategy with body prior and a simplified TTA4 method on the final model M_{OT3} to build the final submitted docker image. In Table 6 and Table 7, we report the efficiency evaluation results from the official platform.

Table 6. Quantitative evaluation of segmentation efficiency in terms of the running time and GPU memory consumption. Total GPU denotes the area under GPU Memory-Time curve. Evaluation GPU platform: NVIDIA QUADRO RTX5000 (16G).

Case ID	Image Size	Running Time (s)	Max GPU (MB)	Total GPU (MB)
0001	(512, 512, 55)	19.28	2468	31332
0051	(512, 512, 100)	26.05	2468	49968
0017	(512, 512, 150)	38.61	2468	54208
0019	(512, 512, 215)	23.93	2468	43972
0099	(512, 512, 334)	27.27	2468	51457
0063	(512, 512, 448)	31.75	2468	59780
0048	(512, 512, 499)	34.23	2468	65627
0029	(512, 512, 554)	38.02	2468	73601

Table 7. Efficiency evaluation results of our submitted docker. All metrics reported are the average values on 20 validation cases.

Time	GPU Memory	AUC GPU Time	CPU Utilization	AUC CPU Time	RAM	AUC RAM Time
26.7	2504.6	49352.9	66.67	916.63	6283.97	126713.2

4.4   Results on Final Testing Set

Our method achieved seventh place out of 37 submissions in the final testing set. Tables 4 and 8 show the detailed evaluation metrics of our method in the final testing set.

Table 8. Testing results of our proposed method. All metrics reported are the average values on 400 testing cases.

Organ DSC	Organ NSD	Tumor DSC	Tumor NSD	AUC GPU Time	Time
0.8985	0.9607	0.6321	0.5222	33804	18.53

4.5   Limitation and Future Work

We used a simple but effective iterative training strategy to gradually improve the quality of pseudo-label generation, but there may be noise in the pseudo-labels, which can limit or even degrade the segmentation performance of the model. Therefore, we will investigate the latest pseudo-label selection strategy in our future work to form a positive feedback loop in iterative training.

5   Conclusion

In this paper, we iteratively train a model capable of segmenting both abdominal organs and whole-body pan-tumors on a mixed-labeled dataset based on the nnU-Net framework, which combines fully supervised, semi-supervised, and multi-task learning. In addition, this paper designs a sliding window strategy based on the body prior and a simplified test-time augmentation to trade-off efficiency and accuracy during inference. The results of the public validation set of FLARE2023 show that the method has good segmentation performance and computational efficiency.

Acknowledgements. The authors of this paper declare that the segmentation method they implemented for participation in the FLARE 2023 challenge has not used any pre-trained models nor additional datasets other than those provided by the organizers. The proposed solution is fully automatic without any manual intervention. We thank all the data owners for making the CT scans publicly available and CodaLab [15] for hosting the challenge platform.

References

1. Bilic, P., et al.: The liver tumor segmentation benchmark (LiTS). Med. Image Anal. **84**, 102680 (2023)
2. Clark, K., et al.: The cancer imaging archive (TCIA): maintaining and operating a public information repository. J. Digit. Imaging **26**(6), 1045–1057 (2013)
3. Gatidis, S., et al.: The autopet challenge: towards fully automated lesion segmentation in oncologic PET/CT imaging. preprint at Research Square (Nature Portfolio) (2023). https://doi.org/10.21203/rs.3.rs-2572595/v1
4. Gatidis, S., et al.: A whole-body FDG-PET/CT dataset with manually annotated tumor lesions. Sci. Data **9**(1), 601 (2022)
5. Heller, N., et al.: The state of the art in kidney and kidney tumor segmentation in contrast-enhanced CT imaging: results of the kits19 challenge. Med. Image Anal. **67**, 101821 (2021)
6. Heller, N., et al.: An international challenge to use artificial intelligence to define the state-of-the-art in kidney and kidney tumor segmentation in CT imaging. Proc. Am. Soc. Clin. Oncol. **38**(6), 626 (2020)
7. Huang, Z. et al.: Revisiting nnU-Net for iterative pseudo labeling and efficient sliding window inference. In: Ma, J., Wang, B. (eds.) Fast and Low-Resource Semi-supervised Abdominal Organ Segmentation. FLARE 2022. LNCS, vol. 13816, pp. 178–189. Springer, Cham (2022). https://doi.org/10.1007/978-3-031-23911-3_16
8. Isensee, F., Jaeger, P.F., Kohl, S.A., Petersen, J., Maier-Hein, K.H.: nnU-Net: a self-configuring method for deep learning-based biomedical image segmentation. Nat. Methods **18**(2), 203–211 (2021)
9. Lee, D.H., et al.: Pseudo-label: the simple and efficient semi-supervised learning method for deep neural networks. In: Workshop on Challenges in Representation Learning, ICML, vol. 3, p. 896. Atlanta (2013)
10. Ma, J., et al.: Loss odyssey in medical image segmentation. Med. Image Anal. **71**, 102035 (2021)
11. Ma, J., He, Y., Li, F., Han, L., You, C., Wang, B.: Segment anything in medical images. Nat. Commun. **15**, 654 (2024)

12. Ma, J., et al.: Fast and low-GPU-memory abdomen CT organ segmentation: the flare challenge. Med. Image Anal. **82**, 102616 (2022)
13. Ma, J., et al.: Unleashing the strengths of unlabeled data in pan-cancer abdominal organ quantification: the flare22 challenge. arXiv preprint arXiv:2308.05862 (2023). the FLARE Challenge Consortium, Wang, B.
14. Ma, J., et al.: AbdomenCT-1K: is abdominal organ segmentation a solved problem? IEEE Trans. Pattern Anal. Mach. Intell. **44**(10), 6695–6714 (2022)
15. Pavao, A., et al.: Codalab competitions: an open source platform to organize scientific challenges. J. Mach. Learn. Res. **24**(198), 1–6 (2023)
16. Simpson, A.L., et al.: A large annotated medical image dataset for the development and evaluation of segmentation algorithms. arXiv preprint arXiv:1902.09063 (2019)
17. Wang, Y., et al.: Semi-supervised semantic segmentation using unreliable pseudo-labels. In: Proceedings of the IEEE/CVF Conference on Computer Vision and Pattern Recognition, pp. 4248–4257 (2022)
18. Wasserthal, J., et al.: Totalsegmentator: robust segmentation of 104 anatomic structures in CT images. Radiol. Artif. Intell. **5**(5), e230024 (2023)
19. Yushkevich, P.A., Gao, Y., Gerig, G.: ITK-SNAP: an interactive tool for semi-automatic segmentation of multi-modality biomedical images. In: Annual International Conference of the IEEE Engineering in Medicine and Biology Society, pp. 3342–3345 (2016)

Attention Mechanism-Based Deep Supervision Network for Abdominal Multi-organ Segmentation

Peng An[ID], Yurou Xu[ID], and Panpan Wu[(✉)][ID]

Tianjin Normal University, Tianjin, China
pwu@tjnu.edu.cn

Abstract. In this paper, we present a novel approach to multi-organ segmentation in abdominal CT examinations conducted across multiple centers, various phases, different vendors, and diverse disease conditions. This novel approach use deep learning (DL) and attention. We describe the strategy employed during the Fast and Low GPU Memory Abdominal Organ Segmentation (FLARE) challenge, which was held in conjunction with the International Conference on Medical Image Computing and Computer Assisted Intervention (MICCAI) 2023. To meet the challenge requirements and achieve faster model convergence within the specified time frame, we developed a U-Net architecture. Our U-Net is based on a lightweight network from the VGG family, serving as the encoder, with additional attention mechanisms incorporated into the decoder. The decoder is designed symmetrically to fully leverage forward skip connections. Attention modules were not only integrated within the decoder but also introduced before the final segmentation layer. With this strategy, it enables the model to converge in a short time and has a shorter number of iterations, in order to better cope with the time constraints of the competition. According to challenge rules, encoder and decoder weights are randomly initialized, without relying on any pre-training scheme. To improve the gradient flow and encourage extracting discriminative features, our model leverages multi-stage deep supervision for automatic depiction of tumors and 13 organs such as the liver, right kidney, spleen, etc., providing a new perspective for the interpretation and decision-making of clinical upper abdominal images. Our method achieved an average DSC score of 41.1% and 15.04% for the organs and lesions on the validation set and the average running time and area under GPU memory-time cure are 189 s and 405109MB, respectively.

Keywords: Multi-organ Segmentation · DL · U-Net · VGG · Attention

1 Introduction

The recent development of non-invasive imaging technologies has opened new horizons in studying abdominal structures. Segmentation has become a crucial

© The Author(s), under exclusive license to Springer Nature Switzerland AG 2024
J. Ma and B. Wang (Eds.): FLARE 2023, LNCS 14544, pp. 319–332, 2024.
https://doi.org/10.1007/978-3-031-58776-4_25

task in abdominal image analysis with many applications such as computer-assisted diagnosis, surgery planning, imageguided intervention or radiotherapy [29]. In particular, precise delineation of abdominal solid visceral organs, including the liver, kidneys, spleen, pancreas, and other organs, from Computed Tomography (CT) images, is of critical importance for localization, volume assessment, or follow-up purposes. However, the analysis of abdominal imaging datasets is challenging and time-consuming for clinicians, given the complexity of the abdominal region. Robust and automatic abdominal multi-organ segmentation is required to guide image interpretation, facilitate decision-making, and improve patient care, all while minimizing manual delineation efforts.

In this area, many interactive, semi- and fully-automated methods have been proposed with diverse methodologies including statistical shape models [2], multi-atlas segmentation [33] or machine learning [7,8]. Outstanding performance has been reached in almost all medical image analysis tasks using deep learning (DL) [17]. Despite the large variability in organ shape, size, location and texture, abdominal multi-organ segmentation has naturally benefited from this massive trend [6,12,26]. Compared to conventional machine learning, the need for hand-crafted features no longer remains necessary. In particular, huge efforts have been devoted to automatic segmentation based on variants of Fully Convolutional Networks (FCN) [18]. In the medical image processing community, U-Net [25] is one of the most well-known approach among existing convolutional encoder-decoders. Able to learn from relatively small datasets, U-Net and its derivatives are the most likely to automatically infer high-level knowledge involved by radiologists when interpreting abdominal images.

The Fast and Low GPU Memory Abdominal Organ Segmentation (FLARE) challenge, organized in conjunction with the International Conference on Medical Image Computing and Computer Assisted Intervention (MICCAI) 2023, is an extension of the official competitions held in 2021 and 2022. Due to time constraints, our team is particularly interested in the model [4] that achieved eighth place in the 2021 competition. It is impressive that it managed to secure the eighth position despite its modest configuration, small model size, and low GPU usage. Therefore, our team aims to leverage the attention mechanism, which enhances local features, to improve the convergence speed of their model without significantly affecting its accuracy. In light of our late entry into the competition, our goal is to develop a multi-organ deep learning architecture with faster convergence speed and acceptable accuracy.

2   Method

To ensure faster convergence of the model while maintaining its original segmentation efficiency, we build a U-Net architecture based on a lightweight VGG-13 network from the VGG family [27] as encoder. The decoder adds attention [23] and is constructed in a similar way to obtain a symmetrical construction while keeping long-range shortcuts [5,6] and before the last layer of the neural network, attention is added to obtain a faster Rate of convergence. According to the challenge rules which prevent relying on any pre-training scheme, weights of both encoder and decoder branches are randomly initialized. To further enhance performance, our model, as illustrated in Fig. 1, leverages multi-stage deep supervision [9, 32] and incorporates attention mechanisms [23].

2.1 Preprocessing

Intensity normalization is used as pre-processing step. Thus, each CT volume is clipped to the [1, 99] percentiles of the intensity values. In addition, a z-score normalization is applied based on the mean and standard deviation of the intensity values among the whole training dataset. Neither cropping nor resampling is employed. Not using Data clean also not conducting statistical analysis.

2.2 Proposed Method

Network architecture: Our model comprises an encoder-decoder architecture with forward skip connections from the encoder stages to their corresponding decoder stages. In contrast to the standard U-Net [25], we utilize a simpler yet effective VGG-13 encoder with batch normalization layers (torchvision.models.vgg13_bn).

To avoid large GPU memory consumption, we designed a 2D multi-class segmentation model with $C = 15$ classes dealing with background (bg), liver (li), right kidneys (r-ki), spleen (sp), pancreas (pa), aorta (at), inferior vena cava(i-v-c), right adrenal gland (r-a-g), left adrenal gland (l-a-g), gallbladder (gb), esophagus (ep), stomach (sm), duodenum(dd), left kidney (l-ki), tumor (tm). The network independently processes axial slices to produce 2D segmentation masks which are then stacked together to recover 3D volumes. To exploit spatial relationships between abdominal structures, the model learns to simultaneoulsy delineate the multiple organs instead of relying on several organ-specific models.

The basic layer pattern consists of sequential layers including 3×3 convolutional layers (conv) with 1×1 stride and 1×1 padding followed by batch normalization (BN) and Rectified Linear Unit (ReLU) activation. Such pattern is repeated twice and followed by 2×2 max pooling (MP). The encoder comprises a sequence of 4 [conv, BN, ReLU]x2 + MP patterns (Fig. 2). The first convolutional layer generates 64 channels. The number of channels doubles after each MP layer until it reaches 512. Compared to VGG-13 [27], top layers including fully-connected layers and softmax are omitted. The fifth [conv, BN, ReLU]x2 pattern from original VGG-13 serves as central part to separate contracting and expanding paths.

To get a symmetrical construction while still using forward skip connections, the decoder branch is extended in the similar fashion as the encoder by adding batch normalization layers and more features channels [6] and adding attention mechanism (ReLU+Sigmoid) after concatenate operation (Fig. 2). Additionally, feature maps as outputs of each intermediate decoder blocs are upsampled using bilinear interpolation to the size of the input image. In the same spirit as in [9, 32], a convolutional operation with 3×3 kernel is applied to create 16 feature maps at each level (Fig. 2). These maps then go through deep supervision modules to improve the gradient flow and encourage learning more useful representations [9]. After having performed the concatenation of intermediate outputs (Fig. 1), two convolutional layers including a final one with using attention and softmax activation achieves pixel-wise multi-label segmentation.

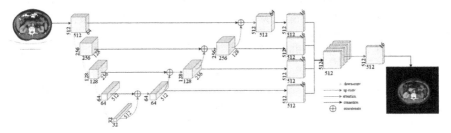

Fig. 1. Overall model framework. In this framework, some repetitive and non-critical details are omitted. Each convolutional block consists of multiple convolution layers. Max-pooling (MP) is used for downsampling, and transposed convolution is used for upsampling. Before upsampling, an attention calculation is performed on the concatenated feature maps, and then upsampling is carried out. Feature matrices obtained from different depth supervision are directly concatenated, followed by attention calculation and convolution to reduce the number of channels.

Loss Function. Our network is trained with the cross-entropy loss function L_{ce} defined below:

$$L_{ce} = \frac{1}{N} \sum_{c=1}^{C} \sum_{i=1}^{N} g_i^c log p_i^c$$

where N is the number of pixels in the axial slices. p_i^c and g_i^c denote respectively the predicted probability and ground truth at pixel i for class label $c \in \{$ bg, li, r-ki, sp, pa, at, i-v-c, r-a-g, l-a-g, gb, ep, sm, dd, l-ki, tm $\}$.

The overall loss function L is the average sum of the cross-entroy losses estimated at different decoder levels involving supervision:

$$L = \frac{1}{M+1} \sum_{j=1}^{M} L_{ce}^j + L_{ce}^f$$

where L_{ce}^j denote the loss for the points of supervision at j layer of the decoder. Following the VGG-13 architecture [27], $M = 4$ intermediate decoder levels are considered. L_{ce}^f correspond to the loss computed at the final network output (f stands for final). Note that level $j = 1$ is closer to the network ending part than level $j > 1$. Because the original model and code used multiple GPUs for deep supervision processing, but our team only had a single GPU to run the program, we made changes to the overall loss function. And after improvement, the performance is similar or even better than the original model, so this method is useful when a single GPU is needed to run. We did not apply the Dice loss function during backpropagation, but rather used it as a visualized indicator. With this indicator and the cross-entropy loss, we performed parameter tuning and other tasks.

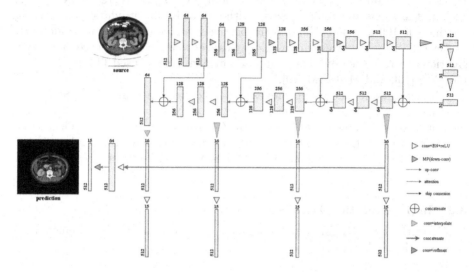

Fig. 2. Detailed convolutional encoder-decoder architecture. In this context, 'up-conv' refers to transposed convolution. 'Attention' is a combination of the ReLU and Sigmoid functions. 'Interpolate' is performed using the bilinear interpolation function.

Number of Model Parameters. Number of model parameters. The number of trainable parameters is 24,496,331 (around 93.5Mb), much less than the 41,268,192 parameters employed in nnU-Net [16].

Unlabeled images were not used and not used the pseudo labels generated by the FLARE21 winning algorithm [15] and the best-accuracy-algorithm [30].

2.3 Post-processing

As post-processing, we keep the largest connected segmented areas for voxels respectively labeled as 13 organs, for example, liver, spleen and pancreas etc. No ensembling method is used.

3 Experiments

3.1 Dataset and Evaluation Measures

The FLARE 2023 challenge is an extension of the FLARE 2021–2022 [20,21], aiming to aim to promote the development of foundation models in abdominal disease analysis. The segmentation targets cover 13 organs and various abdominal lesions. The training dataset is curated from more than 30 medical centers under the license permission, including TCIA [3], LiTS [1], MSD [28], KiTS [13,14], autoPET [10,11], TotalSegmentator [31], and AbdomenCT-1K [22]. The training set includes 4000 abdomen CT scans where 2200 CT scans with partial labels and 1800 CT scans without labels. The validation and testing sets include 100 and 400 CT scans, respectively, which cover various abdominal cancer types, such as liver cancer, kidney cancer, pancreas cancer, colon cancer, gastric cancer, and so on. The organ annotation process used ITK-SNAP [34], nnU-Net [16], and MedSAM [19].

The evaluation metrics encompass two accuracy measures-Dice Similarity Coefficient (DSC) and Normalized Surface Dice (NSD)-alongside two efficiency measures-running time and area under the GPU memory-time curve. These metrics collectively contribute to the ranking computation. Furthermore, the running time and GPU memory consumption are considered within tolerances of 15 s and 4 GB, respectively.

3.2   Implementation Details

Environment Settings. The development environments and requirements are presented in Table 1.

Table 1. Development environments and requirements.

System	Ubuntu 18.04.6 LTS
CPU	Intel(R) Xeon(R) Silver 4210 CPU @ 2.20 GHz
RAM	16 × 4 GB
GPU (number and type)	0 NVIDIA GeForce RTX 2080 Ti
CUDA version	11.3
Programming language	Python 3.7
Deep learning framework	torch 1.7.0+cu92, torchvision 0.8.1+cu92
Specific dependencies	scikit-image, nibabel, torch
Code	https://github.com/0NGU0/FLARE2023-PengAn.git

Training Protocols. Our team utilized only 2200 partially labeled CT scans during the training phase. In the validation stage, we followed a method where 10% of the cases were randomly selected from the pool of 2200 CT scans with partial labels for model validation. The test set was not separated from the initial 2200 labeled CT scans.

Data augmentation methods were not employed in this model, but dropout was utilized. In selecting the optimal model, we used the results submitted to the competition website as the benchmark for determining the optimal weight generation and model selection. This benchmark was primarily based on the DSC (Dice Similarity Coefficient) and NSD (Normalized Surface Dice) indicators for tumor assessment in the website results (Table 2).

Table 2. Training protocols.

Network initialization	normal initialization
Batch size	2
Patch size	512 × 512 (full axial slices)
Total epochs	5
Optimizer	Adam
Initial learning rate (lr)	10^{-5}
Lr decay schedule	no decay
Training time	27 h per iteration and the 5 generation took a total of 135 h
Loss function	
Number of model parameters	93.55M
Number of flops	212.95G
CO_2eq	/

4   Results and Discussion

From the current situation, the improved model has achieved similar or better results with fewer iterations and less time.

Possible reasons for segmentation errors or incompleteness include:

The model may not have fully converged, and certain features may not have been learned effectively. Although improvements have been made in the convergence speed of the model, the original model's limitations in segmenting closely located organs have not been addressed. Due to the limited number of tumor cases in the training set and the random occurrence of actual tumors, the model's performance in predicting tumors may not achieve the same level of segmentation accuracy as for other organs.

4.1   Quantitative Results on Validation Set

In Table 3, we present the Dice and NSD scores for the validation of specific organs and tumors. We did not utilize unlabeled data for training, validation, or prediction. This decision was made because when our team became aware of the competition, a month had already passed since it began. To expedite all stages of the process, we opted to use only 2200 CT scans with labeled data for training. (This choice was made because more raw data would require additional preprocessing time, and we needed to experiment with various preprocessing strategies.) As a result, no ablation experiments were conducted to investigate this aspect (Table 4).

Table 3. Quantitative evaluation results.

Target	Public Validation		Online Validation		Testing	
	DSC(%)	NSD(%)	DSC(%)	NSD(%)	DSC(%)	NSD (%)
Liver	93.27 ± 2.78	92.01 ± 2.96	87.91	86.94	64.83	62.06
Right Kidney	86.8 ± 2.42	86.18 ± 2.54	86.37	85.27	66.25	66.34
Spleen	89.54 ± 4.36	89.41 ± 4.64	84.64	84.41	64.53	63.68
Pancreas	71.39 ± 1.6	83.79 ± 1.61	69.69	81.86	50.9	58.83
Aorta	15.31 ± 7.57	15.62 ± 7.64	16.86	17.46	8.14	7.36
Inferior vena cava	12.54 ± 6.63	12.26 ± 6.25	18.31	17.62	7.39	6.58
Right adrenal gland	4.22 ± 3.96	5.05 ± 5.43	12.87	16.85	5	5.84
Left adrenal gland	2.11 ± 2.26	2.48 ± 3.04	7.14	9.26	3.5	3.8
Gallbladder	17.95 ± 7.88	17.65 ± 7.68	29.1	28.72	18.01	17.15
Esophagus	10.76 ± 4.92	14 ± 6.42	13.05	16.47	5.44	5.91
Stomach	10.2 ± 4.09	10.77 ± 4.32	10.85	11.53	3.38	3.19
Duodenum	6.6 ± 4.75	10.92 ± 4.96	13.27	17.49	4.98	6.09
Left kidney	83.38 ± 3.75	83.14 ± 3.72	84.18	84.76	67.91	68.62
Tumor	12.56 ± 2.69	7.69 ± 1.58	15.04	9.23	8.22	4.23
Average	36.9 ± 4.26	37.93 ± 4.49	41.1	42.97	28.48	28.88

Table 4. Quantitative evaluation of segmentation efficiency in terms of the running them and GPU memory consumption. Total GPU denotes the area under GPU Memory-Time curve.

Case ID	Image Size	Running Time (s)	Max GPU (MB)	Total GPU (MB)
0001	(512, 512, 55)	39.59	2218	75269
0051	(512, 512, 100)	60.07	2218	121299
0017	(512, 512, 150)	98.89	2218	206949
0019	(512, 512, 215)	122.14	2218	258027
0099	(512, 512, 334)	185.31	2218	397158
0063	(512, 512, 448)	307.15	2218	665363
0048	(512, 512, 499)	347.57	2218	754546
0029	(512, 512, 554)	351.28	2218	762258

4.2 Qualitative Results on Validation Set

Figure 3 depicts two simple cases (upper part) and two challenging cases (bottom part) from the validation set. The source axial slices, ground truth, and predicted label maps are presented from left to right. The liver, kidneys, spleen, pancreas, and other organs are color-coded in red, green, blue, yellow, and other colors, respectively. Taking into consideration the limited computational resources, our model demonstrates strong performance in segmenting larger or distinct organs. However, in cases where diseased tissues are present, or when certain organs are in close proximity to others, the segmentation effectiveness correspondingly diminishes.

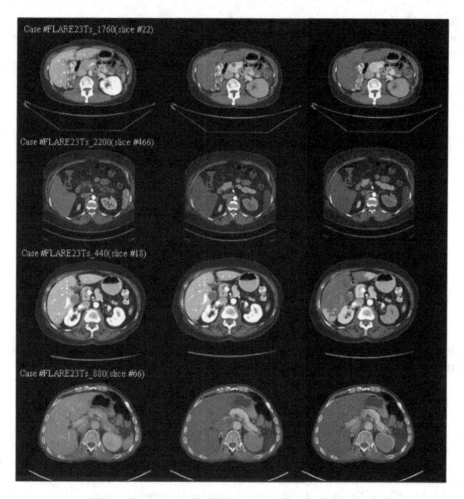

Fig. 3. Source axial slices, ground truth and predicted label maps are shown from left to right.

4.3   Segmentation Efficiency Results on Validation Set

Based on the data presented in Table 5, our model performs equally well or better than the eighth-place model within the same total time frame.

4.4   Results on Final Testing Set

The final test results, including DSC and NSD metrics, are shown in the 'Testing' column of Table 3. The average time for case predictions is 83.03 s, and the GPU memory usage is 169,244. Although the final test results are lower compared to the online validation results, this was expected. On the one hand, the uncertainty in the location and shape of tumors has led to a decrease in tumor prediction

Table 5. The table shows the data comparison between our improved model and the unmodified model. The data in the table comes from the submission results of the website.

Model Category	Organ		Tumor		Iterations
	DSC(%)	NSD(%)	DSC(%)	NSD(%)	
Origin	32.95	33.31	6.03	1.6	1
Origin	39.23	40.44	8.13	2.76	3
Origin	43.9	45.35	8.1	3.29	5
Origin	38.24	39.29	11.83	7.03	7
Origin	40.64	42.07	15.23	9.58	9
Add attention	40.43	41.54	14.12	8.42	1
Add attention	35.97	37	11.61	7.03	2
Add attention	40.16	41.58	7.69	4.9	3
Add attention	37.18	38.39	14.32	8.86	4
Add attention	41.1	42.97	15.04	9.23	5

accuracy. On the other hand, the lack of model convergence and poor generalization have resulted in reduced accuracy in the segmentation of non-tumor organs.

4.5   Limitation and Future Work

During the competition, our model did not fully converge, and the prediction time for larger cases exceeded 60 s due to personal and time constraints. However, the results from the previous iterations demonstrate the effectiveness of the improvements. When compared to the previous model, it achieves better or similar results with fewer iterations and shorter processing times.

Recently after the competition, we made further improvements based on the proposed model during the competition and achieved better results. Specifically, for loss calculation, we provided deep supervision with different optimal weights for losses calculated at different scales. Regarding the attention module, we updated the composition of the attention module to improve its performance in segmenting multiple organs. Moreover, about the model training, instead of trainig all the all 2200 label data to obtain the final trained model, we conducted two stages of training. In the first stage, a rough trained model was acquired based on the whole, 2200 label data. In the second phase, the rough trained model is further trained from 251 cases containing at lease 13 abdominal orgain labels to obtain the final fine trained model. Comparions of the results of different training methods are shown in Table 6. As can be observed, significant improvements are achieved with our latest updated model.

In the future, our team will try to integrate multimodal, domain adaptive and other techniques to improve the model performance and enhance the model

Table 6. The results come from 50 prediction cases published during the competition. Because our team is still improving the model, the DSC results here only show the part about organs.

Case ID	No change DSC result(%)	Change DSC result(%)
0001	81.15	91.92
0003	78.84	88.88
0005	73.19	85.01
0007	66.56	85.65
0009	73.59	82.74
0011	79.27	86.02
0013	73.19	83.41
0015	68.16	87.32
0017	63.96	71.16
0019	65.03	77.74
0021	27.81	86.48
0023	64.2	78.23
0025	73.6	78.83
0027	76.73	86.18
0029	60.57	85.8
0031	77.21	92.35
0033	70.68	89.87
0035	56.28	67.44
0038	77.55	82.26
0039	70.88	86.25
0041	69.58	84.71
0043	81.01	93.37
0045	70.11	88.92
0048	57.92	79.48
0049	64.24	81.39
0051	65.04	76.55
0053	71.33	86.49
0055	79.64	89.36
0057	41.52	43.9
0059	77.76	89.79
0061	70.88	84.04
0063	68.04	89.31
0065	80.97	91.34
0067	42.17	49.31
0069	65.38	86.37
0071	65.75	81.55
0073	81.01	90.56
0075	72.54	87.13
0077	59.95	79.95
0079	68.82	78.24
0081	69.81	88.55
0083	60.84	71.17
0085	73.28	87.13
0087	66.45	73.57
0089	77.01	88.34
0091	70.07	80.2
0093	58.14	85.59
0095	55.47	60.83
0097	75.59	86.71
0099	71.49	85.31
Average	68.2	82.2

generalization. Additionally, the lightweight model will be developed to ensure that each test case, regardless of its size, can be predicted in 60 s.

5   Conclusion

The multi-center, multi-phase, multi-vendor, and multi-disease CT data were segmented using deep learning and an attention mechanism. This work demonstrates that there is still room for improvement in the convergence speed of The eighth model of flare competition in 2021, under the same number of iterations, and our team has provided a solution for this. Standard pipelines have been extended to lightweight convolutional encoder-decoders with deep supervision and attention mechanisms. Preliminary results suggest that the attention we have incorporated has played a significant role in accelerating the model's convergence, thereby avoiding the need for resource-intensive computational processes in clinical practice. While our approach accurately processes many images containing healthy organs or organs with small lesions, the presence of large tumoral areas is a critical factor affecting delineation performance. Additionally, the segmentation task for the pancreas and other organs warrants further investigation to enhance the capacity of deep learning models in handling the substantial inter-patient anatomical variability in terms of size, shape, location, and texture.

Acknowledgements. The authors of this paper declare that the segmentation method they implemented for participation in the FLARE 2023 challenge has not used any pre-trained models nor additional datasets other than those provided by the organizers. The proposed solution is fully automatic without any manual intervention. We thank all the data owners for making the CT scans publicly available and CodaLab [24] for hosting the challenge platform.

References

1. Bilic, P., et al.: The liver tumor segmentation benchmark (LiTS). Med. Image Anal. **84**, 102680 (2023)
2. Cerrolaza, J.J., Reyes, M., Summers, R.M., González-Ballester, M.Á., Linguraru, M.G.: Automatic multi-resolution shape modeling of multi-organ structures. Med. Image Anal. **25**(1), 11–21 (2015)
3. Clark, K., et al.: The cancer imaging archive (TCIA): maintaining and operating a public information repository. J. Digit. Imaging **26**(6), 1045–1057 (2013)
4. Conze, P.H., Andrade-Miranda, G., Singh, V.K., Jaouen, V., Visvikis, D.: Current and emerging trends in medical image segmentation with deep learning. IEEE Trans. Radiat. Plasma Med. Sci. 7 (2023)
5. Conze, P.H., Brochard, S., Burdin, V., Sheehan, F.T., Pons, C.: Healthy versus pathological learning transferability in shoulder muscle MRI segmentation using deep convolutional encoder-decoders. Comput. Med. Imaging Graph. **83**, 101733 (2020)
6. Conze, P.H., et al.: Abdominal multi-organ segmentation with cascaded convolutional and adversarial deep networks. Artif. Intell. Med. **117**, 102109 (2021)

7. Conze, P.H., et al.: Scale-adaptive supervoxel-based random forests for liver tumor segmentation in dynamic contrast-enhanced CT scans. Int. J. Comput. Assist. Radiol. Surg. **12**, 223–233 (2017)
8. Cuingnet, R., Prevost, R., Lesage, D., Cohen, L.D., Mory, B., Ardon, R.: Automatic detection and segmentation of kidneys in 3D CT images using random forests. In: Ayache, N., Delingette, H., Golland, P., Mori, K. (eds.) MICCAI 2012. LNCS, vol. 7512, pp. 66–74. Springer, Heidelberg (2012). https://doi.org/10.1007/978-3-642-33454-2_9
9. Dou, H., et al.: A deep attentive convolutional neural network for automatic cortical plate segmentation in fetal MRI. IEEE Trans. Med. Imaging **40**(4), 1123–1133 (2020)
10. Gatidis, S., et al.: The autopet challenge: towards fully automated lesion segmentation in oncologic PET/CT imaging. preprint at Research Square (Nature Portfolio) (2023). https://doi.org/10.21203/rs.3.rs-2572595/v1
11. Gatidis, S., et al.: A whole-body FDG-PET/CT dataset with manually annotated tumor lesions. Sci. Data **9**(1), 601 (2022)
12. Gibson, E., et al.: Automatic multi-organ segmentation on abdominal CT with dense v-networks. IEEE Trans. Med. Imaging **37**(8), 1822–1834 (2018)
13. Heller, N., et al.: The state of the art in kidney and kidney tumor segmentation in contrast-enhanced CT imaging: results of the kits19 challenge. Med. Image Anal. **67**, 101821 (2021)
14. Heller, N., et al.: An international challenge to use artificial intelligence to define the state-of-the-art in kidney and kidney tumor segmentation in ct imaging. Proc. Am. Soc. Clin. Oncol. **38**(6), 626 (2020)
15. Huang, Z., et al. Revisiting nnU-Net for iterative pseudo labeling and efficient sliding window inference. In: Ma, J., Wang, B. (eds.) Fast and Low-Resource Semi-supervised Abdominal Organ Segmentation. FLARE 2022. LNCS, vol. 13816, pp. 178–189. Springer, Cham (2022). https://doi.org/10.1007/978-3-031-23911-3_16
16. Isensee, F., Jaeger, P.F., Kohl, S.A., Petersen, J., Maier-Hein, K.H.: nnu-net: a self-configuring method for deep learning-based biomedical image segmentation. Nat. Methods **18**(2), 203–211 (2021)
17. Litjens, G., et al.: A survey on deep learning in medical image analysis. Med. Image Anal. **42**, 60–88 (2017)
18. Long, J., Shelhamer, E., Darrell, T.: Fully convolutional networks for semantic segmentation. In: Proceedings of the IEEE Conference on Computer Vision and Pattern Recognition, pp. 3431–3440 (2015)
19. Ma, J., He, Y., Li, F., Han, L., You, C., Wang, B.: Segment anything in medical images. Nat. Commun. **15**, 654 (2024)
20. Ma, J., et al.: Fast and low-GPU-memory abdomen CT organ segmentation: the flare challenge. Med. Image Anal. **82**, 102616 (2022)
21. Ma, J., et al.: Unleashing the strengths of unlabeled data in pan-cancer abdominal organ quantification: the flare22 challenge. arXiv preprint arXiv:2308.05862 (2023). the FLARE Challenge Consortium, Wang, B
22. Ma, J., et al.: Abdomenct-1k: is abdominal organ segmentation a solved problem? IEEE Trans. Pattern Anal. Mach. Intell. **44**(10), 6695–6714 (2022)
23. Oktay, O., et al.: Attention U-Net: learning where to look for the pancreas. ArXiv Preprint ArXiv:1804.03999 (2018)
24. Pavao, A., et al.: Codalab competitions: an open source platform to organize scientific challenges. J. Mach. Learn. Res. **24**(198), 1–6 (2023)

25. Ronneberger, O., Fischer, P., Brox, T.: U-Net: convolutional networks for biomedical image segmentation. In: Navab, N., Hornegger, J., Wells, W.M., Frangi, A.F. (eds.) MICCAI 2015. LNCS, vol. 9351, pp. 234–241. Springer, Cham (2015). https://doi.org/10.1007/978-3-319-24574-4_28
26. Roth, H.R., et al.: Hierarchical 3D fully convolutional networks for multi-organ segmentation. ArXiv Preprint ArXiv:1704.06382 (2017)
27. Simonyan, K., Zisserman, A.: Very deep convolutional networks for large-scale image recognition. ArXiv Preprint ArXiv:1409.1556 (2014)
28. Simpson, A.L., et al.: A large annotated medical image dataset for the development and evaluation of segmentation algorithms. arXiv preprint arXiv:1902.09063 (2019)
29. Summers, R.M.: Progress in fully automated abdominal CT interpretation. AJR Am. J. Roentgenol. **207**(1), 67 (2016)
30. Wang, E., Zhao, Y., Wu, Y.: Cascade dual-decoders network for abdominal organs segmentation. In: Ma, J., Wang, B. (eds.) Fast and Low-Resource Semi-supervised Abdominal Organ Segmentation. FLARE 2022. LNCS, vol. 13816, pp. 202–213. Springer, Cham (2022). https://doi.org/10.1007/978-3-031-23911-3_18
31. Wasserthal, J., et al.: Totalsegmentator: robust segmentation of 104 anatomic structures in CT images. Radiol. Artif. Intell. **5**(5), e230024 (2023)
32. Xie, S., Tu, Z.: Holistically-nested edge detection. In: Proceedings of the IEEE International Conference on Computer Vision, pp. 1395–1403 (2015)
33. Xu, Z., et al.: Efficient multi-atlas abdominal segmentation on clinically acquired CT with simple context learning. Med. Image Anal. **24**(1), 18–27 (2015)
34. Yushkevich, P.A., Gao, Y., Gerig, G.: ITK-SNAP: an interactive tool for semi-automatic segmentation of multi-modality biomedical images. In: Annual International Conference of the IEEE Engineering in Medicine and Biology Society, pp. 3342–3345 (2016)

Teacher-Student Semi-supervised Strategy for Abdominal CT Organ Segmentation

Chong Wang[✉], Wen Dong, and Rongjun Ge

College of Computer Science and Technology, Nanjing University of Aeronautics and Astronautics, Nanjing, China
wangchong9905@163.com

Abstract. Semi-supervised abdominal multi-organ segmentation is a challenging topic. In recent years, many methods for automatic segmentation based on fully supervised deep learning have been proposed. However, it is very expensive and time-consuming for experienced medical practitioners to annotate a large number of pixels. Therefore, more researchers focus on semi-supervised learning in abdominal organ and tumor segmentation. In this paper, we adopt a classical Teacher-student semi-supervised strategy to perform the task of abdominal organs and tumor segmentation. Unet is used as the architecture for the segmentation network. Based on the Unet network structure, we add the Inception block and SEBlock to achieve more accurate segmentation. Inception block is its ability to simultaneously capture features at multiple different scales. By introducing SEBlock, the model can better focus on specific information relevant to the task while reducing attention to noise or irrelevant information. Besides, we combine Cross Entropy Loss and Dice Loss as loss functions to improve the performance of our method. We apply a teacher-student model with exponential moving average (EMA) strategy to update the network model parameters. The organs and tumor mean DSC on the public validation set was 85.39%, 18.30% respectively, the organs and tumor mean NSD was 89.36%, 6.44% respectively. And the average running time and the area under GPU memory-time curve 35.54 s, 38175.35.

Keywords: Semi-supervised · Abdominal organ segmentation · FLARE2023

1 Introduction

The field of abdominal multi-organ segmentation has witnessed significant advancements in recent years, primarily driven by the rise of fully supervised deep learning methods. However, the reliance on fully annotated datasets, which demand considerable time and expertise from medical professionals, has become a bottleneck in further progress [18]. Semi-supervised learning uses existing labeled samples to pseudo-label the remaining unlabeled data, thus mining useful

J. Ma and B. Wang (Eds.): FLARE 2023, LNCS 14544, pp. 333–345, 2024.
https://doi.org/10.1007/978-3-031-58776-4_26

information from unlabeled samples [2,4], which is more practical for the current background. Therefore, more and more researchers begin to pay attention to semi-supervised learning

In this paper, we present a novel approach that leverages the classical Teacher-student semi-supervised strategy to tackle the intricate task of segmenting abdominal organs and tumors. Our methodology is founded on the robust architecture of U-Net [15], a popular choice for image segmentation tasks. Based on the U-Net framework, we introduce Inception block [17] and SEBlock [7] to enable our model to fully understand the belly structure and effectively filter out noise and irrelevant data, thus selectively focusing on relevant information needed for segmentation tasks.

Moreover, we employ a combined loss function approach, merging Cross Entropy Loss and Dice Loss, aimed at augmenting the performance of our method. To facilitate the learning process, we adopt a teacher-student model enriched with an exponential moving average (EMA) strategy for network parameter updates. We evaluated our proposed method on the MICCAI FLARE 2023 challenge dataset, and the experimental results demonstrated the validity of the individual components of our method.

The main contributions of this work are summarized as follows:

– We adopt a two-stage segmentation method, which utilizes a coarse model and a fine model, and adopt a Teacher-Student training strategy of semi-supervised learning to improve the utilization of unlabeled data to achieve robust segmentation results.
– We added Inception blocks and SEBlocks to enhance the ability of the network to capture features at different scales, while enabling the network to learn useful features more efficiently.

2   Method

2.1   Teacher-Student Model

We propose a method as shown in Fig. 1. We use the coarse model to obtain approximate segmentation results from the input CT scan, and then obtain the region of interest(ROI) coordinates of the abdomen from the coarse segmentation. Then we crop the area, and use the fine model for segmenting, and finally restore the inference results to the original cropped area according to the ROI coordinates. In previous deep learning works, network structure and parameters often need to be adjusted according to practical application. U-Net can achieve good results in most cases. Therefore, we respectively constructed two Unet [15] structural networks with the same architecture and different initial parameters as our coarse model and fine model.

In order to leverage the unlabeled data, we adopt the Mean Teacher model training strategy to achieve semi-supervised learning. Specifically, we first train a teacher model using labeled data and then predict segmentation results for unlabeled data with the trained teacher model as pseudo-labels. Then the student

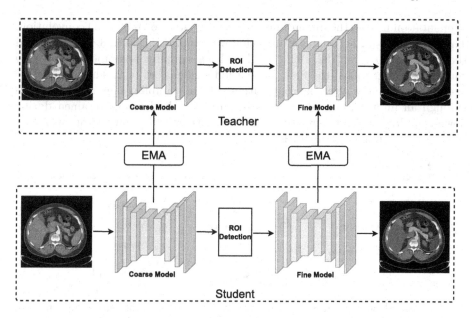

Fig. 1. Coarse-to-fine segmentation framework. Coarse and Fine are model inference processes: crop means cutting the approximate position of the organ from the original image according to the result of coarse segmentation, and restore means place the result back to the position before cropping.

model training in labeled and unlabeled data set with labels and pseudo-labels. The EMA algorithm is used to update the teacher model parameters during the training process.

2.2 Preprocessing

We regroup the 2200 labeled samples and 1800 unlabeled samples to form two datasets. The first dataset containing all 1800 samples is used to train the teacher model, and the second dataset containing only the 4000 labeled and unlabeled samples is used to train the student model for coarse and fine segmentation.

- Reorientation image to target direction.
- For two datasets, we adjust the window width to [−325, 325]. Then the intensities of each CT sample are normalized to have a mean of 0 and a variance of 1 using the individual mean and standard deviation.

2.3 Proposed Method

Network architecture. We use a UNet structure model as our model as shown in Fig. 2. For the coarse segmentation model, the dimensions are first adjusted to 16 by a 3D convolution. Then, the number of channels after each downsampling is [32, 64, 128, 256], and the input patch size of [160, 160, 160]. For the fine segmentation model, the dimensions are first adjusted to 16 by a 3D convolution. Then, the number of channels after each downsampling is [64, 128, 256, 512], and the input patch size of [192, 192, 192]. The down-sampling is composed of two 3D convolution operations, the first convolution stride is set to 2. The features are one-half size smaller after the convolution. The up-sampling operation first goes through an interpolation operation, concatenates the features retained during down-sampling through skip connections, and then a 3D convolution operation to adjust the number of channels.

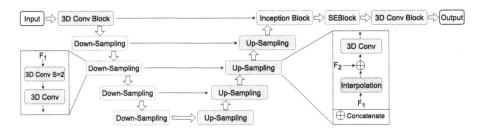

Fig. 2. Network architecture. A UNet structure is used and the outputs are used to compute loss. For the coarse segmentation model and the fine segmentation model, we use the same model architecture, but we use different parameters above the model parameters, for the fine segmentation model, we use a deeper model to extract higher dimensional information in the data.

For the segmentation of abdominal organs, which are numerous and vary greatly in size, we propose a method that combines the Inception block and SEBlock with the final segmentation head to enhance the model's feature-capturing ability at different scales. As shown in Fig. 3. One of the primary advantages of the Inception block is its ability to simultaneously capture features at multiple different scales. This is highly beneficial for processing images of organs, ranging from small to large, and contributes to enhancing the model's understanding and segmentation performance on abdominal images. The fundamental concept of SEBlock involves adaptively adjusting the weights of each channel to enable the model to more effectively learn useful features. It consists of two main steps: Squeeze (Compression): In this step, SEBlock calculates importance scores for each channel through global pooling operations. This means it considers the average value of each channel across the entire feature map to obtain a weight vector. Excitation: In this step, SEBlock employs a small feed-forward neural network (typically a fully connected layer) to learn how to adjust the feature responses of each channel based on their importance scores. This learning process can adaptively increase or decrease the weights of each channel. By introducing SEBlock, the model can better focus on specific information relevant to the task while reducing attention to noise or irrelevant information.

Loss Function. We use the summation between Dice loss and cross-entropy loss because compound loss functions have been proven to be robust in various medical image segmentation tasks [9].

Training Strategies. First, train a teacher model on all the labeled data D_l. During the training process of the student model, for the labeled data $(x_l, y_l) \in D_l$, input it into the student model obtain $\hat{y}_l$, calculate the loss, and update the network parameters. For unlabeled data $x_u \in D_u$, input it into the teacher model to obtain pseudo-labels y_p, and then input it into the student model to obtain predictions $\hat{y}_u$. Calculate the loss using these predictions and pseudo-labels, and then update the parameters of the student network. The parameters of the teacher model are updated using the Exponential Moving Average (EMA) algorithm. And the student model is used in the inference process.

Strategies for Using Partially Labeled and Unlabeled Data. For the partially labeled data, we don't incorporate pseudo-tags provided by the organizer. For unlabeled data, we input it into the teacher model to obtain pseudo-labels.

Improve Inference Speed and Reduce Resource Consumption. The anisotropic convolution, anisotropic pooling and coarse-to-fine strategy are used to reduce inference time and GPU memory usage.

2.4   Post-processing

To avoid the impact of noise, the connected component analysis is used, and we choose the maximum connected component as the final segmentation results.

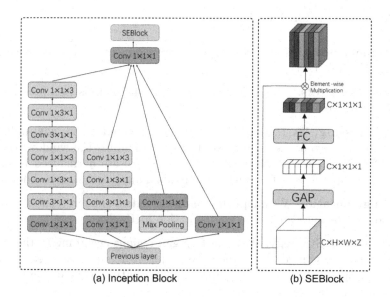

(a) Inception Block   (b) SEBlock

Fig. 3. Inception block and SEBlock. Inception block is its ability to simultaneously capture features at multiple different scales. By introducing SEBlock, the model can better focus on specific information relevant to the task while reducing attention to noise or irrelevant information.

3 Experiments

3.1 Dataset and Evaluation Measures

The FLARE 2023 challenge is an extension of the FLARE 2021–2022 [11,12], aiming to aim to promote the development of foundation models in abdominal disease analysis. The segmentation targets cover 13 organs and various abdominal lesions. The training dataset is curated from more than 30 medical centers under the license permission, including TCIA [3], LiTS [1], MSD [16], KiTS [5,6], and AbdomenCT-1K [13]. The training set includes 4000 abdomen CT scans where 2200 CT scans with partial labels and 1800 CT scans without labels. The validation and testing sets include 100 and 400 CT scans, respectively, which cover various abdominal cancer types, such as liver cancer, kidney cancer, pancreas cancer, colon cancer, gastric cancer, and so on. The organ annotation process used ITK-SNAP [19], nnU-Net [8], and MedSAM [10].

The evaluation metrics encompass two accuracy measures-Dice Similarity Coefficient (DSC) and Normalized Surface Dice (NSD)-alongside two efficiency measures-running time and area under the GPU memory-time curve. These metrics collectively contribute to the ranking computation. Furthermore, the running time and GPU memory consumption are considered within tolerances of 15 s and 4 GB, respectively.

3.2 Implementation Details

Environment Settings. The development environments and requirements are presented in Table 1.

Training Protocols. The Training protocols and details are presented in Table 2 and Table 3.

Data Processing. We regroup the 1800 labeled samples and 2200 unlabeled samples to form two datasets. For two datasets, we adjust the window width to [–325, 325]. Then the intensities of each CT sample are normalized to have a mean of 0 and a variance of 1 using the individual mean and standard deviation.

Data Augmentation. We adopt the common random enhancement of contrast and random rotation as our data augmentation methods.

ROI Detection Strategy. We identify organ regions according to the output results of the coarse model, and then the proper RoI can be inferred by calculating the weighted average coordinates and distribution scope of the predicted organ voxels.

Optimal Model Selection. Regarding the selection of the optimal model, we did not set the validation set in the experiment, and we selected the network parameters saved in the last epoch as our optimal model.

Table 1. Development environments and requirements.

System	Ubuntu 20.04.1 LTS
CPU	Intel(R) Xeon(R) Platinum 8160 CPU @ 2.10 GHz
RAM	4 × 32 GB
GPU (number and type)	2*NVIDIA 3090 24G
CUDA version	12.0
Programming language	Python 3.7
Deep learning framework	Pytorch (torch 1.8.2)
Specific dependencies	SimpleITK, numpy
Code	https://github.com/code-Porunacabeza/flare23

Table 2. Training protocols for the coarse model.

Network initialization	"he" normal initialization
Batch size	2
Patch size	160 × 160 × 160
Total epochs	150(pretrain on labelled dataset 50 epochs)
Optimizer	SGD with nesterov momentum($\mu = 0.99$)
Initial learning rate (lr)	0.01
Lr decay schedule	Halved by 50 epochs
Training time	34 h
Loss function	Cross-entropy loss, Dice loss

Table 3. Training protocols for the fine model.

Network initialization	"he" normal initialization
Batch size	2
Patch size	192 × 192 × 192
Total epochs	200(pretrain on labelled dataset 50 epochs)
Optimizer	SGD with nesterov momentum($\mu = 0.99$)
Initial learning rate (lr)	0.001
Lr decay schedule	Halved by 50 epochs
Training time	58 h
Loss function	Cross-entropy loss, Dice loss

4   Results and Discussion

4.1   Quantitative Results on Validation Set

Table 4 shows the results of this work on the validation set. Among the evaluated organs, the liver and spleen demonstrate outstanding segmentation accuracy,

Table 4. Quantitative evaluation results.

Target	Public Validation		Online Validation		Testing	
	DSC(%)	NSD(%)	DSC(%)	NSD(%)	DSC(%)	NSD (%)
Liver	96.81 ± 1.84	95.28 ± 4.85	94.91	93.46	95.21	93.77
Right Kidney	89.56 ± 20.26	87.88 ± 21.03	94.36	92.70	93.42	91.56
Spleen	95.48 ± 7.45	95.10 ± 9.78	93.53	92.73	93.74	93.09
Pancreas	78.33± 12.53	89.58 ± 12.87	76.75	86.57	77.52	87.23
Aorta	94.95 ± 4.77	96.49 ± 5.97	95.72	97.83	95.75	97.86
Inferior vena cava	88.22 ± 14.70	88.41 ± 16.29	86.93	87.31	87.46	87.89
Right adrenal gland	80.14 ± 18.61	90.19 ± 19.80	67.28	75.51	68.33	76.50
Left adrenal gland	81.95 ± 14.57	91.94 ± 14.60	74.72	82.28	75.14	82.65
Gallbladder	76.78 ± 28.12	77.66 ± 28.07	77.08	78.26	78.23	79.40
Esophagus	77.10 ± 19.65	86.27 ± 20.94	82.16	91.08	82.42	91.26
Stomach	85.70 ± 15.60	86.97 ± 15.66	87.06	87.78	87.47	88.20
Duodenum	76.38 ± 12.34	89.14 ± 11.52	75.69	87.70	76.11	87.85
Left kidney	89.09 ± 19.72	86.78 ± 21.16	94.08	87.04	93.06	90.89
Tumor	18.30 ± 25.14	6.44 ± 9.62	18.39	6.86	18.22	6.83
Average	80.59 ± 25.16	83.44 ± 27.32	79.91	82.36	79.73	82.20

with DSC scores exceeding 95%, indicating precise delineation of these critical structures. However, challenges arise in the segmentation of pancreas, gallbladder and tumors, reflected by DSC scores below 80%. This suggests opportunities for further refinement of the segmentation model for improved tumor detection. On average, our method achieves a commendable DSC score of 80.59% ± 25.16% and NSD score of 83.44% ± 27.32% across all organs and tumors, highlighting the effectiveness of our approach.

4.2   Qualitative Results on Validation Set

Figure 4 shows some representative good segmentation results. In Case 0029 and Case 0073 examples, our method successfully identified all organs, and the final predictions are almost the same with the ground truths. The poor segmentation

Table 5. Quantitative evaluation of segmentation efficiency in terms of the running them and GPU memory consumption.

Case ID	Image Size	Running Time (s)	Max GPU (MB)	Total GPU (MB)
0001	(512, 512, 55)	29.61	3080	298264
0051	(512, 512, 100)	16.77	3096	235758
0017	(512, 512, 150)	36.28	3100	396605
0019	(512, 512, 215)	30.03	3130	493118
0099	(512, 512, 334)	32.07	3134	550114
0063	(512, 512, 448)	43.88	3154	776612
0048	(512, 512, 499)	49.49	3110	890207
0029	(512, 512, 554)	58.49	3300	1056456

results are shown in Fig. 5. In Case 0043 and Case 0059, we can see that there are some under-segmentation and over-segmentation errors in our prediction results. We believe that these poor segmentation results from the ambiguous boundaries of the lesion. Our method performs well in segmenting organs. For healthy organs, we can segment each organ relatively accurately. However, for tumors, our method does not perform well. This may be because tumors are easily confused with organs, leading to the wrong segmentation of organs as tumors.

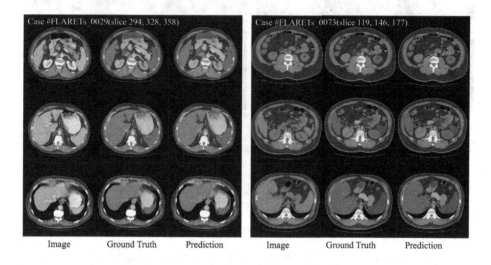

| Image | Ground Truth | Prediction | Image | Ground Truth | Prediction |

Fig. 4. Good segmentation results

4.3   Segmentation Efficiency Results on Validation Set

In this paper, our segmentation efficiency evaluation is obtained in the development environment shown in the Table 1. The segmentation efficiency results are shown in the Table 5. The computing resources and time required for samples of different sizes vary. Case 0051 is the fastest at 16.77 s and Case 0029 is the slowest at 58.49 s. This highlights the trade-off between segmentation speed and image complexity, and a similar situation applies in terms of total GPU memory consumption.

4.4   Ablation Study

Table 6 shows the ablation study results of this work on the validation set. We trained on the first dataset and verified our segmentation results on the validation set, our method achieves a mean DSC of 79.21% and an NSD of 81.89%. On the second dataset, the semi-supervised training strategy of the teacher-student

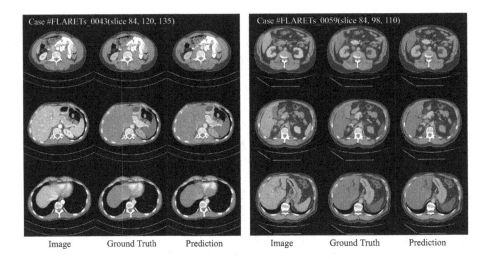

Fig. 5. Bad segmentation results

Table 6. Ablation study on public validation.

Target	Without unlabeled		With unlabeled	
	DSC(%)	NSD(%)	DSC(%)	NSD(%)
Liver	96.11	92.26	96.81	95.28
Right Kidney	88.54	86.65	89.56	87.88
Spleen	92.46	89.67	95.48	95.10
Pancreas	79.18	89.82	78.33	89.58
Aorta	93.81	95.20	94.95	96.49
Inferior vena cava	88.06	88.12	88.22	88.41
Right adrenal gland	80.01	90.14	80.14	90.19
Left adrenal gland	81.82	91.92	81.95	91.94
Gallbladder	74.58	75.97	76.78	77.66
Esophagus	76.64	85.91	77.10	86.27
Stomach	85.35	84.90	85.70	86.97
Duodenum	74.04	89.35	76.38	89.14
Left kidney	86.97	84.00	89.09	86.78
Tumor	11.36	2.52	18.30	6.44
Average	79.21	81.89	80.59	83.44

Table 7. Ablation study of SEBlock and Inception Block on public validation training with unlabeled data.

Variant	Modules		DSC	
	SEBlock	Inception Block	Organs	Tumor
Baseline	✗	✗	84.63	16.77
w/o SEBlock	✓	✗	85.07	17.62
w/o Inception Block	✗	✓	85.12	18.39
Full Version	✓	✓	85.38	18.30

model is adopted, and both DSC and NSD are improved, achieving mean DSC of 80.59% and NSD of 83.44%. As shown in Table 6, by using unlabeled data, both DSC and NSD are significantly improved and the indicators of all organs improved. It shows that unlabeled data and semi-supervised learning can make the model achieve better performance.

We verified the SEBlock and Inception Block separately using three different network configurations. We summarize the experimental results in Table 7. We used Unet as the Baseline, compared with w/oSEBlock, the DSC of the organs and tumors was improved. This is due to the channel attention of SEBlock, which makes the model focus on the relevant channels that can improve the segmentation performance. The addition of InceptionBolock enables the model to effectively capture image features at different scales and improves the expressive power of the network, making it more adaptive and able to learn complex image features. The DSC of the DSC of the organs and tumors improve to 85.07% and 18.39%, respectively.

4.5   Results on Final Testing Set

The test results are shown in Table 4. In the test dataset, we achieved an average DSC of 84.46% and NSD of 88.0% for all organs. At the same time, the average inference time of our method is less than 30 s with 44236 GPU memory on average. However, for tumor segmentation, we achieved DSC of 18.22% and NSD of 6.83%. There is still much for improvement.

4.6   Limitation and Future Work

The proposed method works well in most organs. However, the segmentation results of tumors are still unsatisfactory, it has large room to be further improved. Perhaps treating tumor segmentation as a separate task and designing multiple decoders is an effective solution, which is left for future work.

5   Conclusion

In this paper, we adopt a Teacher-Student semi-supervised strategy for the abdominal organ segmentation task. We develop and test the whole framework on the FLARE 2023 challenge dataset. The network consists of a coarse segmentation model and a fine segmentation model. We adopt a Teacher-Student semi-supervised learning strategy to leverage a large amount of unlabeled data. We use Unet as the basic network framework and the Inception block [17] and SEBlock [7] combined with the Unet network. The whole framework of our method acquires 79.95% mean DSC and 82.79% mean NSD on the FLARE 2023 challenge validation dataset.

Acknowledgements. The authors of this paper declare that the segmentation method they implemented for participation in the FLARE 2023 challenge has not used any pre-trained models nor additional datasets other than those provided by the organizers. The proposed solution is fully automatic without any manual intervention. We thank all the data owners for making the CT scans publicly available and CodaLab [14] for hosting the challenge platform.

References

1. Bilic, P., et al.: The liver tumor segmentation benchmark (LiTS). Med. Image Anal. **84**, 102680 (2023)
2. Chen, X., Yuan, Y., Zeng, G., Wang, J.: Semi-supervised semantic segmentation with cross pseudo supervision. In: Proceedings of the IEEE/CVF Conference on Computer Vision and Pattern Recognition, pp. 2613–2622 (2021)
3. Clark, K., et al.: The cancer imaging archive (TCIA): maintaining and operating a public information repository. J. Digit. Imaging **26**(6), 1045–1057 (2013)
4. French, G., Laine, S., Aila, T., Mackiewicz, M., Finlayson, G.: Semi-supervised semantic segmentation needs strong, varied perturbations. arXiv preprint arXiv:1906.01916 (2019)
5. Heller, N., et al.: The state of the art in kidney and kidney tumor segmentation in contrast-enhanced CT imaging: results of the kits19 challenge. Med. Image Anal. **67**, 101821 (2021)
6. Heller, N., et al.: An international challenge to use artificial intelligence to define the state-of-the-art in kidney and kidney tumor segmentation in CT imaging. Proc. Am. Soc. Clin. Oncol. **38**(6), 626 (2020)
7. Hu, J., Shen, L., Sun, G.: Squeeze-and-excitation networks. In: Proceedings of the IEEE Conference on Computer Vision and Pattern Recognition, pp. 7132–7141 (2018)
8. Isensee, F., Jaeger, P.F., Kohl, S.A., Petersen, J., Maier-Hein, K.H.: nnU-Net: a self-configuring method for deep learning-based biomedical image segmentation. Nat. Methods **18**(2), 203–211 (2021)
9. Ma, J., et al.: Loss odyssey in medical image segmentation. Med. Image Anal. **71**, 102035 (2021)
10. Ma, J., He, Y., Li, F., Han, L., You, C., Wang, B.: Segment anything in medical images. Nat. Commun. **15**(1), 654 (2024)
11. Ma, J., et al.: Fast and low-GPU-memory abdomen CT organ segmentation: the flare challenge. Med. Image Anal. **82**, 102616 (2022)
12. Ma, J., et al.: Unleashing the strengths of unlabeled data in pan-cancer abdominal organ quantification: the flare22 challenge. arXiv preprint arXiv:2308.05862 (2023). the FLARE Challenge Consortium, Wang B

13. Ma, J., et al.: Abdomenct-1k: is abdominal organ segmentation a solved problem? IEEE Trans. Pattern Anal. Mach. Intell. **44**(10), 6695–6714 (2022)
14. Pavao, A., et al.: Codalab competitions: an open source platform to organize scientific challenges. J. Mach. Learn. Res. **24**(198), 1–6 (2023)
15. Ronneberger, O., Fischer, P., Brox, T.: U-Net: convolutional networks for biomedical image segmentation. In: Navab, N., Hornegger, J., Wells, W.M., Frangi, A.F. (eds.) MICCAI 2015. LNCS, vol. 9351, pp. 234–241. Springer, Cham (2015). https://doi.org/10.1007/978-3-319-24574-4_28
16. Simpson, A.L., et al.: A large annotated medical image dataset for the development and evaluation of segmentation algorithms. arXiv preprint arXiv:1902.09063 (2019)
17. Szegedy, C., et al.: Going deeper with convolutions. In: Proceedings of the IEEE Conference on Computer Vision and Pattern Recognition, pp. 1–9 (2015)
18. Yu, L., Wang, S., Li, X., Fu, C.-W., Heng, P.-A.: Uncertainty-aware self-ensembling model for semi-supervised 3D left atrium segmentation. In: Shen, D., et al. (eds.) MICCAI 2019. LNCS, vol. 11765, pp. 605–613. Springer, Cham (2019). https://doi.org/10.1007/978-3-030-32245-8_67
19. Yushkevich, P.A., Gao, Y., Gerig, G.: ITK-SNAP: an interactive tool for semi-automatic segmentation of multi-modality biomedical images. In: Annual International Conference of the IEEE Engineering in Medicine and Biology Society, pp. 3342–3345 (2016)

A Semi-supervised Abdominal Multi-organ Pan-Cancer Segmentation Framework with Knowledge Distillation and Multi-label Fusion

Zengmin Zhang[1,2], Xiaomeng Duan[1], Yanjun Peng[1,2]($\boxtimes$), and Zhengyu Li[1,2]

[1] College of Computer Science and Engineering, Shandong University of Science and Technology, No. 579, Qianwan'gang Road, Qingdao 266590, China
pengyanjuncn@163.com
[2] Shandong Province Key Laboratory of Wisdom Mining Information Technology, No. 579, Qianwan'gang Road, Qingdao 266590, China

Abstract. The segmentation of abdominal organs and tumors plays a crucial role in computer-aided diagnosis of medical images. To achieve high-precision segmentation while maintaining efficiency, especially in semi-supervised learning, we propose a novel semi-supervised knowledge distillation framework. The framework consists of the teacher model and the student model. In the first step, we design an attention nnU-Net with a dual convolutional attention decoder as the teacher model to generate high-quality tumor pseudo-labels for unlabeled tumor data. The dual attention decoder enhances attention to the regions of interest and highlights the most relevant channels, improving the model's ability to optimize features. Additionally, we design an effective 2D sliding window inference strategy to accelerate the inference speed of the teacher model. We utilize partial labels, organ pseudo-labels provided by the FLARE2022 winner, and tumor pseudo-labels for multi-label fusion, ensuring the fusion results closely resemble the ground truth. In the second step, we employ a lightweight nnU-Net as the student model to achieve efficient segmentation. Our method achieved an average DSC score of 88.53% and 30.47% for the organs and lesions on the validation set and the average running time and area under GPU memory-time cure are 15.85 s and 15601 MB, respectively. Our code is available at https://github.com/zzm3zz/FLARE2023.

Keywords: Knowledge Distillation · Dual Attention · Multiple labels fusion · Semi-supervised learning

1 Introduction

Abdominal organs are commonly affected by cancer, such as colorectal cancer and pancreatic cancer, which rank as the second and third leading causes of

J. Ma and B. Wang (Eds.): FLARE 2023, LNCS 14544, pp. 346–361, 2024.
https://doi.org/10.1007/978-3-031-58776-4_27

cancer-related deaths [20]. Therefore, it is necessary to accurately depict abdominal organs and cancerous lesions. However, manual annotation of organs from CT scans is time-consuming and subjective. As a result, obtaining a large number of fully annotated cases is often impractical. In recent years, deep learning models have achieved state-of-the-art performance in multi-organ or abdominal organ and tumor segmentation tasks, and semi-supervised knowledge distillation has emerged as an important solution to address this issue. FLARE2023 is a competition aimed at efficiently segmenting 13 abdominal organs and pan-cancer lesions in large-scale CT images. In addition to evaluating the accuracy of organ and tumor segmentation, efficiency metrics such as inference time and resource utilization are also taken into consideration. Compared to FLARE2022, FLARE2023 faces the greater challenge of simultaneously segmenting 13 abdominal organs while addressing various lesion tasks associated with abdominal cancers. Furthermore, it explores how to improve segmentation performance using only partially labeled and unlabeled data while maintaining efficient inference.

In recent years, significant efforts have been devoted to exploring image segmentation with partially labeled and unlabeled data. For partially labeled image tasks, a straightforward strategy is to train separate networks on each partially labeled dataset, but this approach leads to longer inference times and higher complexity in post-processing. Recent research has focused on training a single unified model using multiple partially labeled datasets. Zhou et al. [25] proposed the Prior-aware Neural Network (PaNN), which utilizes prior anatomical knowledge of organ sizes estimated from fully labeled datasets to regularize organ distributions in partially labeled datasets. However, this approach requires at least one fully annotated dataset and may not generalize well. Some studies have attempted to design adaptive loss functions that can be directly applied to partially labeled data [3,19]. Fang et al. [3] introduced the Target Adaptive Loss (TAL), treating unlabeled organs as background. Furthermore, some works have explored the use of training with pseudo-labels, which is also applicable to unlabeled image tasks. Liu et al. [12] proposed training individual models on each partially labeled dataset to generate pseudo-labels for unlabeled organs, followed by supervised training using a pseudo multi-organ dataset. Feng et al. [4] introduced a Knowledge Distillation (MS-KD) framework where a pre-trained teacher model on each partially labeled dataset generates soft pseudo-labels.

We summarize the mainstream approaches in recent years and propose a novel semi-supervised self-training knowledge distillation training framework. It achieves comprehensive segmentation of all organs and lesions while maintaining efficiency. Specifically, we first design a teacher model attention nnU-Net with a dual convolution attention decoder to provide pseudo-labels for tumors. The spatial attention module utilizes dual-path gating to enhance attention to regions of interest, particularly challenging pan-cancerous tumors. The channel attention module adaptively calibrates the connections between low-level and high-level features, emphasizing the most relevant feature channels [7]. Additionally, to accelerate the generation of pseudo-labels for tumors, which may lack annotations in a large number of samples, we propose an effective 2D sliding window inference strategy to speed up the teacher model's inference. Furthermore, considering that tumors may be occluded by genuine organ annotations and that pseudo-labels from organs may overlap with genuine organ annotations, we design two methods for pseudo-label fusion for partially labeled datasets and unlabeled datasets. Finally, considering efficiency, we employ the small nnU-Net proposed by [10] as the final student model for efficient inference and segmentation. Our main contributions are summarized as follows:

- We propose a novel knowledge distillation training framework, which enables high-precision segmentation and maintains efficiency in a semi-supervised set-ting.
- We design a teacher model attention nnU-Net that incorporates a dual-convolution attention decoder to achieve high-quality segmentation of regions of interest.
- We propose an effective 2D sliding window inference strategy using prior knowledge of abdominal organ slices to significantly enhance the inference speed of the 2D nnU-Net framework.
- We have devised two label fusion methods to address the issues of inaccuracy and overlap in multi-label scenarios.

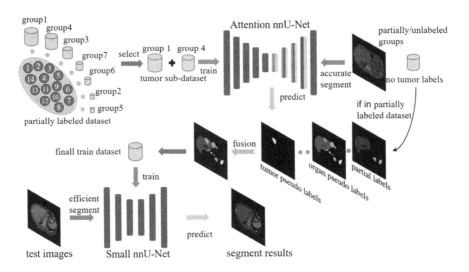

Fig. 1. Overview of our proposed framework. It comprises partial label data selection, teacher model attention nnU-Net for tumor segmentation, multi-label fusion methods, and student model small nnU-Net for efficient segmentation.

2   Method

The semi-supervised knowledge distillation framework is shown in Fig. 1. We divided the partially labeled data of 2,200 cases into 7 groups to represent different combinations of organ or tumor labels based on our careful analysis.

We employ pseudo-labels provided by the highest-precision method [22] from FLARE2022 to label the images that miss organ annotations. To address missing tumor annotations, we train the teacher model attention nnU-Net using group 1 and group 4 data with tumor labels to generate tumor pseudo-labels for the remaining samples in the partially labeled dataset and unlabeled dataset. Section 2.1 elaborates on the methodology that fuses ground truth partial labels, tumors pseudo-labels, and organs pseudo-labels. Finally, we train a small nnU-Net model by use of the final datasets with 4,000 samples to achieve high accuracy and efficiency in the segmentation process.

2.1 Preprocessing

The first 2,200 data samples contain partial labels of organs and lesions. Hence, we categorize the data based on the annotation distribution of segmentation targets to train the labeled tumor data. The dataset partitioning results are shown in Table 1.

Table 1. Results of partitioning the partially labeled dataset based on targets annotations. The abbreviations used in Table 1 are as follows: RK, Spl, Pan, Aor, IVC, RAG, LAG, Gall, Eso, Sto, Duo, LK are short for Right Kidney, Spleen, Pancreas, Aorta, Inferior Vena Cava, Right Adrenal Gland, Left Adrenal Gland, Gallbladder, Esophagus, Stomach, Duodenum, Left Kidney.

Group	Total	Liver	RK	Spl	Pan	Aor	IVC	RAG	LAG	Gall	Eso	Sto	Duo	LK	Tumor
group1	888														✓
group2	6	✓	✓	✓	✓										
group3	447	✓	✓	✓	✓									✓	
group4	609	✓	✓	✓	✓									✓	✓
group5	4	✓	✓	✓	✓	✓	✓	✓	✓	✓	✓	✓	✓		
group6	24	✓	✓	✓	✓	✓	✓	✓	✓		✓	✓	✓		
group7	222	✓	✓	✓	✓	✓	✓	✓	✓	✓	✓	✓	✓	✓	

We perform image reorientation to align the images with the target orientation for each modality-specific data. The resource-intensive teacher model is expected to generate high-quality tumor pseudo-labels, which inevitably leads to higher resource consumption. Therefore, we adopted a 2D method with a smaller memory footprint. A more effective 3D method is employed for segmentation in the lightweight student model. Our configuration information is provided in Table 2. Intensity normalization is conducted using the default method of nnU-Net [11]. We set intensity values below 14 to 0 in the ground truth of group 1 and group 4, and intensity values of 14 to 1 to improve the accuracy of tumor segmentation in the teacher model. This conversion transforms the task of multi-organ tumor segmentation into a binary tumor classification. Subsequently, the labeling intensity is adjusted during the label fusion process.

Table 2. Comparison of different strategies. The first one is the default 3D nnU-Net configuration. The input patch sizes and inter-axis spacing are denoted as (z, y, x) or (y, x).

Setting	Default	Attention nnU-Net	Small nnU-Net
method	3D	2D	3D
channels in the first stage	32	32	16
convolution number per stage	2	2	2
downsampling times	5	7	4
input patch size	(40, 224, 192)	(512, 512)	(32, 128, 192)
input spacing	(2.5, 0.8, 0.8)	(0.8164, 0.8164)	(4, 1.2, 1.2)
test time augmentation	yes	no	no

2.2 Proposed Method

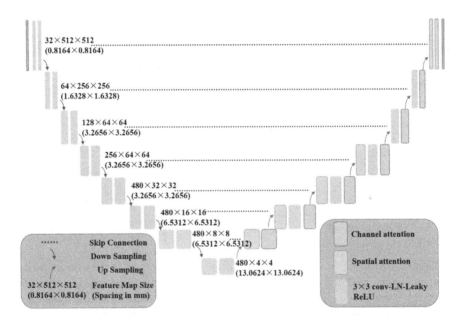

Fig. 2. The network architecture of Attention nnU-Net

Resource Intensive Attention nnU-Net. We design attention nnU-Net to label tumor pseudo-labels more effectively. As shown in Fig. 2, our attention nnU-Net expands upon the 2D nnU-Net architecture by incorporating a dual attention mechanism comprised of spatial attention (SA) and channel attention (CA) in the decoder [7]. The spatial attention utilizes dual-path gating to enhance attention towards regions of interest, particularly challenging pan-cancer tumors. The channel attention module dynamically adjusts the connections between low-level and high-level features, enabling higher coefficients to be assigned to more relevant channels, thereby emphasizing the most pertinent feature channels.

Our SA block is a type of dual-path spatial attention that utilizes two attention gates simultaneously to enhance attention to regions of interest and reduce noise in the attention maps. Figure 3(a) illustrates the detailed information of a single attention gate pathway. Here, z^l represents the low-level feature map in the encoder, while z^h represents the high-level feature map upsampled from the decoder. Both z^h and z^l are compressed with 1×1 convolutions, with the output channels C, and then summed and passed through a $ReLU$ activation function. The activated feature map is then fed into another 1×1 convolution with one output channel, and the resulting attention coefficients $\alpha \in [0,1]^{H \times W}$ on a pixel level are obtained through the $Sigmoid$ function. Subsequently, z^l is calibrated by multiplication with α. In the dual-path attention gate, the spatial attention maps in the two pathways are represented individually as $\hat{\alpha}$ and $\tilde{\alpha}$, as shown in Fig. 3(b), and the output of the dual-channel attention gate is obtained as:

$$Output = ReLU\left[\varphi^C((z^l \cdot \hat{\alpha})\copyright(z^l \cdot \tilde{\alpha}))\right] \tag{1}$$

where $\copyright$ indicates channel concatenation and φ^C represents a 1×1 convolution with C output channels.

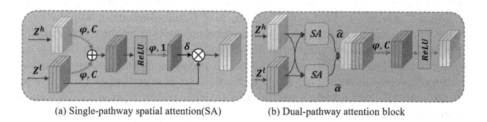

(a) Single-pathway spatial attention(SA)   (b) Dual-pathway attention block

Fig. 3. Details of our spatial attention(SA).

To better utilize the most informative feature channels, we introduce channel attention to automatically emphasize relevant feature channels while suppressing irrelevant ones. Our channel attention (CA) block primarily combines the low-level features from the encoder, calibrated by spatial attention, and the high-level features from the decoder, as shown in Fig. 4. Let z represent the input features with C channels. We use global average pooling P_{avg} and global max pooling P_{max} to obtain the global information for each channel, resulting in $P_{avg}(x) \in \mathbb{R}^{C \times 1 \times 1}$ and $P_{max}(x) \in \mathbb{R}^{C \times 1 \times 1}$, respectively. The channel attention coefficients β are obtained using a multilayer perceptron (MLP) and can be represented as $\beta \in [0,1]^{C \times 1 \times 1}$. The results are summed and input to $Sigmoid$ to obtain β, and the output can be represented as:

$$Output = z \cdot \beta + z \tag{2}$$

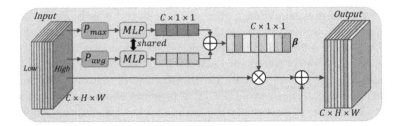

Fig. 4. Details of our channels attention(CA).

We use the summation between Dice loss and cross-entropy loss because compound loss functions have been proven to be robust in various medical image segmentation tasks [13].

Fusion Strategy for Partial Labels. The simple fusion method performs direct fusion of partial labels, organs, and tumor pseudo-labels, and chooses to use the value of the partial label if the positions overlap when the annotation is not zero. However, the simple fusion method ignores the inaccuracy of organ pseudo-label edges and the fact that tumors can be masked by organ labeling. We therefore perform dual fusion on partial labels to obtain a more comprehensive and reasonable distribution of target annotations. Specifically, for group i, where $i \in \{2, 3, 5, 6, 7\}$, there may be missing tumor annotations. We incorporate high-quality tumor pseudo-labels generated by the teacher model for fusion. As real tumors can be masked by organ annotations, when there is an overlap between organ annotations and tumor pseudo-annotations, we prioritize the tumor pseudo-annotations. The specific method is described in Eq. 3, where θ_p represents the ground truth partial annotations, and θ_t represents the tumor pseudo-annotations.

$$\hat{\theta}^{(z,x,y)} = \begin{cases} \theta_p^{(z,x,y)}, & \theta_t^{(z,x,y)} = 0 \\ \theta_t^{(z,x,y)}, & \theta_t^{(z,x,y)} \neq 0 \end{cases} \tag{3}$$

Subsequently, for group j where $j \in \{1, 2, 3, 4, 5, 6\}$ with remaining missing organ annotations, we fuse $\hat{\theta}^{(z,x,y)}$ with corresponding organ pseudo-labels [22] using the approach outlined in Eq. 4. θ_o represents organ pseudo-labels. λ represents the annotated organ categories in group j.

$$\theta^{(z,x,y)} = \begin{cases} \hat{\theta}^{(z,x,y)}, & \hat{\theta}^{(z,x,y)} \neq 0 \\ \theta_o^{(z,x,y)}, & \hat{\theta}^{(z,x,y)} = 0 \wedge \theta_o^{(z,x,y)} \neq \lambda \\ 0 & otherwise \end{cases} \tag{4}$$

Different from the tumor pseudo-label fusion strategy, there are two scenarios for organ pseudo-label fusion. (1) When the organ pseudo-annotations overlap with the foreground of the $\hat{\theta}^{(z,x,y)}$, we use the annotations of $\hat{\theta}^{(z,x,y)}$ in overlapping regions. (2) In the background region of $\hat{\theta}^{(z,x,y)}$, if the corresponding position in the organ pseudo-label is annotated as a missing organ in $\hat{\theta}^{(z,x,y)}$, we use the organ annotations labeled by the organ pseudo-label. However, if the corresponding position is annotated as background or as an already annotated organ in $\hat{\theta}^{(z,x,y)}$, it is considered as background.

Fusion Strategy for Unlabeled Images Pseudo-labels. For unlabeled images, similar to the partial label fusion strategy, in cases of overlap at the same location, we give priority to the tumor pseudo-label. The fusion method is described in Eq. 5.

$$\theta^{(z,x,y)} = \begin{cases} \theta_o^{(z,x,y)}, & \theta_t^{(z,x,y)} = 0 \\ \theta_t^{(z,x,y)}, & \theta_t^{(z,x,y)} \neq 0 \end{cases} \qquad (5)$$

Efficient 2D Sliding Window Inference. We employed a precise configuration and trained using a large-scale 2D attention nnU-Net to infer tumors. This inevitably leads to higher resource consumption and longer inference time. Based on [10], we have designed an efficient 2D sliding window inference method. The default sliding window strategy is designed with separate steps for the X and Y axes, using a nested two-layer for loop to iterate over the image. However, a significant portion of 2D slices in the entire 3D image does not contain the abdominal organs and tumor regions, especially in whole-body CT images. Moreover, the abdominal organs and tumors should be located in the middle of the slice plane. Therefore, we use 2×2 windows on each cross-sectional plane, with a window size of 512×512. As shown in Fig. 5, since the resized 2D slices have similar dimensions to the window size after resampling, we start by performing inference on the first window. We can skip the remaining three windows if this window does not contain any foreground regions.

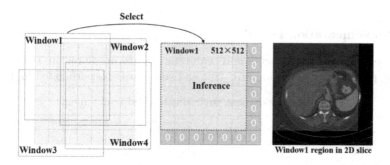

Fig. 5. On the left is the default inference strategy of 2D nnU-Net. The middle image illustrates our proposed strategy. The image on the right demonstrates that window 1 covers a large portion of the abdominal area. The inference of the remaining three windows depends on whether window 1 detects the target.

2.3   Post-processing

Our method does not utilize post-processing operations because techniques such as connected component analysis and testing time augmentation tend to introduce significant computational overhead during the prediction phase.

3   Experiments

3.1   Dataset and Evaluation Measures

The FLARE 2023 challenge is an extension of the FLARE 2021–2022 [15,16], aiming to aim to promote the development of foundation models in abdominal disease analysis. The segmentation targets cover 13 organs and various abdominal lesions. The training dataset is curated from more than 30 medical centers under the license permission, including TCIA [2], LiTS [1], MSD [21], KiTS [8,9], autoPET [5,6], TotalSegmentator [23], and AbdomenCT-1K [17]. The training set includes 4000 abdomen CT scans where 2200 CT scans with partial labels and 1800 CT scans without labels. The validation and testing sets include 100 and 400 CT scans, respectively, which cover various abdominal cancer types, such as liver cancer, kidney cancer, pancreas cancer, colon cancer, gastric cancer, and so on. The organ annotation process used ITK-SNAP [24], nnU-Net [11], and MedSAM [14].

The evaluation metrics encompass two accuracy measures-Dice Similarity Coefficient (DSC) and Normalized Surface Dice (NSD)-alongside two efficiency measures-running time and area under the GPU memory-time curve. These metrics collectively contribute to the ranking computation. Furthermore, the running time and GPU memory consumption are considered within tolerances of 15 s and 4 GB, respectively.

3.2   Implementation Details

The development environments and requirements are presented in Table 3. The training protocols of attention nnU-Net and small nnU-Net are listed in Table 4.

Table 3. Development environments and requirements.

System	Ubuntu 20.04.3 LTS
CPU	AMD EPYC 7T83@3.50 GHz
RAM	1×90 GB; 320MT/s
GPU (number and type)	1 NVIDIA RTX 4090 24G
CUDA version	11.3
Programming language	Python 3.8.10
Deep learning framework	torch 1.12.1, torchvision 0.13.1
Specific dependencies	nnunet 1.7.0
Code	https://github.com/zzm3zz/FLARE2023

During the training process, we employed data augmentation techniques such as dynamic additive brightness, gamma adjustment, rotation, scaling, and elastic deformation. Mirror data augmentation is not used in either of the networks since test-time augmentation (TTA) involving flipping is not performed during inference.

After training on group 1 and group 4 and obtaining high-precision pseudo-labels for all potentially missing tumor annotated samples, we conducted four experiments. In the first experiment, we obtained fused labels for the first 2,200 data using a simple label fusion method and conducted training evaluation using the teacher model. In the second experiment, we utilized the proposed label fusion method and continued the evaluation using the teacher model. In the third round, based on the data from the previous round, we conducted an evaluation using the student model. In the fourth round, different from the third experiment, we employed all 4,000 samples and used the student model to conduct an evaluation.

Table 4. Training protocols for the refine model.

Model	Attention nnU-Net/Small nnU-Net
Network initialization	"He" normal initialization
Batch size	4/2
Patch size	$512 \times 512/32 \times 128 \times 192$
Total epochs	1000/1500
Optimizer	SGD with nesterov momentum ($\mu = 0.99$)
Initial learning rate (lr)	0.005/0.01
Lr decay schedule	Poly learning rate policy: $(1 - \text{epoch}/\text{Total epochs})^{0.9}$
Training time	$19\,h/17\,h$
Number of model parameters	62.96M/5.64M
Number of flops	114G/70G

4   Results and Discussion

4.1   Quantitative Results on Validation Set

Table 5 shows our final submission result. We trained 4,000 cases of train data by using the student model small nnU-Net with the proposed label fusion method and achieved an average DSC score of 84.83% and an average NSD score 89.60% on the public validation set. Similarly, on the online validation set, we achieved an average DSC score of 84.38% and an average NSD score 89.28%.

Table 6 shows the results of our ablation experiments on the online validation set, corresponding to the four experiments mentioned above. Comparing the first and second columns, our label fusion method improved the segmentation accuracy of tumors by 9.62%. When comparing the second and third columns, the attention nnU-Net teacher model outperformed the small nnU-Net student

Table 5. Quantitative evaluation results of our final submitted model.

Target	Public Validation		Online Validation		Testing	
	DSC(%)	NSD(%)	DSC(%)	NSD(%)	DSC(%)	NSD (%)
Liver	97.12 ± 2.38	98.25 ± 4.45	97.06	98.24	95.93	96.68
Right Kidney	93.83 ± 7.25	94.64 ± 9.05	93.07	94.06	94.77	95.36
Spleen	96.34 ± 1.41	97.92 ± 3.73	95.38	97.16	95.83	97.88
Pancreas	85.19 ± 6.36	96.36 ± 5.86	83.24	95.10	87.48	96.46
Aorta	95.36 ± 2.53	98.72 ± 2.76	95.40	98.63	96.01	99.60
Inferior vena cava	91.01 ± 4.93	93.12 ± 5.43	90.80	92.69	91.82	94.20
Right adrenal gland	81.22 ± 16.9	93.15 ± 19.1	82.46	94.91	83.33	95.86
Left adrenal gland	83.20 ± 5.78	96.02 ± 3.27	82.59	94.96	84.05	96.08
Gallbladder	83.22 ± 23.6	84.40 ± 24.7	82.56	83.54	80.23	82.57
Esophagus	80.57 ± 15.9	91.16 ± 16.4	81.55	92.59	87.26	97.27
Stomach	92.88 ± 4.65	96.43 ± 5.38	93.26	96.83	93.13	96.62
Duodenum	81.55 ± 8.25	94.55 ± 5.46	81.53	94.44	84.77	95.82
Left kidney	91.73 ± 14.3	92.52 ± 15.7	92.02	93.07	94.71	95.83
Tumor	34.46 ± 34.6	27.21 ± 29.0	30.47	23.67	36.49	24.22
Average Organs	88.71	94.40	88.53	94.32	89.95	95.40
Average All	84.83	89.60	84.38	89.28	86.13	90.31

Table 6. Ablation experimental results on online validation leaderboard. Data denotes the number of training samples we used. Labels denote the way we fused the labels. The first experiment uses simple fusion. The last three times used our proposed method.

Method	Att nnU-Net		Att nnU-Net		Small nnU-Net		Small nnU-Net	
Data	2,200		2,200		2,200		4,000	
Labels	Simple Fusion		Our Method		Our Method		Our Method	
Target	DSC(%)	NSD(%)	DSC(%)	NSD(%)	DSC(%)	NSD(%)	DSC(%)	NSD(%)
Liver	98.25	98.14	98.27	97.49	96.58	97.42	97.06	98.24
RK	92.30	92.12	92.30	91.54	89.58	88.98	93.07	94.06
Spleen	95.38	94.85	98.00	97.33	95.07	96.69	95.38	97.16
Pancreas	85.08	94.61	85.76	94.80	81.50	94.27	83.24	95.10
Aorta	97.24	98.94	96.53	98.31	95.25	98.35	95.40	98.63
IVC	90.58	90.88	89.77	89.61	89.24	90.60	90.80	92.69
RAG	87.80	96.59	86.54	94.99	79.86	92.62	82.46	94.91
LAG	84.74	92.83	83.75	91.58	79.95	92.71	82.59	94.96
Gallbladder	87.37	87.82	84.93	85.01	79.54	79.39	82.56	83.54
Esophagus	83.68	93.48	83.99	93.64	79.98	91.69	81.55	92.59
Stomach	93.79	95.49	93.34	94.66	91.96	95.35	93.26	96.83
Duodenum	82.72	94.37	80.59	93.28	77.32	92.57	81.53	94.44
LK	90.73	90.56	92.64	91.98	91.40	91.14	92.02	93.07
Tumor	25.18	19.53	34.80	26.01	24.81	16.89	30.47	23.67
Avg Organs	88.97	93.90	89.72	93.40	86.71	92.44	88.53	94.32
Average All	85.34	88.58	85.80	88.58	82.29	87.04	84.38	89.28

model with higher scores of 3.51% and 1.54% in DSC and NSD, respectively. Additionally, comparing the third and fourth columns, including an additional 1,800 cases resulted in a 2.09% and 2.24% improvement in DSC and NSD, respectively.

Table 7. Ablation for tumor segmentation on public validation set

Method	Tumor DSC(%)	Tumor NSD(%)
2D nnU-Net	34.28	27.29
Attention nnU-Net	36.75	29.51

Table 7 demonstrates the ablation experiments for tumor segmentation ability. We use group1 and group4 contained 1497 cases with tumor label to evaluate the ability of tumor segmentation. It can be seen that the addition of the dual convolution attention decoder improves the model's ability to segment tumors compared to the regular 2D nnU-Net resulting in a 2.47% and 2.22% improvement in DSC and NSD, respectively.

We compared the effectiveness of the model and sample selection. It can be observed that using a larger number of samples improves the segmentation results of organs and lesions. The utilization of resource-intensive models yields better segmentation performance compared to smaller models by using more parameters and calculations. Additionally, there is significant room for improvement in lesion segmentation. After balancing accuracy and performance, we ultimately selected the student model with 4,000 train cases that exhibited the most comprehensive performance as our submission result.

4.2 Qualitative Results on Validation Set

Figure 6 shows our final four representative segmentation results on the validation set. Additionally, we present the segmentation results using small nnU-Net training 2,200 partially labeled data for comparison. For Case #43 and Case #81, our network achieved high-precision recognition of all organs and lesions. However, for Case #35, it is evident that our model exhibits segmentation defects for tumors and struggles to correctly identify the targets in cases with multiple overlapping objects. Additionally, for Case #67, we found that our model has difficulty recognizing the esophagus.

We believe that there are two factors contributing to the suboptimal segmentation results. Firstly, for small organs and lesions, the target regions are small, exhibit significant shape deformations, and have low contrast and unclear boundaries. In particular, as lesions can occur within different organs, accurately determining their precise locations becomes challenging. Some lesions only occupy a small portion of the entire sample, making it difficult for our model to differentiate them. Additionally, we attribute these issues to the inaccuracies in the mixed annotations labels, as well as the loss of important details due to the lower resolution resulting from image resampling.

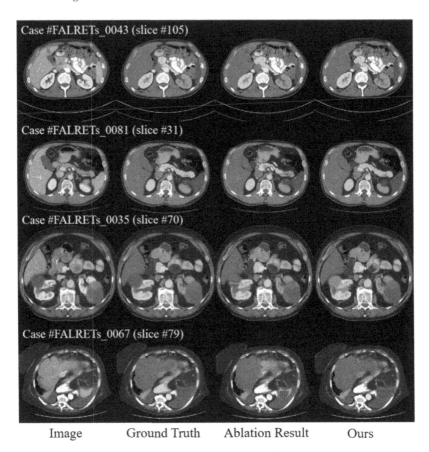

Image   Ground Truth   Ablation Result   Ours

Fig. 6. Qualitative results of our small nnUNet and ablation comparative experiment on two easy cases (Case #43 and Case #81) and two hard cases (Case #35 and Case #67)

4.3 Segmentation Efficiency Results on Validation Set

Table 8 presents the evaluation results of our validation dataset Docker submission, including all running time, max GPU memory usage, and total GPU memory.

4.4 Results on Final Testing Set

We submitted the docker of our final solution and was evaluated by the Flare official. The results on final testing set are shown in Table 5.

Table 8. Quantitative evaluation of segmentation efficiency in terms of the running them and GPU memory consumption. Total GPU denotes the area under GPU Memory-Time curve. Evaluation GPU platform: NVIDIA QUADRO RTX5000 (16G).

Case ID	Image Size	Running Time (s)	Max GPU (MB)	Total GPU (MB)
0001	(512, 512, 55)	18.21	2562	16305
0051	(512, 512, 100)	15.03	1694	15786
0017	(512, 512, 150)	26.23	3704	21449
0019	(512, 512, 215)	14.21	2562	14479
0099	(512, 512, 334)	15.20	1978	15303
0063	(512, 512, 448)	17.86	1694	18322
0048	(512, 512, 499)	19.55	1694	20940
0029	(512, 512, 554)	21.16	3704	22890

4.5 Limitation and Future Work

Due to the large number of data samples and limited experimental resources and time, the quality of pseudo-labels is not satisfactory, resulting in suboptimal results. In future work, we will reference the latest research advancements to improve efficiency and enhance segmentation quality.

5 Conclusion

In this paper, we followed a semi-supervised knowledge distillation strategy and proposed a novel semi-supervised knowledge distillation framework. This framework consists of the teacher model and the student model. In the first step, we design a resource-intensive teacher model, attention nnU-Net, which incorporates a dual convolutional attention decoder, to generate accurate tumor pseudo-labels. Additionally, we designed an effective 2D sliding window inference strategy to accelerate pseudo-label generation. Subsequently, we devised a method for multi-label fusion to enhance target segmentation accuracy. In the second step, we employ a lightweight nnU-Net as the student model to achieve efficient segmentation. Experimental results on the FLARE2023 validation set demonstrated that our method exhibits excellent segmentation performance and efficiency. In the future, we will continue to optimize the framework to further improve the model's segmentation performance and enable fast, low-resource inference.

Acknowledgements. The authors of this paper state that the methods implemented for participating in the FLARE2023 challenge do not utilize any pre-trained models, nor do they involve data augmentation or additional manual annotations. The proposed approach is fully automated and does not require any human intervention. We thank all the data owners for making the CT scans publicly available and CodaLab [18] for hosting the challenge platform.

References

1. Bilic, P., et al.: The liver tumor segmentation benchmark (LiTS). Med. Image Anal. **84**, 102680 (2023)
2. Clark, K., et al.: The cancer imaging archive (TCIA): maintaining and operating a public information repository. J. Digit. Imaging **26**(6), 1045–1057 (2013)
3. Fang, X., Yan, P.: Multi-organ segmentation over partially labeled datasets with multi-scale feature abstraction. IEEE Trans. Med. Imaging **39**(11), 3619–3629 (2020)
4. Feng, S., Zhou, Y., Zhang, X., Zhang, Y., Wang, Y.: MS-KD: multi-organ segmentation with multiple binary-labeled datasets. arXiv preprint arXiv:2108.02559 (2021)
5. Gatidis, S., et al.: The autopet challenge: towards fully automated lesion segmentation in oncologic PET/CT imaging. preprint at Research Square (Nature Portfolio) (2023). https://doi.org/10.21203/rs.3.rs-2572595/v1
6. Gatidis, S., et al.: A whole-body FDG-PET/CT dataset with manually annotated tumor lesions. Sci. Data **9**(1), 601 (2022)
7. Gu, R., et al.: CA-Net: comprehensive attention convolutional neural networks for explainable medical image segmentation. IEEE Trans. Med. Imaging **40**(2), 699–711 (2021)
8. Heller, N., et al.: The state of the art in kidney and kidney tumor segmentation in contrast-enhanced CT imaging: results of the kits19 challenge. Med. Image Anal. **67**, 101821 (2021)
9. Heller, N., et al.: An international challenge to use artificial intelligence to define the state-of-the-art in kidney and kidney tumor segmentation in CT imaging. Proc. Am. Soc. Clin. Oncol. **38**(6), 626 (2020)
10. Huang, Z., et al.: Revisiting nnU-Net for iterative pseudo labeling and efficient sliding window inference. In: Ma, J., Wang, B. (eds.) Fast and Low-Resource Semi-supervised Abdominal Organ Segmentation. FLARE 2022. LNCS, vol. 13816, pp. 178–189. Springer, Cham (2022). https://doi.org/10.1007/978-3-031-23911-3_16
11. Isensee, F., Jaeger, P.F., Kohl, S.A., Petersen, J., Maier-Hein, K.H.: nnU-Net: a self-configuring method for deep learning-based biomedical image segmentation. Nat. Methods **18**(2), 203–211 (2021)
12. Liu, P., et al.: Universal segmentation of 33 anatomies. arXiv preprint arXiv:2203.02098 (2022)
13. Ma, J., et al.: Loss odyssey in medical image segmentation. Med. Image Anal. **71**, 102035 (2021)
14. Ma, J., He, Y., Li, F., Han, L., You, C., Wang, B.: Segment anything in medical images. Nat. Commun. **15**(1), 654 (2024)
15. Ma, J., et al.: Fast and low-GPU-memory abdomen CT organ segmentation: the flare challenge. Med. Image Anal. **82**, 102616 (2022)
16. Ma, J., et al.: Unleashing the strengths of unlabeled data in pan-cancer abdominal organ quantification: the flare22 challenge. arXiv preprint arXiv:2308.05862 (2023). the FLARE Challenge Consortium, Wang, B
17. Ma, J., et al.: Abdomenct-1k: is abdominal organ segmentation a solved problem? IEEE Trans. Pattern Anal. Mach. Intell. **44**(10), 6695–6714 (2022)
18. Pavao, A., et al.: Codalab competitions: an open source platform to organize scientific challenges. J. Mach. Learn. Res. **24**(198), 1–6 (2023)
19. Shi, G., Xiao, L., Chen, Y., Zhou, S.K.: Marginal loss and exclusion loss for partially supervised multi-organ segmentation. Med. Image Anal. **70**, 101979 (2021)

20. Siegel, R.L., Miller, K.D., Fuchs, H.E., Jemal, A.: Cancer statistics, 2022. CA Cancer J. Clin. **72**(1), 7–33 (2022)
21. Simpson, A.L., et al.: A large annotated medical image dataset for the development and evaluation of segmentation algorithms. arXiv preprint arXiv:1902.09063 (2019)
22. Wang, E., Zhao, Y., Wu, Y.: Cascade dual-decoders network for abdominal organs segmentation. In: Ma, J., Wang, B. (eds.) Fast and Low-Resource Semi-supervised Abdominal Organ Segmentation. FLARE 2022. LNCS, vol. 13816, pp. 202–213. Springer, Cham (2022). https://doi.org/10.1007/978-3-031-23911-3_18
23. Wasserthal, J., et al.: Totalsegmentator: robust segmentation of 104 anatomic structures in CT images. Radiol. Artif. Intell. **5**(5), e230024 (2023)
24. Yushkevich, P.A., Gao, Y., Gerig, G.: ITK-SNAP: an interactive tool for semi-automatic segmentation of multi-modality biomedical images. In: Annual International Conference of the IEEE Engineering in Medicine and Biology Society, pp. 3342–3345 (2016)
25. Zhou, Y., et al.: Prior-aware neural network for partially-supervised multi-organ segmentation. In: 2019 IEEE/CVF International Conference on Computer Vision (ICCV), pp. 10671–10680 (2019)

Author Index

J. Ma and B. Wang (Eds.): FLARE 2023, LNCS 14544, pp. 363–364, 2024.
https://doi.org/10.1007/978-3-031-58776-4